CONSTITUTIONAL AND ADMINISTRATIVE LAW
BASIC PRINCIPLES

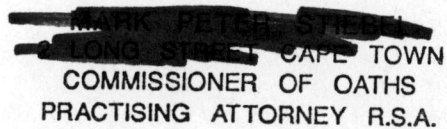

Constitutional
and
Administrative Law
Basic Principles

LAURENCE BOULLE
BEDE HARRIS
CORA HOEXTER

Juta & Co, Ltd

CAPE TOWN WETTON JOHANNESBURG

First Edition 1989
Second Impression 1993

© Juta & Co, Ltd 1989
PO Box 14373, Kenwyn 7790

Cover illustration by Caroline Cullinan
Cover design by Joy Wrench

ISBN 0 7021 2316 1

SET, PRINTED AND BOUND IN THE REPUBLIC OF SOUTH AFRICA
BY THE RUSTICA PRESS (PTY) LTD, NDABENI, CAPE
D2188

To Students

Contents

Preface

This work is intended for use in the teaching of constitutional and administrative law at South African universities. This intention is reflected in the scope of the work, the level at which it is presented, its annotation, analytical content and style.

While the content, orientation and level of presentation of constitutional and administrative law courses differ from institution to institution, they do contain many common features for which, it is hoped, this book will cater. In particular, we have taken account of the fact that in many instances the two subjects are taught as a combined credit course. For this reason, apart from any others, the work has two overriding objectives: to provide an introductory but balanced text for students making their first integrated approach to the subject-matter; and to indicate the underlying importance of constitutional principles in the development of administrative law doctrine, and the formative effect of administrative law practice on constitutional principle. The centrality of these objectives has resulted in a tripartite division of the material.

Part I is designed to introduce students to the basic principles of public law in a social, theoretical and historical context. It is intended to be used as an introduction to either constitutional law or administrative law or both, and it therefore emphasises the theoretical and legal connections between the two academic disciplines. An eclectically comparative approach is used to provide a broad base for the consideration of constitutional and administrative law issues.

Part II is intended to introduce students to the most important aspects of the South African Constitution and South African constitutional law. Where it is appropriate to modern conditions, detailed reference is made to aspects of constitutional history.

University courses in administrative law tend to focus on judicial review to the exclusion of the other controls on the administrative process, which are (understandably) regarded as belonging to constitutional law. While we have had to acknowledge this fact, we hope to avoid giving students the impression that judicial review is the only significant cog in the public-law machine—an impression often reinforced by textbooks on administrative law, particularly those coming from common-law jurisdictions. Thus Part III gives an account of the most important features of South African administrative law as determined by the courts, including the limited role of the system of judicial review.

Part I has been written by Laurence Boulle, Part II by Bede Harris and Part III by Cora Hoexter. However, the authors accept collective responsibility for all the Parts and chapters. We have taken account of developments in law and practice up to the end of September 1989.

While this work adopts an original approach to many aspects of its subject-matter, it owes an appreciable debt to those writers who have made significant contributions to the development of South African constitutional and administrative law in recent years; in particular, to Dion Basson, Lawrence Baxter, Gretchen Carpenter, Henning Viljoen and Marinus Wiechers.

We thank Val Rencken for her efficient processing of Part II. Our thanks go also to the staff of Juta & Co and the Rustica Press for their speedy transformation of electronic manuscript into print. We are grateful to Richard Cooke and Madeline Lass for their enthusiastic supervision of the project. We acknowledge with appreciation the cover illustration, a commissioned work by Caroline Cullinan. It symbolises *Power* in an African context, which is what our book is all about.

Laurence Boulle, Bede Harris and Cora Hoexter
Pietermaritzburg
October 1989

Principal Works Cited

Mark Aronson and Nicola Franklin *Review of Administrative Action* Sydney: The Law Book Company (1987)

Dion Basson and Henning Viljoen *South African Constitutional Law* Cape Town: Juta (1988)

Lawrence Baxter *Administrative Law* Cape Town: Juta (1984)

Vernon Bogdanor *Constitutions in Democratic Politics* Aldershot: Gower (1988)

L J Boulle *South Africa and the Consociational Option* Cape Town: Juta (1984)

A W Bradley *Constitutional and Administrative Law* London: Longman 10 ed (1985)

Gretchen Carpenter *Introduction to South African Constitutional Law* Durban: Butterworths (1987)

William Connolly (ed) *Legitimacy and the State* Oxford: Blackwell (1984)

Hugh Corder *Judges at Work* Cape Town: Juta (1984)

P P Craig *Administrative Law* London: Sweet & Maxwell (1983)

Kenneth Culp Davis *Discretionary Justice* Westport, Conn.: Greenwood Press (1971)

A V Dicey *The Law of the Constitution* London: Macmillan 10 ed (1959)

C F Forsyth *In Danger for Their Talents* Cape Town: Juta (1985)

H R Hahlo and Ellison Kahn *The Union of South Africa: The Development of its Laws and Constitution* Cape Town: Juta (1960)

Carol Harlow and Richard Rawlings *Law and Administration* London: Weidenfeld and Nicolson (1984)

J W Harris *Legal Philosophies* London: Butterworths (1980)

H L A Hart *The Concept of Law* Oxford: Clarendon Press (1961)

W A Joubert (ed) *The Law of South Africa* multi-vol Durban: Butterworths (1978)

Lord Lloyd of Hampstead and M D A Freeman *Lloyd's Introduction to Jurisprudence* London: Stevens & Sons 5 ed (1985)

Anthony S Mathews *Freedom, State Security and the Rule of Law* Cape Town: Juta (1986)

Patrick McAuslan and John F McEldowney (eds) *Law, Legitimacy and the Constitution* London: Sweet & Maxwell (1985)

Charles Howard McIllwain *Constitutionalism: Ancient and Modern* Ithaca, N.Y.: Cornell University Press rev ed (1947)

Edward McWhinney *Constitution-making: Principles, Process, Practices* Toronto: University of Toronto Press (1981)

Dan Meir-Cohen *Rights, Persons and Organizations—A Legal Theory for Bureaucratic Society?* Berkeley: University of California Press (1986)

Phillipe Nonet and Philip Selznick *Law and Society in Transition: Towards Responsive Law* New York: Harper & Row (1978)

J Roland Pennock and John W Chapman (eds) *Constitutionalism* New York: New York University Press (1979)

O Hood Phillips and Paul Jackson *O Hood Phillips' Constitutional and Administrative Law* London: Sweet & Maxwell 7 ed (1987)

L A Rose-Innes *Judicial Review of Administrative Tribunals in South Africa* Cape Town: Juta (1963)

Alan Rycroft (ed) *Race and the Law in South Africa* Cape Town: Juta (1987)

Geoffrey Sawer *Modern Federalism* Carlton, Vic.: Pitman 2 ed (1976)

Bernard Schwartz *Lions Over the Throne* New York: New York University Press (1987)

Philip Selznick *Law, Society and Industrial Justice* New Brunswick, N. J.: Transaction Books (1980)

Harry Street and Rodney Brazier *S A De Smith's Constitutional and Administrative Law* London: Penguin 5 ed (1985)

C F Strong *Modern Political Constitutions* London: Sidgwick & Jackson 8 ed (1972)

Jérold Taitz *The Inherent Jurisdiction of the Supreme Court* Cape Town: Juta (1985)

Laurence H Tribe *American Constitutional Law* Minneola, N.Y.: Foundation Press (1978)

Aryeh L Unger *Constitutional Development in the USSR* London: Methuen (1987)

M J C Vile *Constitutionalism and the Separation of Powers* Oxford: Clarendon Press (1967)

E C S Wade and A W Bradley *Constitutional and Administrative Law* London: Longman 10 ed (1985)

H W R Wade *Administrative Law* Oxford: Clarendon Press 6 ed (1988)

K C Wheare *Modern Constitutions* Oxford: Oxford University Press 2 ed (1966)

Marinus Wiechers *Administrative Law* Durban: Butterworths (1985)

Table of Cases

Page

W

Part I

Theoretical Foundations of Constitutional and Administrative Law

1 Introduction

This book is about aspects of public law. At a formal level public law is concerned with the powers and duties of three organs of government known as the legislature, the executive and the judiciary, with the legal relationships among these bodies, and with their relationships with private individuals and organisations. At a deeper level public law has to do with the nature of the state system and the way in which society operates and is regulated; all writing on public law makes some assumptions about the nature and extent of the power which the state exercises in society.[1] As this is predominantly a legal text it focuses mainly on the first level of public law, with some attention to the second.

This chapter provides a basic introduction to concepts and terms used in constitutional and administrative law. Each topic warrants a more elaborate analysis, but is dealt with at its most elementary level so as to provide the preliminary understanding necessary to make progress in the field. More advanced treatment can be found in the specialised texts referred to in the list of works cited. The chapter ends with a glossary of public law terms, some of which have been introduced or referred to in the narrative text. Specialised concepts, such as sovereignty, the Rule of Law, and checks and balances, are explained in the chapters in which they are first introduced.

I THE STATE, SOCIETY AND LAW

Constitutional and administrative law are concerned with the state, society and law. While the same can be said to some extent of other branches of law, the combination of these three elements is a special and distinctive feature of constitutional and administrative law.

A State

The term state is a contentious and disputed concept. It is also used in a variety of senses.[2] In international law it means an independent, politically organised community which is identified with a defined territorial area. In political science it is used to refer to the institutions of government and organised political power. A classic sociological definition identifies the state as a human community that claims the monopoly of the legitimate use of physical force within a given territory.[3] Some jurists use it synonymously with the

---

[1] See Martin Partington in Patrick McAuslan and John F McEldowney (eds) *Law, Legitimacy and the Constitution* (1985) 191 at 192.

[2] See generally Gianfranco Poggi *The Development of the Modern State* (1978); Kenneth Dyson *The State Tradition in Western Europe* (1980).

[3] Max Weber in William Connolly (ed) *Legitimacy and the State* (1984) 32 at 33. See also Rodney Barker in Carol Harlow (ed) *Public Law and Politics* (1986) 3–22.

legal order.

In the present context the term is understood to mean the organised authority of a defined social system which manages its public affairs, both internally and externally. The modern state has numerous different branches and institutions: in fact it can only act through its various organs or agents. (For this reason some writers refer to the 'state system' rather than the state.) They exercise a wide variety of functions in the name of the state: they create law, resolve disputes, maintain order, regulate the economy, plan for development, engage in commercial activity, provide social services, and uphold individual rights. The state is also a massive consumer of goods and services. Some of these bodies and the functions they perform are traditionally dealt with in the subject of constitutional law and others in administrative law. These subjects provide a partial insight into the complex way in which state systems operate. They emphasise the state's dependence on law but tend to underplay its reliance on force.

The most prominent agency of the state is the government. (This term is defined further below.) It is the government in which state power is formally invested and which speaks on behalf of the state, and it is so conspicuous an institution that it is often regarded as being identical with the state. This is an incorrect perception.[4] Not only does the state comprise many institutions other than the government, but in practice the government may not be the most influential power-holder. One of the important modern rivals to the government is the administration, which is also defined below. In few contemporary countries is the state system fully cohesive and co-ordinated; its different parts provide competing centres of power and influence. Thus both the judiciary and the government are part of the state, but the judiciary is usually relatively independent of the government. The balance of power among different state institutions shifts continuously.

Traditionally the state has been portrayed as a neutral set of institutions which do not intrinsically favour any group or class of people. In classical liberal theory the state merely provides an impartial structure within which groups can compete for political power. Much contemporary writing has sought to refute this view by exposing the partiality of state systems. Thus in the Marxist tradition it is held that the state system intrinsically benefits the dominant economic class and is used as an instrument for the domination of the working class. Other intellectual traditions also emphasise the instrumental nature of the state and its role in benefiting certain interests at the expense of others. The new perception of the state can be attributed partly to the changed understanding of the political process, which now goes behind formal structures in order to come to grips with the real dynamics of the political system.

[4] See R Milliband *The State in Capitalist Society* (1969) 46–7.

It can also be attributed to fundamental changes in the functions of the modern state. Whereas its traditional functions were to maintain law and order, resolve disputes, conduct foreign affairs and organise the defence of the country, its modern functions go further and include the regulation of many aspects of social and economic life.[5] For these reasons it is said that we live in the age of the 'welfare state' or the 'administrative state'. People live in awe of the state's agents with their potentially coercive and repressive powers: the policeman, the inspector, the official. They require protection from their actions and intermediate organisations—such as trade unions, churches, political parties, and other voluntary associations—serve as buffers between individuals and the apparently omnipotent state. However, the uniqueness of the state's powers and strength should not be exaggerated.[6] Private organisations, such as large corporations, can also wield awesome powers and if the state is democratic it might be the only guardian of individual interests against oppression from these bodies.

The term state does not refer only to the government of a country but also by implication to those who are governed. It suggests a two-way political relationship between the two entities. In theory the state personifies the interests of its citizens, and it claims to exercise power in the public or national interest. Suspected criminals are arrested and prosecuted in the name of the state in its capacity as the representative of the community, and economic and environmental policies are presented as being in the state interest. Of course it does not always happen that organs of the state act in the genuine public interest, and there are often conflicts of interest between the state and its subjects, but the principle of the national interest, or public good, is an important one in the field of administrative law and in interpreting the laws of the country.

In South Africa the term state appears in many statutes, including the Constitution Act 110 of 1983. It is used in several different senses which are impossible to reconcile into a single public law theory of the state. The courts are also inconsistent in their use of the term. However, it is, whenever necessary, possible to recognise the legal identity of the state, for example when one of its organs does something illegal or where someone is employed by the state. There are developed rules and principles of law which prescribe how an individual or group of individuals can deal with the state, or be dealt with by it, in these situations. It is even possible for one branch of the state to sue another branch where it has allegedly acted unlawfully.[7] In practice the concept of the state does not provide many juristic problems in South African public law.

[5] See Anthony Black *State, Community and Human Desire* (1988) 95ff.
[6] See Dan Meir-Cohen *Rights, Persons and Organisations—A Legal Theory for Bureaucratic Society* (1986) 165.
[7] See below, 229–30.

B   Society

By society we mean an organised community of persons within a defined territorial area. For some purposes society can be regarded as a single entity, for example when we speak about a society being affected by a natural disaster; for other purposes it can be regarded as a collection of different groups, for example when there is discrimination against one sector; and for yet other purposes it can be regarded as a collection of individuals, as when a single citizen seeks a social benefit. Traditional societies were regulated by a variety of institutions, such as religion and culture, and, as long as they remained small and economically undeveloped, they could cope very well without a state system. However, modern societies are more complex, and the state is their most important instrument of social order and control. The state achieves its control through planning, regulation, economic distribution and coercion.

Traditionally society has been seen to begin where the state system ends. Each has its own, independent realm. Thus while the state is concerned with public institutions such as government and politics, society is concerned with private institutions such as culture, religion and the economy. This has led to a traditional contradistinction between politics and economics. Politics is presented as public and political, and economics as private and non-political. In the classic liberal state the clear distinction between public and private was crucial to its legitimacy: the private sphere was supreme while the public was charged primarily with facilitating the activities of the private sphere.[8] The contrast between state and society is central to the development of constitutionalism,[9] which is dealt with in the following chapter.

In the contemporary era, however, these distinctions have become blurred. The state and society are intimately connected: there could be no society without the existence of a state system, and the state system would be superfluous without an organised society. Moreover the line dividing state and society is becoming increasingly difficult to draw. This is because, on one hand, the state no longer only maintains order but intervenes extensively in all facets of society, and even takes on many of the economic and other functions traditionally regarded as being within the province of the non-state sector. On the other hand society is producing giant commercial and social entities with considerable power; they not only rival the state's authority in certain fields but they act increasingly like state institutions (as some commentators put it, as 'private governments'[10]) or actually 'capture' and control a department of the state. Such power can be, and frequently is, abused. For historical reasons public law focused on the state's considerable power and the need for

[8] See Norman Lewis in McAuslan and McEldowney op cit n 1 at 110.
[9] See O Gierke *Political Theory of the Middle Ages* F W Maitland transl (1958) 61–2.
[10] See Philip Selznik *Law, Society and Industrial Justice* (1980) 33ff.

individual protection from it and was not concerned with the potential dangers of private power, against which the state may sometimes be the only source of protection.[11] Orthodox constitutional theory and doctrine recognises the existence of two entities, government and the individual, and nothing intermediate in the way of groups or associations is envisaged.[12]

The relationship between state and society is one of the major predicaments of model social structure. One of the important political issues of recent years concerns the relinquishment by the state of a portion of its powers, either through privatising some of its former functions, or by deregulating activities which were previously strictly controlled.[13] These initiatives are motivated in terms either of efficiency, or simply the need to limit the range of government activities. They increase the functions and powers of private enterprise, and assume that 'regulation' will be effected through market forces. Public law is at the heart of this debate between the advocates of state regulation and private enterprise.[14]

C Law

As regards law the tendency is for short definitions to be simplistic and for lengthy definitions to become over-complex. The problem is that law performs a variety of functions in society. It is concerned with advancing the welfare of the public, with resolving disputes, maintaining social control, planning and development, the conferral and control of power, the protection of rights, and the regulation of politics and the economy. Sometimes law is also concerned with justice. These different functions account for its different understandings. In some respects law is a system of rules and procedures which ensure that promises are kept and losses are made good; these rules and procedures are mainly enforced by the courts. In other respects it is a tool of the dominant group which uses it to give effect to its social policies, and to control and sometimes suppress subordinate groups; in this manifestation it is enforced mainly by non-court bodies, often known as tribunals. While neither branch can be simplistically related to one or other function, *private law* tends to be defined more in terms of the former function and *public law* at least partly in terms of the latter.

These two branches of law can be distinguished in the following way: Public law involves the state acting in its authoritative capacity and one or more other entities—an individual, another state body, a private company, and so on. The state acts in an authoritative capacity when it exercises power in the public domain which it alone can exercise. This can range from making laws to issuing licences,

---

[11] See Meir Cohen op cit n 6, at 96.
[12] For an attack on this theory see Arthur Miller *The Modern Corporate State* (1976).
[13] See below, 80–3; 103.
[14] See Tony Prosser 1982 *Journal of Law and Society* 1; Laurence Boulle (1987) 104 *SALJ* 104.

imprisoning citizens and regulating the price of milk. Public law consists of rules, but it also admits within its ambit policy and discretion. It is created mainly by legislatures and officials of the state. Indeed there is increasing recognition in public law of the codes, guides, rules and directives issued and followed by government agencies which are not legal rules in the strict sense but which have an important practical effect and must be taken account of in the theory and practice of public law.[15]

Private law, by contrast, regulates the relations between two or more non-state entities in all matters of private conduct—ranging from the enforcement of contracts, to the provision of compensation for losses suffered, to the protection of property rights. Where the state is involved with other legal entities in a non-authoritative capacity, that is in the same way as a private person or company, then we classify it as a matter of private and not public law—for example when it purchases supplies or hires a lawyer. Private law consists of rules and procedures, but unlike public law tends to disguise its elements of policy and discretion. Private law is also known as 'lawyers' law' in that it has been created mainly by lawyers, namely the courts, and is the branch of the law which most practitioners and law teachers have felt comfortable with: contract, delict, company law, property, and so on.[16]

Not only is the exact nature of the distinction between public and private law in dispute, but so its very existence. Just as the gap has narrowed between state and society and between politics and economics, so too has it narrowed between public law and private law; nowadays much 'private law' is laid down by the state and principles of public law have come to extend their ambit to private institutions.[17]

In some European civil-law systems the distinction is both clear and meaningful in that there is a separate set of courts, rules and procedures for each branch. In the English system there is only a single over-arching set of courts for deciding matters of both public and private law, and although there are some differences in their rules and procedures, many jurists argue that there is no justification for drawing a distinction between public and private law. Though Roman law made use of the distinction, South Africa, as is shown in chapter 4, has adopted the English model, with its limited criteria for distinguishing between public and private law.

This work is concerned only with public law, and specific aspects of the subject. Public law has a positive side, which is concerned with conferring power on state bodies, and a negative side, which

---

[15] See Partington op cit n 1 at 196; see also below, 86–7.
[16] See L G Baxter (1985) 1 *Natal University Law and Society Review* 15 at 17–18.
[17] See Roberto Mangabeira Unger *Law in Modern Society* (1976) 58–65.

imposes procedural rules on these bodies and provides means for making them accountable for their actions.[18]

There are three different ways in which public law is relevant to the way in which states regulate society. In the first place law legitimises the structure and very existence of the state. It does this by suggesting that its powers come from an external, impersonal source and not from the state itself. As the law has a high esteem in most societies a state system with a legal pedigree is more likely to be accepted and obeyed by the citizens; if state actions are widely accepted there is less need for coercive action to enforce them. There are other sources of legitimacy in modern societies, but law is the most important. It is primarily the law of the Constitution which provides this sanctity for the state system, and the appeal to pre-existing law is of the essence of constitutionalism. However, not all constitutionally enshrined systems will be regarded as legitimate if they do not satisfy requirements other than having a legal source; the activities of the state must also conform to minimum standards of morality and social acceptability. Indeed, while the older definitions of legitimacy concentrated on the element of law or right, more recent definitions focus on the belief or opinion of the people subject to the existing institutions of the state—if they regard them as appropriate and proper then they are legitimate.[19] Public law is a necessary factor for providing legitimacy to the state, but it is not a sufficient one.

Second, the state uses law as a means of regulating society, that is it passes specific laws which sanction and validate the policies and actions it wishes to pursue. It is true that all modern states use many means other than law for this purpose, including economic measures and propaganda, and they sometimes even act outside the law, or in contravention of it, to achieve their social designs. However, law has the advantage of providing legitimacy for individual actions of the state, and for the force it will use if they are not accepted. This is because the law is depicted as a neutral social institution, not influenced by special interests in society. As a general rule people tend to accept, follow and obey the law. Again, not all exercises of lawful authority will be regarded as legitimate, for example if the state seems to be manipulating the law or the law itself is discriminatory. Thus law is a minimum requirement for state legitimacy, but not the only requirement. A large part of administrative law is concerned with this aspect of state activity.

Law, however, is not only used by state bodies, it can also be used against them. This is because law has certain values, policies and procedures which the state must respect if it uses law as a form of regulation and control—the very idea of law connotes limitation.[20]

[18] Cf Partington 194.
[19] See John H Schaar in Connolly op cit n 3 at 104; and Patrick McAuslan and John F Eldowney in McAuslan and Eldowney 1.
[20] See Frederic S Burin (1966) 15 *The American University Law Review* 313 at 334.

Even if the state tries to circumvent these standards they can still be upheld to some extent because public law and the institutions which enforce it, such as the courts, have a certain measure of independence from the other state institutions. Therefore the third area in which law is relevant is in controlling and limiting the state. This is apparent in both the constitutional and administrative law fields where the state is both the promulgator of the law and is itself a party in disputes in which the law must be applied. Most modern states, other than dictatorships, find it necessary to subject themselves to the law.

Thus in different ways public law mediates relations between the state and society. In this work attention is given to two branches of public law, constitutional law and administrative law. In each branch there is a constant interaction between the state, society and the law. Even if a legal dispute is formally only between the state and an individual there is always a third dimension to the issue—namely society, or the public interest. This is an important theme in public law.

II CONSTITUTIONAL LAW

A Its definition

Constitutional law as traditionally understood has three elements. In the first place it is the law which regulates the principal organs of the state, in the sense of describing their composition, powers and duties, and procedures.[21] These organs are the legislature, the executive and the judiciary. Secondly, it regulates the relationships among these branches when they come to exercise their powers. Where more than one authority is exercising power in the same system, rules are necessary to resolve disputes among them and these are provided by constitutional law. Thirdly, it regulates some of the relationships between the various institutions of the state and its citizens; this aspect is often dealt with under the topic of civil liberties. In all its elements constitutional law is concerned with the system of government, but each one focuses on a different facet.

The definition and subject-matter of constitutional law overlap with that of other disciplines, most obviously political science. But while political science is also concerned with the state and its powers and processes it is not restricted only to the legal aspects but looks as well, and inevitably more so, to the political, social and economic forces in society. While these factors should be taken account of in constitutional law they do not play as prominent a part as the legal component. Indeed constitutional law is a cornerstone of any legal system in that its rules identify the lawmaking authorities themselves, namely the legislature, the courts and various administrative

---

[21] See E C S Wade and A W Bradley *Constitutional and Administrative Law* 10 ed (1985) 4ff.

authorities.[22] However, the preoccupation with law entails that constitutional law provides a very deficient and sometimes misleading picture of how the state and politics actually operate.

The question is asked whether constitutional law, so termed, is really law; or, to put it differently, whether constitutional law is a practical legal subject: can one become a practising constitutional lawyer? The reason for the question is that in countries like South Africa there does not seem to be much judicial activity in the field. Here the answer will depend upon the nature of the particular legal system. In some jurisdictions the disputes arising in each of the above three areas will be resolved by the courts, thereby providing practising opportunities for lawyers. But in other systems many of them are resolved outside the courts by political or administrative bodies and are not the subject of legal practice. Thus in the United States the drawing of electoral boundaries is a constitutional issue, periodically litigated before the courts, while in the United Kingdom (and South Africa) it is treated as a political issue. (The reasons for these differences will become apparent later.) But the fact that there is no court-based practice in an area does not mean that there is no law. Much law is not enforced by the courts but is still influential; an example is the customs and privileges of Parliament which are enforced not by the courts but by Parliament itself. Therefore constitutional law can still be regarded as law despite the fact that the courts do not often pronounce on its principles.

B Its scope

As its definition implies, the scope of constitutional law is highly flexible, depending on factors which change over time and vary from country to country. The first factor is the extent to which the state intervenes in social and economic matters. Activities directly regulated by the state in some countries will in others be left to private social and economic forces. The scope of public law, including constitutional law, will be greater in the former than in the latter. The second factor concerns which of its institutions regulate the matters under state control; if they are the subject of political and administrative processes the scope of constitutional law will be less than if they are under the jurisdiction of the courts. The third factor is the role of the courts; the greater their powers in enforcing the constitution and upholding basic rights, the wider will be the scope of constitutional law. In some countries everything from family matters to pollution to school transport can be brought within the sphere of constitutional law. Historically speaking the scope of constitutional law has evolved gradually with the growth of the state, though currently the greater growth is experienced in the field of administrative law.

[22] O Hood Phillips and Paul Jackson *O Hood Phillips' Constitutional and Administrative Law* 7 ed (1978) 10.

C Its sources

In any branch of the law it is practically important to know the different places where its rules and principles can be found. Here we are referring to the sources of the law. In time you will know intuitively where to find the law in a certain area but at this stage it is important to explain the rudiments of the process. The matter is complicated to some extent by the fact that there is dispute as to the exact boundaries of constitutional law.

1 Statute

The first source of constitutional law in most countries is a statute or statutes. In South Africa it is the Republic of South Africa Constitution Act 110 of 1983. In this country the Constitution Act has the same legal status as any other Act of Parliament, though in many jurisdictions it has a higher status and provides a set of standards by which other laws and acts of government can be measured. The nature of modern documentary Constitutions is dealt with in chapter 3. Besides the Constitution Act there are normally other statutes which provide the source of constitutional law in respect of specialised matters, such as the electoral process or public finance system.

2 Common law

This is not a major source of constitutional law in the countries of the world. This is because most countries have enacted Constitutions relatively late in their political history and these have replaced principles enunciated by common-law writers. A second reason for the relative unimportance of common law is that constitutional law by its nature is political and controversial and therefore not appropriate for common-law regulation. In South Africa both the English and Roman-Dutch common law have had potential relevance for constitutional law, but it is the English common law which has been more important in practice. This topic is dealt with comprehensively by Carpenter.[23] In general it can be said that South Africa follows the fashion of according very little significance to common law in the constitutional domain.

3 Case law

This is the third important source of constitutional law. In jurisdictions where the courts have an active constitutional role, case law is the most important source. In South Africa case law is important in certain areas, such as citizenship,[24] the status of the homelands and the interpretation of some sections of the Constitution Act, and its importance is likely to increase over time. However case law has only a conditional status in that it can be easily

[23] Gretchen Carpenter *Introduction to South African Constitution Law* (1987) 18–25.
[24] See below, 234–6.

circumvented by other institutions of the state. The constitutional reasons for this situation, and the different arrangements elsewhere, are explained in later sections of the book.

4 Custom

This is the oldest source of law in that originally law derived from the well-worn and well-accepted practices of the community. To be legally binding, a custom must have been generally observed over a long period; if it is reasonable, by modern standards, and certain in its ambit it will then be enforceable, provided it has not been superseded by some other form of law. Constitutional conventions, which are of importance to the practical operation of the constitutional system, were originally based on custom, but are now generally held not to constitute 'law' in the strict sense of the word. Conventions are dealt with in more detail in chapter 3. In South Africa only a few important conventions of the constitution are still intact.

III ADMINISTRATIVE LAW

A Its definition

The definition of administrative law overlaps with that of constitutional law. It is also the law which regulates state institutions, their interaction with one another, and their relationships with individuals, but it is concerned mainly with one branch of the state system known as the administration or bureaucracy. In some definitions the emphasis is on the control of administrative power and the protection of the individual; in others it is on the need for rules which will ensure that administrative bodies perform their functions effectively.[25]

Baxter divides administrative law into general and particular categories.[26] He defines general administrative law as

'the general principles of law which regulate the organisation of administrative institutions and the fairness and efficacy of the administrative process, govern the validity of and liability for administrative action and inaction, and govern the administrative and judicial remedies relating to such action or inaction'.

Particular administrative law he defines as

'the legislation governing, and legal principles and policies developed in respect of, specific areas of administration'.

An analogy from the law of contract clarifies this distinction. All contracts are governed by certain basic principles of common law and statute, but some contracts, such as those involving the sale of land or purchase of goods on credit, have in addition their own specific rules. Thus all administrative acts will be governed by the general principles of administrative law but most administrative

---

[25] See P P Craig *Administrative Law* (1983) 1.
[26] Lawrence Baxter *Administrative Law* (1984) 2.

bodies will also have their own body of administrative law—for example planning bodies, licensing authorities or the state's security forces. Part III of this book deals with aspects of general administrative law in South Africa.

In the case of administrative law there is also recurring doubt as to whether it is properly law. Here the reason for doubt is that branches of the government other than the courts manage to enforce much 'administrative law' and many of the remedies for those who feel unhappy with the decision of a public authority must be sought from another administrative body, rather than from the courts. These bodies, moreover, appear not only to apply the law but also to exercise discretions and even to enforce the policies of the department or the government. But the truth is that law is no less law because it is not enforced by the courts. In fact in some legal systems all administrative law is enforced by bodies other than the traditional courts,[27] whereas in our system it is a basic principle of the public law system that the courts have some say over all administrative bodies. It is also worth remembering that historically the courts did not have a monopoly on judging—they were one of a range of sources of justice. The modern trend is for the courts to be losing the monopoly which they had developed in this century, partly in the face of administrative-law developments.

B Its scope

The scope of administrative law is so vast that it is easier to describe the matters it deals with than to define it. These matters include the granting of licences, the planning of towns, the building of roads, the collection of taxes, the censorship of literature, the arrest of criminal suspects, the protection of the environment, the development of the economy, the provision of education and health services, and so on. In all cases the administrative bodies concerned are subject to a mass of rules and principles. However there are differences in the degree to which these various functions are under the control of law—and hence of lawyers and the courts. One of the basic issues in administrative law is how far the administrative process should be regulated by law.[28] Its scope is partly dependent on this flexible and sometimes controversial factor.

C Its sources

1 Legislation

In practice this is the most important source of administrative law. The rise of the administrative state and governmental intervention into almost all facets of life is a relatively recent phenomenon and it is necessarily regulated by statute. Furthermore governments use legislation as the main instrument for giving effect to their social

[27] See below, 93–5.
[28] Gavin Drewry *Law, Justice and Politics* 2 ed (1981) 75.

policies which inevitably involve more power for public authorities; examples would include the group areas and other apartheid legislation in South Africa, or national health schemes in other countries. In these cases it is mainly the conferment of administrative authority which has a statutory source. In South African administrative law all powers of public authorities must be expressly or impliedly conferred by statute, otherwise they will be disallowed by the courts; there are so few exceptions to this rule that it can be regarded as 'Principle 1' of the administrative-law system. However the power of the administration need not derive only from Acts of Parliament—it could also be conferred by other kinds of legislation such as municipal by-laws, regulations or orders, all of which are known as subordinate legislation. In many cases the only obvious source of law for an administrative-law problem might be a terse regulation buried in the pages of the *Government Gazette*. However, it is important to bear in mind that while the regulation will be the immediate legal source, it takes on its meaning and significance from the wider legal context in which it is found.

2 Case law

In most administrative-law systems decisions of the courts will be a significant source of administrative law. They will be particularly important where the courts are the main institutions which control administrative bodies. Court decisions will be important in two broad areas. The first is in interpreting and defining the ambit of authority conferred on public authorities by statute. The second is in imposing limits and constraints on those powers. The second function is seen as the courts' unique contribution to administrative law, particularly in those jurisdictions where the legislature imposes few restraints on public authorities and where the political process provides no real checks on their activities. South Africa is one such country, and here many administrative-law principles have been developed through the process of judicial review. The courts often invoke common-law principles in exercising their supervisory powers and frequently create law to deal with unique problems. However, the extent of the courts' ability to develop principles for the regulation of public authorities is a matter of controversy. The normal rules of precedent apply to this source of administrative law; decisions of other jurisdictions, especially those from English law, can be very influential in South African courts and therefore constitute an indirect source of administrative law. It will be shown in Part III of this work that much administrative law is decided by bodies other than courts and these administrative tribunals are also a source of law.

3 Common law

This is a more important source in administrative than in constitutional law. Although administrative law is a very modern branch of the law and derives mostly from statute and judicial interpretation, there is an important part which comes from the common law.[29] In South Africa Roman-Dutch common law provides a range of rules and principles of interpretation which are important in determining the nature and scope of a public authority's power. The most important of these are the presumptions of interpretation which are enforced on administrative bodies—for example that legislation does not have retrospective effect and that it is enacted in the public interest. From the English common law comes the head of state's prerogative power which allows the executive to perform certain administrative actions; these are now few in number but not without significance.[30] Of more importance are the principles of natural justice which apply to the method of administrative decision-making; these principles are dealt with in Part III of the book. In all cases the administrative-law principles derived from the common law have been defined and modified by the courts. It is through the courts' inherent power to review administrative actions, and in the process to interpret and apply the legislation conferring power on public authorities, that common law affects the body of administrative law. Their effect will usually be to limit and contain public authorities, but in some cases their powers are amplified to give effect to the object of the legislation. However, in the administrative-law context the common-law principles can be, and frequently are, overridden by legislation. The interface between common law and statute gives rise to a creative and at times controversial element in administrative law.

4 Custom

Although custom is the oldest source of law it might not be expected to have relevance in the administrative law context.[31] As indicated above, the normal requirements for a custom to give rise to binding law are that it be reasonable, have been followed by for a considerable period of time and be well-known in the relevant community. In the administrative law context this would involve the question of whether long-established administrative practices and procedures which were relied on by the public could be recognized by law. In South Africa it has been understood that there is virtually no scope for this source; not only is the branch of law relatively modern, but the administrative process is highly regulated by statute and common law. However, in a recent decision the Namibian Supreme Court suggested that custom could in some circumstances be a source of administrative law.[32] Moreover, while custom can hardly give rise to new rules of administrative law, it can affect the

---

[29] See the fuller treatment of this topic in Marinus Wiechers *Administrative Law* (1985) 33–6.

[30] See below, 175–82.

[31] See Wiechers op cit n 29 at 40–1.

[32] *Ndisiro v Mbanderu Community Authority* 1986 (2) SA 532 (SWA).

way in which existing rules are interpreted and understood—that is, the courts will be influenced by past practices of the authority concerned, particularly where they have been relied on by the public. Finally, quasi-legislation[33] can also have a formative effect on administrative-law practice. However, generally in South Africa administrative custom is not an important source of law.

IV THE CONNECTION BETWEEN CONSTITUTIONAL AND ADMINISTRATIVE LAW

The above definitions have attempted to show the theoretical and practical differences between constitutional and administrative law. It is also important to show the connectedness of the two.[34] One of the functions of the constitutional process is to create a government through the prescribed process of election, nomination and appointment. The government of the day is able to give effect to its policies, firstly by securing the enactment of legislation through the prescribed parliamentary procedures. After this preliminary step the process of implementing and administering that policy begins. This involves a vast range of public authorities at the national level of government, and others at the regional and local levels. In the course of implementing policy these bodies have a range of powers: they implement, they make subsidiary rules, they formulate additional policy within the framewok of the umbrella policy contained in the legislation, they exercise discretions, and they even settle disputes—that is, they adjudicate.

Thus while constitutional law is concerned with the establishment of the governing system and the initial formulation of policy, administrative law is concerned with the daily business of government. They both have to do with the way in which power is distributed in the state system and the ways in which it is exercised, but with different areas of focus. It is sometimes said that constitutional law is concerned with the state system at rest and administrative law with it in motion,[35] but this metaphor is not wholly appropriate. It is better to see administrative law as a specialised part of constitutional law. In practice it is also the most important part as public administration impinges daily and directly on the lives of all citizens. Nevertheless the constitution provides the basic framework within which administrative law operates and evolves. In chapter 4 specific attention is given to the dependence of the system of administrative law on constitutional principles.

V THE ELEMENTS OF PUBLIC LAW

In this section a brief description is provided of the common terms of constitutional and administrative law. The objective is again to

---

[33] See below, 86–7. Cf Baxter 399.
[34] See S A de Smith *Constitutional and Administrative Law* 5 ed (1985) 533ff.
[35] Holland *Jurisprudence* 13 ed (1924) 374.

provide the basic tools required for further progress. In reality many of the terms have a wide range of meanings, some of which overlap with one another; some are ambiguous, and others are used inconsistently in legislation and textbooks.[36]

State has been defined in terms of the system of authorities which regulate society. *Government* is sometimes used synonymously with the state, from which it should be clearly distinguished, or in the sense of the whole system of 'government', including that at local and regional levels. Here it is understood in a narrower and more accepted sense as relating to the 'government of the day'. In this sense the government is the group which controls the most important state institution, the executive branch or cabinet (see below), though it may control other branches as well. The government is concerned with the making of policy in the constitutional system and it undertakes a programme of law-making and administration to give effect to that policy. The government has less permanence than the state and may change from time to time without the state system being affected in any way. The political group which attempts to replace the government in power is referred to as the *opposition*, in contradistinction to the government, and where there is more than one group the strongest rival of the government is known as the *official opposition*.

The term *executive* also has a wide and narrow meaning. In its narrow sense it denotes the formal constitutional body which is often referred to as the executive council and in practice means the ministers of state together with the chief executive (president, prime minister) acting in their official policy-making capacity. This body, or sometimes a smaller component of it, is also known as the *cabinet*. (In South Africa the executive authority consists of the national cabinet and three ministers' councils.) In its wider sense executive denotes the whole of the implementing branch of government, that is the cabinet, ministers' councils, administrative departments, boards, tribunals and semi-government bodies (parastatals). Thus while the cabinet (or government) is primarily concerned with policy-making, the rest of the executive is primarily concerned with the implementation of laws. In this work *executive* (or political executive) is used to signify the narrower meaning, which is similar to government, and *administration* is used to refer to all executive bodies other than the cabinet. (In some countries the term administration is used to identify a specific leader and cabinet, as in 'the Reagan administration', but this sense is infrequently used in South Africa.) *Bureaucracy* has a similar sense to administration, but nowadays it has a derogatory connotation, as suggesting unnecessary or inefficient forms of public administration.

The *legislature* means the central law-making organ of government with power to make laws with national effect. As the legislature is

---

[36] See generally on these terms L G Baxter (1982) 99 *SALJ* 212.

usually a representative body, the term *Parliament* is a more accurate one because representative bodies do more than just make legislation. However, in practice the term Parliament is used only for some legislatures, usually those modelled on the British Parliament, and alternative terms such as Congress or National Assembly are used for others. In this work the term legislature is used to designate the central representative assembly in any constitutional system. *Bicameralism* is the term used to indicate that a legislature has two separate parts, usually known as houses or chambers. Traditionally the term 'lower house' is used for the larger body which is more directly representative of the electorate and which can prevail over the less representative upper house. The 'upper house' is often called the Senate, but other terms such as Legislative Council are also used; in Britain the upper house is the House of Lords. The lower house can also be known by different terms; in Britain it is House of Commons and in other countries House of Assembly or House of Representatives. (No particular significance attaches to the different terminology.) Where neither house in a bicameral legislature is more powerful than the other, the terms upper and lower house are not used; thus the United States Senate, which is smaller and less representative than the House of Representatives, does not have to give way in cases of conflict, and in some matters is even the more influential body. *Unicameralism* indicates that the legislature has only one house or chamber. In 1983 South Africa introduced a new term into the constitutional lexicon when it established a *tricameral* Parliament. Tricameralism is not a common feature in the world's constitutions.

In its narrow sense the *franchise* denotes the right to elect and be elected to the central representative assembly, but in a looser sense the term means entitlement to political rights. A universal adult franchise signifies that all adults, regardless of race, gender, language or religion, have political rights, subject to disqualification on grounds of insanity, criminality, and the like. A qualified franchise accords political rights to those who satisfy certain educational or property requirements. The collection of individuals who have the franchise in a country is known as the *electorate*.

A *statute* is a written law which has been passed by the central legislature and ratified by the head of state; it is also sometimes known as an *enactment* or an *Act*. A Bill is a draft statute which is still in the process of being considered by the legislature or is awaiting ratification by the head of state. Sometimes statute (as in statute law) is used in a wider sense and as the equivalent of *legislation*, which denotes all law enacted by a competent law-making body, and is contrasted with common law which is pronounced by the courts. *Delegated legislation* is made by one or other authority which is subordinate to the national legislature; it is known by various terms such as regulations, rules, orders or by-laws, none of which has any intrinsic difference to the others. To become effective legislation must be assented to, often by the head of state, and be *promulgated* in an official publication, the *Government Gazette*.

The *judiciary* is the adjudicative, or dispute-resolving branch of government. In its normal understanding judiciary has a narrow scope, referring only to the higher courts, such as the Supreme Court in South Africa, which is staffed by judges. However, it is sometimes used more widely to include lower courts, such as Magistrates' Courts, the personnel of which are not judges but officials of the Department of Justice.

The terms *review* and *appeal* each have several meanings, some of which overlap, and they are sometimes used interchangeably.[37] Here the terms are defined according to their general meaning in the South African constitutional system, and in the sense in which they are used in this word unless the contrary is indicated. Both denote a judicial-type remedy, but with different powers and consequences. In a review the courts can scrutinise the procedure adopted by a public authority and determine whether it conforms to that required by statute and laid down by the courts. In an appeal the court will scrutinise the merits of the previous decision with a view to determining whether it was correctly decided on the evidence. Clearly the distinction between these two functions can at times blur. There is also a difference in the courts' respective powers. On review the court can usually only refer the matter back to the original authority which took the decision with the directive that it reconsider the matter and follow the correct procedure in doing so. On appeal the court can, depending on its assessment of the evidence, substitute its own decision for that of the public authority. Again you will encounter exceptions to both these general rules. At common law the Supreme Court has an inherent right of review over all decisions of administrative bodies, though the right may be removed or curtailed by statute. However, a right of appeal does not exist at common law and must be expressly provided by statute. It should also be borne in mind that bodies other than the courts may be granted powers of review or appeal by statute.

Discretion denotes the right to choose between two or more courses of action, or between action and inaction. It is an important part of administrative law because governments claim more and more discretionary power to be able to cope with the complexities of modern society. State discretion is a very necessary ingredient of modern life, but it also requires supervision and control, some of which is provided by administrative law. Note here that there can be no such thing as a completely unfettered discretion; that is, there will always be limits to discretionary power, no matter how widely it is conferred. This is borne out by common usage, as in 'she acted with discretion', meaning in a careful, discerning and responsible fashion. *Policy* has different meanings in different branches of the law. In

---

[37] On this distinction see further at 251–5 below.

public law it denotes a communal goal, for example to preserve mountain catchment areas, and it is closely related to the concept of public interest. Governments and administrative bodies are allowed to decide matters of policy (though of course they might not do so in the genuine national interest) and policy can be an influential factor in discretionary decision-making. In administrative law there is a tension between what are seen as the competing demands of law, on one hand, and discretion and policy on the other.

Jurisdiction means lawful authority. (Sometimes it refers to a legal system, as in the American jurisdiction.) The term is used to define the powers and capacities of all public authorities, including the executive and the courts. The term *ultra vires* means 'beyond lawful authority'.[38] The ultra vires doctrine is of crucial importance in administrative law as it provides the justification for the courts' power to intervene in the administrative process,[39] namely that they are acting beyond their legal authority. The term *justiciability* denotes the extent to which adjudication in an appropriate or feasible way of solving disputes. The degree of justiciability of an issue will depend partly on its nature (for instance, issues with a high policy content are less justiciable than those issues governed by legal rules) and partly on the judges' attitudes to their position and role in government.[40]

Legality is the cornerstone of public law. In its narrow sense it means that all acts of state institutions must be permitted by law, and this provides the justificatory basis of judicial review. In its wider senses it means not only that acts of public authorities must be legally authorised, but they must in addition conform to certain minimal standards of justice—fairness, equality before the law, and absence of arbitrary administrative action.[41] Where they have not been tampered with by statute these standards provide for creative development in administrative law. The principle of legality is part of the wider doctrine of constitutionalism which is dealt with in the following chapter.

[38] See below, 259–64.
[39] See Baxter op cit n 25 at 303–12, and below, 262–4.
[40] Cf Baxter 320ff.
[41] Cf Selznik op cit in 10 at 11, Baxter 78, and below, 255–9.

2 Constitutionalism

The doctrine of constitutionalism has to do with the state, society and law. While the doctrine is a relatively modern one its roots can be identified in the earliest forms of government. Over the centuries its meaning has evolved and modified; as constitutional structures have changed, so have the theories used to explain, evaluate and justify them. The essence of the doctrine is that the power of the state should be defined and limited by law in order to protect the interests of society;[1] it upholds the notion of limited government as opposed to arbitrary rule. The principle of limitation applies in two areas: first, in restricting the range of things which a government can do, and second, in prescribing the procedures it must follow in doing those things within its competence. There have, however, been very different emphases during its evolution and different institutional arrangements have arisen for giving effect to its requirements.

Constitutionalism is a prescriptive and not a descriptive doctrine; it indicates how state power should be exercised and not how it is exercised in practice. It is normative, that is it denotes which set of values should be upheld in the governing process. These values require more than just a set of constitutional rules: as is often observed, not every country with a Constitution upholds the principles of constitutionalism. The fact that it is prescriptive and normative does not make constitutionalism something that is not 'real'; its principles do influence the practice of government and are a significant ingredient in the constitutional systems of the world. They provide a standard by which the record of individual governmental systems can be measured, and by which one can be compared with another. It has some influence on those who operate the state system: policy-makers, administrators, and most importantly, judges. However, it does not describe how political systems actually work in practice.

After a description of the general development of constitutionalism, the doctrine is examined within the historical context of three specific traditions of constitutional thought. While there are other traditions, such as those associated with Islamic and African public law, the analysis is restricted to the English, American and socialist systems. The greatest attention is given to English constitutionalism because of its historical relevance in South Africa.

I ANCIENT INFLUENCES

A Cave-dwellers

Cave-dwellers did not make a lasting contribution to the develop-

---

[1] Cf the definition of Charles Howard McIllwain *Constitutionalism: Ancient and Modern* rev ed (1947) 21–2.

ment of the doctrine of constitutionalism. However, even without constitutions, courts or law books, cave-dwellers displayed certain principles of social organisation which are intrinsic to constitutional government. The first is a regular pattern of authority and obedience, the second is social order, and the third is legitimacy. These principles were upheld by custom, religion, superstition, and force. Custom and force are still a part of modern constitutional government but the contemporary standard of legitimacy is the formal constitution. (Some constitutional preambles[2] retain elements of superstition.)

B The Greeks

In Greek political philosophy there was a vigorous debate about the respective virtues of a government of men and a government of law.[3] For Plato the ideal system of government consisted of the philosopher-king, a wise and superior being who, through divine wisdom, knew what was in the common good and who was not subject to any controls in pursuing it. Law had a minimal role in this conception of government. Plato appreciated that legally controlled government would always be weak compared with an arbitrary system; because it did not have the freedom to do evil, it would also be precluded to some extent from doing good. For Aristotle, however, a government by laws was superior to a government by men because even the best of persons could be perverted by power. Law had the advantages of being rational and dispassionate, and Aristotle advocated a limited doctrine of the supremacy of law. He was the first to emphasise the importance of law for the notion of the state.[4]

The differences in these views were not extreme. Plato was mindful of the dangers of arbitrary government and conceded that his ideal must give way at times to government of laws, to which all citizens owed obedience, and Aristotle considered that certain individuals of exceptional quality and ability should be above the law, and should even be granted unlimited power and unconditional obedience. Moreover, in both instances the reflections on government occurred in the absence of any clear notion of the state and in a social system with a very undeveloped system of law, in the technical sense. Although the procedural side of constitutionalism was developed in the Greek city-states, there was no notion of the constitution being a form of higher law, which is a characteristic of modern constitutionalism. Nor, for the Greek philosophers, was there any opposition or conflict of interests between the individual and the state.[5]

Besides providing the origins of a modern debate within constitutionalism, ancient Greece inspired later conceptions of

[2] See below, 58.
[3] McIllwain op cit n 1 at 23–40.
[4] Cf A P d'Entreves *The Notion of the State* (1967) 74.
[5] C F Strong *Modern Political Constitutions* 8 ed (1972) 15.

constitutional government. Aristotle distinguished between three constitutional forms, which involved rule, respectively, by the monarchy, the aristocracy, and the polity (by which he meant a middle class-dominated democracy). The best constitution was the one which blended the three forms so that each element of society participated in the system of government. This notion was later refined by the idea that each part of government, as opposed to each social class, should exercise a different function, a principle which subsequently came to be known as the separation of powers. It was also in ancient Greece that the notion first emerged that law could be altered by the legislature, an idea which matured in the later Middle Ages[6] and became a commonplace feature of constitutional thought. The model for man-made laws was provided by the laws of nature, a concept which led to the later development of natural law theories. Greek philosophy and law first developed the principle of the equality of men—but not of women or slaves—under the law, which became a major influence in later theories of constitutional government. One of the consequences of equality was the right of citizens to participate directly in law-making in the city-state.

Greek political theory operated at the level of the city-state. This limited its relevance for the future nation-states. Furthermore its practice of government did not measure up to the constitutional theories of its philosophers. It was the philosophical ideas of Greece rather than its system of government which had a lasting influence on constitutionalism. Thus a question posed by Aristotle remains of fundamental concern to modern constitutionalism: how much control over officials and the decision-making process is desirable and how should it be exercised?[7]

C The Romans

McIllwain suggests that modern constitutional theory begins with Rome.[8] After the monarchy had been abolished an important principle emerged during the period of republican government. The system comprised three elements, a 'monarchical' element, namely the two consuls, an aristrocratic element, the Senate, and a democratic element, the meetings of the people. This arrangement recalled Aristotle's tripartite system. There was a balance of power among these elements so that no one branch could function without some assistance from the others. In this way different class interests in society participated in government through separate institutions and acted as a check on one another. Later commentators interpreted this as a system of 'mixed government', which was identified in the English constitutional system and influenced the development of separation of powers thinking in constitutional theory. It also

---

[6] Cf F Hayek *Law, Legislation and Liberty* vol 1 (1973) 73.
[7] *Politics* III, 15–16 (transl Barker (1946) 140–8).
[8] McIllwain 41ff.

provided the foundations for the modern doctrine of checks and balances.[9]

Other aspects of the Roman constitutional-legal system were also influential. For the first time it was accepted that enacted law derived its legitimacy from the fact that it was consented to by the people. Conversely it was understood that whatever the appropriate law-making bodies enacted was the law. These principles both became prominent in the English constitutional system centuries later. There was also an early system of rights, in the sense of claims which the individual could enforce through appropriate legal remedies. Some indication of the advanced nature of this system is the general right which was available to the private citizen to vindicate the common rights of all, a remedy which is not generally available in contemporary South African law.[10] (In the later republic even ex-governors could be tried for malpractice at the suit of an aggrieved citizen.) Finally, the Roman system of law, including its doctrines of equity and legal equality, provided a rational and systematic institution which had a formative effect on the development of Western civilization.[11] It inspired not only later legal systems but provided some of the basic concepts for subsequent principles of legally controlled government—for example, the principle of the generality of law became a cornerstone of the Rule of Law doctrine. The distinction between public and private law can also be traced to Roman law.

Despite the sophistication of Roman law and government, there was no developed conception of natural rights—that is, universal and immutable standards with a higher authority than human laws. Enacted law could not be invalidated on the ground that it did not conform to natural-law standards. On the contrary, law pronounced by the supreme authority was binding.[12] In theory the supreme authority derived its power through delegation from the people; the people, acting through the constitutional processes, were the ultimate source of legal authority. This implied a notion of supreme power which in later constitutional theory evolved into the doctrine of sovereignty. Rudimentary notions of natural law were, however, prevalent in Roman jurisprudence. Cicero has been described as the first natural lawyer to argue that enacted laws should be struck down if they contravene natural law.[13] In a famous phrase he defined natural law as 'right reason in agreement with nature'.[14] However, in practice there was no notion of supreme norms to which laws were subject.

The reality of the Roman state was not always in keeping with constitutional theory—constitutional principles were swept aside by

[9] See below, 43–4..
[10] It is known as the actio popularis and is dealt with below, 266–7.
[11] Cf H J Wolff *Roman Law* (1951) 3–6.
[12] *Quod principi placuit legis vigorem habet.* Digest I, 4, 1.
[13] Lord Lloyd and M D A Freeman *Lloyd's Introduction to Jurisprudence* 5 ed (1986) 108.
[14] *De Republica* III, xii, 33.

authoritarian rulers in much the same way as they are today. The constitution remained essentially that of a city-state and for Rome's subject peoples provided only authoritarian control. The Roman system of government did, however, establish law as one of the conditions of the state's existence. It also espoused the theory, even during imperial times, that legislative power derived fron the people. One of the reasons for the lapse into autocracy was that even when the empire extended into remote regions there was no system of representation in the constitutional scheme. This principle emerged only many centuries later in constitutional practice.

II THE MIDDLE AGES AND THE RENAISSANCE

A Descending theories of power

There is uncertainty about the theories and practices of government during the early Middle Ages. Generally, however, this period was characterised by a descending theory of power.[15] Under the influence of the church, the most powerful social institution of the times, the idea prevailed that original power was located in God. The government was regarded as having a divine origin and its main function was to apply and interpret pre-ordained law, and not to create it. Obedience to law was part of man's obedience to God. Bad government was God's way of punishing sin. These conceptions were well-suited to a monarchical form of government and there was no room for the notion of popular consent to law and the governing process.

During the thirteenth century Bracton drew a distinction which is still relevant to constitutional thought. Some functions of government were recognised to involve more than the mere application of law but to require the active discretion of the king.[16] Within this sphere of power the king was absolute and his acts were beyond the law and popular control. Beyond this sphere, however, the king could not act autocratically because he was subject to the law, and to the assemblies of the people which were then emerging. If he acted beyond these constraints his actions were ultra vires and invalid, a basic notion of constitutional government. Unfortunately, however, there was no effective remedy against the monarch if the constitution was overridden! Although Bracton was writing about the English system of government, the distinction applied also in the continental systems. Subsequent centuries saw the narrowing of those areas of government beyond the reach of the law and, more importantly, the development of effective remedies for invalidating illegal acts of government. Nevertheless, to this day governments attempt to place some of their actions and practices beyond the reach of the law, the

---

[15] The 'descending' and 'ascending' theories of power were first used by Walter Ullmann *Law and Politics in the Middle Ages* (1975) 225ff.

[16] The concepts of 'gubernaculum' and 'jurisdictio' are elaborated on by McIllwain 77ff.

courts and the constitution—for example, international treaties and the conduct of foreign affairs.

One of the checks on the power of the king during the medieval period was the church. The 'doctrine of the swords'[17] which endured until the Reformation, held that the church and the secular government had co-ordinate powers. Although their powers were co-ordinate there was a limited participation by each in the functions of the other. This provided a crude medieval form of separation of powers between the two institutions, each of which acted as a check and balance on the other.

B Feudalism

Feudal society introduced a system of mutual rights and obligations which produced a greater degree of social and political organisation than had existed in tribal society. In essence the system produced a hierarchical social ordering based on land tenure. Allegiance and service were owed to those above one in the hierarchy, and protection and the maintenance of peace was owed to those below. At the apex of this pyramid stood the feudal monarch or emperor. One of the effects of feudalism was to bond society together in anticipation of the modern state. Law became an important feature of feudal society, and in theory was binding on all, irrespective of status. The development of law entailed an important new function for the king, namely the administration of justice. Despite its hierarchical ordering, feudalism also created a mutual dependence between the feudal monarch and his chief barons. In practice they were consulted on matters of government, including the promulgation of law, and in time their consent became a political necessity, particularly in financial matters. Strong suggests that feudalism was a kind of medieval constitutionalism.[18]

One of England's best-known constitutional products of the feudal era was Magna Carta. This document was approved by King John in 1215, but as he was under a heavy threat of arms it was an assent he could not refuse. Magna Carta was a feudal document in that it set out the grievances and rights of various classes of the community, in accordance with their status and needs. Not surprisingly, it protected the interests of the most powerful barons, who had compelled John to accept it. But it also made provision for the Church, the cities, the freemen, and even the serfs. Some of its better-known sections read as follows:

'No freemen shall be taken or imprisoned . . . or in any way destroyed, nor will we go upon him nor send upon him, except by the lawful judgment of his peers and by the law of the land';
'To no one will we sell, to no one will we refuse or delay, right or justice';

---

[17] See G Sabine *A History of Political Theory* (1951) 198ff; cf W G Andrews *Constitutions and Constitutionalism* (1963) 19.
[18] Strong op cit n 5 at 20.

'We will appoint as justices, constables, sheriffs, or bailiffs only such as know the law of the realm and mean to observe it well'.[19]

While there was not much of substance that was new in Magna Carta it evidenced an attempt to restore the legal limits on the monarchy, which had in the past been disregarding them, through the force of a constitutional document. Although there was yet no legal remedy for enforcing its provisions, Magna Carta was imbued with the spirit of constitutionalism, and its provisions relating to access to justice and due process of law are seen as providing the origins of the Rule of Law doctrine. Its practical effects on the governing process were not, however, impressive and its importance was mainly symbolic. Nevertheless it was re-enacted on several occasions and some of its provisions are still on the English statute book.[20] They remain binding on the executive but have never been binding on the legislature. The rights first embodied in Magna Carta were also reproduced in modified form in the early constitutions established on American soil.

In other feudal systems, such as France, charters similar to Magna Carta of England were also promulgated. In each case they were the earliest forms of documentary constitutionalism. Thus while feudalism did not dispense with the descending theories of power, it did pave the way for the modern constitutional state. It was particularly those feudal systems with powerful kings which became highly centralised and provided the basis for the subsequent nation states.

C Taxation, representation and ascending theories of power

Taxation had a significant influence on the development of constitutional theory. Governments in the Middle Ages were no less dependent on revenue than those of modern times, and taxation was an obvious source of money. In order to legitimise taxation measures, medieval kings summoned assemblies of the people to secure their acceptance. In countries such as England and France these assemblies were representative of more than just the chief barons, though they were not genuinely representative by modern standards.

These developments led to one of the earliest principles of modern constitutionalism, later encapsulated in the slogan 'no taxation without representation'. It became accepted practice for the medieval Parliaments to be consulted on and to approve taxation measures, failing which they would not be enforced. With the growing financial needs of the central administration, this provided early parliamentary assemblies with considerable leverage over the king. In time they extended their influence to legislation, in respect of which they came to be consulted—though not always followed. This facilitated

---

[19] See William Sharp McKechnie *Magna Carta—A Commentary on the Great Charter of King John* 2 ed (1914) 375ff.

[20] E C S Wade and A W Bradley *Constitutional and Administrative Law* 10 ed (1985) 10ff. Magna Carta was not strictly a statute but was treated as such by the courts and Parliament.

the development of ascending theories of power and the notion that the legitimacy of government depended on the consent of the governed. This was a major development in the evolution of constitutionalism. It led to the replacement of the absolutist monarchy by the constitutional monarchy, in terms of which the Crown was understood to be politically dependent on representatives of the people and constitutionally subject to the law—though at this stage the constitution did not provide any method for enforcing the law against the Crown. Ascending theories of power led subsequently to parliamentary and republican systems of government.

D The Renaissance and the national state

The Renaissance revived interest in the systems of government and political theories of the ancient cultures. It witnessed a new intellectual interest in the rights of the individual and human liberty. These cultural and philosophical developments coincided politically with a strong assertion of national integrity and the drawing of territorial boundaries in Western Europe. The nation-state emerged with a strong central authority, the monarchy. But now the Crown held sway independently of the competing barons from feudal times. It also attempted to govern without the assistance of the representative assemblies which had emerged in the medieval period. For the purposes of getting the business of government done there emerged strong centralised bureaucracies under the close supervision of the Crown.

This was not, in continental Europe, a fertile time for theories of constitutional government.[21] It was the period of the absolutist state which upheld the principle of the divine right of kings. The Crown held itself to be above the law and citizens had little in the way of legally protected rights. Theorists such as Bodinus developed extreme theories of sovereignty to justify the Crown's authoritarian actions. Any conflict between the government and constitutional rules was resolved in favour of the former.[22] In some countries the absolutist state was eradicated only through revolution. One of its lasting contributions to constitutional theory was the notion of sovereignty. In essence this involved the identification of the supreme power in a state system, to which all other authorities were subordinate. This concept was not easily reconcilable with the constitutionalist emphasis on the division and limitation of state power, but its legacy is still felt in many constitutional systems, including the South African.

E The social contract and natural law

The social contract is a theory of the state and society. In its

[21] One of the principal theorists of the time was Machiavelli who published *The Prince* in 1513.
[22] Cf Gordon J Schochat in J Roland Pennock and John W Chapman (eds) *Constitutionalism* (1979) 1 at 2.

developed form it provided grounds of justification for those wishing to break the absolutist systems and the concept of the divine right of kings which legitimated them.[23] Some of its best-known exponents were Thomas Hobbes, John Locke and Jean Jacques Rousseau.[24] In its simplest terms the social contract held that the state is formed when persons fictionally agree to come together to end the insecurity of a dangerous state of nature caused by the clash of individual interests. In the enduring words of Hobbes, human life in a state of nature, and without the social contract, is 'solitary, poor, nasty, brutish, and short'.[25] The authority of the king, or government, was said to have rested on a contract made between him and the people in terms of which he would perform the duties of his office and they would obey. In entering the contract the people abandoned certain natural rights with the object of preserving others. The contractual basis of government entailed that if either party broke the pact, the other would be released from its obligations. Most pertinently, if the king broke the fundamental laws of the system the citizens were entitled to disobey and, in extreme circumstances, overthrow him. In short, the social contract held that sovereignty passed from the ruler to the people and the authority of the ruler was circumscribed by law. This was an attractive notion for the architects of the 'revolutionary constitutions' of the eighteenth century.[26]

Although social contract theory was developed out of the specific circumstances in which its adherents found themselves, it was claimed to be of universal application. At the time it was seen as a radical doctrine, particularly in respect of its condonation of disobedience to the state in certain situations. But ultimately the social contract theory was based on a colossal fiction and in its classical form it was no longer propounded after the eighteenth century.[27] However, the theory had a lasting effect on the doctrine of constitutionalism. One of its legacies was the principle that only through his or her consent can a person be subjected to the authority of the state and its agents. This led to the development of representative institutions of government, and ultimately to the universal franchise. Another was the emphasis on the protection of private property, which, together with the preservation of other individual rights, came to be regarded as the predominant function of the constitutional state. The social contract theory also freed state governments from their former close relationship with the church. In its wake popular sovereignty replaced the absolutism of the sixteenth and seventeenth centuries. The prevalence of the written Consti-

---

[23] See Strong 29–33.
[24] Hobbes published *Leviathan* in 1651, Locke *Treatises of Civil Government* in 1690, and Rousseau *Social Contract* in 1762.
[25] *Leviathan* ch 13.
[26] See below, 43.
[27] A sophisticated modern form is found in the writings of John Rawls *A Theory of Justice* (1973).

tution was an indirect product of the development of popular sovereignty.

The development of natural law also affected the shape of constitutionalism.[28] It complemented the theory of the social contract, although its roots went further back in history and its fruits are still evident today. In medieval times natural law was regarded as having a divine origin, but it could be determined by man through the powers of moral reasoning.[29] Despite its divine source the principles of natural law were based on the nature of man: they included self-preservation, propagation, education, and social life. Natural law later took on a more secular form which emphasised the value and sanctity of the human being.[30] In all its forms it claimed to be of universal application and to transcend barriers of time, geography and culture, and in particular of human laws. It was also applied to relations between nation states. It became the moral vehicle for a theory of natural rights for the individual and legal limitations on the power of the state.

The relevance of natural law for constitutionalism is that it provided standards on which the limitations of government could be based. Whereas in its undeveloped form in Greek political theory it provided only a vague intellectual ideal, in modern constitutionalism it provided the basis for concrete judicial decisions. It introduced a new dimension to the constitutional equation, namely the individual as the bearer of rights, and inspired the notion of the 'higher law' of the constitution.[31] What has been called 'basic-rights' constitutionalism[32] was brought to fruition in the American constitution; the natural rights of moral philosophy were translated into basic rights of the positive law in the constitutional amendments of 1787. Natural law also influenced the French Declaration of the Rights of Man of 1789. To this day, legal rights entail an appeal to underlying considerations of morality, though it is only in rare situations, such as Irish constitutional law, that natural law is expressly invoked to provide specificity to the general language of constitutional rights.[33]

The theories of the social contract and natural rights lent support to the constitutional revolutions in England in the seventeenth century and France and America in the eighteenth, which swept away the notion of the divine right of kings. This cleared the way for the emergence of modern forms of constitutional government. In

[28] For a basic introduction to natural law theories see J W Harris *Legal Philosophies* (1980) 6–23.

[29] One of the best-known theological proponents was Thomas Aquinas in his thirteenth-century work *Summa Theologiae*.

[30] Among the exponents of this form of natural law were Hugo Grotius and Samuel Pufendorf, seventeenth-century jurists whose works are still influential in South Africa.

[31] See on this theme the well-known work by Edward S Corwin *The 'Higher Law' Background of American Constitutional Law* (1955).

[32] See Klaus Stern (1985) 18 *CILSA* 187 at 192.

[33] See Desmond M Clarke (1982) 17 *The Irish Jurist* 187.

particular it presaged the emergence of modern documentary constitutionalism.[34]

III ENGLISH CONSTITUTIONALISM

A Evolution

One of the striking features of English constitutional development is its evolutionary nature. English constitutional structures and procedures developed gradually and progressively without any break in legal continuity. This may be contrasted with the American constitutional experience which witnessed the deliberate creation and implementation of a constitutional system, involving a legal as well as a political break with the past. Most modern constitutional experience has followed the American pattern.

Evolutionary constitutional development has no necessary relevance for the doctrine of constitutionalism. However, in the English context it does require a historical approach to the understanding of the constitutional system. In broad terms English constitutional development has involved the movement of authority and power from one institution to another, the gradual emergence of new institutions and replacement of the old, and the incremental development of corrective devices to keep the current wielders of power in check. In some cases the development of formal institutions occurred only long after a significant change in power relations had taken place. Here only the briefest outline can be provided of that complex process.

B Constitutional monarchy

The term 'constitutional monarchy' denotes that a monarch has the trappings of political authority but in reality has a very circumscribed role; it is a term of art, and one would not encounter its opposite—an unconstitutional monarchy.

The institution which spans the whole of English constitutional development is the monarchy.[35] In Anglo-Saxon times the king existed at the pleasure of the people, and some kings were elected. The functions of the Crown were restricted and were more of a religious than a secular nature. There was a very limited law-making function and the relatively small king's household had no effective means of law enforcement. It was accepted that the king was subject to the law. He was assisted by a council of the wise. The introduction of feudalism after the Norman invasion increased the power of the monarchy by providing a more close-knit and centralised society. To assist him the king summoned a king's council, comprising the most powerful barons. The council was the King's effective instrument of government and had legislative, executive and judicial functions. It

[34] Strong 32.
[35] See generally S B Chrimes *English Constitutional History* 4 ed (1967); T P Taswell-Langmead *English Constitutional History* 11 ed T F T Plunkett (1960).

also became the practice to summon more representative assemblies for specific purposes, such as assenting to royal taxes; these assemblies, the future Parliament, also assisted the Crown in supervising local affairs. The king retained the right to make law through the council, but by the fourteenth century the assemblies began to petition the king for legislation and gradually to assume the initiative in the law-making process. While the king had the final say in all legislation, and was virtually unrestricted by the assembly or council in the implementation of law, there was a rudimentary balance of power between the Crown and Parliament. It was still accepted during these developments that the monarch was subject to the law.

The picture changed during the time of the Tudor monarchs, the best known of whom was Henry VIII. Not only were some of the kings and queens autocratic and high-handed, but the Crown was a rejuvenated institution, in part because of the establishment of new organs of executive power.[36] One of these was the Privy Council, a nominated body which was consulted by, but was also under the influence of, the monarch. It had a wide range of functions in public and private life. One of its committees, the Star Chamber, was notorious for its prosecution and punishment of political opponents of the Crown, though it also served a more admirable purpose in upholding the rights of the working person and cutting the nobility down to size. The Tudor Parliaments were submissive towards the dominating Crown, which avoided summoning them where possible. Nevertheless, for tactical reasons the Crown introduced the concept of 'king-in-parliament', which implied that the Crown could not afford to assert its will purely through the armed forces but required the approval of Parliament. By the end of the Tudor period Parliament was becoming more assertive. In the celebrated *Case of Monopolies*[37] the House of Commons (the 'lower' house in the English Parliament) was able to put an end to the abuses of Queen Elizabeth I who had been granting exclusive import monopolies to her favourites. Parliament also regained its share in the legislative process and forced a partnership between the two institutions.

During the seventeenth century there was a prolonged dispute between Parliament and the Stuart kings as to where sovereignty lay. James I adopted the prevailing continental doctrine of the divine right of kings inherent in the hereditary monarchy and instead of a partnership with Parliament he strove for more absolute powers. He was opposed by the Commons, and by Chief Justice Coke who in the *Case of Prohibitions*[38] proclaimed that the king was subject to both God and the law. The king regarded it as treasonous to suggest that

---

[36] See D Lindsay Keir *The Constitutional History of Modern Britain 1485–1957* 2 ed (1943) 94ff.
[37] (1602) 11 Co Rep 84, 77 ER 1260.
[38] (1607) 12 Co Rep 63, 77 ER 1342.

he was subject to the ordinary law and dismissed Coke, emasculating the courts in the process. In order to avoid the opposition of the Commons he ruled for long periods without a Parliament, attempting to legislate by proclamation. When James was succeeded by Charles I the position deteriorated further, and in 1628 the Commons rebelled and submitted a Bill known as the Petition of Right. This was an attempt to terminate various unlawful practices of the Crown and to guarantee certain rights and privileges. Charles was forced to accede to the Petition under duress, but effectively ignored its contents and did not summon Parliament for eleven years. When it was eventually called, Parliament exacted some concessions from the Crown, such as the right to assemble at least once every three years (the Triennial Act), but this was not sufficient to prevent civil war between the royalists and parliamentarians, resulting in a short period of republican government under Oliver Cromwell. During this period an attempt was made for the first and only time to codify the principles of the English constitution.

The monarchy was restored in 1660, and both Charles II and James II held themselves to be above the law and the other institutions of government, but it was clear that never again could there be the royal absolutism of the past. The culmination of the struggle occurred towards the end of the century when James II was forced into exile, and in terms of the revolution settlement the throne was offered to William and Mary of Orange (the present-day Netherlands). While the transition was referred to as a 'great and glorious revolution' it all took place quite peacefully; the settlement was 'revolutionary' in the sense that it involved a break in legal continuity with the past. The settlement was accompanied by the Bill of Rights of 1689, which listed a number of ways in which James II had abused his powers and declared them to be illegal. The Crown could no longer suspend the operation of a law, and the sole power to levy taxation was vested in Parliament. Also significant was the Act of Settlement of 1701, which effected a profound and permanent change in the monarchy. It was now provided with a statutory basis which not only required the Crown to act subject to the ordinary law, but also regulated succession to the throne. Intellectual support for this innovation was provided by John Locke in terms of his social contract theory. Another feature of this period which had lasting implications for English constitutionalism, and administrative law, was that the executive power of the Crown was broken; it was not, as in countries such as France, simply transferred to another institution.[39] The abolition of the conciliar courts, such as the Star Chamber, meant that there were no longer any rivals to the ordinary common-law courts, in which alone the supervision of government legality was vested.[40]

Thus from the early eighteenth century there has been a constitutional monarchy in England. Its legislative powers have been

[39] On the remaining prerogative powers of the Crown see below, 70 and 175–8.
[40] See J D B Mitchell *Constitutional Law* 2 ed (1968) 97–8.

restricted to the right to veto legislation, but this right was last exercised in 1707. Its executive power has been circumscribed by law, save for the prerogative powers which came to be exercised by convention; prerogatives and conventions are dealt with in the following chapter.[41] Its judicial power has been transferred to the courts. While the Crown has retained some political influence over the centuries, its constitutional powers have been rendered mainly ceremonial.

C Parliamentary sovereignty

The institution which rivalled and came to surpass the English Crown was Parliament. Its early predecessors were the councils of the wise which assisted the king in declaring the law. There were in Anglo-Saxon times early assemblies which advised the king, but they were summonsed purely at his pleasure. In 1295 under Edward I there was a meeting of what is, with hindsight, called the first Parliament, in the modern sense of the term. At this stage it was still part of the king's court, and was used to strengthen the Crown's hand in struggles with powerful barons. It was also used by the Crown to pledge financial aid through various forms of taxation. While laws could still be made by the king in his council, the early parliaments considered less important laws and matters of taxation. In the fourteenth century Parliament divided into the Lords and Commons, and the latter began to develop a clearer view of its role and functions, particularly as far as the initiation of legislation was concerned. It was able to do this partly because of the fact that it was not as unrepresentative as the Lords. Parliament began to sit more regularly and to claim some of its privileges—that is, rights and practices which could not be interfered with by the Crown or courts. By the end of the fourteenth century a distinction was apparent between 'ordinances', which could be proclaimed by the King, and 'statutes', which required the approval of Parliament.

During the Tudor period, Parliament was dominated by the Crown and its influence was usurped by royal committees such as the Privy Council. However, because Parliament was no real threat to the Crown there was no resistance during this period to the development of its privileges—in particular, freedom of speech and freedom from arrest. The privileges were designed to reduce royal influence over Parliament, but their presence was also exploited by the Crown. In his conflicts with the Pope, Henry VIII was able to claim that he could not interfere in laws confiscating church property because they had been enacted by Parliament, which had unassailable constitutional privileges—notwithstanding the fact that in reality he controlled it closely. This was also the time during which the concept of 'king-in-parliament' developed and it provided the foundation for the principle that legislative power was shared between the two

[41] See below, 67–70.

institutions. When the Stuart kings attempted to legislate by prerogative without Parliament, the courts supported the Commons and invalidated the legislation.[42] Even before the civil war it became evident that the Crown could not rule for long without Parliament, in particular as far as financial matters were concerned. The enactment of the Petition of Right and the Triennial Act, to which Charles I was opposed, foreshadowed the eventual dominance of Parliament in the legislative domain.

The statutory enactments during and after the 1689 Revolution and the Settlement which followed it signified the final triumph of Parliament over the Crown. While the Crown continued to wield considerable influence, the terms of its tenure were now statutorily based in laws enacted by Parliament. It was subordinate in both domestic and external affairs to the overarching constitutional dominance of Parliament. In the legislative field, parliamentary approval was required for all laws, royal approval becoming only a formality; the monarch retained virtually no power to legislate independently of Parliament. In the nineteenth and twentieth centuries Parliament became a more representative body and the relationships between its constituent parts were regularised.

During the eighteenth and nineteenth centuries commentators drew attention to the legal implications of Parliament's constitutional dominance. Blackstone asserted not only that Parliament was the ultimate legal authority in the constitutional system, but that its laws were subject to no limitations: '. . . what the Parliament doth, no authority upon earth can undo.'[43] This doctrine was elaborated on by Dicey,[44] who justified its apparent extravangance in terms of the 'representative nature' of Parliament. The doctrine remains a central and characteristic feature of the modern British constitution.

The doctrine incorporates two principles, which are really different sides of the same coin. The first is that of parliamentary sovereignty, which has mainly political connotations and denotes that there is no constitutional authority whose powers can prevail over those of Parliament. While there are other kinds of legislative bodies, and bodies with other kinds of authority, they are all subordinate to the national Parliament. The second is that of legislative supremacy, which has mainly legal implications and denotes that the laws of Parliament can regulate any matter whatsoever and cannot be invalidated by the courts. However, both terms are nowadays understood in qualified senses. The fact that sovereignty vests in Parliament does not say anything about where real power in a political or sociological sense is to be found.[45] In fact many modern writers avoid the term sovereignty altogether because of this

---

[42] *Case of Proclamations* (1611) 12 Co Rep 74, 77 ER 1352.
[43] William Blackstone *Commentaries on the Laws of England* vol 1 4 ed (1876) 66.
[44] A V Dicey *An Introduction to the Study of the Laws of the Constitution* 10 ed (1959) 82–5.
[45] See S A de Smith *Constitutional and Administrative Law* 5 ed (1985) 64.

deception, and also because of the absolutist connotation which it has. Legislative supremacy is also understood in qualified terms. Even Dicey conceded that there were political and practical limitations on Parliament's law-making powers.[46] In the English context the constitutional implications of membership of the European Economic Community and proposals for a devolution of power to Scotland and Wales have also led to a reassessment of the doctrine during the last decade. Already a European court can determine whether the British government has violated the European Convention on Human Rights (as it frequently has); and in terms of its treaty obligations such a finding requires the British Parliament to change a statute or the common law. More important is the acceptance that a composite body such as Parliament must follow various constitutional procedures before it can be said to have enacted a law, and the courts have some say over whether these procedures have been correctly followed or not. This was an important factor in the South African 'constitutional crisis' of the 1950s.[47] Parliament is thus bound by the rules regulating its composition and procedure, and it can change these only if it follows the existing rules in doing so.

Modern commentators emphasise that the doctrine of sovereignty should be restricted to the legal and not the political dimension.[48] Political power is by no means concentrated in Parliament in the English constitution, and modern lawmaking is a complex process involving a range of institutions, only one of which is Parliament. Nevertheless the doctrine does retain very practical consequences. It means that in the normal course of events Parliament can enact, amend or repeal legislation as and when it pleases. It is not limited by a Bill of Rights, international law or natural law, and its legislation cannot be repudiated by the courts. It also means that the latest expression of Parliament's will prevails, in cases of inconsistency, over earlier expressions, an important principle of the operation of the legal system.[49] For the doctrine of constitutionalism, with its emphasis on the limitation of government, this apparent absence of legal restrictions on a political body poses a continual problem.

D Parliamentary government

Before the Revolution of 1688 the executive power in the English system of government vested in the Crown. It was exercised by members of the king's household and council, and by committees such as the Privy Council. The executive function was under the overall control, if not direct supervision, of the Crown, and those

[46] Dicey op cit n 44 at 39–86.
[47] See below, 132–43.
[48] See Carol Harlow in Patrick McAuslan and John F McEldowney *Law, Legitimacy and the Constitution* (1985) 62ff.
[49] The principle is sometimes expressed in terms of the Latin maxim *leges posteriores priores derogant*.

administering government were responsible to the Crown alone. There was only a remote accountability to the emerging Parliament, through the mechanism of impeachment: the Commons could bring a charge against a servant of the Crown which was heard by the House of Lords; a conviction could result in the official being removed from his post, and in some cases in his head being removed from his body. The mere threat of impeachment could achieve results—for example in persuading the autocratic Charles I to sign the Petition of Right in 1628—but generally the executive branch of government, including the military, was subordinate to the king and an instrument of his will. However much the Crown needed Parliament in the legislative domain, it was not accountable to it for the administration of the state.

After the Settlement of 1688, executive authority continued to vest in the Crown, but by convention it came to be exercised in accordance with the wishes of the king's ministers. Whereas before the Settlement ministers were appointed in the monarch's discretion, afterwards they were appointed only from Parliament. As the convention became more defined, it became necessary to appoint as ministers those who had the support of the majority of members of Parliament. This choice was facilitated by the fact that after the Restoration of 1660, political groupings had begun to form in Parliament, and from these groupings emerged the distinct political parties which exist today. During the eighteenth century the king's ministers began to meet alone, thereby strengthening their position vis-à-vis the Crown. While individual monarchs retained influence in the appointment of ministers until the late nineteenth century, it became recognised that, for the administration of their departments, ministers were accountable to Parliament and not to the Crown. This came to be known as the system of cabinet government: a committee from the majority party in Parliament formed the effective executive organ, and the ministers retained their membership of the legislature. The system is also known as parliamentary government (or parliamentary executive) to distinguish it from the system of presidential government which arose in the United States. In the twentieth century, countries which incorporated this feature of the British constitutional system were said to be adopting the 'Westminster model'. The system of parliamentary government is a distinctive contribution of the English system to the doctrine of constitutionalism.

In its developed form parliamentary government requires that members of the executive be members of Parliament, or become so within a period of grace, and that they retain the confidence of the majority party or coalition of parties. Once this confidence has been lost they must either be replaced by the head of state or the Parliament must be dissolved and re-elected. The system is supported by two conventions, collective and individual responsibility.[50] The collective or joint responsibility of the executive means that all ministers are responsible for policy decisions of the cabinet and must support them publicly. If the executive falls, all ministers fall with it. The individual responsibility of ministers means that each member of the executive must account to Parliament both for the policy decisions taken by the relevant government department, and for its administration; the minister is both its political and administrative head. Parliament has various mechanisms for enforcing these conventions: it can censure the cabinet, or an individual minister; it can table questions and demand information about activities of a department; it can audit and scrutinise departmental accounts; and it can deny funds to the government or withhold a minister's salary.

While the theory of parliamentary government is that the legislature controls the executive, and thereby the administration, the reality is the converse of this. In practice the mechanisms of ministerial responsibility are not effective, and the cabinet controls Parliament.[51] There are several reasons for this. The most important is the strength of the party system in modern constitutional systems.[52] Political parties are organised on a hierarchical basis and enforce strict discipline which gives party leaders immense influence in the caucus and control over party members. This helps the cabinet, through the majority party, to dominate Parliament—by definition the governing party has the majority of members of Parliament, and the cabinet usually consists exclusively of members from the same party. In parliamentary practice, decisions are taken along party lines, and the conventions of joint and individual ministerial responsibility are only as effective as the majority party and the cabinet allow them to be. In the words of one commentator, 'The House of Commons no longer behaves like [a] deliberate body. . . [It is] a collection of two sets of whipped dogs, who follow their masters . . .'.[53] In addition the cabinet has the capacity to dissolve Parliament and force a general election, with which it can threaten the legislature in order to get its way.

The second reason is that in all modern constitutional systems power has shifted away from cabinet ministers to the bodies and officials which make up the administrative branch of government. The administration's power to administer includes the capacity to make policy, at least in minor ways. The principles and institutions of parliamentary government are quite inadequate to keep a mammoth and powerful bureaucracy under control and to bring it to account. Ministers, even if they wished to, are unable to keep abreast of developments in their departments, and there is a tendency for

---

[50] On conventions see further below, 67–9.
[51] On the South African experience see below, 154–8.
[52] On the party system see further below, 66–7.
[53] C J Hughes in G Walker *Initiative and Referendum: The People's Law* (1987) 31.

them to be denied information about its activities. The problem is exacerbated by the rule of 'public service anonymity' which is part of the doctrine of parliamentary government: it entails that Parliament cannot call individual public servants directly to account for their actions, but only indirectly through their minister. The system has led to government becoming closed and secretive: because the responsible minister could, theoretically, be called to account in Parliament, no other rights of public access to information were developed. As is indicated below,[54] these deficiencies in the system of parliamentary government have led to the development of alternative mechanisms for ensuring the accountability of ministers and the administration. Some of these are constitutional bodies, and others extra-constitutional institutions, such as a free press.

From this analysis it can be seen that 'responsible government' is a term of art: it does not mean that the government acts responsibly, but that the executive must maintain political support in the legislature if it is to remain in office. Provided it does so, it can provide strong cohesive leadership. In those countries (Australia, Canada and India) in which responsible parliamentary government has been combined with federalism, which attempts to disperse and limit authority, the two constitutional principles tend to conflict and executive leadership is less powerful.

E   The Rule of Law

The Rule of Law, in constitutional theory, compensates for the apparent absence of legal limitations on the British Parliament deriving from the principle of legislative supremacy. In the sixteenth century the English courts seemed prepared to invalidate laws which were in conflict with natural law. In *Dr Bonham's Case*[55] the Royal College of Physicians was empowered to fine medical practitioners, and to keep one half of the fine for itself. The College, very conveniently, had a financial interest in its own judgment. In the face of this iniquity, Chief Justice Coke held that the common law could control Acts of Parliament, which would be void if against 'common right and reason' or 'impossible to be performed'. This approach was followed in a few subsequent cases. However, by the eighteenth century the doctrine of parliamentary sovereignty held sway and there was no scope for the invalidation of laws on the basis of their repugnancy to natural law or morality. Nevertheless in English constitutional law the notion has always been current—whether or not it has been actually practised—that the law is supreme over the government of the day. This finds expression in the doctrine of the Rule of Law which provides a more discreet check on the powers of government than the Bill of Rights system introduced into the United States constitution. It really involves the principle of 'auto-

[54] At 95–7.
[55] (1610) 8 Co Rep 113, 77 ER 647.

limitation',[56] that is, the recognition by governments that there are some actions they should not take—such as enacting outrageous legislation. The constitution rather paradoxically purports to uphold rights by ignoring them, and by relying instead on conventions and tradition, sometimes vague and sometimes open-ended.

The beginnings of the Rule of Law doctrine are usually traced to Magna Carta, the Petition of Right and the Bill of Rights. In different ways these documents asserted the supremacy of law over government. However, as long as the procedures for enforcing the 'rights' which they enumerated remained undeveloped, they had no real significance. Thus it was only after the Restoration that the procedure in connection with the writ of habeas corpus was improved, and thereafter it developed into an effective remedy in terms of which the High Court could order the release of those unlawfully imprisoned, unless the state could show sufficient cause for their further detention. Dicey first established the Rule of Law as a coherent doctrine in the nineteenth century. He described it in terms of three main principles.[57] The first principle was the absolute supremacy of regular law as opposed to arbitrary power; this implied that no person could be punished unless there had been a breach of the law, a principle with particular application to criminal law. The second principle was equality before the law; this implied that all individuals should be subject to the same laws and to the jurisdiction of the ordinary courts. The third principle was that the constitution was the result of the ordinary law of the land; this implied that constitutional principles such as personal liberty and freedom of speech were the product of the ordinary remedies of common law provided by the courts, and not of the enforcement of a constitutional charter of rights.

The Diceyan conception of the Rule of Law implied certain requirements for laws and their methods of enforcement: they must be clear, pre-announced, general in their application, and impartially enforced by the independent courts of the land according to fair procedures. These features were designed to serve one overriding objective—the protection of basic human rights. Subsequent versions of the doctrine developed the human rights element according to modern notions, and with due regard to the conditions under which they might be restricted.[58] In this form the Rule of Law has implications for the activities of the legislative, executive and administrative branches of government. However, there are several other versions of the doctrine besides that of Dicey. A narrow, formalistic version reduces the Rule of Law to the bare requirement that the government act in accordance with a promulgated law,

[56] See McAuslan and McEldowney op cit n 48 at 8.
[57] Dicey op cit n 44.
[58] See Anthony S Mathews *Freedom, Security and the Rule of Law* (1986) 1–30, and in Ellison Kahn (ed) *Fiat Iustitia—Essays in Memory of Oliver Denys Schreiner* (1983) 294.

regardless of its procedural or substantive qualities. This version has sometimes been propagated by the state in South Africa.[59] A somewhat more sophisticated version, known as the principle of legality, requires in addition that the laws according to which state actions are taken be general, prospective, clear and relatively stable and that various procedural standards be met in their enforcement, but has no regard to the content of the laws or their human rights implications.[60] An expanded version propagated by the International Commission of Jurists defines the Rule of Law in terms of a range of substantive economic, educational and social rights which are required for the individual to realise his aspirations and dignity.[61] In all its versions the Rule of Law is a normative doctrine and does not prescribe any specific institutional arrangements for the constitutional system. It is used to categorise systems of government according to whether they tend towards authoritarian and arbitrary rule or towards legally constrained government and respect for basic rights.

Despite the different understandings of the doctrine, the Rule of Law is a prominent notion in modern constitutionalism. It is another distinctively English contribution, though a similar set of constitutional principles is signified by the German term 'Rechtsstaat'. However, it is also a controversial notion. If measured by the actual practice of civil rights in the United Kingdom, the Rule of Law is only partially effective in its jurisdiction of origin.[62] It has been criticised for concealing political and social-economic values behind the façade of legality, and as being an 'invaluable concept for those who wish not to change the present set-up'.[63] It is also inadequate to cope with the realities of the modern administrative state. Its emphasis on the primacy of ordinary law and the regular courts is not easily compatible with the discretionary elements of administrative law, and it overlooks the fact that most law is, quite necessarily, interpreted and enforced by bodies other than the courts. The Rule of Law advocated the generality of law as a safeguard against the singling out of individuals for special treatment, and this remains an important principle; however, the greater the involvement of the state in social and economic management, the greater the need for discrimination among individuals and groups, and therefore for particularised rules as well as general ones.[64] The system of checks

---

[59] See the references in John Dugard *Human Rights and the South African Legal Order* (1978) 43ff.

[60] See J Raz (1977) 93 *Law Quarterly Review* 195; cf Lon L Fuller *The Morality of Law* (1964) 46–94.

[61] See the references in Mathews op cit n 58 at 15–22.

[62] For a highly critical account of the Rule of Law, and other constitutional principles, in the contemporary United Kingdom see Ian Harden and Norman Lewis *The Noble Lie — The British Constitution and the Rule of Law* (1986). See also the essays in Jeffrey Jowell and Dawn Oliver (eds) *The Changing Constitution* (1985).

[63] J A Griffith (1979) 42 *Modern Law Review* 1 at 15.

[64] See T S Allan (1988) 44 *Cambridge Law Journal* 111 at 116.

and balances and Bill of Rights, which the United States contributed
to constitutionalism, provide more concrete means of achieving the
normative aims of the Rule of Law.

F Judicial independence

The independence of the judiciary is a factor implied by the Rule of
Law doctrine, though it is not unique to the English constitutional
system. In this context independence should be distinguished from
bias; it refers to the institutional position of the courts and not to the
personal or collective preferences, conscious or otherwise, of the
judges.

The Crown's courts were originally just another state department
and its members enjoyed no institutional independence from the
monarch. Judges exercised their power in the name of the king.
Under the leadership of Chief Justice Coke, the court asserted its
independence, as against the king's perception of the judges as his
servants. After Coke's dismissal the courts again came under the
direct influence of the Crown. The Act of Settlement of 1701 was a
landmark in the development of institutional independence for the
courts in Westminster constitutions. It improved the position of the
judges by providing that they could not be dismissed during good
behaviour, thereby preventing the executive from exercising the
kind of threat which had proved effective in the past.

In modern Westminster systems the independence of the courts is
secured by several factors. Although judges are appointed by the
political executive, there is usually informal consultation with
existing members of the bench before an appointment is made. Once
appointed, a judge cannot be removed from office except by
resolution of both houses of Parliament, and then only on grounds of
unfitness or misconduct. The remuneration of judges is fixed directly
by Act of Parliament, and it is not possible to reduce a judge's salary
during his or her tenure. There are restrictions on the right to bring
legal proceedings against judges, and even if an incorrect judgment
is given negligently the judge cannot be held liable. Contempt of
court principles insulate them from public denigration, and prevent
certain kinds of public comment on matters before court. These
arrangements are designed to prevent undue influence on judges
from the other branches of government or from the public, both
generally and in respect of particular cases. While institutional
conditions vary from country to country the principle of judicial
independence is now an established feature of modern constitutional
thought, and is much-vaunted in South Africa.[65]

G Representative government and the party system

The principle of political representation was evident in the earliest
assemblies of the people in Anglo-Saxon times; in order not to leave

[65] See below, 200–6.

its property unprotected, each community sent a representative to London on its behalf. During the feudal period the King's Council consisted only of the chief barons summonsed by the king. Only when the king wanted to strengthen his hand against the barons did he call up four representatives from each county. The Parliaments in the thirteenth century included the barons, representatives from the counties, and representatives from the cities and boroughs. The idea took root that Parliament should reflect interests more representative than those only of the Crown.

Nevertheless, as has often been said, English government was constitutional long before it was democratic. This means that the structure and procedures of the constitutional system were developed at a time when Parliament and the government were, by modern notions, still remarkably unrepresentative of the people governed. It was only in the nineteenth century that the franchise was extended in any meaningful way. This was brought about by a number of Reform Acts, in particular those of 1832 and 1867. Even then there remained massive discrepancies in the system of representation because of the way in which the boundaries of electoral constituencies were drawn. The right to vote and be voted for was extended to women only in 1918, and plural voting, which gave some electors more than one vote, was abolished only in 1949. Even in the present day the principle of 'one vote one value' is not fully upheld in the English constitutional system.[66]

The party system arose in the seventeenth and eighteenth centuries, and was reinforced by the franchise reforms of the nineteenth century. The governments of the day wanted to widen their appeal among the newly enfranchised citizens. To meet the expectations of their supporters the government had to be in control of Parliament, and this could be achieved only through a rigid party system.[67] The plurality electoral system[68] produced two predominant parties which filled the roles of government and opposition, elections being partly concerned with whether the main parties should exchange these roles. Politics became a competitive, adversarial contest between government and opposition, with Parliament the main site of the competition. Ironically, the more 'representative' Parliament became, the more its representative character was subordinated to the dynamics of the party system.[69]

The English electoral and party systems provided the basis for the majoritarian nature of the Westminster constitution. Majoritarianism

---

[66] See A H Birch *The British System of Government* 4 ed (1980) 69–71.

[67] See below, 66–7.

[68] That is, the candidate with the most votes in each constituency is elected, even though she may have an overall minority of support where there are more than two candidates. On electoral systems see D Lakeman *How Democracies Vote—A Study of Majority and Proportional Electoral Systems* 3 ed (1970), and G Hand, J Georgel and C Sasse *European Electoral Systems Handbook* (1979).

[69] See further below, 66–7.

exists where the political group which wins an electoral contest is able to dominate the main institutions of the state to the exclusion of other parties. Where this domination is not temporary, majoritarianism poses a threat to the principles of constitutionalism.[70]

IV AMERICAN CONSTITUTIONALISM

A Revolutionary contract

The theoretical assumptions of American constitutionalism are different from those of the English version. The American war of independence was fought partly over the long-established constitutional principle that taxation could be levied only with the consent of those who paid it; the colonies rebelled against the obligation to pay taxes to an English government in which they had no representation. After the war's successful outcome, and the constitutional break with England, the need arose for an appropriate legitimating theory of government. This was provided in part by the social contract.[71] The 1787 constitution, which unified the thirteen individual colonies, was the product of a deliberate process of constitution-making. Delegates at the federal convention drafted the constitution on the assumption that they were representative of the people and that it reflected the popular will. For greater credibility it was approved by the representative bodies in the different colonies. In reality this whole process was biased in terms of class, colour and gender, but the social bias of the framers has not prevented their product from enduring for many generations. The process gave rise to a revolutionary doctrine of constitutionalism, namely that a constituent assembly has the power to create and enact a Constitution and accord it the force of law. This new conciousness was apparent in the opening words of the United States Constitution, 'We the people of these several states . . .'. France also followed the line of 'revolutionary constitutionalism' in the eighteenth century.

B Separation of powers

In a classic work Vile describes the separation of powers as the most significant constitutional device of the modern era, alongside representative government, for the limitation of state power.[72] The separation of powers principle has traditionally been regarded as the fundamental feature of the American Constitution, and one of its distinctive contributions to the doctrine of constitutionalism. While separation of powers thinking had been evident in the systems of government and political theory of earlier ages, the principle was given more consistent expression in the constitution of 1787. It was also given a coherent theoretical justification, in particular in the

---

[70] See Boulle *South Africa and the Consociational Option* (1984) 1–11, and the references cited there.
[71] See above, 27–30.
[72] M J C Vile *Constitutionalism and the Separation of Powers* (1967) 1–2.

Federalist Papers which were published at the time of the constitutional convention. The authors were able to refer to the recent writings of the French commentator Montesquieu, who had argued that the control of state power depended on it being divided among different governmental institutions.[73] The very form and organisation of the American Constitution reflected this emphasis.

Unlike the British system of parliamentary government, the United States Constitution provides for the almost complete separation of the personnel of the legislative and executive branches. Legislative power vests in the Congress. It comprises the House of Representatives, which is popularly elected, and the Senate, which has two representatives from each state. Executive power vests in the President who is directly elected by the people[74] and retains office for four years, whether or not he has the political support of Congress. No member of the President's cabinet may simultaneously be a member of Congress. Thus not only is there a strict separation of personnel between the two institutions, but each has a separate political mandate and neither can remove the other from office. Judicial power vests in the Supreme Court, the judges of which have permanent tenure, and in other courts established by Congress.

The United States Constitution did not embody the pure theory of separation of powers which had been espoused in the American colonies.[75] It was amalgamated with the doctrine of checks and balances, according to which each branch of government should be subject to some influence and control from the others. In this way none can act completely independently, but requires the 'support' of at least one other branch. While Congress has the primary law-making power, legislation can be vetoed by the President and invalidated by the courts, thereby making them subordinate partners in this constitutional activity. The President and other members of the cabinet have executive power, but some executive actions require approval by the Senate—for example, cabinet appointments and the ratification of treaties—and others are susceptible to invalidation by the courts. In addition the President can be removed by Congress through the impeachment process. The Supreme Court has the highest judicial power but the judges are appointed by the President, with Senatorial approval, and can be impeached by Congress; the Court's structure and jurisdiction are subject to the authority of Congress and judges are dependent on the executive to give effect to their decisions. These and other checks and balances are either stipulated by the Constitution or have developed through convention. They ensure that while the exercise of each power is entrusted to one institution, there is scope for minor participation by the other.

The basic structures of separation of powers and checks and balances have remained intact since their incorporation into the

---

[73] His classic work *De l'Esprit des Lois* (The Spirit of the Laws) was published in 1784.
[74] On the convention defining this process see below, 68.
[75] See Vile op cit n 72 at 18.

United States Constitution. They have given rise to a number of subsidiary constitutional doctrines.[76] In practice, however, they have not always produced a balanced system of government, and over time different institutions, in particular the presidency and the Supreme Court, have usurped powers well beyond their constitutional allocation. Nor should they be seen as politically or socially neutral institutions. The separation of powers doctrine was a reaction against the political experiences in the colonies and the authoritarian nature of English rule, and it continues to be based on a distrust of government; in modern social conditions the restrictions which it imposes on government could favour a vested élite over a disadvantaged majority. However, the separation of powers remains an important safeguard and protection in the constitutional practice of the United States, and in other systems of government which have adopted it. One of the reasons for its continued relevance is the strong system of judicial review in the United States which allows the courts to invalidate Congressional legislation.

C   Federal division of power

At its simplest, federalism assumes two levels of government within the same constitutional system, each having powers in its own right and affecting directly the citizens.[77] The principle of federalism was not conceived in the American context, but it was first given a juridical basis in the United States Constitution. Its emergence was an inevitable outcome of the desire to create a new central government for some purposes, and at the same time to retain the diversity of local governments for others.[78] Thus, besides defining the new national institutions and their powers, the Constitution also ensured the continued existence of the former colonies as political entities by preserving their systems of government, granting them equal representation in the Senate, and making the federal principles in the constitution difficult to amend without their consent. Furthermore, the constitution reserved certain powers for the state governments, and attempted to safeguard them from national encroachment through the same constitutional mechanisms which ensured their existence. Unlike the Westminster system, sovereignty was shared among a number of governmental bodies.[79] While the federal 'balance' between national and state governments has always been affected by political factors, the basic structure has been preserved, in part through the supervision of the courts.

Over time the original federal principles in the American constitution became significantly modified. For two centuries there

[76] See Laurence H Tribe *American Constitutional Law* (1978) 1–19.
[77] See Geoffrey Sawer *Modern Federalism* 2 ed (1976) 1ff.
[78] See J D Lees *The Political System of the United States* (1969) 48ff.
[79] This may be contrasted with a system of 'devolution', in which the central government delegates certain powers to subnational governments, but without relinquishing its sovereignty. On devolution see Vernon Bogdanor *Devolution* (1979).

has been a tension between the competing claims of the national and state governments, and each level of government has, at different times, made inroads on the other. However, in general terms, and particularly in the present century, the trend has been for the national jurisdiction to be enlarged at the expense of the states' jurisdiction; the constitutional division of competence has not prevented the central authorities from exercising power in most important areas of government. This is a partial reflection of the growing complexity of modern government and the need for national treatment of economic, developmental, environmental and industrial matters. The states have also become largely dependent on Washington for their financial viability, and can be encouraged into implementing national policies—for example, no smoking in public places—in exchange for needed revenue. This has made the system decidedly less federal in practice,[80] though without eliminating the significance of the federal principle altogether. In so far as constitutionalism emphasises the limitation and division of state authority, the federal principle is an important manifestation of it and has been incorporated into many modern constitutional systems.

D   Bill of Rights

The American Bill of Rights provided a further means of limiting and restricting state power, and this institution was an original contribution to constitutional government. At first it operated only in respect of the national government, but later provisions were made applicable to the states as well. In essence the Bill of Rights introduced standards according to which acts of government could be tested and, if they fell short, invalidated. These standards incorporated many of the freedoms and liberties which are associated with the various bills of rights documents and the Rule of Law in the English constitutional system. They now include the freedoms of religion, personal liberty, privacy, property and movement, the principle of equality before the law, the right to a fair trial, and protection from inhumane punishment. Should an American legislature provide for indefinite detention without trial, its actions will be declared invalid by the courts as being in contravention of the Bill of Rights. The notion that certain rights are fundamental and inviolable spread to Western Europe and today a justiciable Bill of Rights is a common feature of documentary Constitutions.[81]

A Bill of Rights is not self-executing and it was to a large extent the Supreme Court which determined how effective the American version would be. In its early history it was not incompatible with various fundamental rights abuses, such as slavery, and until the mid-twentieth century it had little limiting effect on discriminatory

[80] See Sawer op cit n 77 at 98–108.
[81] See below, 61–4.

practices against blacks. While the Supreme Court never strayed far from majority social opinion, its interpretation of the various rights was crucial to their impact on the state system. In this additional area the judiciary became a focal institution of American constitutionalism. In no other system of government do the Constitution, the Bill of Rights and the judiciary have as prominent a part as they do in the American system.[82]

E Judicial review and higher law

It has been shown that each of the main principles of American constitutionalism—the separation of powers, federalism, and the Bill of Rights—is dependent on the courts for its enforcement. This is part of a wider judicial role in enforcing and upholding the constitution which gave American constitutionalism a greater degree of legalism than had previously been experienced. This characteristic has remained to the present. The function of the courts is referred to as (constitutional) judicial review. However the constitution itself makes no direct reference to the courts' review powers. The Supreme Court asserted the right to review legislation early in the existence of the Constitution in the famous case of *Marbury v Madison*,[83] and since then judicial review has developed into a major feature of American constitutionalism. The institution is by no means uncontroversial.

Historically the court has adopted two different approaches to constitutional interpretation. On one hand is the 'original intent' approach in which it purports to be discovering the meaning intended by the framers of the Constitution, and on the other hand are various 'organic' approaches in which the court sees its role as interpreting the Constitution according to the contemporary facts of life. While the early theory behind judicial review held that the courts would concern themselves with legal matters and leave political issues to the other branches of government, during certain periods, particularly the 1970s, the courts have given decisions on clearly social and political issues such as abortion and the electoral system. Instead of merely 'interpreting' the Constitution the courts became involved in balancing the competing social interests of the day, and thereby assumed a more 'political' role.[84] They were accused of usurping the main policy-making functions in the constitutional system, and of transforming themselves from an institution which protected the minority to one which obstructed the majority. While charges of judicial activism are not generally made of the Supreme Court of the 1980s, there is a considerable literature concerned with

[82] See Vernon Bogdanor (ed) *Constitutions in Democratic Politics* (1988) 11.
[83] (1803) 1 Cranch 137, 1 Sup. Ct. Rep. 60.
[84] See the essays in L J Theberge (ed) *The Judiciary in a Democratic Society* (1979); on the South African courts see below, 242–6.

the reconciliation of judicial review with democratic theory.[85] The extreme position is that no review by an unrepresentative court can be reconciled with democracy.

With the backing of the courts' review powers the American Constitution takes on the nature of a higher law. This means that the provisions of the Constitution will prevail over all other legal or political actions of government which are inconsistent with it: they become null and void on the basis that there was no legal authority for them. This may be contrasted with the English doctrine of parliamentary sovereignty: in the English context Acts of Parliament are legally supreme and the constitution is subordinate, while in the American context the Constitution is supreme. Until the Constitution is amended according to the prescribed procedure, its provisions place certain actions altogether beyond the bounds of all branches of government. The notion of the Constitution as higher, or fundamental, law is a prevalent doctrine in modern constitutionalism. Its status as a supreme legal norm is maintained because it is justiciable by the courts.

V SOCIALIST CONSTITUTIONALISM

A Marxism and socialist legality

Principles of socialist constitutionalism have influenced the constitutional development of several African countries. While there is no single tradition of socialist constitutionalism, the constitutions of socialist systems embody certain principles which together can be contrasted with those of the 'liberal' constitutional tradition, namely British parliamentarism and American presidentialism. These principles must be understood within the framework of Marxist theories of law and the state,[86] a subject of considerable complexity which cannot be done justice here.

The Marxist tradition holds that for a proper understanding of society it is necessary to focus on its economic basis, and that historically the primary forces which have shaped social institutions in all societies have been economic, and they have determined the nature of the political, constitutional and cultural systems, and even of moral codes. History has witnessed a succession of class struggles, with one form of economic organisation giving way to another. In this theory of society neither the state nor law is a 'neutral' institution; they are designed to reinforce the position of the dominant economic class and to suppress the subordinate classes. The real nature of law and the state as instruments of class oppression is disguised in ideological rhetoric, and the Constitution gives a false picture of social reality. In some Marxist writings it is

---

[85] Cf L H Tribe op cit n 76 at 50ff; J H Ely *Democracy and Distrust—A Theory of Judicial Review* (1980) 180ff.

[86] On Marxist theories of law and society see J W Harris *Legal Philosophies* (1980) 245–58 and Hugh Collins *Marxism and the Law* (1982). See also D M Davis in Hugh Corder (ed) *Essays on Law and Social Practice in South Africa* (1988) 65–92.

argued that although the dominant function of law and the state is to preserve class rule, there is a degree of relative autonomy within each institution which precludes it from being used in a purely instrumental way.[87] In dogmatic Marxist theory it is held that when the conflict between economic classes has been eliminated through the advent of socialism, and finally communism, there will be no need for law and the state and they will wither away. During the lengthy transition to a classless society, law and the state will remain but will be used for a specific end, namely to protect the authority of the working class against the remaining capitalist elements. The Communist Party is the body through which the working class will organise itself during this period.

Against this background it can be understood why socialist Constitutions tend to be more programmatic than liberal Constitutions, in the sense of postulating aims or standards which are to be realised at some stage in the future. The stated objective is to serve the working people and to provide a weapon in the fight for socialism—as opposed to liberal Constitutions which are seen to safeguard the interests of the ruling classes. In this context constitutionalism has an essentially different purpose: whereas liberal constitutionalism emphasises the need for limiting power and restraining rulers, socialist constitutionalism is concerned with creating the conditions for socialist society.[88] In what follows attention is given to constitutionalist principles in the Soviet Union and the systems inspired by its Constitution.[89] The western socialist and welfare-state systems operate with more traditional liberal Constitutions.

B Popular sovereignty

The notion of popular sovereignty is a fundamental one in socialist constitutional systems. Power is held to derive from the people and to be exercised through their democratically elected representatives at all levels of government. The highest policy-making body is the Supreme Soviet, which usually comprises two chambers elected through a system of universal adult franchise and which can make laws on all matters. However, there are some restrictions on this body: for example in the Soviet Union all laws are supposed to be in conformity with the Constitution, and constitutional amendments require the approval of two-thirds of the members of the two chambers.

C The role of the party

The role of the Communist Party is also central in socialist constitutionalism. The Communist Party is claimed to represent the

---

[87] A frequently cited work is E P Thompson *Whigs and Hunters* (1975).
[88] See A Unger *Constitutional Development in the USSR* (1987) 2–3.
[89] See generally David Lane *State and Politics in the USSR* (1985).

working class and the peasantry and to give effect to the 'dictatorship of the proletariat'. Many socialist Constitutions permit the legal existence of only this one party, and expressly stipulate that its representatives must fill various key positions in the state. At every level of the Constitution the various organs of the party have a direct influence on the relevant organs of the state in their policy-making and administrative functions. The theory underlying this pre-eminence is that because the party is open to and representative of the great majority of people, it provides for a more democratic system of government than the dictatorship of the dominant class which is disguised by the illusion of multi-party democracy in the western constitutional systems. However, as with all constitutional theory, that underlying the one-party systems is not realised in practice, and experience in countries such as Poland and the Soviet Union shows that the single-party system does not lead to representative government, is intolerant of dissent, and cannot cope with high levels of conflict or divisions of interest.

D   Absence of a separation of powers

In official doctrine the exercise of state power is 'one and indivisible'.[90] Each branch of government is seen to derive its authority from the same source, namely the will of the people as reflected in the highest popularly elected assembly. This view renders unnecessary any separation of powers principle, which is expressly repudiated, and as it applies in liberal constitutionalism it is regarded as a mere façade which conceals the reality of exploitative class rule. Thus socialist Constitutions tend to concentrate the three traditional powers of government so as to maximise the legal authority of the various representative bodies.[91] In practice, however, there is a division of functions in the socialist state systems, but it does not have the juridical basis which exists where the separation of powers is an entrenched constitutional principle.

As far as the federal division of powers is concerned many socialist systems, including the Soviet Union, have a federal framework. The framework incorporates several of the federal principles associated with liberal federal Constitutions, including the integrity of the unit governments and the reservation to them of powers not conferred on the central government. In practice these principles are subject to the same centralising tendencies encountered in the western federations, which are reinforced to some extent by the unifying role of the party. They are also subject to the countervailing principle of hierarchy, in terms of which lower bodies are subordinate to higher bodies. The lack of meaningful functional and territorial divisions of power entail that in practice the Communist Party has the decisive influence in legislating, administering and adjudicating. While the liberal state is

[90] Unger op cit n 88 at 273.
[91] See S E Finer *Five Constitutions* (1979) 29.

susceptible to being 'captured' by powerful private interests, such as large corporations, there are individual safeguards against state power, whereas the socialist state is in the permanent 'capture' of the party but such safeguards are not provided.

E Human rights

In socialist constitutional thought there is no doctrine of fundamental rights, in the sense of a code which can be enforced against the government. This derives partly from the view that the interests of society as a whole are more important than, and should prevail over, the interests of the individual. Thus the social ownership of the means of production is regarded as a more important principle than the protection of private property.

Nevertheless most socialist constitutions contain lists of basic rights, which show several resemblances to western Bills of Rights—equality before the law, freedom from arbitrary arrest, and privacy. Other rights, such as those to property, are less prominent, but in their stead is a heavy emphasis on socio-economic rights: the right to work, to health protection, to housing and to education. While all state bodies are obligated to give effect to these rights and freedoms, they are not legally enforceable as in the western Bill of Rights systems; their realisation depends more directly on political and economic factors. Another significant characteristic of the socialist rights systems is the linking of rights to duties and obligations. The Soviet Union Constitution requires all citizens to observe the Constitution, to work in a socially useful occupation, to protect socialist property and to respect the rights of other citizens. These are again more in the nature of social guidelines than legally enforceable norms.

It is thus a consistent feature of socialist constitutionalism that constitutional rules and principles do not comprise a system of higher norms against which actions of government can be tested.[92] While the form and style of socialist Constitutions are sometimes remarkably similar to those of liberal Constitutions, they are deviated from in a more drastic and consistent way. The separation of powers, Rule of Law, powers of the courts and even the legislative competence of the central soviet are all susceptible to the political intrusion of the supreme organs of government. The division between law and politics is a very vague one. In contemporary socialist systems there is a serious reappraisal of constitutional and legal matters, with fresh consideration being given to western notions of constitutional legality.

VI TWENTIETH-CENTURY TRENDS

The second half of the nineteenth century has been described as the heyday of documentary Constitutions, as the countries of Europe,

[92] See E L Johnson *An Introduction to the Soviet Legal System* (1972) 77–104.

displaying great faith in constitutions, followed the American precedent of codifying their rules of government.[93] After the First World War there was the first outburst of twentieth-century Constitution-making to accommodate the redrawn boundaries of Europe. After the Second World War there was a further wave of Constitution-making in Western and Eastern Europe to reconstitute governments or accommodate boundary changes. This was followed by the decolonisation era in Africa and other colonised regions of the world, during which new Constitutions were drafted to herald independence and to provide a fresh political start from the former colonies. In many instances, from Ghana in 1957 to Zimbabwe in 1980, the predominant influence was the British constitutional experience, but in other cases presidential or socialist constitutional principles were introduced. Finally, even in stable western systems there has been a recent tendency to renew constitutional structures. Over two-thirds of the world's Constitutions have been drafted in the past three decades.

Frenetic Constitution-making has not, however, signified the successful advance of constitutionalism. In the twentieth century the principles of constitutionalism have been severely battered by authoritarian governments of various kinds. The accession to power of totalitarian regimes in Germany and Italy led to periods of centralised autocracy in these countries and to the temporary destruction of democratic constitutionalism in numerous others, such as France and Netherlands. In many developing countries, such as Uganda, the Philippines and Brazil, constitutional niceties did not prevent the emergence of highly authoritarian regimes, and in some cases the overthrow of the constitutional order by military dictatorships, as in Nigeria and Paraguay. The concept of the Constitution as 'higher law' has not been well served in practice. One of the consequences of the discrepancy between constitutional theory and political reality is that the term 'constitutionalism' fell into disrepute.[94] All modern states justify their actions by reference either to written Constitutions, or to the drastic actions needed to safeguard the constitutional system. Where oppressive policies can be justified in terms of principles of constitutional government, the concept loses its normative significance.

In response to these excesses there has been renewed emphasis on human rights in the contemporary phase of constitutionalism.[95] This has been promoted in part by international developments—for example, the Universal Declaration of Human Rights adopted by the United Nations in 1948—and the activities of bodies such as Amnesty International. These developments have provided a major challenge for constitutionalism, namely how to protect and enhance

[93] See Strong op cit n 5 at 36.
[94] See Schochat op cit n 22 at 5.
[95] See below, 61–4.

human rights in a manner which is compatible with democratic principles.[96] Since the mid-1980s these notions have begun to impact on the South Africa constitutional debate.

Modern expressions of constitutionalism have also had to take account of the massive transfer of power to the executive and a corresponding decline in the importance of Parliaments. This has occurred across the range of constitutional models, giving rise to the 'imperial presidency' in the United States, the 'elective dictatorship' of the prime minister in the United Kingdom, and the totalitarianism of the one-party system. In many jurisdictions there has emerged within the executive an 'alternative' constitution which is secret, authoritarian and centralised. The control of the executive has always been the main challenge for constitutionalism, and in the present era it has been met in part by new powers for the courts. Judicial review has never before been a more prominent element in constitutional government. However, the rise of the executive has required the establishment of additional mechanisms of control and accountability to those provided by the courts.

State power has not, however, remained with the executive or government; with the rise of the administrative state it has passed on to the bureaucracy. Modern constitutionalism must also take account of administrative bodies and administrative law. In the regulatory state law performs new functions, not conceived during the historical development of constitutionalism. The theoretical underpinning which served constitutionalism during its evolution, namely the 'necessary evil' theory of government, now has less validity. It has come to be recognised that the modern state must be as able to secure a range of beneficial outcomes for society as it must be restrained from invading the liberty of the individual. The traditional constitutionalist emphasis on the limitation of government has not been favourable for securing a balance between these requirements.

Another challenge for constitutionalism, particularly during the process of decolonisation but also in some 'stable' states of Europe, has been the renewed political significance of cultural and religious pluralism. Divisions of language, class, religion, ethnicity and culture have become prominent in the political process, and have caused intense sectional conflict, social instability, and even the fragmentation of the state system. Constitutional arrangements which allow the majority segment to dominate the political process have been unsuited to these conditions because they lead to discrimination against minority segments, and without any alternation in office to perpetual domination and subordination.[97] Over time certain constitutional principles have become prominent in dealing with these problems: electoral systems which give each group represen-

---

[96] See T S Allan (1988) 44 *Cambridge Law Journal* 111.
[97] According to United Nations materials 124 countries can be classified as having minority problems: J A Singler *Minority Rights—A Comparative Analysis* (1983) 68.

tation in government in proportion to its popular support; the inclusion of all the major political groupings in a coalition government; the availability of a veto for minority groups over government decisions; and allowing the different segments to take decisions over their own affairs. A theoretical model of government known as consociational democracy has been constructed for situations in which these elements are encountered in a constitutional system: proportional representation, grand coalition, mutual veto and segmental autonomy.[98] In some countries (Belgium, Switzerland) consociational institutions have been compatible with political forces and have been successful. In others (Lebanon, Northern Ireland) attempts to establish consociational democracy have failed, thereby demonstrating again the inherent limitations in the constitutional and legal regulation of conflict.

In the twentieth century the concept of constitutionalism has also been broadened to accommodate moves for the greater democratisation of government. While the principle that the governed should participate in government was implicit in earlier expressions of constitutionalism, it was only given the institutional backing of the universal franchise for men and women very late in its historical development (women were enfranchised in Britain in 1918, and in South Africa in 1930). In some constitutional systems a Bill of Rights existed long before the universal franchise! More recently there has been a growing realisation that traditional forms of public participation in government, for example occasional parliamentary elections, do not serve much practical purpose in representing public opinion. New forms of popular participation have been established: referenda, public meetings, prior availability of legislation for comment, access to information, and various forms of consultation. They provide a different perspective to the normal constitutional emphasis on checks and balances, separation of powers, and judicial review. 'Representative government' has come to mean not only choosing in elections who should make policy for society, but also participating directly in the policy-making process. New forms of technology may make this kind of participation in government a more feasible option—where it is desired and tolerated.

Finally, constitutionalism has taken on international dimensions through bodies such as the United Nations and European Economic Community. While some of this must properly be called international law, for example the law of the United Nations, some also impinges directly on national Constitutions and constitutes a new form of constitutional law. As with constitutional government at the national level, these initiatives are designed both to empower and limit transnational authorities in the pursuit of common economic and political objectives. Originally the emphasis was on human rights issues, but now the authorities involved are remarkably

[98] On the principles of consociationalism see L J Boulle op cit n 70 at 45–72.

similar to those encountered in the national Constitutions, having administrative, judicial and law-making powers. While these developments cannot yet be categorised as federal arrangements, they do involve real power for the transnational institutions. In 1986 twelve governments signed a Single European Act which increases the powers of the central organs of European government and allows them to have a direct impact on member states and their citizens in certain circumstances. This suggests the start of a new constitutional and legal order within the tradition of constitutionalism.

In its modern manifestation constitutionalism implies a 'constitution', the nature and content of which is dealt with in the following chapter.

3 Modern Constitutions

The classic constitutional texts point out that the term 'constitution' is used in two senses.[1] In the first it refers to the whole system of government in a country, including all the rules, conventions, practices and customs by which it is conducted—though only some of these are legal rules enforceable by the courts. In this work the term *constitution* is used for this meaning. In the second it denotes a legal document or documents which define the structure of the state, the powers and capacities of its main organs and the interrelationships among its various institutions. These rules are, for the most part, enforceable by the courts. The term *Constitution* is used for this narrower meaning—for example, the Albanian Constitution or the Zambian Constitution. States without such a constitutional document still have a constitution,[2] as in the case of Britain or Israel, but it is one in which the core rules of government have not been codified in a single documentary source. For this reason we would not refer to the British Constitution.

The modern Constitution performs several different functions. It provides a legal framework for the operation of government. It defines the ultimate sources of legal authority, and provides the foundations of the public law system. It is a source of legitimacy for the state and its activities. It indicates the political and legal parameters of the individual's interaction with the state. It operates as a manifesto, a confession of faith.[3] With each of the nearly two hundred independent states and dependencies in the world having Constitutions, and with each Constitution performing this variety of functions, it is to be expected that there is a considerable variation in constitutional content and detail. Generally there is no limit to what Constitutions can contain and attempt to achieve. Nevertheless the formal pattern of documentary Constitutions is remarkably similar. All Constitutions establish public authorities, confer power, impose restrictions on its exercise, indicate which bodies should resolve conflicts, and provide procedures and standards for dispute resolution. In this chapter the focus is on the common features of modern Constitutions.

I HOW THEY EMERGE

Constitutions usually emerge from a critical historical juncture in the political development of a country—colonisation, a revolution,

---

[1] For example, K C Wheare *Modern Constitutions* (1966) 1–13.

[2] Afrikaans is more helpful in this regard as *grondwet* can be used for Constitution and *konstitusie* for constitution; cf Dion Basson and Henning Viljoen *Suid-Afrikaanse Staatsreg* (1987) 20.

[3] See Wheare op cit n 1 at 46.

independence, unification of separate territories, the dissolution of a political entity, and so on.[4] In each case there is a break in institutional continuity with the past, and political leaders initiate a fresh start by drawing up a Constitution which describes the new system of government and prescribes how it should operate in the future. In South Africa new Constitutions were produced to mark important political settlements during the course of the nineteenth century, at the time of unification in 1910, to effect the transition to a republic in 1961, and during a period of intense social instability in 1983.

How Constitutions are drafted and put into effect is important for their future legal and political status. In some cases they are imposed by the dominant group through force and coercion, in others they are drafted after consultation, of varying degrees, with those whose lives they will influence. Occasionally a body purporting to represent the people, known as a constituent assembly, drafts the document and puts it into effect.[5] Where a constituent assembly is used for drafting the Constitution, this fact is sometimes reflected in a rigid amending procedure (see below) which notionally reinvokes the constituent assembly for the purposes of changing the Constitution. However, whatever the origin of a Constitution it is—as a matter of simple logic—authoritative because it is generally adhered to in practice, rather than being adhered to because of its own claims to authority. Under which circumstances a Constitution will be generally adhered to is a complex issue.

The political and social background of Constitutions determines the extent to which they adopt constitutional norms from the past, or attempt to establish wholly new norms of government in reaction against the past. Generally constitutional systems are remarkably resilient, even at times of radical political change, and the Constitutions of today reflect the characteristics of those of yesterday—though there are of course exceptions. Its social history will also determine the extent to which a Constitution goes beyond merely regulating the powers and duties of government agencies and prescribes rules of personal conduct to be followed by citizens.[6] Even the style and prose of a Constitution will be affected by its social origins. While many Constitutions have a formal, impersonal quality, drafting styles vary considerably—from a broad and general approach whose language can be interpreted to accommodate social change without itself being amended, to the detailed and specific approach which invites a formal legalistic approach to constitutional interpretation. The American Constitution reflects the word-economy approach, and the Indian Constitution that of extravagant prolixity.

[4] See generally Edward McWhinney *Constitution-making: Principles, Process, Practice* (1981).
[5] See above, 43.
[6] See S E Finer in Vernon Bogdanor *Constitutions in Democratic Politics* (1988) 17.

II WHAT THEY CONTAIN

A   A preamble

Constitutions are usually introduced to readers by way of their preambles. Preambles are included in Constitutions for symbolic and ideological purposes. One of the functions of Constitutions is to legitimise the state and government, and preambles, together with national symbols such as the flag, motto and anthem, are prominent in this objective. They are usually constructed in the grand rhetorical style and provide a glorification of the country's history, its struggles and its champions. Reference is invariably made to the almighty guidance bestowed on the state in the past, and to the benevolent principles by which it will be governed in the future. A modest example is provided in the Swiss Constitution:

> 'In the Name of Almighty God the Swiss Confederation with the intent of strengthening the alliance of the Confederates and maintaining and furthering the unity, strength and honour of the Swiss nation, has adopted the following Federal Constitution . . .'

With a few exceptions this declamatory part of the Constitution does not have any legal significance, in the sense of being binding on the government or enforceable by the courts. As you become familiar with those closest to hand, you will realise that they usually do not have much political significance either. While on one hand Constitutions often fail to disclose what is important, on the other they flaunt what is insignificant. Thus while Constitutions are a form of statute law, they do more than just define rights and prescribe procedures, but also, in their preambles, espouse values and principles, such as democracy, justice and equality. It goes without saying that these values may not be easy to uphold in practice.

B   A chart of the state system

On the operational side a constitutional system is concerned with the way in which public authority is distributed, exercised and controlled, and with the accession to and succession in office of those responsible for its exercise. The greater part of modern Constitutions is therefore taken up (metaphorically speaking) by an organisational chart which accounts for these elements.[7] This chart includes matters of both substance and procedure. In the majority of cases the contents are organised according to the principle of constitutional tripartism, the legislature being dealt with first and the executive and judiciary thereafter; this is because the legislature is supposedly representative of the people and therefore a more important body than the other two, though in practice it is executives which are in command and many parliamentary activities have become merely symbolic.

[7] Cf the first chapter of Ivo D Duchacek *Power Maps—Comparative Politics of Constitutions* (1973) 3–16.

Usually the structure and composition of the legislature is described in some detail: the sizes of the constituent chambers, the way they are elected or nominated, their internal organisation, how they relate to each other, and qualifications for electing members or being elected as a member. Then it is necessary to specify the powers of the legislature, which need not be restricted to lawmaking. The way in which laws can be passed, amended or repealed is an important procedural aspect of the organisational chart. The Constitution will define the situations in which the legislature must share the law-making function with other bodies, such as with the electorate through a referendum (Switzerland, Denmark) or with regional, community or economic councils (Belgium, South Africa, France). It is usual for the Constitution to define the bodies which may initiate legislation, the role of parliamentary committees in the law-making process, and the requirements for assent to and promulgation of statutes. However, the Constitution seldom defines the internal procedures and codes of behaviour of the legislature.

The office of head of state is usually dealt with in some detail: qualifications for office, method of election, tenure, and powers and duties. But the other organs of government, such as the judiciary or bureaucracy, tend to be described only in outline, with the particulars being provided in separate statutes or by administrative practice. Because of their importance in the political system it is sometimes felt necessary to define the reciprocal relationships between the executive and legislature—for example, when the government can dissolve Parliament, or when Parliament can bring down the government, though a clear picture might only be provided if conventions are taken into account as well. The executive's vast powers, however, tend at best to be merely enumerated in the Constitution, and some far-reaching powers, such as that of making delegated legislation, may not even be referred to at all. In federal and decentralised systems, the authority chart will outline the powers and duties of the governments at different levels to ensure a territorial distribution of power. However there can be endless variety in this part of the Constitution; in the lengthy Indian Constitution of 1949 there is a provision which directs the government to make an annual grant for the upkeep of temples, whereas in the concise United States Constitution of 1787 there is no reference at all to the mighty White House. Nevertheless in all cases the organisational chart is the most important operational part of the Constitution.

C An amending provision

The amending provision in a Constitution has been likened to a safety valve to release the pressure which might threaten its violent destruction. Expressed more moderately, the amending provision allows the present generation to modify the ground rules which it has inherited from the past, without rejecting the whole system of government. In a few cases this provision allows amendments to be made in the same way as any other law; the Constitution is then described as flexible (see below). But in order to prevent amendments from being made too often, or for reasons of temporary political expediency, the amending procedure is usually an extraordinary one which precludes the government of the day from acting alone and too hastily. Where the Constitution is more difficult to amend than other laws, it is said to be rigid (see below) and its provisions are entrenched. Here there are numerous variations in relation to the initiation, validation and ratification of amendments: a special quorum requirement (for example, ninety per cent of the members present and sober), a qualified majority in the legislature (for example, three-quarters of the members supporting the amendment), the approval of a body outside the legislature (for example, regional governments or the electorate), and so on. In some countries, such as Switzerland, the citizens can initiate constitutional amendments; in several (West Germany, the Soviet Union) a special majority is required in the legislature; and in a few (Australia, Switzerland) citizen approval in a referendum is necessary. In France a referendum is required only if there is a sixty per cent majority in the legislature favouring a constitutional amendment. In each case it is the amending clause of the Constitution which defines the requirements and procedures. This clause is usually, but surprisingly not always, made rigid itself, so that a system of double entrenchment operates; the New Zealand constitution has an incongruous exception to this rule.

Many Constitutions, such as the South African, provide different amending procedures for different provisions or sections. Occasionally the amending clause will provide that certain sections of the Constitution cannot be changed at all; this indicates that the principles or values they embody are considered so important that the Constitution could not continue to exist without them. It could be the federal principle which is thus entrenched—s 79(3) of the 1949 Basic Law (Constitution) of the Federal Republic of Germany stipulates that amendments to the Constitution which affect the participation in principle of the Laender (the different states or provinces) in national legislation are wholly inadmissible, and there is a similar provision in the United States[8] and Brazilian Constitutions. In other cases it is the principle of republican (non-monarchical) government, as in Italy, or territorial integrity, as in France, which is made inviolable.

A Constitution without any amending provision is a rarity, but this was the case in Canada where there was no express provision for the amendment of the original Constitution, the British North

---

[8] In the case of the United States this revolves around a rather theoretical interpretation of art V of the Constitution. Cf Laurence H Tribe *American Constitutional Law* (1978) 3ff, 50–1.

America Act of 1867. Until an amending provision was introduced in 1949 it was assumed that the only method of amendment was through a statute of the British Parliament—which had enacted the original document. From 1949 the Canadian Parliament could amend some provisions, but only in 1982 with the 'patriation' of the Constitution was the British Parliament's competence to legislate for Canada terminated and a comprehensive domestic amending procedure introduced. A contemporary example of a Constitution with no formal amending provision is the 1979 Constitution of the Islamic Republic of Iran. Of course in terms of practical possibilities Constitutions and entrenched clauses could be destroyed in the course of the overthrow of the state system, or if a new basic norm were generally accepted, but in either case constitutional lawyers would say that a constitutional revolution had taken place. In general it is not wise to make constitutional provisions too difficult to amend; as Lord Bryce said many years ago, Constitutions that do not bend will soonest break.[9]

Formal amendment is not the only way in which Constitutions can be changed. In some cases the courts alter them substantially over the years through their powers of constitutional interpretation.[10] In this way, clauses drafted in an earlier age can be given meanings relevant to the present. Even sections of highly rigid Constitutions can be transformed over the years through judicial interpretation—for example the 'trade and commerce' clause of the United States Constitution has been given an expansive meaning in the present century which allows the national government to regulate numerous aspects of trade and industry, from marketing systems to safety standards. Constitutions can also be changed through custom and usage.[11] Here it is the political branches of the state which render the change without formal amendment.

D Bill of Rights

Most modern Constitutions contain a Bill of Rights. It is usually in a prominent early part of the document so that it can be noticed even by the reader recovering from the preamble. So regular and normative a feature of modern Constitutions is the Bill of Rights, that some commentators are reluctant to use the term Constitution unless it is present. The oldest Bill of Rights, in the modern sense of the term, is in the United States Constitution, but in the present century they have been incorporated into the Constitutions of countries as diverse as West Germany, Japan and Zimbabwe. Bill of Rights provisions are usually consolidated in a self-contained part or chapter of the Constitution, but occasionally, as in Australia, are scattered among its clauses.

A Bill of Rights can be of either a normative or a 'rights' kind. The

[9] James Bryce *Studies in History and Jurisprudence* vol 1 (1901) 12ff.
[10] See Wheare 100–20.
[11] See Wheare 121–36.

normative kind declares the way in which the government ought to operate but provides no sanction if it fails to do so; here it is up to the legislature and executive (the political branches of government) to uphold basic rights. Thus in the Indian Constitution there is a list of directive principles of state policy which the legislatures are required to apply when enacting law, but which are not enforceable by the courts. Although such arrangements are in one sense only a symbolic reminder to those in office to behave, their political, cultural and educational significance can be quite considerable. The 'rights' kind allows a non-political institution, the judiciary, to invalidate acts of government which are in contravention of its provisions. It is the enforceable Bill of Rights which has become the characteristic feature of documentary Constitutions in the latter twentieth century.

There is wide variety in the content of Bills of Rights. It is possible to distinguish at least four general categories of rights: civil rights (property, religion, person and contractual), political rights (voting, speech, assembly, association), economic rights (employment, housing, social security, pension) and social rights (marriage, family life, privacy and leisure). Most Bills enumerate the 'traditional' liberal rights such as property, person, assembly and expression; these are 'negative' rights which take power away from government. But modern Bills of Rights also reflect the changed nature of the state in that they also 'constitutionalise' social and economic rights, such as claims to health, social security and education, and in some cases they require affirmative action from the state for their realisation.[12] These are positive rights which impose obligations on government— a problematic factor as regards their implementation. Bills of Rights in developing countries and socialist systems usually accord priority to the right to work and the right to social welfare, while liberal Bills of Rights emphasise the freedoms of property and contract. This difference reflects an opposition in philosophical stance between the view that liberal rights are a sham unless basic economic and social conditions have been ensured, and the view that civil rights and liberties are themselves prerequisites for the establishment of social and economic rights.[13] However, there is also much common ground in between the extremities as regards personal, political and civil rights, inspired in part by the existence of international rights codes such as the Universal Declaration of Human Rights which was passed by the United Nations in 1948.

As one set of rights can always come into conflict with another, the Constitution should indicate in such circumstances which are to be preferred and which to be superseded—and which body is to enforce the rules.[14] A contemporary phenomenon is for Bills of Rights to qualify the rights which they enumerate, allowing for their

[12] See Danny Pieters (1987) 2 *SA Public Law* 68.
[13] See Alex Amankwah (1988) 21 *CILSA* 190ff.
[14] Cf art 20 of the Constitution of the Federal Republic of Germany.

non-enforcement in certain circumstances. The Declaration of Rights in the 1980 Zimbabwe Constitution contains numerous savings provisions designed to relieve the government of the obligation to comply with the relevant clauses. However, there is an additional judicial discretion to override official reliance on some of the savings clauses if it could not be 'reasonably justifiable in a democratic society'. A similar compromise is apparent in respect of the 1982 Canadian Charter of Rights. Section 1 of the Charter is a general limitation clause which expressly stipulates that the rights in the Charter are not absolute and can be limited by the legislature as long as the limits are 'reasonable and demonstrably justified in a free and democratic society'. The Zimbabwean and Canadian formulations are remarkably similar, but their open-ended standards must be evaluated by different bodies—in the Zimbabwean case by the judiciary, and in the Canadian case by the legislature.

Just as important as the Bill of Rights is the composition and power of the judicial body which the Constitution mandates to enforce it. This can be either the ordinary courts, as in the United States, or a specialist tribunal, such as the Constitutional Court in the Federal Republic of Germany. Inevitably the knowledge citizens have of the Bill's provisions and the procedures by which they can bring matters to the constitutional court is important in determining how effective it will be; here a Constitution should, though seldom does, play an educative role. However, the most critical factor in an enforceable Bill of Rights is the attitude and approach of the relevant court towards its task, since it is invariably a flexible and adaptable tool in the hands of judges. The Bill of Rights allows for the development of law and practice beyond that which the legislature and executive are able to bring about,[15] provided the courts accept this creative responsibility. Judges interpreting the new Charter of Rights and Freedoms in the Canadian Constitution have in their judgments used literary and philosophical sources such as Shakespeare, Gandhi and St Thomas Aquinas, none of them customary legal references.[16] This reveals the need for innovative approaches to constitutional interpretation once the courts are directly involved in policy, and political, issues. Of course all institutions of the state are involved in interpreting the Constitution in everyday practice, but only the courts' interpretations are authoritative and binding.

A correlate of the Bill of Rights, found mainly in socialist Constitutions, is the statement of fundamental duties owed to others or to the state. The 1986 Nicaraguan Constitution, for example, provides that all persons have duties to their families, the community, the homeland and humanity. These abstract duties are not easily susceptible to legal enforcement—as opposed to the duties to pay taxes or perform national service which are encountered more

[15] See Michael Zander *A Bill of Rights* 3 ed (1985) 38ff.
[16] See Eric Colvin (1988) 52 *Saskatchewan Law Review* 191 at 241.

regularly in modern Constitutions. The Japanese Constitution has rights and corresponding duties side by side in the same sections. Where socio-economic rights are mentioned in the Constitution, some obligation to provide them is usually imposed on state institutions. However, their enforcement will depend on political and economic factors, and not on the courts.

While the South African Constitution has never tolerated the judicial enforcement of basic rights, the possible introduction of a Bill of Rights has become a central issue in the constitutional debates in the late 1980s.[17]

E   Financial provisions

While financial provisions may not have the greatest prominence in documentary Constitutions, they require one of the most important constitutional functions of modern governments—the supervision of the national budget. There are two kinds of financial measures, those which generate revenue for the state, such as customs duty, income taxation and sales tax, and those which allow moneys already collected to be spent by state departments, that is to be 'appropriated'. The 'budget' is an annual exercise in which the government estimates the proposed revenue and expenditure for the forthcoming year, and submits the estimates to Parliament for approval. In a few countries the budget is approved through exactly the same procedure as is followed for normal legislation.[18] However, in most countries the Constitution stipulates different procedures for financial measures, which curtail the rights of Parliament and its individual members to consider and modify their contents. This is an ironic tendency, as it has been shown[19] that one of the oldest principles of the British constitutional system is that the government cannot levy money from the people without the approval of Parliament. In modern Westminster-style Constitutions only the executive can introduce Bills dealing with finance, and these Bills may deal only with financial matters. In a great number of countries Parliament can propose reduction but not increases in expenditure, and in a few cases Parliament cannot even demand an increase in taxation.[20] A number of Constitutions limit the debating time of Parliament and its committees for financial measures, in the interests of continuity of government and its services. These various measures ensure that the government of the day has the predominant position in relation to the budget, which is regarded as a major instrument of its policies. This political significace of financial measures is illustrated in the South African Constitution, which provides that the State President must dissolve Parliament (or resign) if each of the three houses

---

[17] See below, 112.
[18] See Inter-Parliamentary Union *Parliaments of the World* (1986) 1091ff.
[19] See above, 26–7 and 32.
[20] Ibid.

rejects an appropriation Bill for the central government departments.[21]

F Other matters

Constitutions can have transitional provisions, special provisions and temporary provisions; they can also have schedules and appendices containing detailed lists of information. There are isolated examples of these in many Constitutions of the world but the lengthy Indian Constitution of 1949 contains them all. It is also possible for the constitutional amendments to be included at the end of the document in chronological sequence—as in the French and United States systems—instead of being consolidated into the original charter, as in South Africa and Mongolia. In a few cases there are definition sections and provisions which direct the courts how to interpret the Constitution Act. With the modern preference for lengthy rather than concise constitutional documents, there is a tendency for ever more exotic material to be included.

III WHAT THEY DO NOT CONTAIN

It has already been indicated that modern Constitutions often say little or nothing about the most important aspects of public power and its exercise. This is why political scientists and sociologists say that they provide only a one-dimensional view of the state and the governing process. Not only is a single dimension deficient, but it can be positively misleading in that the lay person might come to a faulty understanding of the constitutional process from a reading of the Constitution alone. The 1972 Constitution of the Kingdom of the Netherlands, for example, devotes nearly one third of its provisions to the status and authority of the king, yet the Dutch have a constitutional monarchy which confers mainly ceremonial powers and little political influence on the Crown. Conversely the Constitution may say nothing at all about important constitutional factors, such as the institutionalised influence of business, religion or cultural bodies on legislative policymaking. Moreover, many important constitutional matters, such as the electoral system, tend to be regulated by ordinary legislation, or occasionally the common law. Often history and tradition determine what is included in the Constitution and what is dealt with elsewhere: for example, in some Westminster-style Constitutions there is no constitutional Bill of Rights but instead extra-constitutional administrative bodies have been introduced to enforce anti-discrimination principles or matters of race, colour or gender.

What follows is a description of some of the significant matters which are not dealt with in most modern Constitutions.

[21] Sec 39(2)(*b*)(ii).

A   Party system

The party system is a major factor in the operation of constitutional systems.[22] The way citizens organise themselves into political groups determines how and in whose interests power is exercised, who is appointed to government positions, and how much real governmental accountability there is to the people. Thus Westminster-type Constitutions allow the person with majority support in the legislature to become the head of the executive. This might give the false impression that the legislature considers various contenders and, after due deliberation, expresses its preference. In reality the legislature comprises not only individuals but also readily definable political parties, and the leader of the larger or largest party becomes the chief executive—yet how he or she is elected (or even appointed) as party leader is a purely 'domestic' matter not regulated by the Constitution. The same applies to the nomination of candidates for parliamentary election. If one party is so strong in a constituency that its candidate is certain to win the election, then the decisive issue is who the party nominates as its candidate, a process which may take place in smoky backrooms or dark corridors. The actual election by voters follows the constitutionally prescribed procedures, but is just a formality. Another example concerns cabinet appointments: in many systems these will always be made from the majority party alone, though this is not required by the Constitution. In each case party formation and solidarity makes the Constitution operate in a way not apparent from its formal provisions.

Party formation and predominance will depend in part on the electoral system. In broad terms electoral systems can have one of two outcomes: a 'two-party system' in which there are two major parties filling the roles of government and opposition, with other parties, if any, filling very minor roles in the political system, and a 'multi-party system' in which there is a number of political parties represented in government in rough proportion to their support among the electorate. (The two-party and multi-party systems can both be contrasted with the one-party system[23] in which the formation of political parties in opposition to the officially sanctioned one is prohibited.) The two-party system in encountered, again in general terms, in Westminster constitutional systems, and multiple-party systems are found in the European countries. In the former the parties tend to be much stronger because they are organised on a strict hierarchical basis and operate through a caucus system.[24] The hierarchy ensures substantial power and influence for party leaders, and the fact that generally only parties have the funds and organisational capacity to secure the election of candidates to

---

[22] See above, 37.

[23] See above, 49–50.

[24] The United States provides an exception in that although the electoral system throws up two dominant parties, the absence of national party organisation and leadership makes the parties significantly weaker than in Westminster systems.

Parliament means that ambitious politicians must accept the party line as dictated by the leadership. The caucus consists of the members of the particular party who have been elected to the legislature. It confers several organisational and resource benefits on members, and is the crucible in which their promotion prospects are decided—in return for which they have to support publicly all decisions taken by the caucus.

While the parties in a two-party system have to be broad-based and cohesive if they are to attain power, those in a multiple-party system sometimes revolve around sectional religious, linguistic or cultural interests, or single social issues. This accounts for the existence in various countries of religious and cultural parties in the past, and the rise of the Greens (environmental issues) and the Greys (old age issues) in the present. It is said of such systems that power is too diffused among the various parties for electoral outcomes to be decisive; there are no clear-cut lines of accountability for governments, and the systems tend to be politically unstable. The two-party system, by contrast, allows electors to choose not only the members of the legislature but also which party is to constitute the government. Lines of accountability are clearer and the political system is more stable. There are, of course, exceptions to both of these tendencies.

Despite the importance of political parties, Westminster-type Constitutions make virtually no references to them at all. In this respect, South Africa falls within the Westminster category. This again gives the false impression that the systems are operated by free-thinking individuals who make decisions on rational grounds and appointments on merit. Another class of Constitutions makes some reference to political parties, but without describing or prescribing their role in government—for example, the 1983 Turkish Constitution. It is only the one-party systems, such as those of Malaŵi or Yugoslavia, which openly acknowledge and define the role of party. Here the Constitution provides that there shall be only one political party and the electoral laws stipulate that all candidates for Parliament must be members of the party. In some cases the organisation of the party and the election of the leadership is also directly regulated by the Constitution, so that the party is liable to follow prescribed procedures and practices. Clearly such systems exclude the freedom of political association encountered in multi-party systems.

B Constitutional conventions

The term convention was given constitutional currency by A V Dicey, an influential commentator on the English constitution in the nineteenth century.[25] Under the influence of Dicey, subsequent

---

[25] A V Dicey *An Introduction to the Study of the Law of the Constitution* 10 ed (1959) 417ff.

writers devoted considerable energy to defining and describing the conventions of the constitution.[26] Unfortunately, in the modern state the definition and the practice of conventions is not so easy to characterise. They are traditionally defined as the non-legal rules of the constitution, which means that although they are treated as binding by the political branches of government they are not legally enforceable by the courts. They nevertheless form a very real part of the constitution in that they are faithfully observed in the normal course of affairs—so much so, that if a government breaks a convention we would say that it is acting unconstitutionally, albeit not illegally. The sanction for breaking conventions is political, that is censure by Parliament, dismissal from office, loss of public support, and so on. Some writers argue that conventions are legal rules in that they are enforced by Parliament and afforded passing recognition by the courts, but this debate does not have much practical significance and the orthodox view is that conventions must be distinguished from law. They are also different to mere usages or traditions, such as the wearing of suits in parliament, since they are regarded as more binding and have real political significance; the wearing of shorts and sunglasses in the legislature would be neither illegal nor unconstitutional, although it might contravene the rules of parliamentary procedure.

The significance of conventions can be illustrated through three international examples. In the monarchical systems of Sweden and the Netherlands, the Crown has the constitutional right to veto legislation by refusing to sign it. In practice this power is never exercised because by convention the head of state acts on the government's advice and legislation comes into force—although there could be no appeal to the courts if a Bill was vetoed by the Crown. In the United States the Constitution provides for the election of the president by a college of electors which represents all the states. Largely through the operation of convention, the college has no independent discretion but merely reflects the results of the popular vote for the presidency, and formalises the outcome. In Switzerland places on the national executive are distributed to the four main parties in the proportion of 2:2:2:1, a so-called 'magic formula' which is not constitutionally prescribed but is the most important feature of the political system. All these conventions go to the heart of the constitutional systems concerned. They show how conventions can nullify the power conferred on one body and transfer it to another, thereby supplementing and modifying the written word of the Constitution.[27] For Dicey, the overall purpose of conventions was to ensure that effect was given to the wishes of the electorate. Unfortunately, like many of his other insights, this one

---

[26] For a good modern analysis of constitutional conventions see Geoffrey Marshall *Constitutional Conventions: The Rules and Forms of Policital Accountability* (1984).
[27] On South African constitutional conventions see below, 153.

has only limited current validity. If conventions do have any overall role it is, as another English writer suggests, to adapt structure to function.[28]

Conventions can be of a strong or a weak kind. The three already described are extremely strong. However, the strains of modern government and the growth of party systems have weakened others considerably, and the sanctions for breaking them are often non-existent. For example, in Westminster-type Constitutions there is a convention that cabinet ministers are responsible to the legislature for the management and administration of their departments. This means that the minister must take the political blame for maladministration, ineffeciency or corruption, for which the sanction, in an extreme case, should be loss of office. This convention still has some effectiveness in the United Kingdom but in many Westminster systems it has become very weak. South Africa is one country where ministers avoid furnishing Parliament with information about their departments,[29] deny any responsibility for their faulty operation, and are seldom forced to relinquish office. As the convention depends for its operation on publicity and open government, it is quite unsuited to constitutional systems which have become closed and secretive. Rather than the legislature controlling the government, as the convention suggests, the government can, through the party system, control the legislature.[30] This suggests that the convention has become inappropriate for modern conditions of government and does not serve its immediate function of checking the executive, and far less the Diceyan vision of reflecting popular wishes.

As with customary law, conventions come into being through long and recognised usage. This means that unlike the prerogatives (see below), new conventions can emerge over time, though exactly when they assume the status of conventions can be difficult to determine. It is also difficult to say at which point a convention weakens to such an extent that it can no longer be regarded as a convention. The clearest way to terminate a convention is through the enactment of legislation which is incompatible with it, and therefore overrides it. Another way in which a convention can come to an end is if it is codified in the Constitution or other statute; here it is by definition no longer a convention because it becomes a legal rule, enforceable by the courts, but the overall effect is to reinforce and not undermine the previous practice.

[28] O Hood Phillips and Paul Jackson *O Hood Phillips' Constitutional and Administrative Law* 7 ed (1987) 30ff.
[29] This allegation can be tested by reading a random series of Questions and Replies in Hansard, the transcript of parliamentary proceedings.
[30] Commentaries often underplay this reality despite the insights of orthodox writers such as Ivor Jennings *Cabinet Government* 3 ed (1959) 472–3.

C Prerogative powers

Some countries with documentary Constitutions still have a common law of the constitution, especially if they are derived from the Westminster system. The prerogatives are common-law powers residing in the supreme executive authority. In English constitutional law they represent the residue of the Crown's rights, powers and privileges which remained intact after the royal power had been broken by Parliament.[31] They include various powers in respect of foreign affairs, war, peace and travel, and various domestic powers relating to the conferment of honours, the operation of Parliament and the appointment of commissions of enquiry. By definition there cannot be any new prerogatives, and many have been reduced to statutory form, where they lose their status as common-law powers. Moreover, in modern practice prerogatives are not exercised by the head of state personally but by convention on the advice of another body—usually the cabinet or a minister, but in some cases the legislature. Partly through Dicey's fault they have in the past been seen as immune from judicial review, but when he referred to the prerogative powers as 'discretionary' he meant that they do not have any statutory legal basis, not that they are arbitrary and uncontrollable. In the administrative law context the prerogative is the only significant non-statutory source of power for public authorities; the extent to which the South African prerogatives are subject to judicial control is discussed elsewhere.[32] There you will also encounter the modern reincarnation of the ancient prerogative in the form of the wide discretionary powers of ministers and state officials (the so-called 'statutory prerogative'). Only a few traditional prerogatives continue to play an important role in modern constitutional systems.

D The administrative branch

The most striking omissions from modern Constitutions is any significant reference to the administrative branch of government (that is the bureaucracy). There are two related reasons for this oversight. First, the pattern of documentary Constitutions was established at an historical juncture when the bureaucracy was not a major autonomous force in government and politics; and secondly, in constitutional theory the bureaucracy continues to have only a limited and dependent function, namely to put into effect policy decisions taken by the executive and legislature and court orders made by the judiciary.

In reality the modern administration is a powerful and 'independent' branch of government with the ability to formulate policy as well as implement it, and in many respects it has the organisation, resources and information to dominate the other branches. Not only has constitutional theory been slow to adjust to this reality, but the

[31] See further below, 175–8.
[32] See below, 180–1 and 248–9.

constitutional tripartism of Constitutions has not been modified to bring the bureaucracy within their ambit. There are some exceptions—for example the 1980 Zimbabwe Constitution regulates the qualifications for and method of appointment of certain high-ranking officials—but they tend to be of limited significance. Generally the composition, appointment, powers and accountability of the administrative branch are not regulated by the Constitution and are largely within the competence of the bureaucracy itself. The result is that bureaucracies to some extent operate extra-constitutionally, in the sense that they are not directly subject to the checks and balances which the Constitution imposes on the executive, legislature and judiciary. The rules of administrative law provide some order and control over the activities, but they have been developed only late in the history of constitutional government and they do not reach into all areas of the administrative process.

E Other aspects

It is self-evident that judicial interpretations of the Constitution will not be reflected in the document itself, despite the fact that they are more authoritative than the original provisions, and in some cases might even be in apparent conflict with them. There are several other aspects of the constitutional system which modern Constitutions tend not to describe. It has been indicated that this is often the case with the electoral system, which, despite its crucial importance in the political system, is usually regulated by a separate Act: in South Africa it is the Electoral Act 45 of 1979. Others are the forms of government at local and regional level, matters of public finance, and the regulation of nationality and citizenship. It is also not often that the economic system is described or regulated in any detail. The internal procedures of all three branches of government are normally left to be developed by these bodies themselves—parliamentary orders by the legislature, rules of court by the judiciary, and procedures and the correct forms to fill in by the administration. These omissions are quite defensible in that if matters requiring detailed regulation were included, the Constitution would assume the length of a telephone directory. However, they contribute to the relative unreliability of the documentary Constitution as a guide to the workings of the state system.

IV WHAT THEY SHOULD INFORM YOU

Whatever the variation in Constitutions and the information they conceal or confuse, they should provide some basic information to political actors, constitutional lawyers and the public. For political actors the Constitution has a self-evident function: it describes the procedures and processes which must be followed for officials to accede to office and for their actions to be regarded as legal and, provided the Constitution is broadly accepted, legitimate. For citizens the Constitution should describe the rights and conditions of political participation in different institutions, and the remedies for redress of civil and social rights—though citizen ignorance of such matters is probably the norm and not the exception. For the constitutional lawyer the Constitution should reveal the juridical basis of the constitutional-legal system. While the Constitution is itself a legal document and constitutes the 'law behind the law',[33] it should also indicate the highest form of law in the system and the way in which conflicts between laws are to be resolved. This requirement has several important elements.

A Ultimate authority

First, a Constitution should indicate the ultimate authority in the constitutional-legal system. All other rules and principles will be derived from the ultimate legal source. For lawyers this feature is important because it identifies the 'rules of recognition'[34] on which the validity of the whole legal system is based, and it indicates the juridical status of the Constitution itself within the legal system. Where a Constitution has evolved through evolutionary processes the ultimate rule of recognition will contain a reference to pre-existing rules of legislative competence and change—that is, the principles which validate the existing constitutional system, whether they be the pre-existing Constitution or, in the colonial context, imperial authorities.[35] In a revolutionary situation, in which constitutional continuity is broken and power is usually said to derive from the people, the rule of recognition will be a 'first cause' in the sense that it is not derived from another legal source.[36] Thus if a post-revolutionary Constitution stipulates that Acts of Parliament are the ultimate source of law, then the source of the rule that statutes have the force of law is historical and political, not legal.[37] This does not, of course, detract from the legality of the Acts of Parliament.

In practical terms the Constitution should indicate which body, or combination of bodies, has the final say on constitutional and legal matters. This reintroduces the doctrine of sovereignty,[38] which is both a legal principle and a political reality. There are broadly two models which can operate here. The legislature can have the capacity to make laws on any subject-matter without regard to constitutional

---

[33] S A de Smith *Constitutional and Administrative Law* 5 ed (1985) 16.

[34] See H L A Hart *The Concept of Law* (1971) 97–106. For Hart the 'rule of recognition' specifies 'some feature or features possession of which by a suggested rule is taken as a conclusive affirmative indication that it is a rule of the group to be supported by the social pressure it exerts' (92).

[35] See R D Lumb (1988) 15 *University of Queensland Law Journal* 3 at 5.

[36] See J M Finnis in A W B Simpson (ed) *Oxford Essays in Jurisprudence* 2nd series (1973) 44 at 49. As a matter of practical logic, the law cannot proceed ad infinitum in tracing the descent of its principles and ultimately legal authority rests on political force. Cf John Salmond *Jurisprudence* 2 ed (1907) 49.

[37] No statute can confer law-making power on Parliament, because this would be to assume the very power which is conferred.

[38] See above, 33–5; and see further, below, 125–32

norms or judicial review; the legislature is then the sovereign authority on constitutional mattters, subject only to the requirement that it act according to the 'manner and form' prescribed by the constitution. This is the situation in jurisdictions such as the United Kingdom and New Zealand. Alternatively, if the Constitution is supreme, it is binding on all organs of government and is enforced by the courts through their power to review, and declare invalid, acts of the executive and legislature which appear to be in conflict with constitutional standards. This is the situation in jurisdictions such as the United States and Italy. Sovereignty then vests in a combination of bodies which, when acting according to a complex set of procedures, can alone amend the rigid Constitution. There is a third possibility, namely that the highest executive authority can act as final arbiter in the constitutional system, as is provided for in the Constitution of Iran; but this is not a frequent arrangement.

The constitutional amending procedure will be an important element in the rules of recognition. In some cases the Constitution may indicate more than one basic rule of change,[39] for example where there are different procedures for amending different provisions. In others there is need for more elaborate compromises. In Canada the introduction of a justiciable Charter of Rights in 1982 necessitated a compromise between the prevailing Westminster principle of legislative sovereignty and the new principle of constitutional supremacy. This was achieved in s 33(1):

> 'Parliament or the legislature of a province may expressly declare in an Act of Parliament or the legislature . . . that the Act or a provision thereof shall operate notwithstanding a provision included in s 2 or ss 7 to 15 of this Charter.'

This provision served to preserve legislative supremacy as the dominant constitutional principle, provided the relevant legislature is prepared to take the political risk of invoking it publicly; even then the statute lasts for only five years and further publicity will surround its renewal. In all other cases the Charter predominates, and is a standard of validity for government actions. Commentators suggest that in its first years this compromise has resulted in the effective endorsement of civil rights without any large-scale abandonment of legislative supremacy.[40] Another variety of compromise is found in the situations where a Bill of Rights is introduced into the Constitution but there is a period of grace before it becomes enforceable: in Tanzania a recent amendment to the 1987 Constitution incorporated a Bill of Rights but stipulated that it would not be justiciable for a transitional period of three years after commencement. This is designed to allow the government a reasonable period to amend offending laws, and to avoid a hiatus in the statute book.[41]

[39] See 59–61, above.
[40] See B L Strayer 1988 *Public Law* 347.
[41] See D Z Lubuva 1988 *Commonwealth Law Bulletin* 853.

Where the period of grace does not apply, there can be some uncertainty as to the implications of a new Bill of Rights for pre-existing laws, as occurred in the case of Bophuthatswana.[42]

While all Constitutions indicate the ultimate authority in the constitutional-legal system this should clearly not be seen as synonymous with the most powerful political body, such as the cabinet or party caucus, which in turn might be influenced by organised business interests, trade unions, a religious grouping, or a sporting board.

B The judicial role

Secondly, the Constitution must define the role of the courts. Regardless of where ultimate authority lies, the constitutional system should, particularly from the perspective of the constitutional lawyer, identify the role of the courts in relation to the functions of other branches of government and the rights of citizens. The courts could police the distribution of authority between different levels of government (as in a federal system), enforce basic rights (where there is a justiciable Bill of Rights), or uphold the whole Constitution (where there is judicial review of a rigid Constitution). Where the courts have a dominant constitutional function there exists a system of judicial supremacy, which can operate in terms of two broad institutional models.[43] The first is the decentralised American model in which every judicial body has the authority to review legislation in the ordinary course of litigation. The second is the centralised European model in which there is a specially-designated constitutional court which alone has the power of review, but can exercise it regardless of whether there is an actual dispute before it.[44] In both cases constitutional adjudication is different to normal litigation between two private parties in that the outcome, for example the invalidation of a statute or government practice, will have implications for the whole state system and all its citizens. The West German Constitutional Court is in a unique constitutional position in that it is empowered to recommend and demand legislation of the legislature, which often responds obligingly.[45] This arrangement is in harmony with the constitutional system because the German Constitutional Court, as with other central bodies, is an elective, and therefore democratically legitimate, institution.

The type of administrative law which a country has will be foreshadowed by the role which the Constitution confers on the courts. However, the Constitution itself might play only an initial part in defining the judicial role, which will also be shaped by the common law and the courts themselves—and as with the fashions it

---

[42] See G Devenish in M P Vorster, Marinus Wiechers and D J van Vuuren *Constitutions of Transkei, Bophuthatswana, Venda and Ciskei* (1985) 85ff.
[43] See above, 63.
[44] See M Cappelletti *Judicial Review in the Contemporary World* (1971) 46ff.
[45] See Gisbert Brinkman 1981 *Public Law* 83.

is likely to fluctuate over time. Here a persistent theme can be restated from a slightly different perspective. While the Constitution's description of the role of the courts is a significant factor, ultimately the effectiveness of judicial review and constitutional restraints will depend not on what the Constitution prescribes, but on extra-constitutional factors such as the political process, the regularity of elections, and the periodical alternation, or at least its possibility, of parties in government.[46]

C Hierarchy of legal norms

Thirdly, the Constitution should not only identify the ultimate sources of law but should also indicate how conflicts among different kinds of laws are to be resolved. A situation of legislative supremacy implies that laws of the central Parliament will prevail over all other laws, and that if two Acts of Parliament are in conflict the latter will prevail over the earlier;[47] both these rules have exceptions which you will encounter in more specialised contexts. In a situation of constitutional supremacy the Constitution itself, and its Bill of Rights in particular, constitutes the highest legal norm against which all other laws can be tested. In a federal system the Constitution must indicate whether, in cases of conflict, the laws of the federal government, on one hand, or the state or provincial governments, on the other, should prevail. It must also indicate the legal relationship between the national Constitution and the individual state Constitutions. There are other possibilities as well: for example, the 1983 South African Constitution[48] stipulates that some 'own affairs' laws are subject to norms and standards laid down in 'general affairs' laws; the latter will therefore prevail over the former in cases of conflict. As regards delegated legislation, this is subject to the Constitution, to limitations imposed in the empowering legislation, and to other standards imposed by the courts in the exercise of their common-law review function; in addition modern Constitutions often provide for its review by Parliament, or a Parliamentary committee, which can also result in its invalidation. The courts will usually supervise and enforce the rules of legal hierarchy expressed or implied in the Constitution.

D Emergency powers

Finally, the Constitution should, expressly or impliedly, indicate the position concerning its own suspension, or concerning a deviation from some of its provisions. This might seem a contradiction in terms, but most constitutional systems incorporate a principle of

---

[46] See Bogdanor op cit n 6 at 12.
[47] Lawyers mystify this principle by stating it in Latin: *leges posteriores priores derogant.*
[48] Schedule 1.

'self-preservation'[49] in terms of which constitutional principles and processes can be overridden where the security of the state is at stake.[50] Both martial law and a state of emergency are recognised situations in which this suspension can occur, and in many systems they can be proclaimed by the head of state at common law. In other jurisdictions the power of constitutional suspension is conferred by the Constitution—those of France and the Ivory Coast, for example, have emergency provisions which allow the head of state or political executive to take exceptional measures involving the temporary suspension of constitutional norms. While emergency powers are designed to be used only in cases involving a threat to public safety or national crisis, there is always a suspicion that they are used primarily for political purposes. Sometimes this has ironic consequences: the emergency powers adopted by the Smith government in Rhodesia were used in independent Zimbabwe by those who had been previously subjected to them. There are only a few instances, such as the Constitution of Belgium, where there is an express prohibition on the complete or partial suspension of the Constitution. There are other Constitutions which, with a supreme sense of optimism, stipulate that they do not lose their effect even if their observance is interrupted by force and that they will automatically resume operation once there is a return to normality—this is often the case in South American countries, for example the 1961 Venezuelan Constitution.

V HOW THEY ARE CLASSIFIED

Much ink has been used in describing the classifications of Constitutions,[51] yet it is widely agreed that the traditional classification system indicates little about an individual system. Here an outline only is provided of the conventional classifications, some of which relate more to the government system than to the Constitution.

A Codified and uncodified

A country has a codified Constitution if the most important rules and principles of government have been assembled in a single statute-like document. If there is no such document, the constitution is uncodified. Of the approximately 160 member-states of the United Nations all have codified Constitutions, save for the United Kingdom, Israel and New Zealand. Because there are so many codified Constitutions the classification is very broad and uninformative. The terms written and unwritten are sometimes used for codified and uncodified, respectively, but they are misleading in that

---

[49] The principle is sometimes expressed in terms of the Latin maxim *salus populi suprema lex est*.

[50] See Edward McWhinney op cit n 4 at 81–5.

[51] See, for example, Leslie Wolf-Phillips *Comparative Constitutions* (1972).

'unwritten' constitutions may have many documentary elements, such as a statute regulating elections, and 'written' Constitutions may have many unwritten elements, such as conventions.

B Rigid and flexible

If a Constitution is easy to amend it is classified as flexible, and if it is difficult to amend it is classified as rigid or inflexible. The uncodified constitutions are all flexible. Most codified Constitutions are rigid, but in varying degrees: a special legislative majority, or electoral ratification, or approval by provincial or state governments, is required for their amendment. However, despite these variations, the formal amending procedure gives no necessary indication of how often a Constitution will be amended in practice. The Swiss Constitution is formally more rigid than the American, but is amended far more frequently in practice. Notwithstanding the formal amending procedure, a Constitution can also be rendered flexible where it is changed in other ways, such a through the development of conventions or judicial interpretation; it is particularly when constitutional provisions are 'vague and general' that this kind of modification can occur.

C Unitary and federal

A Constitution is unitary if it gives the central authorities the predominant role in the process of government, including the right to prevail over any regional or local authorities. A Constitution is federal if it gives some autonomy to subnational bodies and protects them against central intrusion, through devices such as constitutional rigidity and judicial review. In a federal system the subnational authorities derive their power directly from the Constitution, whereas in a unitary system power derives from (and can be resumed by) the national legislature. There is again a potential discrepancy between the presence of federal characteristics in a Constitution and the actual realisation of federal government in political and economic practice.

D Parliamentary and presidential

A parliamentary Constitution requires the executive to be drawn from the members of the legislature. This provides the basis for a system of parliamentary or responsible government, in which there is a stable pattern of legislative/executive relationships, which revolves around the fact that the same political party controls both branches. A presidential Constitution establishes a greater separation of powers between the legislature and executive, and it precludes the president and other members of the political executive from simultaneously being members of the legislature; here there is a set of reciprocal checks and balances between the two institutions, each of which has a separate political mandate. Hybrid arrangements are catered for by categorising the Constitution as semi-presidential or semi-parliamentary. The parliamentary/presidential distinction has real implications for the principles of constitutionalism and the system of administrative law.

E   Other classifications

Socialist Constitutions seek to locate state power in the hands of the working people by stipulating that ownership of natural resources and factories vests in the people collectively;[52] they are programmatic, in that they provide a programme for the further transformation of society. *Non-socialist* (bourgeois or liberal) Constitutions tend to be status-quo oriented and non-programmatic, depict state institutions as neutral instruments which can be controlled by any organised interest, and emphasise individual ownership and property rights.

A *Multi-Party* Constitution authorises the formation and operation of multiple political parties, whereas a *One-Party* Constitution, of which there are socialist and non-socialist varieties, legalises only a single named political party and prohibits the existence of other parties.

A *Monarchical* Constitution provides for the head of state to be identified according to hereditary tenure, whereas a *Republican* Constitution provides for a directly or indirectly elected head of state. A Republican Constitution can be further categorised according to the executive arrangement, namely, as to whether it is *Parliamentary* or *Presidential*.

VI   WHETHER THEY MATTER

For some time it has been fashionable to suggest that Constitutions no longer matter.[53] Unlike previous centuries, and even earlier decades, there is now a more sceptical attitude towards the role and significance of documentary Constitutions.[54] This is because political scientists and sociologists have shown that they sometimes provide an inaccurate reflection of state power, and political actors have shown that they can be ignored in practice. They are perceived as both incomplete and ineffective—hence the complaint that they are not worth the paper they are written on. Of Constitutions in developing countries it is said that they can only be understood in the context of global politics and the forces of a world economy. The 'anti-constitutionalist' thesis resulted in only constitutional lawyers seeing any merit in the analysis and discussion of documentary Constitutions.

While there is much substance in these criticisms of documentary Constitutions, they also involve an overreaction. Constitutions do

---

[52] In practice though, ownership and control effectively vest in the state.
[53] Cf S E Finer *Five Constitutions* (1979) 15–20.
[54] See above, 65ff.

provide some of the foundation stones for the system of public law: they enfranchise citizens, they confer authority, they provide some constraints on government, and they establish court systems and judicial power. The prevalance of constitutional crises and constitutional revisions in many countries suggests a new significance for documentary Constitutions, as political factors and as objects of study. They should not be treated with too much reverence, but must also not be underestimated in their significance.

4 The Constitution and the Administrative-Law System

Administrative-law systems are given primary shape by the constitution. Here the term administrative-law system is used in a wide sense to include the structure of the administrative branch of government, the principles, rules and procedures by which administrative bodies operate, and the ways in which they are controlled and held accountable. In each area the constitution provides a basic framework for the development of the administrative-law system. The framework provides some latitude for these developments, but this latitude is sometimes insufficient and the framework comes under strain from the dynamics of administrative law in practice. Thus while the constitution provides the initial foundation for administrative law, the actual practices of the system sometimes require a redefinition of constitutional principles themselves.

In this chapter, an overview is provided of different models and principles of administrative law, and the way in which they are influenced by the constitutional context in which they operate. For lawyers, an awareness of this overview is an important point of departure when approaching an administrative-law problem. To express it in other words, no administrative-law problem should be seen separately from the basic principles of the constitutional framework. However, this relationship is never completely harmonious, and some of the basic tensions are referred to in the last section of the chapter.

I APPROACHES TO ADMINISTRATIVE POWER

In the critical literature one encounters different approaches to the desirability and optimal scope of the state's power to administer. Each approach has different implications for the administrative-law system.

Some theorists have a negative view of state power and believe that it should be restricted to a very limited range of social functions, such as law and order, internal security, and external defence. In this 'necessary evil' view of government the state should not be involved in regulating the economy and economic factors, in providing welfare services, and in undertaking entrepreneurial activities, all of which should be left to private enterpise and market forces. The role of public law generally, and administrative law in particular, should be to provide legal controls over state power to ensure that it is correctly exercised and confined to its 'proper' province. This view has been referred to as the 'red-light' theory of public law in which the emphasis is on the control, limitation and supervision of the state and its power, primarily through the institutions of the law.[1]

Another group of writers subscribes to a more positive view of state power. These theorists regard it as an instrument for giving effect to social policies which will benefit either the general public or specifically defined communities. Unlike the market and private power, which are used for the pursuit of short-term, individual goals, state power can be used to develop and implement long-term social and economic policies for the benefit of the public—the development of economic infrastructure, the exploitation of natural resources, the preservation of the environment and the implementation of the comprehensive social programmes. It can be used for ensuring a minimum platform of educational, health and welfare services for all members of society, for redressing economic inequalities, and for controlling powerful and unaccountable interests in the private sector. In this view the institutional mechanisms which ensure that public power is used to promote collective policies and objectives are best located not in the legal domain but in the political system. This group, which upholds a 'green-light' theory of public law, advocates the development of institutions which ensure greater political (that is, democratic and public) control of state power, and does not place much reliance on law as a mechanism of control and accountability.

There is a third position, which is espoused by the adherents of an 'amber-light' theory of public law. In common with the second group, they acknowledge the need for extensive state power in many areas of social and economic life. However, they differ from them in their perception that even developed political institutions will not alone be adequate to control state power and make it accountable. Administrative law principles and procedures must also be developed to supplement the democratic, political controls over those who exercise state power. This implies an important, but restricted, role for the courts and judicial review. An optimal balance is sought among internal administrative controls and external political and judicial controls over the administrative process.

The traffic-light metaphor is useful in highlighting some of the assumptions of those who advocate either more or less judicial review of administrative action. Those advocating extensive judicial review operate with a model of the minimal state with circumscribed powers, whose main function is to provide social stability so that the free market can operate. Those advocating restricted judicial review operate with a model of the state as the embodiment of the collective welfare, as a social planner, a provider of benefits and a safeguard against private power. The first group sees the main function of the

---

[1] On this metaphor see Carol Harlow and Richard Rawlings *Law and Administration* (1984) 1–59. For the South African judiciary's version of this theory, and a switch of metaphor, see below, 243ff, on the 'watchdog' theory of review.

legal system as being the protection of private rights, such as individual freedom and personal property, the second as being the advancement of social utility and the common good. The metaphor is also useful in its juxtaposition of the legal and political elements in administrative law: it focuses attention on the fact that whatever the merits of judicial review it cannot claim to be the most *democratic* method of controlling the state and its administrative powers.

The majority of lawyers are either red- or amber-light theorists and advocate a more rather than a less extensive constitutional role for the courts. If the courts cannot take decisions themselves, they should at least be able to supervise those taken by administrative bodies. The decisions of administrative bodies will be condoned, broadly speaking, if they have acted in a judicial manner.[2] This implies a preference for the legal method of decision-making and dispute-resolution over the administrative method—though as is suggested below, lawyers tend to be relatively ignorant of the way in which administrators operate. Most administrative-law systems, including the South African, have this orientation. In consequence, they focus more on the protection of individual rights by the courts than on the implementation of collective social policies by public authorities. A smaller group of lawyers, together with other 'green-light' critics, point out that the courts are unrepresentative, unaccountable and in some cases unresponsive institutions, which should have only a limited role in administrative law. At its most refined level this view holds that judicial review can never be justified in terms of democatic principles.[3] This 'anti-judicial review' thesis assumes the existence of a range of genuinely representative and democratic political institutions, an assumption which does not hold good for many repressive societies.

The three theoretical constructs described above postulate three different models of administrative law, though in practice no administrative-law system will conform wholly to one construct. The extent to which one or other tendency predominates within a particular legal jurisdiction depends partly on the constitutional basis of the system. Thus in the United States the constitution manifests a distrust of government and state power in the many ways in which it attempts to divide, limit, share and control state authority. The constitutional checks and balances, the Bill of Rights and the courts' powers of review contribute to a highly judicialised form of administrative law. Constitutions in developing countries, on the other hand, tend to remove restrictions on state authority so that it can be used to implement social and economic policies; this leads to a less judicialised system of administrative law. The Australian constitution provides a wide range of institutions for bringing administrative action under political, administrative and

[2] See Allan Hutchinson (1985) 48 *Modern Law Review* 293.
[3] See Hutchinson ibid 296.

legal controls, in an attempt to integrate and balance the political and legal dimensions of the administrative-law system. However, the constitutional basics are only a partial indicator of administrative-law tendencies. The British constitution places its theoretical faith in a legally omnipotent central Parliament, yet in practice the administrative-law system has become highly judicialised.[4]

II THE STRUCTURE OF THE PUBLIC ADMINISTRATION

Modern state systems are large and complex organisations. Because of their size and complexity there is an infinite variety of ways in which public officials and administrative authorities can be arranged. These arrangements are not always cohesive and coherent: different branches of the state can have different interests, can be in competition with one another, and can even become embroiled in legal and political disputes. The structure of the public administration is an important element in an administrative law system, but the formal Constitution is usually reticent on this matter.[5]

In a federal system there are two levels of administrative authorities, with institutional links to the other branches of government at the relevant level, national or regional. The state or provincial bureaucracies may be subject to controls by federal authorities, either directly or, as is more likely, indirectly through financial or political factors. In a unitary constitutional system the structure of the bureaucracy is more hierarchical, though with vastly different degrees of centralisation or decentralisation. At the local level there can be different forms of municipal government. In some cases their status and powers are guaranteed by the Constitution, they have independent sources of revenue, and they are autonomous sites of policy-making; in others they are creations of the central government with no independent resources and little autonomy in matters of policy. Likewise in their composition municipal councils can vary according to whether they are locally elected or centrally appointed—or a combination of both. In all cases a local bureaucracy administers local affairs.

The most prominent administrative institutions are the national government departments. The primary repository of administrative power in a specific area is usually a member of the political executive, in most systems known as a minister of state. The minister is the political and administrative head of a hierarchical departmental structure which is staffed by public servants. In some systems all officials are permanent, in the sense that they retain their positions when the government, and relevant minister, lose office. This is when the rule of public service anonymity operates.[6] In other

---

[4] See the recent comparative analysis in Bernard Schwartz *Lions Over the Throne* (1987).
[5] See above, 70–1.
[6] See above, 38.

systems, top-ranking officials are replaced when the governing party loses office, and their positions are regarded as having a political nature. The United Kingdom provides a prominent example of the former system, and the United States of the latter.

Besides the traditional 'public servant' state departments, there can be a variety of boards, tribunals, councils and other agencies which exercise different state powers. For some state undertakings specific institutions are created which seem best suited to the needs in question: an example is the public corporation for commercial and entrepreneurial ventures. Modern states also establish a range of quasi-government institutions, or parastatals,[7] in which state and private resources are combined for a specific purpose. Here the edges of the state system become blurred and it is difficult to say where the public sector ends and the private sector begins.

A specifically American feature is the semi-autonomous agency which is not part of the orthodox departmental structure in that it is created by the legislature, to whom it is responsible.[8] These agencies are sometimes said to constitute the 'regulatory branch' of government. They are acknowledged to have not only administrative powers but also legislative, financial and judicial powers. Because they combine these powers their constitutional position is an awkward one.[9] While they have institutional links with the other branches of government, they have an additional mechanism for rendering them responsible and responsive to the public, namely procedures for public participation in their policy-making functions.[10] Further reference is made to this dimension of administrative law below.

Each of these variations in state structure has implications for the system of administrative law. It is important to be aware of the constitutional and political position occupied by different public authorities so that appropriate legal standards can be applied to them.[11] Members of the cabinet are apparently subject to the most direct political controls in respect of their administrative actions, and the courts extend them greater leeway and do not lightly intervene in their actions. More lowly officials are remote from political control and are likely to be called to account more readily by the courts. Where administrative bodies are elected, as with municipal councils, the courts will be less likely to intervene, particularly where their policy decisions are challenged on the grounds of unreasonableness. These varying consequences provide some rationale for what might

---

[7] See below, 194.

[8] Under Prime Minister Thatcher's reform proposals for the British civil service new executive agencies will be created outside the departmental structure, and may even be private agencies. They will undermine ministerial control and traditional forms of accountability to Parliament. See R Baldwin (1988) 51 *Modern Law Review* 622.

[9] See R Baldwin and R McCrudden *Regulation and Public Law* (1987) 3.

[10] See on this topic L J Boulle 1986 (2) *TSAR* 136.

[11] See P P Craig *Administrative Law* (1983) 1ff.

otherwise appear to be inconsistent tendencies in administrative-law systems, though they are mostly a matter of sound common sense. Unfortunately, changes in institutional relationships are not always recognised in time: a belief in the effectiveness of parliamentary control of ministers moved the English courts to constrain their own powers of control, whereas had they understood the realities of parliamentary life they may have been more ready to develop principles of public law.[12]

However, the administrative branch of government is not all that it might appear to be. Beneath the prominent positions, such as ministers, government departments and tribunals, is a more shadowy form of public administration. All modern states have 'hidden' branches of government which operate in secrecy as to their actions, funding, and even existence, but which nevertheless have real influence on matters of policy and administration. In South Africa this phenomenon is exemplified by the existence and influence of the National Security Council and Joint Management Committee systems.[13] While these bodies have limited formal authority, they wield immense real power. The hidden branches of the public administration are clearly not subject to the legal and political controls which operate elsewhere. Thus a formal description of the bureaucracy and its control might overlook important elements of administrative life.

III KINDS OF ADMINISTRATIVE POWER

The powers of the administrative branch can be divided into various categories. A feature of the modern state is that the administration is the most active branch of the state system, and in terms of the extensive authority delegated to it performs all of the functions which characterise contemporary government: formulating policy, regulating, policing, providing services, settling disputes, acting entrepreneurially, consuming, and controlling the economy. The principle of constitutional tripartism provides one basis for classifying this wide range of functions: legislative, executive, judicial.[14] For administrative lawyers this categorisation is significant because different legal consequences attach to the different 'constitutional' categories of administrative acts. In some cases further refinement of the categories is necessary, but here attention is paid mainly to the 'separation of powers' categories.

A Legislative

In most countries the bulk of legislation is produced by administrative authorities. Legislation not made by the central Parliament is known as subordinate legislation, and if the power to legislate has

[12] See J D B Mitchell 1965 *Public Law* 95.
[13] See below, 195–7.
[14] Cf Lawrence Baxter *Administrative Law* (1984) 344ff.

been delegated in a specific statute it is known as delegated legislation. (In practice the terms subordinate and delegated are used interchangeably in this context.) A further array of terms is used for different kinds of delegated legislation: regulations, rules, orders, directives, decrees, by-laws and schemes. These terms are not used consistently, and although different legal consequences are attached to some forms of delegated legislation, nothing hinges on the different terms themselves—they merely lend variety to the statute book, and confuse its users.

Legislation is the easiest of the administrative acts to identify, partly because of the 'statutory' form in which it is produced—title, numbered clauses, bilingual text, and so on. Formal appearance, however, is not always conclusive. Legislation differs substantively from other administrative acts in that it contains rules of general application which apply impersonally to the whole society, or to a specific community within it. Unlike adjudication, legislation is concerned not with resolving individual disputes but with implementing social policies which are intended to advance the general interest. Legislation usually operates prospectively, that is it has legal conseqences for developments which occur after its promulgation, but in some cases it operates retrospectively, that is it changes the legal consequences of pre-existing circumstances. Legislation is usually intended to remain in force for an indefinite period, though there is a developing tendency in many countries for delegated legislation to lapse after a specified number of years, by virtue of so-called 'sunset' laws.[15] Unlike other administrative acts, legislation requires publicity in an official publication (for example, *Government Gazette*) to become valid, and it is sometimes preceded by procedures which allow for public comment on its content. Many legislative acts require further administrative action for their application:[16] a discretion will have to be exercised, a sanction enforced, or an investigation undertaken. They can therefore be regarded as incomplete administrative acts. This has important implications. When a policy is formulated in legislation it purports to advance the collective good and individual rights are not taken account of. But when it is implemented in a concrete situation, then individual rights are liable to be affected, and the constitution and administrative law system provide various safeguards for persons whose interests are at stake.

The term 'quasi-legislation' is used to describe 'rules' which are developed by administrative authorities, and generally acted upon by them, but which lack the formality and legal authority of regular

---

[15] That is a law which provides that delegated legislation lapses automatically after a defined period, unless it is renewed by the appropriate body. Emergency regulations in South Africa require annual renewal.

[16] Baxter op cit n 14 at 350.

administrative legislation.[17] It is a kind of 'no-name brand' of legislation. Quasi-legislation can include departmental circulars, policy directives, guidelines, and codes of conduct—for example, the policy statements put out to the public by the taxation authorities of South Africa. In some cases quasi-legislation is made available to the public and in others it is kept within departmental bounds. Quasi-legislation cannot add to the authority of the administrative body, nor should it serve to fetter its discretions. A more complex issue is whether members of the public can place any reliance on it in organising their affairs, and if so what legal remedies they have against the public authority concerned. In English law there is a growing tendency for public authorities to be subject to judicial review where they depart from their own quasi-legislation, or misapply it, and a member of the public has had a reasonable expectation of it being observed.[18] Despite uncertainties of this nature, and the absence of direct constitutional authority for quasi-legislation, it performs a useful function in the modern administrative state in that it limits discretion and makes its exercise more consistent and predictable.

B Adjudicative

Adjudication involves the resolution of a dispute by an authoritative institution: courts are obvious adjudicative (or 'judicial') bodies. However, in contravention of the separation of powers doctrine, adjudication is becoming an increasingly prevalent form of administrative activity. Numerous commentators have pointed to the fact that just as administrative bodies make more legislation than the legislature, so too do they resolve more disputes than the judges. Courts are unable to adjudicate on many specialist matters[19] and administrative bodies are able to do this more informally, quickly, cheaply and expertly, and not necessarily any less justly. Administrative adjudication can be undertaken not only by specialist bodies, known as administrative tribunals, but also by a range of other public authorities and individual administrative officials.

Adjudication by administrative bodies assumes a different character to adjudication by the courts. Traditionally adjudication is understood in terms of an impartial court acting as a passive arbiter in resolving a dispute in the light of existing rules and precedents and in such a way as to affect only the parties to the dispute. Even court adjudication is departing from this formalised model, but administrative adjudication differs in respect of each element. First, many administrative bodies are sufficiently specialised to allow them to take a more active role in the adjudicative process than do the

---

[17] See Gabriele Ganz *Quasi-Legislation: Recent Developments in Secondary Legislation* (1987) on this subject.
[18] See Baldwin op cit n 8.
[19] See the Justice-All Souls Report *Review of Administrative Law in the United Kingdom* (1981) 3.

courts—for example bodies which deal daily with planning matters, monopolistic conditions, and civil aviation. Second, in so far as their orders are binding on large administrative hierarchies, administrative courts are involved not only in resolving a past dispute between two parties but also in regulating administrative conduct for the future. (This assumes that public authorities will adhere to decisions affecting their activities.) Third, the role of precedent is not as prominent in administrative adjudication, as the process is as much concerned with contemporary social policy as it is with past decisions. Because of these differences, constitutional systems often provide for the regular courts to supervise the adjudication of administrative bodies through a system of appeal or review.

In English and South African law the term 'quasi-judicial' has for a long time been a term of art. It denotes an administrative action which is undertaken by a public authority according to a process partly resembling that of a traditional court. At times the categorisation of an administrative action as 'quasi-judicial' has had important implications for the courts' powers to review such decisions. Where this significance remains, it is dealt with in Part III of this book.

C Administrative

An administrative act is one which implements or gives effect to a policy, a piece of legislation or an adjudicative decision. This is the operational side of the state: since policies, laws and judgments are not self-executing, they have to be put into operation by the public authorities responsible for administering them. Administrative acts include every conceivable aspect of state activity—granting a licence, promoting a clerk, stamping a passport, arresting a suspect, paying out a pension. Here the term administrative act is used widely to include both the decision as to what to do and the action itself.

In their attempts to explain the variety in administrative actions commentators, and some judges, have referred to certain acts as 'purely administrative'. One leading work uses this description for all administrative acts which are not legislative or judicial.[20] However, this is just a residual definition which is not particularly helpful. Some assistance is provided by the terms 'ministerial' and 'discretionary'. The term ministerial administrative act (while it could refer to the act of a minister of state) is used to describe the situation where an official or public authority is legally required to perform a duty in respect of which there is no element of choice or discretion.[21] Examples of ministerial acts are the admission of local scholars to state schools, the refund of overpaid tax, and the grant of a dog licence. Because of the absence of discretion in these activities, they are sometimes referred to as 'mechanical' administrative acts and are usually performed by subordinate officials. However, the

[20] Marinus Wiechers *Administrative Law* (1985) 115.
[21] See S A De Smith *Constitutional and Administrative Law* 5 ed (1985) at 525.

term 'mechanical' underlines the limited usefulness of this concept, since very few acts will involve no independent judgment at all on the part of the administrative organ.[22]

The term 'discretionary act' is often used in juxtaposition to 'ministerial act' to denote that the relevant administrative organ has a wide choice as to its decision and course of action. Where there is an extremely wide choice the term 'unfettered' is sometimes used to describe the discretion. This is an unfortunate term, since it is close to the notion of arbitrariness. In reality an 'arbitrary discretion' is a contradiction in terms; any rational choice—and the state is assumed to be a rational actor—must be based on identifiable criteria, otherwise it becomes purely whimsical. In some cases the criteria on which the judgment is made may be very meagre, but it is difficult to conceive of an administrative act involving judgment unrelated to objective criteria. However, sometimes it may be intended that the public authority should itself be the evaluator of the criteria, to the exclusion of the courts, and here it is appropriate to describe the act as discretionary. These discretionary acts provide continual problems for the courts, and for constitutional theory. In South African law there are many examples relating to security matters, and these come frequently before the courts.[23]

D Other administrative acts

Administrative acts can also be categorised on a functional basis, though these categories have less relevance in law. One such category is that of *police acts*, which embraces all administrative activities undertaken in the ostensible pursuit of internal order and external defence. While police acts are not inherently different to other administrative actions, they have important constitutional implications in that they involve wide powers which can impinge drastically on the freedoms and rights of individuals and organisations; moreover, the executive frequently attempts to free them from external constraints, both political and judicial. Then the bureaucracy performs many *investigative* functions, ranging from small internal investigations to large-scale public inquiries. In countries such as Britain the public inquiry has been an important mechanism for making the minister better informed when taking a decision, and for allowing some public input into the policy-making process. Investigations usually result in recommendations being made to policy-making bodies. In other countries, including South Africa, commissions of inquiry are frequently presided over by judges and some are used for a more devious purpose, namely to put contentious political issues on ice.[24] Modern states also engage in *entrepreneurial* activities in a wide range of commercial fields, where state undertakings use both official authority derived from statute and the

[22] Wiechers op cit n 20 at 137.
[23] See below, 314ff.
[24] See below, 206–7.

common-law rights enjoyed by private undertakings. Finally, the state and its agencies frequently establish *contractual* legal relations with other enterprises, and although these relations are covered mainly by non-administrative-law principles they can be an important means of implementing official policy.[25]

E   Administrative non-action

In some cases the failure of an administrative organ to exercise its power is a significant factor in itself.[26] The failure may be due to inadvertence, negligence, or wilful omission—for example the deliberate failure to institute criminal prosecutions against those who commit offences against government opponents. According to norms of sound administrative practice, the failure to make decisions is in principle no different to the making of incorrect decisions. However, in most administrative-law systems there are only limited remedies available in respect of administrative non-action; even where an official can be ordered to exercise a discretion, it is difficult to stipulate how it should be exercised. In any event administrative non-action is necessarily difficult to detect or diagnose.

IV   THE EXERCISE OF ADMINISTRATIVE POWER

It is emphasised in this work that most administrative authority has a statutory source. As far as the exercise of administrative power is concerned, the general principle is that public authorities can devise their own procedures. These procedures can be flexible and informal. This allows a public authority to tailor its procedures to what is appropriate in terms of available time and resources, the complexity of the issues, and the rights and expectations of those who will be affected. Flexibility and informality are necessary ingredients in the exercise of administrative power because of its intrinsic nature: it has to do with changing social policies, it must be applied in vastly differing circumstances, it must take account of the public interest, and it is discretion-based. Administrative bodies also tend to make 'institutional decisions', involving many hands and minds at different levels of the bureaucracy, though only the highest ranking official is formally responsible for it.[27] It is thus to be expected that administrative decision-making will differ from that of legislatures and the courts. The differences present a problem when legal standards are imposed on administrative practices: there is a conflict between the flexible and informal discretion of the administration and the fixed and general principles of the law.

Where the source of authority is statutory, there will often be expressed or implied provisions which prescribe the procedures the

[25] See below, 187–90.
[26] See Kenneth Culp Davis *Discretionary Justice* (1971) 42ff; see also below, 306ff.
[27] See J Mashaw and R A Merrill *Adminstrative Law: The American Public Law System* (1985) 229.

public authority must follow: notice to be given, forms to be completed, quorums to be met, and so on. The general principle is that these procedural requirements must be satisfied to validate the particular exercise of power. If they are not complied with the administrative actions will be ultra vires and invalid. Where there are no procedural formalities prescribed by statute, public authorities might still be required to follow procedures required by the courts. The most important of these are referred to collectively as the principles of natural justice, or fairness, which may in appropriate circumstances require that an affected party be given a hearing before an administrative decision is taken, or be furnished with reasons once it has been taken. These principles are dealt with in detail, in respect of South African law, in Part III.[28] The major shortcomings in the administrative process are a lack of uniform standards and no guarantee of procedural fairness; in England the first problem has been addressed by legislation which fosters the standardisation of tribunal procedures,[29] and in Canada the second has been tackled by stipulating minimum procedural rules for a wide range of tribunals.[30]

Lawyers tend not to be much concerned with the attributes of good, as opposed to lawful, administrative decision-making, leaving the subject to the disdained discipline of public administration. This is to the detriment of both disciplines. On one hand the attributes of judicial decison-making will always have some significance for the administrative process: a correct understanding of the law, a purposive interpretation of the legislation conferring authority, the furnishing of reasons for individual decisions, and the rigorous discipline of legal reasoning. As regards the furnishing of reasons, this is a fundamental element of the judicial process, and, provided the reasons are adequate and intelligible, such a requirement would improve administrative decision-making, even if the reasons could not always be furnished at the time of the decision. On the other hand there are two elements of administrative decision-making which are becoming increasingly relevant to the judicial process. The first is in determining the correct influence of policy, whether embodied in legislation or formulated by the executive, in decision-making. Since policy may change from situation to situation, it brings an element of flexibility into administrative decision-making which is not always formally countenanced in the judicial process. The second is in determining which factors are relevent in exercising administrative discretions and can thus be legitimately relied upon by the administrator, and, conversely, which are irrelevant and illegitimate. In this regard the aversion to discretion which lawyers

---

[28] See below, Chapter 15.
[29] Through the offices of the Council of Tribunals to which procedural requirements must be referred.
[30] See Baldwin and McCrudden op cit n 9 above, 32ff.

have traditionally exhibited has made it difficult for the courts to determine what are the sufficient or necessary grounds which must exist to constitute a good administrative decision.

Most persons would agree that it is better to have good primary administrative decision-making, rather than indifferent primary decisions and a sophisticated system of legal review and appeal. Given this view, it would seem preferable to place greater emphasis on the proper contribution of the legal process to primary administration. It has been pointed out that there is a continual tension in the exercise of administrative power between social concerns, as represented by public policy, and individual interests, such as autonomy and property. If deployed in the correct manner, law can assist in the resolution of this conflict in social administration. Commentators are now questioning whether lawyers should not be more involved in building accountable systems of administration which ensure more open and better informed decisions, rather than continuing to be concerned with better reactive systems.[31]

V JUDICIAL CONTROL AND SUPERVISION: TWO MODELS

When it comes to the control and supervision of administrative actions, it is possible to distinguish between two different models or formats,[32] of administrative law. The distinction is based on the role of the ordinary courts in reviewing administrative action, though it should be borne in mind that this is by no means the only way of controlling state organs. The distinction can be traced to basic principles in the constitutional system.

The first model is found in English law and those systems, such as the South African, based on it. Its distinctive feature is that administrative bodies are subject to supervision by the ordinary courts of the land. The historical explanation for this is found in the fact that the Court of King's Bench early developed remedies for controlling administrative authorities and when the rival administrative courts, such as the Star Chamber, were abolished in the seventeenth century it assumed the supervisory role in all respects. A modern justification for the system was provided by the Diceyan doctrine of the Rule of Law with its emphasis on the subordination of both citizens and public authorities to the regular courts. Dicey also contributed to the English suspicion of the specialised administrative courts which had developed in France. The result was that lawyers in these systems tended to assume that 'administrative justice' was in all respects inferior to 'judicial justice' and attempted wherever possible to mould it to a legalistic likeness. However, one of the criticisms of judicial review is that the courts cannot assess the merits of the matter under review; it pays too much attention to

[31] See Patrick McAuslan 1988 *Public Law* 402.
[32] See Baxter 17ff.

procedural due process and too little substantive due process.[33] This derives from the basic constitutional principle that the role of review is to check the unauthorised use of administrative authority, but that if the court substitutes its own view for that of the authority, it is usurping the latter's power. Nevertheless there are signs in English administrative law that judges are beginning to abandon their traditional preference for dealing with the technicalities of cases rather than the principles governing sound administration and individual rights.[34] Moreover, in the English system judicial review has always been supplemented by political controls over the executive, which are referred to in the following section.

The second model is found in French law and those systems modelled on it. Its distinctive feature is that administrative authorities are subject to supervision by special administrative courts and not by the ordinary courts. This too can be explained historically in terms of the fact that at the time of the French Revolution executive power was not broken but was merely transferred to a new class of rulers and officials.[35] A rigid separation of powers notion served to preclude the post-Revolution courts of law from 'interfering' in legislative and executive action; they were denied jurisdiction to control administrative authorities, the supervision of which was seen as being a matter of political and not legal concern.[36] A Council of State was established to hear citizens' complaints against officials; its powers and procedures became formalised over time and it came to operate as an administrative court with final jurisdiction in all administrative matters. The Council is now the highest court of appeal in a developed hierarchy of administrative courts. The modern justification for the system is found in the fact that the Council, and other administrative courts, have qualified specialists who have developed a sophisticated body of administrative law appropriate to the nature of disputes between individuals and the organs of the state.

As with so many legal 'models', those based on the English and French systems are not watertight. In some English-influenced systems there has been a movement towards the establishment of administrative courts. A notable example is in Australia where the Administrative Appeals Tribunal (AAT) was established in 1975 to replace the proliferation of appeal tribunals which had previously existed.[37] The AAT has appellate jurisdiction in respect of all administrative issues in a wide range of matters. (The decisions of some public authorities cannot be taken on appeal to the AAT.) What is striking about its jurisdiction is that it provides for a full rehearing on the merits: unlike a court of review, the AAT can investigate the

[33] See the Justice-All Souls report op cit n 19 above.
[34] See Jefferey Jowell 1988 *Public Law* 365.
[35] See C E Hoexter (1985) 48 *THRHR* 152.
[36] See Mauro Cappelletti (1981) *Monash University Law Review*.
[37] See Mark Aronson and Nicola Franklin *Review of Administrative Action* (1987) 221ff.

merits of a public authority's decision, and after considering the facts of the matter, the relevant law, and the policy which was applied, substitute what it regards as the preferable decision for that from which the appeal is brought.[38] In theory the AAT can operate informally and without the constraint of normal legal procedures, though in practice it has been dominated by lawyers and acts in a court-like way. The ordinary courts still retain a right of review over AAT decisions, and the tribunal is neither subject to political control through the Minister, nor is it part of the regular administrative branch. The system does not therefore resemble the French model where administrative courts have exclusive control over administrative authorities. Its main advantages have been in providing the aggrieved individual with what he or she wants, namely a rehearing on the merits, whereas judicial review looks at only part, and sometimes only the technical aspect, of the administrative decision. It also serves to unify the administrative process and ensure greater predictability in dealing with different officials and departments. In other countries operating with the English model, such as New Zealand, separate divisions of the regular courts have been established to hear administrative cases; this has entailed administrative-law specialisation, but again within the same basic format of public law.

Separate mention should again be made of the American model of administrative law, which has distinctive features deriving from its constitutional background. The most important constitutional feature bearing on the administrative system is the justiciable Bill of Rights which allows the courts to impose procedural standards on public authorities—similar to those which the English courts demand according to the rules of natural justice. There is also an important variation in the wide range of agencies with regulatory and investigative powers which are largely autonomous of the formal executive branch, and are responsible to Congress which created them. These bodies have legislative, executive and judicial functions, the separation of powers doctrine notwithstanding. There are both political and legal controls over them. However, the need for judicial review is reduced by the fact that a federal statute, the Administrative Procedure Act, provides a detailed code for different kinds of decision-making by the agencies. These requirements are closely modelled on judicial procedures, and the officials involved in formulating policy according to the Act are now called 'administrative-law judges'. Thus within each agency there is a kind of administrative court, but its decisions remain subject to judicial review by the ordinary courts.

Inevitably, each model of administrative law has its strengths and weaknesses, and these have been extensively analysed in the comparative literature. Here it is relevant to refer to one weakness of

[38] Ibid.

the English model which has practical implications for South African administrative law. This is the tendency to approach administrative-law disputes from a private law perspective.[39] Law and litigation have been shaped in the image of the individual human being.[40] The concept of the individual human actor is used for both natural and juristic persons, regardless of the size, functions and powers of the latter. As legal actors, humans are, to outward appearances, all equal in that they enjoy the benefit of two feet and a single head. The model of litigation developed to resolve disputes between two notionally equal parties is applied to disputes involving the state and private parties. This model is inappropriate for administrative-law matters in two respects. First, it overlooks the fact that the state is by far the predominant party, in terms of power, resources and information, over most other litigants, which renders the accustomed adversarial procedures and system of remedies inappropriate. French administrative law has acknowledged this imbalance in inverting the normal onus of proof and requiring the administration to prove its case in all disputes. Second, there is an additional dimension to administrative law disputes, as represented by policy and the public interest, which is not easily accommodated within the boundaries of traditional bipolar litigation. Thus a dispute between a licensing authority and a prospective commercial fishing concern may be determined not only according to the applicant's fishing abilities, but also in terms of the public interest in maintaining stocks of fish for the future. Adjudication by the courts is therefore not always the ideal model for dealing with all administrative issues, and alternatives such as regulation (referred to in the next section) are being developed in many jurisdictions.

VI POLITICAL AND ADMINISTRATIVE CONTROLS

Review, whether by the regular courts or specialist tribunals, remains the most prominent form of control over the administration. Judicial and non-judicial review, on one hand, can be contrasted with political controls over the administration, on the other. Broadly speaking, the former are legal forms of supervision in that they are dominated by legally trained personnel, use processes associated with the courts, and impose legal remedies. The political controls, by contrast, are associated with the legislature and executive, they revolve around factors of representative politics and bureaucratic hierarchy, and their 'remedies' are based on public sanction and administrative discipline.

Two basic forms of political control may be identified. The first may be called the 'representative' kind, in that it is undertaken by elected representatives of the public. A familiar example is that of

---

[39] See below, 281–2.
[40] See Dan Meir-Cohen *Rights, Persons and Organisations—A Legal Theory for Bureaucratic Society* (1986).

ministerial responsibility to Parliament, a body which, in democratic systems of government, is regarded as being representative of the people. This principle has conventional roots in Westminster-derived constitutional systems and is sometimes alluded to by courts. Its main instruments are parliamentary question-time, votes of no confidence, public exposure and the interpellation. (The interpellation is a standard parliamentary procedure in terms of which a Minister is required, in the course of a short debate, to explain some action or policy of his department, and it was recently introduced into the South African system.) In reality these instruments have limited contemporary significance; as Parliaments are dominated by modern executives they tend to lack real teeth.[41] Nevertheless, the Westminster system still identifies judicial review and ministerial responsibility as the two basic institutions for controlling administrative authorities.

The second kind of political control is more direct and 'popular' in its nature. It is a manifestation of one of the recent themes in the development of constitutionalism.[42] Institutions have been created whereby individuals, organisations and interest groups can participate in the administrative procedures which precede the formulation of public policy in particular areas. Areas often selected for these procedures are planning and the environment. In order to allow for public participation, policy is formulated in written rules akin to statutes. Like statutes, they must be publicly promulgated before they become effective, and public hearings are held at which all interested parties can be represented and present evidence. The same participatory procedures must be followed before they can be amended. Public funding systems have been set up to assist indigent interest groups to participate in the process. This gives rise to administration through regulation—as opposed to administration through adjudication. It has been prevalent in American administrative law for several decades.

In general terms, there is a continual search for appropriate institutions for checking and controlling administrative power. Such institutions should be susceptible to justification in terms of democratic principles, they should incorporate appropriate legal standards, and they should be compatible with effective government. These are difficult demands to balance. In the process of adjustment, established constitutional principles may be strained. In the United Kingdom the Scandinavian ombudsman system, with local variations, was introduced in 1975 in the form of the Parliamentary Commissioner for Administration.[43] This institution provides a mechanism for the independent investigation of complaints about

---

[41] However, it should not be overlooked that in practice ministers often respond to and deal with complaints brought to their attention by members of Parliament on behalf of constituents.

[42] See above, 54.

[43] See below, 209–11.

the administrative branch and for reporting to Parliament, which can take action thereon. Despite gaps in its jurisdiction and limits on its powers of initiative, it has enjoyed some success in its activities, and local equivalents have been established in different areas. However, it involves a modification of constitutional principle in that the Parliamentary Commissioner can go behind the response given by a minister to Parliament and investigate its reliability. In other Westminster systems specialist parliamentary committees have been established to breathe new life into established constitutional principles such as ministerial responsibility; in matters ranging from public accounts to delegated legislation, these committees scrutinise government and bring maladministration to the attention of the full Parliament.

All the political controls over the administration depend for their effectiveness on a range of supporting constitutional factors, such as a broadly based franchise, a competitive party system, checks and balances between the legislature and executive, the independence of the courts, and the strength of constitutional conventions. These are, however, only minimal requirements. It is becoming increasingly appreciated that for any form of meaningful participation or accountability, citizens require both open government and access to officially held information. Thus in Australia freedom of information legislation is regarded as an indispensable part of the 'new administrative law' in that country. It allows individuals to make application for any information, subject to certain exceptions, held by federal state departments—including material from an applicant's personal file—and provides various mechanisms for enforcing the legislation.[44] Some state governments have duplicated the machinery at the regional level. The freedom of information systems that have been established provide one of the best assurances against maladministration in that knowledge, for those affected by an administrative decision, is the first requirement for relief.

It is also important not to overlook the internal administrative controls, or 'checks and balances', which exist within most public authorities. While the legal and political controls operate at levels of high visibility, and are appropriate for matters of important policy or great expense, the best remedy for an individual feeling badly treated by an official is to request that the matter be referred to a supervisor within the departmental hierarchy. Usually this can be done in the most informal of ways. In some instances there may be a formal system of internal review in a government department, and it may even be necessary to exhaust this remedy before taking legal action. Administrative lawyers should not overlook the simple expedient of internal review.

[44] See Aronson and Franklin op cit n 37 at 272–354.

VII THE CONSTITUTION, ADMINISTRATIVE LAW AND THE COURTS

This chapter alludes to the continual strains which exist between basic constitutional principles and the realities of administrative-law practice. The constitutionalist objective of leaving individuals free to pursue their own goals without intervention by government conflicts with the state's pursuit of collective goals. The separation of powers doctrine implies a very limited participation by each organ of government in the affairs of the others, but the practicalities of government require that all powers be exercised in some measure by the administrative branch. The principle of representative government requires that decisions of policy should be settled by the national Parliament (on the assumption that it is a democratically constituted body), whereas in reality policy is formulated extensively by administrative bodies. The same principle indicates that the courts should not intervene in matters of basic policy, but the distortions which occur in majoritarian politics and the impotence of constitutional checks and balances are used to justify the fact that the courts do modify policy in many ways. The Rule of Law suggests that all administrative actions should be subject to supervision by the ordinary courts, but administrative tribunals of various descriptions are found in all jurisdictions. The Rule of Law also implies that there should only be an official encroachment on common-law rights where it is specifically authorised by law, but the insistence on clear authority can be easily met through the provision of sweeping statutory powers.[45]

These issues are played out not only in the legal, but also in the constitutional and 'political' terrains. It has been an objective of this chapter to emphasise the importance of the non-judicial aspects of administrative law: questions of policy, discretion, political accountability, and responsiveness. Nevertheless, however quantitatively insignificant it might be, judicial review is where the centre of gravity of administrative law is found. For this reason the material in Part III of this work is concerned with the legal rules and processes of judicial review. Here the crucial constitutional issue concerns the basis for, and the proper ambit of, the courts' power to intervene in administrative decisions.

The basic justification for judicial review of administrative action originates in the constitution. In the constitutional state there are, by definition, legal limits to power, and the courts are bestowed with judicial authority, which incorporates the competence to determine the legality of various activities, including those of public authorities. The main source of public authorities' power is an Act of Parliament, which is the primary legal yardstick for determining the validity of its exercise. Thus the main, or umbrella principle, governing the validity of administrative acts is the idea of legality,

---

[45] See T R S Allan (1985) 44 *Cambridge Law Journal* 111 at 121.

the content of which is determined by the courts through their interpretation of Parliament's intention as expressed in legislation.[46] Legality has four basic requirements, authority, regularity, fairness and reasonableness. The requirement of authority entails that every action must be duly authorised by Parliament. The requirement of regularity means that formalities and statutory prescriptions must be complied with. The requirements of fairness and reasonableness mean that administrative action must comply with minimum standards, that is they must be fair and reasonable as these terms have come to be defined in administrative-law doctrine. If a decision is so outrageous in its defiance of logic or of basic moral standards that no sensible person who applied his mind could have arrived at it, then the courts will be likely to interfere and exercise a substantive review jurisdiction.[47] Because these standards are independent of those provided by the statute, the constitutional basis of these principles of legality is less apparent. While reasonableness might seem an intrinsic element in law and legality, it is a controversial requirement because it allows the courts to substitute their own views for those of the administrative body. This entails that the courts can override the constitutionally authorised body on a matter of policy, whereas the orthodox principle is that the higher the policy content of a decision the less susceptible it is to review.[48]

The law–policy distinction remains an important factor in judicial review and the extent to which administrative decisions are reviewable or non-reviewable. However, because the distinction is blurred, this is the site of continual struggle between courts and legislatures. Judges attempt to extend the boundaries of their review jurisdiction, while legislators, acting as the agents of the executive and administration, attempt to immunise decisions from judicial review. Judges assert that they are exercising a purely legal, by which they mean neutral and apolitical, function in ensuring that administrative power is not abused or misused, while legislators point out that by becoming involved in the substantive merits of decisions they are in fact resolving political issues.[49] There can be no precise formula for resolving the conflict. However, there are available criteria for evaluating it. One criterion is that of legitimacy, namely whether constitutional norms tolerate a particular intervention; another criterion is appropriateness, namely whether the judicial method is appropriate for dealing with a specific subject-matter. These criteria would suggest, respectively,

---

[46] Legality is discussed in detail below, 255ff.

[47] See Jowell op cit n 34 at 368.

[48] This principle has been undermined in several Commonwealth countries where the courts have even been prepared to review cabinet decisions, traditionally regarded as having such a high policy content as to be immune from review. See Michael Harris 'The Courts and the Cabinet: Unfastening the Buckle' *Public Law* (forthcoming).

[49] See D J Galligan (1982) 2 *Oxford Journal of Legal Studies* 257.

that the courts should not review decisions in respect of international relations or defence, but that they should review matters relating to personal liberty or punitive action by the state. However, other factors, such as the position of the administrative authority in the constitutional system and the changing attitude of judges, determine the practical resolution of these matters. How they are dealt with in South Africa is referred to in Part III of this work.

5 The Foundations of the South African Constitutional/ Administrative System

This chapter relates the analysis in the preceding chapters to the South African situation. There is a brief description of South African society and the state system, and a general conceptual account of the constitutional and administrative law systems, with reference to standards of constitutional government and human rights.

I THE SOCIETY, THE STATE SYSTEM AND LAW

Like many other countries, South Africa has a society in which there are differences of colour, race, religion, language and culture among the inhabitants.[1] Because these differences appear to create different social communities, it is said that South Africa has a plural society,[2]—that is, one with distinct and separate racial and cultural segments. South African society is also stratified, which means that the various communities have different degrees of access to political power and economic resources. In terms of the official 'racial' categories, whites are, in both economic and political terms, in a position of dominance and blacks are in a position of subordinacy,[3] with coloureds and Indians at different positions in between. While many societies manifest these characteristics of pluralism, stratification and hierarchy, they are very pronounced in South Africa.

The plural and stratified nature of South African society has had direct implications for constitutional development. Successive governments have justified their constitutional policies according to factors of race, colour and tribal affiliation. They have claimed that society consists primarily of a collection of distinct groups which must be accommodated in separate compartments of the constitutional system, and whose rights require protection on a collective group basis. This has resulted in the creation of the apartheid (or separate development) constitution. The group emphasis accounts for the government's brief attraction to the notion of a consociational system of government[4] in the debate on constitutional reform during the last decade.

However, the group formation in South Africa has, to a greater extent than in other plural societies, been artificially imposed and maintained. It has been managed and manipulated by the state

---

[1] For a good, though slightly dated, analysis of South African society see H Lever *South African Society* (1978).

[2] On pluralism in South Africa see L J Boulle *South Africa and the Consociational Option* (1984) 36–9.

[3] On the South African economy generally see Jill Natrass *The South African Economy: Its Growth and Change* (1988).

[4] On consociationalism see above, 53–4; below, 168ff.

through legislation which has defined groups and classified people in terms of race, colour and ethnicity.[5] These legislative definitions have been used as the building-blocks for constitutional development; individuals have been forced to participate politically in terms of the statutorily imposed group definitions—coloured, Indian, Xhosa, and so on. State-imposed definitions have denied individuals any choice of group membership or political affiliation. Over the years political mobilisation and the formation of political parties has been compelled to take place along the prescribed lines, and where it has crossed these lines has been suppressed by the state. The government has exploited real group differences beyond their actual significance to retain its political and economic advantages. The constitutional system has not only reflected group identities, but has also reinforced them. In reality it cannot be assumed that political interests revolve only around factors of colour, race or culture. Other factors, such as class, economic position, ideology or special interests, can be of even greater political significance. In very recent times the South African government has shown a developing acceptance of this reality.

Given the complex and segmented nature of the society, it is not surprising that the state system in South Africa is very powerful and highly centralised. It comprises a vast number of departments, boards, agencies and officials, which operate at the national, regional and local levels of government, and several levels in between. As in other countries, the state bodies perform a wide variety of different functions in South Africa—organising and controlling, funding and policing, providing and managing, watching and reporting. Most state agencies are only too visible to the person in the street, but there is also an invisible part of the state, in particular the security apparatus, which has a significant impact on society.

Although the South African state is immensely powerful, it is not altogether a cohesive and integrated machine; different parts of the state are responsive to different interests and sometimes come into conflict with one another. This is revealed in both constitutional and administrative-law cases. In the past conflicts have occurred among government departments, homeland governments, provincial administrations and local authorities, and between individual officials. As regards the South African courts, they are in a unique position in the state system in that although they are in one respect a part of it, they are in other respects relatively autonomous, and in some instances actually invalidate or obstruct the implementation of government policies. There are also powerful private interests in South Africa in the form of large corporations, some with monopolistic control and extensive economic leverage, which influence and sometimes obstruct state institutions. And of course the state is not

---

[5] The main statutes have been the Population Registration Act 30 of 1950 and the National States Citizenship Act 26 of 1970.

an independent actor in that international law, politics and economics all impose real limitations on its seemingly limitless powers. Thus while the South African state's might is not to be trifled with, it is not a wholly co-ordinated and free-acting leviathan.

Because the society is so divided and the state machine is so powerful, it is of great significance as to who has control of the levers of government. Unsurprisingly, state offices are not equally accessible to all. Historically, the state has been a sectionally dominated institution, serving predominantly the interests of whites, with members of other groups serving in only subordinate positions in its various organs, and experiencing the state more as a controlling than an enabling force. The Constitution has identified those who can obtain keys to the gates of the state kingdom. The principles of constitutional and administrative law have determined the extent to which those operating the state system have been able to give effect to their policies, if necessary through coercion. Generally the public law system has facilitated, rather than inhibited, this capacity. It follows that the South African state system cannot be portrayed as a neutral set of disinterested institutions with a main purpose of enforcing the objective rules of economic and political life.

There is currently an extensive debate about the state system in South Africa. In part the debate is about who should participate in the running and administering the state, but it is also about its very structure and organisation and the division of functions between the state sector and private enterprise. This debate reflects the state's current lack of legitimacy, in the sense that for a vast number of people it is not regarded as an acceptable form of social and political organisation. Here both constitutional and administrative law are at the centre of a dispute between those calling for curbs on state power to protect private rights and interests, and those calling for the emancipation and democratisation of state power for the pursuit of the public good. At present the constitutional and administrative law systems do not advance either objective. The debate about the organisation of the state system has inevitably led to a reassessment of the nature of South African society, and the real significance of group identities.

One of the consequences of the might of the South African state is that it can and does intrude extensively into many spheres, including the law. In order to provide a basis of legitimacy for its actions, the state defines its powers in legal instruments, thereby adding to the body of legal rules and principles. The rules and procedures of constitutional and administrative law are defined largely by the state. Because these branches of the law incorporate state policy, the difference between them and politics is sometimes difficult to identify. This accounts for the perception that South African public law is distinct from private law. Where the latter is supposedy insulated from politics and state involvement, the former is not; where the latter has been created gradually over time by the courts, the former is created overnight by the legislature and executive; where the former is concerned with policy, the latter is concerned with principle. In general terms South African public law tends to be repressive and private law autonomous.[6] However, these contrasts should not be overdrawn. South African private law is also policy-laden, though in a less apparent way. And the principles of South African administrative law show that the courts can to some extent impose judicial values and procedures on public law. While public law is created by the executive, as soon as it comes within the judicial domain it is modified by the courts.

II CONSTITUTIONAL FUNDAMENTALS

The South African constitution[7] is in part imported (made in Britain) and in part of local derivation (autochthonous). There has been an extensive debate about the extent to which the South African system conforms to the Westminster model. The debate often overlooked an elementary truth, namely that the constitutional system consisted of two contrasting, yet complementary, parts. The first part was Westminster-based and catered for whites as political actors. It consisted of an elected Parliament, comprising two houses (until 1980), with Westminster-type powers and privileges. Parliament provided the basis for two Westminster constitutional principles: the supremacy of legislation over all other legal norms, and the (nominal) responsibility of the executive to the legislature. The 'neutral' public service and independent court system also found their genesis in English constitutional history. To complete the Westminster picture, the Constitution was predominantly flexible, there was no Bill of Rights or judicial review, and there was a plurality electoral system.[8] Even the conventions of the constitution, the standards of political morality, were imported from distant shores. However, in South Africa there was always a profoundly different politico-legal culture to that in which the Westminster system developed, most significantly in the extent to which race and colour played a significant part, and the Rule of Law an insignificant part, in the local system. First the conventions, and later other constitutional principles, were victims of the differences in political context.

The foundations of the Westminster constitutional features were laid in the various Constitution Acts of the Union and Republic of

---

[6] This is to use the models of repressive, autonomous and responsive law developed by Philippe Nonet and Philip Selznick *Law and Society in Transition: Towards Responsive Law* (1979). See also below, 244ff.

[7] The most comprehensive constitutional law text is Gretchen Carpenter *Introduction to South African Constitutional Law* (1987). A more thematic approach is found in Dion Basson and Henning Viljoen *South African Constitutional Law* (1988); a more dated text is Marinus Wiechers *Staatsreg* 3 ed (1980).

[8] That is, in a particular constituency election the candidate with more votes than any other is declared the winner, even though he or she may have fewer than the other candidates combined. Proportional representation is an alternative to plurality elections.

South Africa.[9] These were, of course, codified Constitutions, unlike the uncodified Westminster system. They regulated along Westminster lines the main institutions of government, their powers and procedures, and their mutual relationships. They allowed the political party which secured a majority of seats in Parliament to dominate the whole state system and to implement its social policies with little resistance from opposition groups in Parliament. In the absence of a federal division of power, there were also no rival legislative authorities; the abolition of the Provincial Councils in the 1980s is symptomatic of the central Parliament's legislative and political dominance. The courts were unable to review parliamentary legislation, even the drastic legislation which allows for the declaration of the states of emergency[10] which have existed in the second half of the 1980s and have resulted in the suspension of many norms of constitutional government.

The Constitution Acts also established the hierarchy of norms for the constitutional/legal system: statutes of the Parliament in Cape Town would prevail over any other legal rules. As statutes would be the highest legal authority, they would also be the ultimate criteria for determining the validity of other legal instruments. Because legislative supremacy was the highest norm in constitutional law, statutes (and not court decisions) were, and still are, the most important sources of this branch of law. This principle, the most dominant feature of the whole constitutional system, is analysed in detail in the chapter on the historical development of the South African constitution.[11]

The second part of the constitution was not of a Westminster kind. It catered for blacks, coloureds and Indians, not, in the main, as political actors, but as subjects of state power. Its foundations were also laid in the various Constitution Acts—namely the restricted definition of the franchise, which denied blacks, coloureds and Indians the right to elect or be elected to the representative branches of the state system. This part of the constitution was also found in executive decrees and administrative regulations, which served to control the lives of the majority of unfranchised citizens. While coloureds, Indians and blacks were predominantly excluded from the parliamentary franchise, various 'fancy franchise' arrangements were established for them over the years. A series of appointed and elected institutions was constructed, with delegated powers exercised under the control, or potential control, of the central government. These bodies ranged from the Natives Representative Council, established in 1936, to the Coloured Persons Representative Council, disestablished in 1980. In constitutional terms these were essentially

---

[9] The South Africa Act of 1909, the Republic of South Africa Constitution Act 32 of 1961, and the Republic of South Africa Constitution Act 110 of 1983.

[10] Public Safety Act 3 of 1953.

[11] See below, 125ff.

administrative, as opposed to policy-making, bodies and their political objective was to allow disfranchised persons to participate in the state system without giving them any real power. The black homelands system (the national states) was another product of this policy. All these initiatives failed to achieve their political objectives and they introduced numerous constitutional complexities into the state system. By the early 1980s many had been abandoned, or at least seriously reassessed.

This was, and remains, a less conspicuous part of the constitution which does not involve ceremonial openings and media scrutiny. However, the two parts of the constitutional whole were not watertight; the legislative supremacy of Parliament, absence of judicial review and a Bill of Rights, and the non-adherence to the Rule of Law, all had drastic implications in this second part as well. In overall terms, the constitution comprised authoritarian administrative government for Indians, blacks and coloureds and a modified form of Westminster political government for whites. The elaborate system of race classification was a defining feature of the whole system.

The 1983 Constitution Act introduced the current phase of constitutional politics in South Africa. The parliamentary franchise was extended to Indians and coloureds—but it was withheld from all blacks. However, the institutional context in which the new franchise operates ensures that whites retain the dominant position in parliamentary politics. Nevertheless, it was felt necessary to amend some long-standing constitutional principles once the white monopolisation of Parliament had come to an end. The Constitution has been made partly inflexible, the doctrines of parliamentary sovereignty and legislative supremacy have been partially modified, and the principles of parliamentary government have been further undermined. There has also been a shift of power away from parliamentary bodies to new institutions, such as the President's Council and a newly shaped office of the State President. However, the constitution retains a Westminster bias[12] in one important respect—the winning party in the white election is able to dominate the executive, and the executive in turn has the means to dominate Parliament and other constitutional authorities.

The institutional position of the courts has been left largely intact throughout South African constitutional history. The principle of judicial independence has been incorporated from the Westminster tradition in that although there is only a weak separation of powers, judges do have some practical autonomy from other branches of the state.[13] However, while the judges themselves are relatively free from state interference, their powers are not. Successive governments have confined the courts' powers mainly to adjudicating on private

[12] See below, 168ff.
[13] See below, 200ff.

disputes and supervising the regularity of government action,[14] and they have not had the broad constitutional functions associated with modern principles of constitutionalism. Since 1983 judges have had a potentially more active role in policing the Constitution,[15] but they still have no authority to test the validity of legislation. Their powers to review administrative actions have remained formally intact, though the executive has succeeded over the years in immunising various governmental actions from judicial scrutiny. The lack of adherence to the Rule of Law by the executive and legislative branches of the state has further diminished the courts' role. Thus in South Africa the discipline of constitutional law (in the sense of court-applied law) is narrowly defined, and it is in administrative law that the courts have a more significant role.

A detailed analysis of the important features of the contemporary South African constitution is provided in Part II.

III FUNDAMENTALS OF THE ADMINISTRATIVE-LAW SYSTEM

The South African administrative-law system[16] is less idiosyncratic than the constitutional system. Its formal style reflects its English background.[17] It is the product of three Westminster constitutional principles, namely parliamentary sovereignty, legislative supremacy and parliamentary government. The first two principles allow the executive to use Parliament to grant extensive administrative power to itself, and they ensure only a limited review role for the courts. However, they also provide the courts with a justificatory principle for their inclination to review administrative action in spite of executive attempts to the contrary, namely that they are giving effect to the intention of Parliament as reflected in the legislation which is necessary for conferring power on public authorities.[18] An almost exclusive reliance on judicial review is the most prominent feature of the administrative-law system. As in English law, it is the ordinary courts of the land which review administrative action and there is no French-type system of administrative courts; that is, there is no general system of administrative courts, though there are a number of individual tribunals which fit that description.[19] Administrative-law doctrine has been considerably influenced by the importation of English law precedents. One of the disadvantages of this influence is that administrative-law issues, for example the question of standing,[20] tend to be regarded in a private-law light, despite the public-law nature of judicial review.

[14] See below, 255ff.   [15] See below, 146ff.

[16] The most comprehensive administrative law text is Lawrence Baxter *Administrative Law* (1984); the other authoritative work is by Marinus Wiechers *Administrative Law* (1985).

[17] See Baxter op cit n 16 at 30ff.

[18] On the ultra vires doctrine see below, 259ff.

[19] For example the industrial court, the water courts and the tax court.

[20] See chapter 12.

The principle of parliamentary government is responsible for another prominent feature of the administrative-law system, namely the lack of effective political controls over public authorities. In South Africa more reliance is placed on this principle than in its country of origin; ministerial responsibility to Parliament is regarded as the dominant form of political accountability for the South African executive. While the system relies for its operation on parliamentary and public awareness of government activities, there is no institutional means for gaining access to state information. Yet the notion that cabinet Ministers are really accountable to Parliament is occasionally referred to by the courts.[21] A partial exception to this traditional model of political accountability is the system of parliamentary committees, which has been slightly strengthened since the advent of the 1983 Constitution. A less significant exception is the Advocate-General, the office of which was established in 1979.[22] Despite various suggestions over the years, there has been no importation of those institutions developed elsewhere for scrutinising governmental action, such as the ombudsman or parliamentary committees for delegated legislation. Nor has there been the supporting cast, in the form of legislation requiring open government and access to official information, necessary for bringing government to account. Nor, again, has there been much development towards direct participation in administrative decision-making by interested or affected members of the public.[23]

Another important administrative-law principle which derives from the English constitutional background is that public authorities in South Africa have no inherent power, and all their actions must be authorised by statute. This constitutes 'Principle 1'[24] of the administrative-law system: all governmental power must be rooted in a statutory source. In practice administrative power derives from Acts of Parliament, regulations of the State President and cabinet ministers, departmental rules, homeland statutes, and municipal by-laws. Previously the laws of the Provincial Councils, styled ordinances, were another source of administrative power, and some are still of relevance.[25] There is also the modern phenomenon of quasi-legislation[26] which is used extensively in administrative practice and consists of directives, circulars and departmental guidelines issued by various government offices. However, while these documents indicate how a public authority will exercise its discretion, they cannot add to statutory authority and are not strictly a source of administrative power akin to legislation. The prerogative

---

[21] See *Sachs v Dönges NO* 1950 (2) SA 265 (A), *R v Lusu* 1953 (2) SA 484 (A), and *Kati v Minister of Police* 1982 (3) SA 527 (TkSC).
[22] See below, 211ff.
[23] See L J Boulle 1986 (2) *TSAR* 136.
[24] See above, 12–13; and below, 302ff.
[25] See below, 174–5.
[26] See above, 86–7.

power of the head of state is the only exception to Principle 1—the prerogative is very limited in breadth, but is an important institution within its scope.[27]

Although administrative power and procedure is defined predominantly in legislation, decisions of the courts are a far more important source of administrative than of constitutional law. While there is no review of parliamentary legislation in South Africa, there is review of executive actions, including delegated legislation. This is because the principle of legislative supremacy does not automatically protect administrative action, as it does legislation, and the courts have some leeway for imposing their own standards on administrative decisions and procedures. In South Africa judge-made law is a source of creative development in the administrative law field.

While the constitutional system sets the scene for the administrative-law system, it does this, to some extent, by default: the Constitution Act makes virtually no reference to the administrative branch of government. The furthest it goes is in defining the structure and powers of the various branches of the executive and their relationships with the legislature. Administrative-law principles also find no overt constitutional expression. Even the principle of judicial review, which is so pivotal in the administrative-law system, finds no direct basis in the Constitution Act; it derives from the common law.

While the administrative-law system is modelled on English law as regards the kinds of administrative acts, the forms of judicial and political control, the formalities of judicial review and many administrative-law principles, there are some significant divergences. One is in relation to remedies. Here South African law has never suffered from the formalities associated with the English administrative-law system of remedies which led to some strained forms of classification, the effects of which have never been completely overcome. In practical terms there is only one important legal remedy in respect of alleged unlawful administrative action, namely judicial review.[28] Another divergence is in relation to the scope of judicial review, where the English courts in recent decades have been more intrusive than their South African counterparts. You will recall that the English model of review is a restricted model in that courts are not entitled to scrutinise matters of policy or substance. However, as the courts themselves define the boundaries of policy, it is they who determine degrees of activism and in the South African context they have generally not used their powers assertively.

There are also some tendencies which have been particularly pronounced in South African administrative law, though their existence in other jurisdictions should not be overlooked. One is for

[27] See above, 14 and below, 175ff.
[28] See below, 241; 246ff.

the executive to delegate to itself vast discretionary powers in legislation which it can, if necessary, force through Parliament—for example the Defence Act 44 of 1957 and the Internal Security Act 74 of 1982. Another is for the executive to attempt to immunise its decisions from judicial scrutiny through every possible means—for example by narrowing or ousting the courts' inherent review powers, by conferring administrative power in highly subjective language, or by restricting state liability towards the public. While the constitutional system does not generally provide any basis for checking these tendencies, it does allow the courts to safeguard their own authority to some extent. These matters are dealt with in Part III.

As far as the literature is concerned, South African writers tend to operate with a 'red-light' theory of administrative power.[29] As with other countries which have come under the influence of English law there is a tendency to place the emphasis on judicial review, that is on the cure of bad public administration, rather than on the development of good administration.[30] Liberal lawyers in particular have tended to approach the subject from the perspective of individual rights, and as a system for implementing collective social policies. This inclination may be attributed in part to the offensiveness of many state policies to liberal assumptions—particularly on matters of race and security.[31] These assumptions have not, however, always assisted in developing a coherent approach to administrative-law principles: while ruthless executive action in matters of race and security may cry out for intervention by the courts, it is not always easy to provide a theoretical basis for such intervention which is compatible with other constitutional principles.[32]

A detailed analysis of the important features of contemporary South African administrative law is provided in Part III.

IV CONSTITUTIONALISM

The principles of constitutionalism have not had a noticeable impact on the South African constitutional experience. While there has always been a great deal of constitutional activity, it has generally been of the kind which restricts political activity and condones state action, rather than facilitates political activity and limits state power. To take one example: it has been shown that the separation of powers doctrine was an important landmark in the development of constitutionalism in that it provided a way of limiting, sharing and controlling state power, with the sanction of legal invalidity should it not be upheld. In South Africa the principle has only existed in its weaker form as the executive has always been part of Parliament, and has had the means of dominating the legislature. In this weak form

---

[29] See above, 80ff. On the 'watchdog' approach of the courts, see below, 243–6.
[30] Baxter (op cit n 16) was the first writer to look at the South African administrative process in terms of its internal procedures.
[31] See below, 243–5.
[32] See Laurence Boulle (1987) 104 *SALJ* 104.

the principle has not prevented the executive from assuming dominant roles in lawmaking and law-implementation, and from playing an important role in adjudication. The main vehicle of executive authority is the supremacy of Parliament, which entails that there are no countervailing constitutional norms, which can limit or check executive action—provided only that it is formally sanctioned by an Act. And while the control of the executive is the predicament of all constitutional systems, in the South African context the executive has often been accused of acting in a spirit of lawlessness.

Nevertheless, as was shown in the preceding sections, there is some division of functions in the constitutional system and it is necessary for the appropriate branch of government to function for state actions to be accorded legal validity. Moreover, in the administrative-law system there is something close to a fundamental constitutional norm in the form of the courts' power of review. Not only have the other state authorities found this difficult to eradicate, but its scope and effectiveness is partly determined by the judges themselves,[33] regardless of executive and legislative intent. Here the courts operate with the fiction that Parliament intended some limitation on governmental action, no matter how widely-worded the statutory language might be.[34]

The South African constitutional tradition, for its part, has made no major contributions to the doctrine of constitutionalism. However, the constitutional crisis of the 1950s was a prominent exception. Although the government of the day ultimately succeeded in having its way against the will of the majority of citizens, and against the earlier judgments of the highest court, the crisis did show how an otherwise supreme Parliament could be made subject to procedural requirements contained in rigid provisions of the Constitution. The main court decisions in this saga have been referred to in subsequent international writings on this aspect of the doctrine of constitutionalism.[35]

V RIGHTS AND LIBERTIES

It was shown in chapter 2 that one of the concerns of twentieth-century constitutionalism has been the national and international protection of human rights and liberties. It is not within the scope of this work to examine the issue of human rights and civil liberties in South Africa.[36] Their state and extent is by no means dependent on legal factors alone. However, in so far as they are dependent on the constitutional and administrative-law system, it can be inferred from

---

[33] See below, 242ff.
[34] See below, 256ff.
[35] On the crisis see below, 132–43.
[36] On which see C J R Dugard *Human Rights in South Africa* (1980); A Rycroft, (ed) *Race and the Law in South Africa* (1987).

the preceding analysis that rights and liberties are not provided for in South Africa in any significant way.

The Constitution Acts have set the scene for the human-rights situation. On one hand, they have failed to provide for the legal protection of rights through institutions such as a Bill of Rights, judicial review, or an ombudsman. Thus the courts are denied the effective means of preventing incursions by the state or private groups on human liberties, such as freedom of the person and freedom of movement. On the other hand, the Constitutions have granted to the legislature, and indirectly to the executive and administration, immense power, including the ability to encroach on fundamental rights. The Constitution Acts, themselves statutes of Parliament, illustrate this capacity in so far as they deny basic rights of political expression to many citizens. Numerous other statutes over the years have affected rights and liberties in matters of movement, family life, educational opportunity, due process of law, ownership of property, use of public amenities and entitlement to welfare benefits. In recent years the states of emergency have further eroded civil rights and liberties. The denial of rights has often been overtly based on factors of race and colour. Within this constitutional context, the common law and its rights-values have not had much impact, though one of the contemporary issues in administrative law concerns the extent to which the courts can invoke common-law values to curtail actions and activities of the state.

Legal periodicals in South Africa provide evidence of an extensive current debate about human-rights issues.[37] The debate has revolved mainly around the desirability or otherwise of a judicially enforceable Bill of Rights. In the past human-rights proponents with liberal assumptions have advocated the protection of private property, free speech and religion. The recently revised Freedom Charter of the African National Congress has contributed a new dimension in its promotion of various social and welfare rights. State authorities have also become involved and from their perspective advocated the legal protection of group rights. In 1989 the South African Law Commission issued a far-ranging report,[38] which included a draft Bill of Rights for the country. These contributions have highlighted a wide range of constitutional and legal options for a Bill of Rights regime in a new constitutional order. However, ultimately the human-rights issue cannot be resolved separately from the broader political issue of a legitimate political-constitutional settlement.

VI SUMMARY

South African society has been divided and stratified according to factors of class, race, colour and religion, which through state

---

[37] This development can be attributed in large measure to the launch of the *South African Journal on Human Rights* in 1985, though it has also been evident in other journals.
[38] *Working Paper 25*, Project 58 (1989).

definition and manipulation determine access to economic resources and political power. The state system regulating the society provides a concentrated form of economic resources, bureaucratic strength and coercive power. The constitutional system allows for the sectional domination of this system, and provides an accessible and pliable means for those in government to give effect to their social policies, with little need for accountability and openness towards the governed, though with a veneer of legality attached to most of their actions. The administrative-law system incorporates a basic tension in so far as it provides the means both to implement state policies with limited obstruction, and to check executive discretion and safeguard human rights through judicial review. South African constitutional history has not been influenced in any significant way by the main standards developed in the constitutionalist tradition. Nor has it facilitated the legal protection of human rights and liberties to any significant extent.

Part II
Constitutional Law

6 South African Constitutional History—the Dominance of Legislative Supremacy

The doctrine of parliamentary sovereignty, or legislative supremacy, is British in origin, and is the most important characteristic of the Westminster system. How was this doctrine imported into South African constitutional law? In order to answer this question, it is necessary to trace the constitutional history of the country, province by province, from the time Britain assumed permanent control of the Cape until the achievement of Union in 1910.[1]

I SOUTH AFRICA BEFORE 1910

A Cape Colony

The Cape Colony, the province of the future South Africa with the longest history of British rule, followed the course taken by most British colonies in the nineteenth and twentieth centuries. Having occupied the Cape during the brief period 1795–1803, Britain assumed permanent control in 1806. The territory over which Britain assumed sovereignty enjoyed Crown Colony status. This meant that all executive power was concentrated in the hands of a Governor, who also had the power to legislate by proclamation. The Governor was subject only to Orders in Council[2] and other instructions sent from London. In 1825 it was decided that power should no longer vest in the Governor alone, but in the hands of the 'Governor-in-Council'. In theory this meant that power was wielded by an Advisory Council consisting of the Governor, the Chief Justice, and a few nominated officials from the colony's administration. In reality, all significant decisions continued to be taken by the Governor. From 1827 two 'unofficial' nominees (that is, colonists) also sat on the Council, but this did not satisfy the colonists' increasing demands for more participation in government.

In 1834 a new Constitution was implemented. Two bodies were created: an Executive Council, consisting of the Governor and four senior officials, and a Legislative Council, consisting of the same four officials, the Attorney-General and from five to seven 'unofficial' members nominated by the Governor. The Governor dominated the

---

[1] For a full treatment of South African constitutional history see H Hahlo and E Kahn *The Union of South Africa: The Development of its Laws and Constitution* (1960) 51–127 and Gretchen Carpenter *Introduction to South African Constitutional Law* (1987) 56–73.

[2] These Orders in Council were rules made by the executive branch of the British government (the monarch acting on the advice of the cabinet) in terms of the royal prerogative. To this extent the Cape Colony (like many other colonies) was under the control of the cabinet rather than the British Parliament.

117

Executive Council, just as he had the Advisory Council. Although legislation had to receive the assent of the Legislative Council, this did not mean that the colonists' representatives enjoyed legislative control, as the Governor usually appointed only five 'unofficials'. The Governor also had the power to refuse to assent to legislation. Finally, even if legislation had been assented to by the Governor it could at any time be disallowed (in other words, struck down) by the Crown (that is, by the monarch acting on the advice of the British cabinet) and would in any event lapse after three years if it had not received the royal assent. Britain could still legislate for the Cape by means of Orders in Council.

Political pressure by the colonists led to the promulgation of a new Constitution in 1853. Its most notable feature was that it introduced 'representative government'—the nomination by the Governor of colonists' representatives was now a thing of the past. The Constitution provided for a Parliament consisting of the Governor and a bicameral legislature. The latter was made up of an upper house (the Legislative Council) and a lower house (the House of Assembly). Both houses were elected on a non-racial males-only franchise with a low voting qualification. Any voter could stand for election to the lower house, but a person wishing to stand for election to the Legislative Council had to be at least 30 years of age and had to own unburdened immovable property worth at least £2 000. Once both houses had passed a Bill, the Governor's assent was necessary for it to become law. A Bill which was 'reserved' by the Governor would lapse if not assented to by the Crown within two years. Even those Bills that became law could be disallowed by the Crown within two years of having received the Governor's assent. The granting of representative government meant that it was no longer possible for Britain to legislate for the Cape by means of Orders in Council—an Act of the British Parliament was now necessary. Executive authority was vested in the Executive Council, selected and presided over by the Governor. Its members could not be members of the legislature—in other words there was no responsible government, and thus there was no need for the executive to maintain political support in the legislature.

The denial of responsible government to the Cape Colony was resented by the colonists, the more so as it had been granted in Canada and Australia. Eventually, in 1872, the Cape's Constitution was amended in such a way as to require members of the Executive Council to be members of the lower house and to retain its support. Real executive power now resided not in the Governor but in the Prime Minister and the other members of his cabinet. Their tenure in office now depended on their ability to retain the confidence of the lower house.

The legislative competence of the colony's Parliament was regulated by the Colonial Laws Validity Act of 1865. This Act of the British Parliament had been passed to remove uncertainty regarding the status of colonies with responsible government. In essence it provided that a colonial legislature could amend the common law applicable to its territory, be that English or any other common law, and could also amend any English statutory law that might have been incorporated into the law of the colony. The only restrictions on colonial legislative competence were that colonies could not legislate extra-territorially, and could not amend Acts of the British Parliament which were *expressly or by necessary implication* made applicable to the colony in question. This restriction is sometimes explained in terms of the 'doctrine of repugnancy'—colonial legislation was valid unless it was repugnant to directly applicable British statutes, in which case the colonial legislation was void to the extent of the repugnancy. Finally, a colony could not legislate in contravention of any restriction in its Constitution regarding the subject-matter of legislation or its legislative procedures (the so-called 'manner and form' requirements).[3] The powers of reservation and disallowance were retained. In practice, however, the Crown never used its power of disallowance, and only two reserved Bills failed to obtain Royal assent during the entire history of the Cape Parliament.

The Constitution of the Cape Colony remained substantially unaltered until Union and became the model for the Constitutions of other British colonies in South Africa.

B Natal

Natal's constitutional development was similar to that of the Cape, with representative government being granted in 1856, and responsible government in 1893. However, Natal differed from the Cape in that its franchise was far less liberal, and was further narrowed by an Act passed in 1896[4] which, while not affecting vested rights, effectively barred the enrolment of any new non-white voters.

C Orange Free State

The Constitution of the Orange Free State was drafted shortly after the Republic's independence was recognised by Britain in 1854, and although revised in minor respects in 1866 and 1879, it remained substantially unaltered for its entire history.

The Constitution provided for a unicameral legislature (the Volksraad), and for a directly elected executive president. The Constitution could be amended only by a three-quarters majority of the total membership of the legislature. The franchise was always restricted to white males, although the residence and citizenship requirements for enfranchisement were amended several times.

On paper, the executive seemed to be subordinate to the legislature. The president had no power to veto legislation. The legislature's consent was necessary for a presidential declaration of

---

[3] See 72–3 above and 129–32 below.
[4] Franchise Amendment Act 8 of 1896.

war or peace, as well as for the conclusion of a treaty or convention by the president. The legislature appointed three of the five members of the Executive Council which assisted the president[5] and used this power to select Volksraad members. Moreover the president was responsible to the Volksraad, and the latter could override any executive action. But in reality the president had a virtually free hand, particularly in the conduct of foreign policy, and generally acted first and sought the Volksraad's approval later. The fact that the Volksraad was in session for only a brief period each year, and that its members were generally less sophisticated than the president, meant that Volksraad members of the Executive Council were able to exercise little restraint over him. There was, in any event, no requirement that the president had to act on the advice of the Executive Council, and given the fact that he had a casting vote, he and the other two members could always outvote the three Volksraad representatives. In fact, so great was the prestige of the holder of the presidential office,[6] that he was usually able to use his right to sit and speak (but not vote) in the Volksraad to dominate its proceedings and introduce most legislation, and on no occasion did the Volksraad succeed in overturning an executive act of the president. The only significant power retained by the legislature was that of regulating the finances of the Republic—the Treasurer-General, who presented the budget, was an official appointed by and responsible to the Volksraad, and was not permitted to be a member of the Executive Council.

The Volksraad did not enjoy ultimate sovereignty, as it was subordinate to the Constitution and could not legislate contrary to those of its provisions which guaranteed civil liberties. Furthermore, although the Constitution did not expressly confer upon the courts the right to test legislation and to strike it down if it contravened the Constitution, it gradually came to be accepted that the High Court did have such a testing right.[7]

The Constitution of 1854 was successful in so far as no constitutional crisis of the type which occurred in the South African Republic[8] took place in the Orange Free State. Defeat in the Anglo-Boer War reduced the Free State to the status of a directly governed colony (the Orange River Colony). Nominated legislative and executive bodies were established shortly after the end of the war in 1902, but failed to gain legitimacy within the electorate, who demanded responsible government on the Cape model. This was

---

[5] The other two members were the landdrost of the capital and the Government Secretary.

[6] Especially in the case of President Brand, who served for five terms.

[7] Examples of the court exercising its testing right are provided by *Cassim & Solomon v The State* (1892) 9 *Cape LJ* 58 and *The State v Gibson* (1898) 15 *Cape LJ* 1.

[8] See 121–3 below.

conferred in 1907,[9] but without any revision of the franchise, which remained confined to white males.

D The South African Republic

The South African Republic (modern-day Transvaal) had a more chequered constitutional history than its sister Republic. To begin with, the unification of the various Trekker Republics into one and the drafting of the Constitution lasted six years—from 1854 to 1860.

The Constitution provided for a unicameral legislature (the Volksraad). The franchise was restricted to white males. The Constitution was not entrenched, and given the absence of any special amending procedure, it was presumed that an ordinary enactment sufficed to amend it. Confusion did, however, exist on the very basic question of what was required for the passage of an 'ordinary' enactment: the Constitution required that all legislation receive a three-quarters majority, but in practice the legislature passed Bills by a simple majority, something that was formally legalised only in 1896. A further source of confusion was the fact that three possible methods of legislating were prescribed by the Constitution, and one of these, which provided for the passage of resolutions ('besluiten'), was to give rise to a constitutional crisis in the 1890s. A change in the composition of the legislature occurred in 1890 when unicameralism was abandoned, and a First and a Second Volksraad established in an attempt to satisfy the political demands of unenfranchised foreigners ('Uitlanders'). The Second Volksraad (the only chamber for which 'Uitlanders' could vote) had very limited legislative competence, and could not pass taxation or spending Bills. All legislation that it did pass had to be approved by the First Volksraad and, unlike legislation produced by the First Volksraad, could be vetoed by the president.

The executive consisted of the president and his Executive Council. The president was directly elected on the same franchise as applied to the legislature. After 1890, the franchise in presidential elections was restricted to those who were entitled to vote in elections for the First Volksraad. The Executive Council, whose members were appointed by the Volksraad, consisted of the Commandant-General (who had a vote only when the council was considering military matters), the Government Secretary, and two other citizens. The president had both a deliberative and a casting vote. As chief executive, the president controlled all public officials except the judiciary. However, in the conduct of foreign affairs his power was limited by the requirement that the prior consent of the legislature be obtained before he concluded any treaty or convention.

[9] The responsible government was more conventional than real in nature: members of the Executive Council did not have to be members of the legislature, but conventionally they were. For a detailed discussion of the constitution of the Orange River Colony (and that of the Transvaal) see Hahlo and Kahn op cit n 1 at 110–15.

The president and the members of the Executive Council could sit and speak in the legislature, but had no vote, and the president frequently proposed legislation. As in the Orange Free State, the prestige and the experience of the president was such that he was usually able to dominate the proceedings of the legislature. For the same reason, the fact that the president was stated to be responsible to the Volksraad meant very little in practice—rejection of a Bill proposed by the president did not mean that he was required to resign.

Although any doubts regarding the position of the executive vis-à-vis the legislature were settled fairly early in the history of the Republic, uncertainty surrounded the position of the judiciary relative to the other two branches of government, and this uncertainty led to a constitutional crisis in the 1890s. The seeds of the crisis lay in the failure of the Constitution to specify where ultimate authority lay—was the legislature a creature of the Constitution, and therefore bound to act in accordance with its provisions, or was the Constitution a product of the legislature, which could repeal it either expressly or impliedly (that is by legislating contrary to its provisions)? This constitutional question was given importance by the doubt that surrounded the status of the informal resolutions ('besluiten') which the legislature was in the habit of passing. These enactments were not passed in accordance with the prescribed legislative procedures, but were nevertheless generally thought to be valid, and had been accepted as such by the High Court.[10] However, in *Dom's Trustees v Bok NO*,[11] Jorrison J delivered a dissenting judgment in which he stated that 'besluiten' were invalid because the legislature was subordinate to the Constitution and could therefore not legislate contrary to its provisions. The reaction of President Kruger was to incorporate in a constitutional amendment (Law 4 of 1890) a provision which stated that any 'besluit' published in the official gazette was law. However, in the famous case of *Brown v Leyds NO*,[12] Kotze CJ held that sovereignty vested in the Constitution and not in the legislature, and that the courts could therefore test the validity of legislation against the requirements of the Constitution. He then declared all 'besluiten' invalid on the ground that they had not been passed in accordance with the Constitution, and also struck down Kruger's declaratory amendment. This judgment threw the Republic into confusion, as it nullified much legislation previously considered valid, and raised questions about the validity of the actions of many other institutions of government (including the courts) which had not operated in accordance with the strict letter of the Constitution. Kruger's response was to secure the passage of legislation which proclaimed

[10] *McCorkindale's Executors v Bok NO* (1884) 1 SAR 202.
[11] (1887) 2 SAR 189.
[12] (1897) 4 OR 17.

that the courts had no testing right, and which required members of the judiciary to swear that they would not purport to exercise such a power. Kotze CJ refused to take the oath, and was dismissed by Kruger, who informed the Volksraad that the testing right was a principle invented by the devil! Whether Kotze CJ was right in law is a moot point, but the episode is remembered not for the merits of the decision he made in *Brown v Leyds NO*[13] but rather for the infringement upon judicial independence evidenced by Kruger's dismissal of him.

The Anglo-Boer War brought an end to the South African Republic, and saw the establishment of the British colony of the Transvaal, which was given responsible government in 1906.[14] But this era in the Transvaal's constitutional history was short-lived.

II UNION AND THE SOUTH AFRICA ACT OF 1909

A The establishment of the Union[15]

Proposals for a union of British territories in southern Africa had been made during the nineteenth century, but had met with little success. However, the growing economic interdependence of the colonies after the Anglo-Boer War revealed the need for co-operation between them, and resulted in the establishment of a customs convention in 1903. Disagreements still arose over such questions as import tariffs and the division of railway traffic. A threat by the Transvaal to withdraw from the customs convention led to the calling of an Inter-Colonial Conference in 1908, where it was decided to hold a national convention to draft a Constitution providing for some form of union between the four colonies. The British Government was anxious that the convention should succeed, as it favoured the creation of a strong economic unit which would be part of the British Empire and which would foster reconciliation between whites of English and Afrikaans descent.

The two most controversial issues[16] facing the delegates to the convention were whether the new Constitution should establish a federation or a union, and whether the non-racial franchise of the Cape would be extended to the rest of South Africa. Only Natal, afraid of being dominated by the larger colonies, argued strenuously for federation. The other colonies, who believed that a union would give greater scope for independence from Westminster, carried the day. On this issue, as on many others, the convention adopted the view of the Transvaal delegation. Of the four colonies, it was the only one that could have survived on its own, while the other three (and

[13] Ibid.

[14] The Transvaal's responsible government constitution was virtually a copy of that given to the Orange River Colony; see n 9.

[15] For a comprehensive overview of the history of this period see L Thompson *The Unification of South Africa* (1960).

[16] The language issue, although of comparatively minor importance, also occupied the delegates for a considerable length of time.

in particular Natal) could not survive without the rail traffic generated by the Witwatersrand. Thus, the Natal, Cape and Free State needed union, and for union to succeed the participation of the Transvaal was indispensable. The Transvaal delegation, ably led by Smuts, exploited the strong position afforded by the other colonies' dependence on the Transvaal and by Britain's anxiety that union should be established. Nowhere was this more apparent than on the question of the franchise—the Transvaal (supported by the Orange River Colony) was adamant that the franchise of the Cape should not be extended throughout South Africa, and made it clear that it would not participate in the union unless this point was conceded. Once the issue was stated in those terms, it became inevitable that the Cape would give way, and that the British would abandon whatever hopes they had entertained that liberalism would spread from the Cape to the former Boer republics.[17] Thus it was that Westminster, eager to secure union at almost any price, turned a deaf ear to the pleas made by a delegation representing African opinion, and passed the South Africa Act of 1909.[18] Union was proclaimed on 31 May 1910.

B Prominent features of the South Africa Act of 1909

All four colonies comprising the Union had Constitutions with Westminster features before the convention was summoned. It was therefore in accordance with the prevailing trend in South African constitutional history that the Union Constitution reflected the Westminster pattern. The first Westminster feature was that it was unitary and not federal. The only important concession to federalism was the retention of the separate identities of the four colonies, which became the provinces of the Union. Elements of federalism were also present in s 24 which prescribed that there should be an equal number of senators from each province for at least ten years, ss 18, 19 and 109 which provided for three capitals, s 85(iii) which vested control over school education in the provinces for at least five years, and s 149 which provided that Parliament could change provincial boundaries only if petitioned to do so by the Provincial Councils of the provinces concerned. But provincial powers were limited in that in terms of s 86 no ordinance passed by a Provincial Council would be of any effect to the extent that it was repugnant to an Act of Parliament, while in terms of s 90 ordinances would come into effect only once they had received the assent of the Union cabinet. Responsible government, which had been conferred on all the pre-existing colonies, was provided for by s 14 of the Union Constitution. The legislature was bicameral, consisting of an upper house (the Senate) and a lower house (the House of Assembly). In terms of s 59 Parliament had 'full power to make laws for the peace,

---

[17] For a detailed account of attempts by black politicians to prevent the enactment of the Union constitution see A Odendaal *Vukani Bantu!: the beginnings of Black protest politics in South Africa to 1912* (1984).
[18] 9 Edw 7, c 9.

order, and good government of the Union' and could, subject to certain limitations contained in s 152, amend the Constitution by means of an ordinary enactment. Legislative power was, however, limited by virtue of South Africa's status vis-à-vis Britain: In terms of s 64 all Bills had to be sent to the Governor-General for assent. He then had the option of assenting to the Bill, refusing his assent, or reserving it for the monarch's[19] pleasure. The decision he took depended on the instructions given by the monarch, although in certain instances he (the Governor-General) was bound to reserve legislation.[20] In terms of s 66 a reserved Bill would lapse unless assented to by the monarch within a year of its referral to him. The monarch also had the power of disallowance, s 65 giving him a year within which to disallow a Bill that had received the Governor-General's assent. South Africa was also subject to the Colonial Laws Validity Act of 1865, and could therefore not legislate extra-territorially or repugnantly to any Act of the British Parliament which had been made applicable to South Africa. But, however extensive Britain's power over South Africa may have been on paper, in practice little or no control was ever exercised. The powers of reservation and disallowance were never used,[21] and Britain did not legislate for the Union. The Union Parliament enjoyed much the same relationship with the king (as represented by the Governor-General) as did the British Parliament.

III THE DOCTRINE OF PARLIAMENTARY SOVEREIGNTY

The final and most important feature of the Westminster system included in the Union Constitution was the doctrine of legislative supremacy, often called parliamentary sovereignty. The doctrine was defined by A V Dicey[22] as follows:

'[T]he principle of Parliamentary sovereignty means neither more nor less than this, namely that Parliament[23] has under the English constitution the right to make or unmake any law whatever, and further that no person or body is recognized by the law of England as having a right to override or set aside the legislation of Parliament.'

It is important to note that the doctrine has two cardinal aspects: that Parliament is omnicompetent (that is, can legislate on any subject-matter and in any terms it chooses), and that no other institution constitutes a source of law superior to Parliament or can declare an

---

[19] All references to the monarch are, of course, to the monarch acting on the advice of the British Cabinet.

[20] For example, s 64 compelled reservation where an enactment dealt with ss 32–50 (which governed the composition of the House of Assembly) or the powers conferred upon provincial councils by s 85. In terms of s 106 any Bill touching upon the right to request leave to appeal to the Privy Council would also be compulsorily reserved.

[21] On no occasion was a compulsorily reserved Bill denied the royal assent.

[22] *Introduction to the Study of the Law of Constitution* 10 ed (1959) 70.

[23] Strictly speaking, Dicey ought to have said 'the king in Parliament', as the legislature in Britain consists of the Monarch, Lords and Commons.

Act of Parliament to be invalid. The second aspect of the doctrine is implied by the first: Parliament would not be all-powerful if there was some institution that could create legal rules which were a source of law superior to Acts of Parliament.

The implications of the doctrine of parliamentary sovereignty were clearly spelt out by Lord Reid in the case of *Madzimbamuto v Lardner-Burke*[24] as follows:

> 'It is often said that it would be unconstitutional for the United Kingdom Parliament to do certain things, meaning that the moral, political and other reasons against doing them are so strong that most people would regard it as highly improper if Parliament did these things. But that does not mean that it is beyond the power of Parliament to do such things. If Parliament chose to do any of them, the courts would not hold the Act of Parliament invalid.'

Thus, under the Westminster system, the legislature would be able to pass an Act ordering that all left-handed people be executed, and neither the courts nor any other authority could declare the Act to be invalid. The courts would be obliged to enforce the Act. The doctrine of parliamentary sovereignty is explained on the basis that although Parliament is a common-law body, and derives its authority from the common law, it also has the power to change the common law; and from this it follows that the law (including the law relating to its own powers) is what Parliament says it is. This stands in contrast to countries such as the United States of America where the Constitution, rather than the legislature, is sovereign, and where the courts may therefore strike down legislation which conflicts with the Constitution.

The untrammelled power enjoyed by the British Parliament has been exercised in an unconscionable fashion on several occasions: In terms of the Triennial Act of 1694 parliamentary elections had to be held every three years. A rebellion occurred in Scotland in 1715 and, fearing that voters in Scotland would return anti-government members to Parliament when the next elections were held in 1717, the government secured the passage of the Septennial Act, which provided that, with immediate effect, elections would be held only once every seven years! Parliament again extended its own life, though under less controversial circumstances, in World War I (when the life of the Parliament elected in 1910 was extended to 1918), and in World War II (when the same Parliament sat from 1935 to 1945). Perhaps the most notorious exercise of parliamentary sovereignty in recent times came in the wake of the decision in *Burmah Oil v Lord Advocate*,[25] in which the Court of Appeal held that compensation was payable to a British oil company whose Far Eastern installations had been destroyed by the British Army during World War II to prevent their capture by the Japanese. In order to avoid paying damages, the

[24] [1969] 1 AC 645 at 723B.
[25] [1965] AC 75.

government successfully introduced legislation (the War Damages Act 1965) which, with retroactive effect to World War II, provided that no compensation would be payable for the destruction of civilian property necessitated by the defence of the realm! What is there to stop Parliament at Westminster from passing outrageous legislation, such as that all left-handed people be executed? The answer is nothing, or rather nothing other than the political culture of Britain, which is highly democratic and which would cause a government which introduced tyrannical legislation to lose popular support.[26] The potential for legislative tyranny inherent in the Westminster system provides one of the strongest arguments for the limitation of the power of the legislature by means of a Bill of Rights which is both entrenched (that is, cannot be changed by the legislature) and justiciable (that is, able to be used by the courts to strike down legislation which conflicts with its provisions).

A problem of logic in the doctrine of parliamentary sovereignty arises if the question is asked 'Can Parliament limit itself?' In other words, what would be the position if, in 1980, Parliament had passed an Act imposing a certain fee for dog licences, and that Act had contained a section stating 'No Act shall be passed repealing this Act'? Would an Act passed in 1988 repealing the Dog Licences Act of 1980 be valid? If the answer is 'No', does this not mean that Parliament is not omnicompetent, given that there is something (namely repeal the 1980 Act) that it cannot do? But, on the other hand, if the answer is 'Yes', and the 1988 Parliament *can* repeal the 1980 Act, does this not also mean that Parliament is not omnicompetent in that a prohibition it imposed in 1980 did not bind the Parliament of 1988? It would be impossible for the legislature to function in accordance with the changing needs of society if a prohibition such as the one mentioned in the example were to be effective. The answer therefore is that there is no such thing as an immutable Act of Parliament, and a later Parliament can always repeal what an earlier one has enacted, even if the earlier Parliament purported to deny the later Parliament the power to do so. Thus the sovereignty of Parliament *is* limited in the sense that it is unable to 'bind its successors' by restricting the further exercise of its own powers. Sovereignty is thus said to reside in Parliament as a *continuing institution*. Here lies the paradox inherent in the doctrine of parliamentary sovereignty—the competence of a supposedly supreme institution is limited in order to secure its supremacy in the future. A concrete example of the operation of this rule is provided by the Universities (Scotland) Act of 1853 which repealed a provision of the Union with Scotland Act of 1707 which required that professors at Scottish universities take a religious oath. This repeal took place notwithstanding the fact that article 25(2) of the Union with Scotland Act proclaimed that its provisions would be binding 'in all time coming'.

---

[26] Of course if Parliament abolished elections, the issue of popular political support would become irrelevant!

But in certain cases the inability of Parliament to bind itself gives rise to problems. Examples of this are the Statute of Westminster of 1931, which provided that the British Parliament could no longer legislate for the Dominions unless they requested it, and the various independence Acts (such as the Zimbabwe Act of 1979) in terms of which Parliament asserted that in future none of its legislation would extend to the countries upon which independence was conferred. Does the doctrine of parliamentary sovereignty and the inability of Parliament to bind itself mean that Westminster could resume authority over countries to which it had earlier granted independence? This point was raised in *British Coal Corporation v R*,[27] where Viscount Sankey LC held that in strict theory Parliament *could* repeal the Statute of Westminster and begin legislating for the Dominions once more. However, in *Blackburn v Attorney-General*[28] Lord Denning MR, while declining to decide the issue, expressed the opinion that whatever the theoretical position, in practical terms freedom once given could not be taken away, and that the political realities were such that it would be impossible to resume authority over a former colony.[29] In this instance the realities of international politics would serve to limit the practical effect of parliamentary sovereignty, just as domestic political realities prevent governments from enacting outrageous laws such as that all left-handed people should be killed, even though in theory such legislation could be enacted. Of course countries such as South Africa, which have inherited the Westminster system, but which are *not* democratic, are in an unenviable position, because even if the Parliament of such a country were to pass an Act which established a justiciable Bill of Rights against which future legislation could be tested, it would always be open to a future Parliament to reassert its supremacy by repealing the Bill of Rights. Most authorities agree that one way of limiting the power of the legislature in such a country would be for its Parliament to 'commit suicide' (that is, to pass an Act saying that Parliament was dissolved forever), and for a constitutional convention to draft a new Constitution and Bill of Rights to which the legislature was subordinate.[30]

---

[27] [1935] AC 500 at 520.

[28] [1971] 1 WLR 1037 at 1040.

[29] In any event, the legislation in terms of which British authority was resumed while binding on English courts would probably not be recognised by those of the former colony—the latter could refuse to enforce the British statute by holding that the former colony was an independent state in international law and therefore not subject to British sovereignty. This issue was evidently of concern to countries which gained independence from Britain, as some of them 'took out insurance' and enacted their new status into their own law so as to ensure that that status would continue to be recognised by the British Parliament and by the local courts. An example of such a statute is the Status of the Union Act 69 of 1934 passed by the South African Parliament.

[30] Another way would be for Parliament to pass an Act which subjected Parliament to a legislative restraint, and which was itself protected from amendment or repeal by being 'entrenched'. Entrenchment is discussed at 131 below.

So far as the power of one Parliament to repeal what another has enacted is concerned, it is necessary to mention that that power can be exercised either expressly (as in the examples mentioned above) *or* impliedly. Implied repeal takes place where a later Parliament legislates on the same subject-matter as did an earlier Parliament but without expressly repealing the earlier enactment. In terms of the maxim leges posteriores priores contrarias abrogant later legislation impliedly and automatically repeals the earlier legislation to the extent that the later legislation is inconsistent with it. The doctrine was explained in *Vauxhall Estates Limited v Liverpool Corporation*.[31] In this case the court was faced with a conflict between the Acquisition of Land (Assessment of Compensation) Act of 1919 and the Housing Act of 1925. Section 7(1) of the 1919 Act provided that where land was compulsorily acquired by the State then

'The provisions of the Act or order by which the land is authorized to be acquired, or of any Act incorporated therewith, shall, in relation to the matters dealt with in this Act, have effect subject to this Act, and so far as inconsistent with this Act those provisions shall cease to have or shall not have effect . . .'.

However, s 46 of the 1925 Act was inconsistent with the 1919 Act. The court held that no Act of Parliament could effectively prohibit any future Act from interfering with its provisions, and that therefore any provisions of the 1919 Act that were inconsistent with those of the 1925 Act were impliedly repealed by the later Act to the extent of that inconsistency. In a very similar case, *Ellen Street Estates Limited v Minister of Health*,[32] Maugham LJ held as follows:

'The legislature cannot, according to our constitution, bind itself as to the form of subsequent legislation, and it is impossible for Parliament to enact that in a subsequent statute dealing with the same subject matter there can be no implied repeal. If in a subsequent Act Parliament chooses to make it plain that the earlier statute is to some extent repealed, effect must be given to that intention just because it is the will of the legislature.'

Similarly, in *Government of the Republic of South Africa v Government of KwaZulu*,[33] it was held that the State President's unrestricted power to make laws for self-governing territories, which he enjoyed in terms of s 25(1) of the Black Administration Act 38 of 1927, had been impliedly repealed by s 1(2) of the National States Constitution Act 21 of 1971, which required prior consultation before the State President used his legislative powers to change the boundaries of a self-governing territory.

So far we have concerned ourselves with the doctrine of parliamentary sovereignty as it relates to the inability of any institution (including Parliament itself) to restrict the *subject-matter* upon which Parliament may legislate, or to declare an Act of

[31] [1932] 1 KB 733.
[32] [1934] 1 KB 590 at 597.
[33] 1983 (1) SA 164 (A).

Parliament invalid on the ground of its subject-matter. But are there any circumstances in which a court could declare an Act to be invalid on the ground that it had not been enacted in accordance with the correct *procedure*? Whether Parliament has adhered to the correct procedure really boils down to the question of whether what it has produced is an 'Act of Parliament'. Here the theories of H L A Hart[34] are relevant. According to Hart, every primary rule (such as one embodied in an Act of Parliament) must have a secondary rule of recognition. In other words, before one can say 'This is an Act of Parliament which must be obeyed', one must know that it *is* an Act of Parliament, and this one discovers by enquiring whether the document in question accords with the rule of recognition for an Act of Parliament which, in the case of Britain, is 'something that has been assented to by the House of Commons, the House of Lords and the monarch'. If it is clear that the enactment has received the necessary approval, then the enquiry ends, and a court is bound to accept the Act as being valid. This issue arose in *Edinburgh & Dalkeith Railway Co v Wauchope*,[35] where it was claimed by a landowner that a private Act which had been passed at the instance of the railway company was invalid because he (the landowner) had not received prior notification that legislation affecting his rights was to be passed, as was required by the standing orders (the internal rules of procedure) of the House of Commons. Wauchope's claim was rejected, Lord Campbell holding that

> 'All a court of justice can do is look to the Parliament Roll [the official copy of the Act]: if from that it should appear that a bill has passed both Houses and received the Royal Assent, no court of justice can inquire into the mode in which it was introduced into Parliament, nor what was done previous to its introduction, or what passed in Parliament during its progress in its various stages through both houses'.

In the similar case of *Pickin v British Railways Board*[36] the appellant claimed that the Board had fraudulently misled Parliament into passing a private Act by stating that it (the Board) had complied with the requirements regarding notification to interested parties. The House of Lords cited with approval the decision in *Edinburgh & Dalkeith Railway Co v Wauchope*,[37] and stated that the courts had to obey any enactment that appeared on the face of it to be an Act of Parliament, and did not have the power to examine the internal proceedings of Parliament in order to determine whether the Act had been obtained by irregularity or fraud. Thus, to take an extreme example, even if all the members of the House of Commons were intoxicated when they assented to a Bill, that Bill would still become an Act once assented to by the Lords and the monarch. The same would apply if the House of Commons had failed to comply with its

---

[34] *The Concept of Law* (1961) 77–96.
[35] (1842) 8 Cl & F 710 at 725. This case is also reported at 8 ER 279.
[36] [1974] AC 765.
[37] Note 35.

own Standing Orders in passing the Bill. In both these cases the courts would be unable to inquire into the internal affairs of Parliament, and provided that the official copy of the Act showed that the necessary assents had been obtained, the document would comply with the rules of recognition and would be a valid Act of Parliament. Only if, as in *The Prince's Case*,[38] decided in 1606, the official copy of what purported to be an Act did not contain the words indicating that it had been assented to by Commons, Lords and monarch could the courts declare it to be invalid on the ground that it had not been passed in accordance with the procedures prescribed by the common law.

Given that a purported Act of Parliament could be declared invalid if, on the face of it, it appeared not to have been enacted in accordance with the common law, would it be possible for an enactment to be declared invalid on the ground that it had not been passed in accordance with some special *statutory* procedure? In other words, if Parliament were to pass an Act requiring that all money Bills had to receive a three-quarters majority of the House of Commons, would an Act that appeared on the face of it not to have received the required majority be valid? Or, to put the question another way, would the procedural requirement (often called a requirement of 'manner and form') serve to limit the legislative competence of Parliament? Of course, a simple prohibition such as 'No Act imposing tax shall be valid unless it secures a three-quarters majority of all the members of the House of Commons' would not constitute much of a limitation on the powers of Parliament, as there would be nothing to prevent Parliament from expressly[39] repealing the prohibition itself by a simple majority. However, if the Act imposing the manner and form requirement were phrased as follows: 'No Act imposing a tax, *nor any Act amending or repealing this Act*, shall be valid unless it secures a three-quarters majority of all the members of the House of Commons', the situation would be different. In that circumstance the manner and form requirement would be 'entrenched' in that it would itself be subject to the special legislative procedure which it imposed. Although there is no English case dealing with an entrenched procedural requirement (the South African cases are dealt with below), the Sri Lankan case of *Bribery Commissioner v Ranasinghe*,[40] in which the court declared invalid an Act which had been passed without receiving a two-thirds majority as required by the Constitution, is authority for the proposition that legislation passed in contravention of such a requirement is invalid,

[38] 77 ER 481 at 505.
[39] Whether the prohibition would be held to have been *impliedly* repealed if Parliament simply legislated in contravention of it (in our example, by passing a tax Act by a simple majority) has not been decided by the courts in England. The issue has, however, come before the South African courts and is dealt with at 143–6 below.
[40] [1965] AC 172.

and that manner and form requirements *do* constitute an effective limitation on the sovereignty of Parliament.[41]

IV THE SOUTH AFRICAN CONSTITUTIONAL CRISIS 1927–1957

The doctrine of parliamentary sovereignty has been dealt with at length in the context of the South Africa Act of 1909 because it was relevant to a series of important cases arising out of the Act. In terms of s 59 of the South Africa Act, Parliament had 'full power to make laws for the peace, order and good government of the Union'. These words were customarily used when a Constitution was enacted for a colony to indicate that its legislature had inherited the same supremacy enjoyed by the British Parliament. The sovereignty of the Union Parliament was qualified only to the extent that Britain retained the powers of reservation and disallowance, and the Union Parliament was subject to the Colonial Laws Validity Act of 1865.

As already noted,[42] attempts to have the colour-blind franchise of the Cape Province extended to other parts of the Union failed. The only concession made at the national convention, and incorporated in the South Africa Act, was that the Cape franchise should be 'entrenched': Parliament would be unable to change the franchise except by a two-thirds majority of the total number of members of the House of Assembly and Senate sitting unicamerally.[43] The relevant sections of the South Africa Act were s 35 and s 152, which provided as follows:

's 35: (1) Parliament may by law prescribe the qualifications which shall be necessary to entitle persons to vote at the election of members of the House of Assembly, but no such law shall disqualify any person in the province of Cape of Good Hope who, under the laws existing in the Colony of the Cape of Good Hope at the establishment of the Union is or may become capable of being registered as a voter from being so registered in the province of the Cape of Good Hope by reason of his race or colour only, unless the Bill be passed by both Houses of Parliament sitting together, and at the third reading be agreed to by not less than two-thirds of the total number of members of both Houses. A Bill so passed at such joint sitting shall be taken to have been duly passed by both Houses of Parliament.

(2) No person who at the passing of any such law is registered as a voter in any province shall be removed from the register by reason only of any disqualification based on race or colour.'

's 152: Parliament may by law repeal or alter any of the provisions of this Act: Provided that . . . no repeal or alteration of any of the provisions

---

[41] Although the Sri Lankan Parliament got its authority from a written constitution while the British Parliament gets its authority from the common law, we are still of the opinion that if Westminster changed the common law by enacting a 'manner and form' statute, there is no reason why a court should not reach the same decision as did the Privy Council in the Sri Lankan case and find that Parliament was bound by an Act prescribing a special legislative procedure.

[42] See 124 above.

[43] That is, sitting together as a single-chamber legislature.

contained in this section . . . or in sections thirty-five and one hundred and thirty-seven,[44] shall be valid unless the Bill embodying such repeal or alteration shall be passed by both Houses of Parliament sitting together, and at the third reading be agreed to by not less than two-thirds of the total number of members of both Houses. A Bill passed at such joint sitting shall be taken to have been duly passed by both Houses of Parliament.'

Did these sections constitute an effective limitation on the sovereignty of Parliament? Or, in other words, did the courts have the power to strike down Acts of Parliament? Before going any further, it is of paramount importance to note that in all that follows the word 'court' refers to the Supreme Court, and not to magistrates' courts. Magistrates' courts have no common-law powers (or 'inherent jurisdiction' as it is sometimes called)[45] and can exercise only those powers which have been specifically conferred on them by statute. The review powers of magistrates' courts are governed by s 110 of the Magistrates' Courts Act 32 of 1944. In terms of this section, the only review power conferred upon magistrates' courts is in respect of delegated legislation.[46] Magistrates' courts have therefore never been able to pronounce upon the validity of original legislation such as Acts of Parliament or provincial ordinances.

The first case in which the validity of an Act of Parliament was tested was *R v Ndobe*.[47] This was a criminal appeal which arose out of the refusal of the appellant to surrender title deeds to his land as required in terms of the Native Administration Act 38 of 1927. The appellant's contention was that the Act was 'ultra vires' s 35 of the South Africa Act in that the Native Administration Act empowered the Governor-General to require title deed holders to surrender their deeds and accept in their place title deeds subject to different conditions. As one of the grounds upon which the franchise was granted was the holding of quitrent land, the appellant contended that if a quitrent title deed was taken away and a communal title deed (which did not entitle the holder to the franchise) was substituted in its place, franchise rights would have been affected. The appellant therefore argued that Act 38 of 1927 ought to have been passed by means of the entrenched procedure, and that as it had not, it was invalid. Although the court rejected the argument that the Native Administration Act affected franchise rights, it also rejected the argument advanced by counsel for the Crown that it (the court) did not have the power to declare an Act of Parliament invalid. In the words of De Villiers CJ:[48]

[44] Which provided for the equality of the two official languages.
[45] See 198 below.
[46] The distinction between delegated and original legislation is discussed at 173 below. Note that s 110 also denies magistrates' courts the power to declare invalid proclamations by the State President, even though these are examples of delegated legislation.
[47] 1930 AD 484.
[48] At 496–7.

'Mr *Hoal* on behalf of the Crown contended that the Court cannot enquire whether Act 38 of 1927 was passed by both Houses sitting together in the manner provided in sec 35, as that is a matter of procedure which Parliament alone is competent to decide. This is a contention with which we cannot agree. Under sec 58 of the South Africa Act, each House of Parliament is free to prescribe its own rules with respect to the order and conduct of its business and proceedings. Into the due observance of such rules this Court is not competent to enquire. But whether an Act has been validly passed by Parliament is another matter. . . . If the Act . . . contained a clause offending against sec 35 the Court would have to assume that the clause was ultra vires, in the absence of some indication in the Act or proof aliunde that such clause was passed as contemplated in the section.'

Thus *R v Ndobe*[49] constituted a firm assertion by the Appellate Division that the entrenched sections of the South Africa Act gave it the power to declare invalid a purported Act of Parliament not passed in accordance with those sections.

The next important development was the enactment of the Statute of Westminster of 1931. This Act of the British Parliament provided, among other things, that the Colonial Laws Validity Act of 1865 would no longer apply to South Africa, and that the South African Parliament could legislate repugnantly to any existing or future enactment of the British Parliament. It also provided that Britain would no longer legislate for South Africa, except at the latter's request. In order to ensure that Britain could not effectively resume authority over the Union, the South African Parliament enacted the Statute of Westminster into South African law by means of the Status of the Union Act 69 of 1934.[50]

In 1936 Parliament passed the Representation of Natives Act 12 of 1936. This Act removed black voters in the Cape from the general voters' roll, and placed them on a separate voters' roll for the purpose of electing three white members to the House of Assembly and four white members to the Senate.[51] As they were on a separate roll, black voters would no longer have any effect on elections in white constituencies. Litigation ensued on the validity of the Act, and in the case of *Ndlwana v Hofmeyr NO*[52] the question was again posed as to whether the court had the power to inquire whether an Act had been passed according to the correct procedure. In answering this question in the negative, and declining to overturn the Act, Stratford ACJ provided no explanation other than the following:[53]

'On hearing the Appeal the court requested Mr *Buchanan* to deal with the preliminary question whether this Court had any power at the present time to pronounce upon the validity of an Act of Parliament duly promulgated and printed and published by the proper authority, in as

[49] Note 47.
[50] See n 29 above.
[51] This indirect representation of blacks was itself ultimately abolished by the Promotion of Bantu Self-Government Act 46 of 1959.
[52] 1937 AD 229.
[53] At 236–8.

much as Parliament is now, since the passing of the Statute of Westminster, the supreme and sovereign law making body in the Union. Parliament has moreover, in the Status Act of 1934, defined its own powers and declared them to be "sovereign". . . . Parliament's will . . . as expressed in an Act of Parliament cannot now in this country, as it cannot in England, be questioned by a Court of law whose function is to enforce that will not to question it. . . . It is obviously senseless to speak of an Act of a Sovereign law making body as ultra vires. There can be no exceeding of power when that power is limitless. Now . . . the question then is whether a Court of Law can declare that a Sovereign Parliament cannot validly pronounce its will unless it adopts a certain procedure—in this case a procedure impliedly indicated as usual in the South Africa Act? The answer is that Parliament, composed of its three constituent elements, can adopt any procedure it thinks fit; the procedure express or implied in the South Africa Act is so far as Courts of Law are concerned at the mercy of Parliament like everything else.'

The justification given by the court in support of its finding that it no longer enjoyed a testing right in terms of s 35 was hazy. It seems that the court assumed that because the Statute of Westminster empowered dominion Parliaments to legislate repugnantly to British statutes applicable to them, and because the South Africa Act was such a statute, it followed that the South African Parliament could legislate contrary to the provisions of the Act. While it is true that the South African Parliament could indeed pass an Act which was repugnant to an applicable British statute, this begs the question of what was an 'Act of the South African Parliament'. It is clear that before the South African Parliament could be said to have produced *any* Act that Act would have to conform to the 'rules of recognition'[54] for Acts of the South African Parliament found in the South Africa Act, but the court in *Ndlwana's*[55] case behaved almost as if the Statute of Westminster had *repealed* the South Africa Act! All the Statute of Westminster had done was to empower the South African Parliament to legislate on matters previously denied to it by the Colonial Laws Validity Act, but when it did so legislate it still had to conform with the rules contained in the South Africa Act, including the entrenched provisions. If it did not, then what it produced was not an Act.

To take an example, if the South Africa Act had contained a provision prohibiting the South African Parliament from passing legislation imposing a sales tax, the South African Parliament would have been able to legislate contrary to that prohibition after the enactment of the Statute of Westminster, because the latter Act gave the South African Parliament full legislative competence and removed all restrictions regarding the *substance* of any legislation that that Parliament might pass. But the Statute of Westminster had no effect on *procedural* restrictions contained in the South Africa Act, because these served as 'rules of recognition' which are always

[54] See above at 72 and 130.
[55] Note 52.

needed in order to discover whether what is before one is indeed legislation passed by Parliament. To say that the procedural restrictions were no longer of any force would have meant that there would no longer have been any means by which anyone (and not just the courts) could have identified what was and what was not an Act of Parliament, clearly an untenable situation.

Thirteen years later, and believing that because of the decision in *Ndlwana's* case the entrenched procedures were no longer binding, the National Party government introduced legislation to remove coloured voters from the common roll, and to put them on a separate roll to elect four white members of the House of Assembly. This legislation, the Separate Representation of Voters Act 46 of 1951 (the 'Voters Act') was passed bicamerally and by a simple majority in each House. At this point it is of importance to note that the correctness of the decision in *Ndlwana's* case was crucial to the government, as it lacked the necessary parliamentary support to secure the passage of legislation by a two-thirds majority of both Houses sitting unicamerally.

The validity of the Act was challenged by certain coloured voters who had been removed from the common voters' roll. The Act was upheld by the Cape Provincial Division, which considered itself bound by the Appellate Division decision in *Ndlwana's* case. On appeal, in the case of *Harris v Minister of the Interior*,[56] the Appellate Division overruled the decision in *Ndlwana's* case, holding that the entrenched provisions of the Union Constitution were still binding and that the court therefore did have the power to declare invalid any Act, such as the Voters Act, not passed in accordance with its provisions. What was the basis of the Appellate Division's decision? In delivering the judgment, with which all the other Judges of Appeal[57] concurred, Centlivres CJ examined what effect, if any, the Statute of Westminster had had on the entrenched provisions of the South Africa Act. His conclusion was that where, in s 2(2) of the Statute of Westminster, it is stated that Dominion legislation which was repugnant to Acts of the British Parliament would no longer be invalid on that ground, and that the legislature of a Dominion would have the power to repeal or amend any British Acts applicable to it, the phrase 'Parliament of a Dominion' had to be read subject to the provisions of that Dominion's Constitution. In the words of Centlivres CJ:[58]

> 'But there is nothing in that part of sub-sec (2) of sec 2 of the Statute of Westminster which I am now considering to justify the inference that there was any intention to repeal or modify the provisions of sec 152 of the South Africa Act. There is nothing to prevent the two provisions standing together. The words "Parliament of a Dominion" in the Statute of Westminster must, in my opinion, be read, in relation to the Union, in the

[56] 1952 (2) SA 428 (A).
[57] Greenberg, Schreiner, Van den Heever and Hoexter JJA.
[58] At 463A–E.

light of the South Africa Act. . . . In my opinion one is doing no violence to the language when one regards the word "Parliament" as meaning Parliament sitting either bicamerally or unicamerally in accordance with the requirements of the South Africa Act. . . . There is, in my opinion, no justification for reading the words "Parliament of a Dominion" in the Statute as meaning, in relation to the Union, Parliament functioning only bicamerally.'

Thus the Appellate Division arrived at the conclusion that the entrenched sections were still valid, and that the court did have a testing right, which it used to invalidate the Voters Act . The court's rejection of the theory (implicit in Stratford ACJ's judgment in *Ndlwana's* case) that the Statute of Westminster had nullified the entrenched provisions of the Constitution was based on similar arguments to those presented above: Whereas we approached the question on the basis that the Statute of Westminster did not change the 'rules of recognition' for an *Act* of Parliament, Centlivres CJ made the more fundamental point that the Statute had not changed what might be called the 'rules of recognition' for *Parliament itself*, it being true that in terms of the South Africa Act 'Parliament' meant one thing for ordinary legislation and another thing for legislation dealing with the franchise or the official languages. In deciding whether what was before the court was an 'Act of Parliament' it was still incumbent upon the court, even after the passing of the Statute of Westminster, to inquire whether 'Parliament' had functioned as that body was defined by the South Africa Act—in other words sitting bicamerally in the case of ordinary legislation, and sitting unicamerally and voting by a two-thirds majority in the situations outlined in the entrenched sections. If the body that had purported to pass an Act had not functioned as 'Parliament', then what it had produced could not be considered to be a valid 'Act of Parliament'.

Having been thwarted by the courts in its attempt to change the franchise, the government tried to override the authority of the courts. This it did by securing the passage of the High Court of Parliament Act 35 of 1952. The Act, which was passed by the normal bicameral procedure, purported to establish a body called the High Court of Parliament which would consist of every member of the House of Assembly and Senate. The Act conferred upon this body the power to review and set aside any past or future judgment of the Appellate Division in which that court had declared an Act of Parliament to be invalid. Applications for review of a decision could only be made by a government minister. The decision of the High Court of Parliament would be by majority vote. The High Court of Parliament was summoned, and in due course declared the Appellate Division's decision in *Harris v Minister of the Interior*[59] to be invalid, and upheld the validity of the Voters Act.

The validity of the High Court of Parliament Act was challenged by the same voters who had brought the *Harris* case. The Cape

[59] Note 56.

Provincial Division declared the Act invalid, and the Minister appealed to the Appellate Division in the case of *Minister of the Interior v Harris*.[60] All five Judges of Appeal[61] delivered separate judgments, but were unanimous in declaring the High Court of Parliament Act invalid on the ground that the 'High Court of Parliament' was not a true court of law but rather Parliament sitting under another name and purporting to do by a simple majority what Parliament could only do by a special majority. Centlivres CJ began by comparing the High Court of Parliament with other courts, and identified the following differences between them:[62]

   (i) No legal qualification was required for membership of the High Court.

  (ii) Members of the High Court sat in judgment over what they themselves had done in their capacity as Members of Parliament, thereby transgressing the rule that no man should be judge in his own cause (the nemo iudex in sua causa rule).

 (iii) Only a minister could bring an action before the High Court, whereas any litigant could approach the normal courts.

 (iv) Decisions by the High Court would be of a legislative rather than a judicial character. As an appeal could be brought to the High Court only by a government minister, and only in cases where a lower court had declared a statute to be invalid and the minister wanted it declared valid, if the High Court decided such a case and held the statute to be valid on the ground that s 152 was not binding on Parliament, the effect would be the same as if Parliament had repealed s 152. This would be because all other courts would be bound by the High Court's decision, and no litigant would ever be able to approach the High Court to have that decision overturned, given the rules mentioned in the previous sentence.

Centlivres CJ concluded[63] that:

> 'When, therefore, one looks at the substance of the matter, the so-called "High Court of Parliament" is not a Court of Law but simply Parliament functioning under another name. . . . In my view Parliament cannot by passing an Act giving itself the name of a Court of Law come to any decision which will have the effect of destroying the entrenched provisions of sec 152 of the Constitution.'

The differences between the High Court and normal courts of law also formed the basis of the judgments delivered by Greenberg JA and Van den Heever JA, the latter holding[64] that the effect of the High Court Act was that:

> 'Parliament as ordinarily constituted enacts that Parliament in joint session may change its venue and its name and by a bare majority of those

[60] 1952 (4) SA 769 (A).
[61] Centlivres CJ and Greenberg, Schreiner, Van den Heever and Hoexter JJA.
[62] At 728A–784C.
[63] At 784D–H.
[64] At 792H.

present (the Constitution requires a two-thirds majority of the total number of members of both Houses) and at one reading (the Constitution requires three) pass a declaratory Act as to the meaning of secs 35, 137 and 152 of the South Africa Act.'

The learned Judge of Appeal concluded[65] that

'... in Act 35 of 1952 [the High Court of Parliament Act] Parliament as ordinarily constituted purports to empower Parliament in joint session to ignore the checks limiting the powers of both. The measure is therefore invalid.'

Hoexter JA concentrated on the legislative quality of decisions by the High Court of Parliament (mentioned in (iv) above), and held[66] that

'the effect of the [High Court of Parliament] Act is to abolish the testing power of the Courts, and thereby the testing right of the citizen, in respect of any statute which the High Court has declared valid. There can be no doubt that the decisions of the High Court, being a Court superior to the Appellate Division of the Supreme Court, are binding on that Division. It follows that once the High Court has declared a particular statute valid, the validity of that statute can never be successfully assailed in the Supreme Court. That would not matter if the citizen still had the right to test the validity of that statute in the High Court. But that is the very right which is denied to him by the Act, because the citizen has no right of appeal to the High Court against a judgment of the Appellate Division declaring a statute valid. In the result the Act has abolished the testing right of the citizen in respect of every statute which has been declared valid by the High Court.'

The conclusion reached by Hoexter JA[67] was that

'the High Court of Parliament Act authorizes Parliament to do unicamerally [that is, to repeal s 152] by a bare majority what sec 152 of the South Africa Act says it may do unicamerally only by a two-thirds majority'.

Schreiner JA declared the High Court of Parliament Act invalid on somewhat broader grounds than those referred to by his brother Judges. He found that the Act was invalid not so much because the Court it established differed radically in nature from normal courts, but because any Act which in any way disturbed the protection of entrenched rights provided by the judicial system as it existed at the time s 152 was framed would have the effect of infringing s 152 if it was not passed in accordance with the provisions of that section.

To summarise, the Appellate Division declared the High Court Act invalid on the ground that the High Court was simply Parliament sitting under another name, purporting to make a judicial decision which in reality amounted to an impermissible repeal of s 152 by a simple majority.

The government's final, and ultimately successful, attempt to amend the franchise took place in two stages. The first was the passage of the Senate Act 53 of 1955. This Act (passed by the normal

[65] At 793D.
[66] At 794H–795B.
[67] At 797B.

bicameral procedure) amended the South Africa Act so as to change the composition of the Senate. The number of Senators nominated by the Governor-General[68] was increased from 8 to 16; and the number of elected Senators was changed from an equal number for each province to a number which was in proportion to the number of members sent to Parliament by that province plus the number of councillors on its Provincial Council (a provision that favoured the Transvaal). Furthermore, while each province's Senators would still be elected by its members of Parliament and members of its Provincial Council sitting as an electoral college, voting would no longer be by proportional representation but by simple majority, which meant that the majority party in each province could appoint all the Senators for that province. The practical result was that the old Senate of 48 members which had consisted of 29 government and 19 opposition supporters, was replaced by a new Senate with 89 members, of whom 77 supported the government and 12 the opposition! This dramatic change in the balance of power in Parliament meant that the government was able to muster a two-thirds majority at a joint sitting, and it soon used its new-found strength to pass the South Africa Act Amendment Act 9 of 1956 by the entrenched procedure. This Act repealed the entrenched voting rights in s 35 of the Constitution, amended s 152 so as to make it applicable only to amendments of s 137, and validated the Voters Act. Furthermore, s 2 of the Act declared that:

> 'No court of law shall be competent to inquire into or to pronounce upon the validity of any law passed by Parliament other than a law which alters or repeals or purports to alter or repeal the provisions of section one hundred and thirty-seven or one hundred and fifty-two of the South Africa Act, 1909.'

The purpose of this declaratory section seems to have been to eliminate once and for all the right of the courts to test whether Acts of Parliament had been passed in accordance with the correct procedure.[69]

The validity of the Senate Act and the South Africa Act Amendment Act was challenged by a coloured voter who, having been unsuccessful before the Cape Provincial Division, took the matter on appeal in *Collins v Minister of the Interior*.[70] The basis of the appellant's case was that although in *form* the Senate Act merely provided for the re-organisation of the upper House and could therefore validly be passed by the ordinary procedure, and although the Amendment Act had amended s 35 and s 152 in accordance with the entrenched procedure, in *substance* the two measures together

---

[68] By convention on the advice of the cabinet.

[69] It is doubtful whether it is in fact possible to do this. See the discussion on the effectiveness of s 59(2) of the 1961 Constitution (which in essence re-enacted s 2 of the South Africa Act Amendment Act) at 143–6 below.

[70] 1957 (1) SA 552 (A). For an analysis of this case, see C R M Dlamini (1988) 105 *SALJ* 470.

constituted a single legislative scheme, the purpose and effect of which was to amend sections 35 and 152 by Parliament sitting bicamerally. The case was heard by a full bench[71] of the Appellate Division, and by a margin of 10 to 1 the two Acts were declared valid. In giving one of the majority judgments,[72] Centlivres JA held that the motive behind the Acts was not something into which the court could enquire, and that as each Act had been passed in accordance with the procedures prescribed by the Constitution, they had to be accepted as being valid. As s 152 did not subject to the entrenched procedure constitutional amendments pertaining to the composition of the Senate there was, according to the Chief Justice, no reason to hold that the new Senate was not a real 'Senate' within the meaning of the South Africa Act. The sole dissenting voice was that of Schreiner JA who found the Acts to be invalid on the ground that the Senate established by the Senate Act was not a 'House of Parliament' as contemplated in s 152 of the Constitution. The reason for his finding was[73] that 'the parts of a scheme take their character from the whole', and that where a person takes steps A and B (which are by themselves entirely legal) in order to achieve object C (which is not legal), then steps A and B themselves become illegal because of the unlawful purpose for which they were executed. Although (as Schreiner JA conceded)[74] it would in normal circumstances have been perfectly legal for Parliament to reconstitute the Senate, and for that Senate to participate in a repeal of s 35 and s 152, the reconstitution of the Senate by the Senate Act was not legal because it and the enactment of the Amendment Act were done with the purpose of destroying the protection afforded to the franchise by the entrenched sections at a time when the government lacked the necessary two-thirds majority. According to Schreiner JA where s 152 empowered both Houses of Parliament sitting unicamerally to repeal the entrenched sections, the term 'Houses of Parliament' could not include a Senate constituted with the specific purpose of artificially creating the majority needed to repeal those sections, and that therefore the new Senate was not a 'House of Parliament' within the meaning of s 152. Whether Schreiner JA was correct has long been debated,[75] and this issue remains a moot point.

---

[71] In terms of the Appellate Division Quorum Act 27 of 1955, eleven Judges of Appeal were to sit in cases wherein the validity of an Act of Parliament was in question. This legislation made it necessary to appoint several new judges of appeal, which led to accusations that the government had engaged in 'court packing'. But even if 'court packing' did take place, it turned out to be unnecessary as the decision in *Collins's* case was by a 10–1 margin, with Judges of Appeal who had found against the government in the *Harris* cases finding in its favour in this instance.

[72] Centlivres JA's judgment was concurred in by eight of his brothers. Steyn JA gave a separate concurring judgment.

[73] At 574E.

[74] At 579H–580A.

[75] See Marinus Wiechers in Ellison Kahn (ed) *Fiat Iustitia—Essays in Memory of Oliver Deneys Schreiner* (1983) 383.

The dismissal of the appeal in the *Collins*[76] case marked the end of the constitutional crisis of the 1950s.[77] What conclusions about parliamentary sovereignty can be drawn from this crucial period in South African constitutional history? The first lesson, which is usually lost sight of on account of the fact that the courts lost the struggle with the legislature, is that the entrenchment of a procedural requirement *is* an effective means of restricting the sovereignty of Parliament. The reason why Parliament was ultimately able to destroy the entrenched franchise was not because entrenchment did not work, but because not enough of the Constitution was entrenched. Had the composition of the Houses of Parliament been entrenched it is doubtful whether s 35 would ever have been repealed. Once it is agreed that an entrenched procedural provision constitutes an effective restriction on the sovereignty of Parliament, it follows that such a provision could be used to make legislation on a particular topic virtually impossible. For example, an Act containing a Bill of Rights and providing that Parliament could neither legislate in contravention of the Bill of Rights nor repeal or amend it without the assent of every member of Parliament would for all intents and purposes be immutable. It is important to note that such a provision would *not* breach the common-law rule explained earlier in this chapter[78] that an earlier Parliament cannot bind a later one as to the subject-matter of legislation. An Act which stated that 'Parliament shall not be competent to repeal or legislate contrary to the provisions of the Bill of Rights contained in this Act' purports to place a restriction on the *subject-matter* upon which Parliament may legislate and would thus be invalid. However, an Act which stated that 'Parliament shall be competent to repeal, amend or legislate contrary to the Bill of Rights contained in this Act only with the assent of every member of Parliament' would simply regulate the *procedure* which Parliament had to adopt and would therefore be valid. The practical effect of these two provisions would be virtually the same, but it is important to understand why the one would be legally ineffective and the other effective in restricting the sovereignty of Parliament. The second lesson to be learned is how necessary it is that legislative power be restrained—the franchise legislation was but one part of the vast scheme of apartheid which resulted in the deprivation of so many of the rights that are inherent in the common law. Had South Africa had a well-entrenched Bill of

---

[76] Note 70.

[77] It is a matter of great irony that in terms of the Senate Act 53 of 1960, the Senate was again reconstituted, with the number of nominated senators being reduced, and the elected Senators once more being elected by means of proportional representation. The result of this was that the governing party surrendered its control over constitutional amendment, which it was by then politically safe to do, given that the government had achieved its objective of disfranchising the black and coloured population.

[78] See 127 above.

Rights nothing short of extra-constitutional action would have enabled this scheme to be implemented.

V SECTION 114 AND THE SOVEREIGNTY OF PARLIAMENT

All the cases decided during the constitutional crisis dealt with entrenched sections of the Constitution—that is with sections that not only subjected legislation on a particular topic to a special procedure but which also required that that special procedure be followed if they themselves were to be amended or repealed. The conclusion reached above was that entrenchment does constitute an effective means of restricting the sovereignty of Parliament. But what is the position where the section that imposes the special procedure (say a special majority) is not itself subject to that procedure? It is clear that in such a case Parliament could evade the special procedure by expressly repealing (by an ordinary majority) the section imposing it. But could Parliament *impliedly* repeal that section, simply by legislating in contravention of it? This is the question that was raised but not answered earlier,[79] and which can be rephrased in the form 'Does the doctrine of implied repeal[80] empower the legislature to repeal a procedural restraint by legislating in contravention of it rather than by going through the formality of expressly repealing it?'

This issue might not seem important in view of the fact that an unentrenched procedural provision can always be expressly repealed by a simple majority, but in the event of this formality not being complied with the validity of legislation not passed in accordance with the procedural provision might be called into question. This is what happened in the case of legislation passed in contravention of s 114 of the Republic of South Africa Constitution Act 32 of 1961,[81] the new Constitution enacted when South Africa became a Republic and which replaced the South Africa Act of 1909.

Section 114 provided as follows:

'Parliament shall not—
(a) alter the boundaries of any province, divide a province into two or more provinces, or form a new province out of provinces within the Republic, except on the petition of the provincial council of every province whose boundaries are affected thereby;
(b) abolish any provincial council or abridge the powers conferred on provincial councils under section *eighty-four*, except by petition to Parliament by the provincial council concerned.'

In terms of s 118 Parliament had full power to amend the Constitution by ordinary enactment, with the exception of s 108 (which guaranteed the equality of the two official languages) and

---

[79] See 131 n 39 above.
[80] Discussed at 129 above.
[81] For a discussion of the s 114 controversy see C W Schmidt (1962) 79 *SALJ* 315, L J Boulle (1978) 95 *SALJ* 583, J D van der Vyver (1980) 97 *SALJ* 363, and P Laubscher (1981) 98 *SALJ* 529.

s 118 itself. These two sections could be amended only by a two-thirds majority of the House of Assembly and Senate sitting unicamerally. Section 59(2) of the 1961 Constitution substantially re-enacted s 2 of the South Africa Act Amendment Act by providing that

> 'No court of law shall be competent to enquire into or pronounce upon the validity of any Act passed by Parliament, other than an Act which repeals or amends or purports to repeal or amend the provisions of section one hundred and eight or one hundred and eighteen.'

These sections were relevant to the case of *Nasopie (Edms) Bpk v Minister van Justisie (2)*,[82] in which Basson AJ considered an appeal by the liquor store owner against a decision depriving him of his liquor licence. The decision in the court a quo had been based on the argument that whereas in terms of s 87(1) of the Liquor Act 87 of 1977 the Minister of Justice could grant to the owner of a hotel in any magisterial district a licence to open an off-sales liquor premises in the same district, the Minister had not been entitled to grant a licence in the case in point because the hotel in respect of which the liquor licence was granted was in Bophuthatswana, whereas the off-sales premises were in Kuruman in the Cape Province. One of the grounds upon which the liquor store owner based his application for leave to appeal was the argument that the Black Homelands Constitution Act 21 of 1971 and the Status of Bophuthatswana Act 89 of 1977 (which had created the new state of Bophuthatswana) were invalid because no petition received from the provinces concerned before Parliament had excised Bophuthatswana from their territory, a process which had obviously involved changing provincial boundaries. The applicant therefore contended that the boundary which had had the effect of incorporating part of the old district of Kuruman (the part upon which his hotel stood) into Bophuthatswana did not legally exist, and thus that the hotel and the off-sales store were still in the same magisterial district. Although Basson J's decision to grant the applicant leave to appeal was based on other reasons, he reviewed academic writings on the subject[83] and ventured an obiter opinion that s 114 was not binding on Parliament, agreeing with those writers who held that as Parliament could expressly repeal s 114 there was no reason why it could not impliedly do so. But this argument fails to take account of the difference between procedural and non-procedural limitations on the competence of Parliament. While the latter can always be impliedly repealed in accordance with the doctrine leges posteriores priores contrarias abrogant,[84] the former cannot, because they constitute rules of recognition for an Act of Parliament, and anything passed by Parliament in contravention of them will not be an Act of Parliament and can therefore not impliedly

---

[82] 1979 (4) SA 438 (NC).
[83] At 445H–447H.
[84] Discussed at 129 above.

repeal the procedural provision. Thus, according to this argument, any enactment changing the boundaries of a province passed in contravention of s 114 would not be an Act of Parliament, because the definition of an 'Act of Parliament' (in the case of legislation dealing with the boundaries of provinces and the powers of Provincial Councils) was 'something that has been passed by both Houses of Parliament upon petition by the relevant Provincial Council'. The absence of a petition would mean that the enactment was not an Act of Parliament, and that it could not have had the effect of impliedly repealing s 114.

A further issue raised by the *Nasopie*[85] case was the effectiveness or otherwise of s 59(2) of the Constitution. Even if Parliament was bound by s 114, did s 59(2) not prevent the courts from declaring Parliament's enactment to be illegal? Although at first glance s 59(2) would seem to have ousted the courts' jurisdiction to test the validity of all Acts other than those amending or repealing s 108 or s 118, careful consideration of the wording of the section indicates that this is not the case: Although s 59(2) prohibited the courts from enquiring into the validity of 'any Act passed by Parliament', does logic not dictate that before the court could conclude that what was before it was something into the validity of which it might not enquire it had to be satisfied that what was before it *was* an Act of Parliament? The ineffectiveness of ouster clauses such as that contained in s 59(2) stems from the fact that only once the court has asked itself the question 'Is this an Act of Parliament?', and has satisfied itself that the answer is in the affirmative, will the ouster clause be of effect. If the enactment does not satisfy the rules of recognition for an Act of Parliament, then the ouster clause is of no relevance. The rules regarding the effectiveness of ouster clauses in administrative law are dealt with below,[86] but a single example suffices to illustrate the principle. In *Anisminic Ltd v Foreign Compensation Commissioner*,[87] where the court was faced with a statute which provided that no court should be competent to inquire into a 'determination' by the compensation commission, the court held that in order to discover whether its jurisdiction had been ousted it had first to discover whether what the commissioner had effected was a proper 'determination', and to do this it had to examine what the commission had done.

When the appeal in the *Nasopie* case was finally heard in the case of *Cowburn v Nasopie (Edms) Bpk*,[88] Van den Heever J held[89] (though without giving reasons) that s 114 was binding on Parliament and that s 59(2) did not preclude the courts from enquiring into the validity of enactments produced by Parliament. This finding lends

[85] Note 82.
[86] See 295–8 below.
[87] [1969] 2 AC 147.
[88] 1980 (2) SA 547 (NC).
[89] At 544H–555B.

support to the arguments advanced above, though unfortunately the case was decided on other grounds, and Van den Heever J's statements on s 114 were thus obiter. The last case in which this issue was discussed was *Mpangele v Botha (2)*,[90] in which De Kock J (with Vos J concurring) held that in his opinion any legislation enacted contrary to s 114 would impliedly repeal that section. For this reason the learned judge refused to grant an order restraining Parliament from passing legislation that would give independence to the Ciskei until the necessary petition had been received from the Cape Provincial Council. With respect there is nothing in this judgment which would lead us to abandon the view that Van den Heever J was correct in her findings on s 114 and s 59(2) and (for the reasons already advanced) that even if a procedural restraint is not entrenched it is still an effective limitation on the sovereignty of Parliament. In any event the s 114 controversy was soon made irrelevant by the Republic of South Africa Constitution Second Amendment Act 101 of 1981 which, with retrospective effect to 31 May 1961 (the date the Constitution came into effect), amended s 114 so as to make it applicable only to *inter-provincial* boundary changes and not to boundary changes brought about by the creation of new states.

VI THE SOVEREIGNTY OF PARLIAMENT IN TERMS OF THE 1983 CONSTITUTION

In terms of the Republic of South Africa Constitution Act 110 of 1983, Parliament enjoys supremacy in the same degree as it did in terms of the Constitutions of 1909 and 1961. This is apparent from s 30 of the Constitution, which provides that legislative power is vested in the State President and Parliament, which have

> 'full power to make laws for the peace, order and good government of the Republic . . .'.

Are any limitations placed on the competence of Parliament?[91] Special procedures govern amendments to the Constitution. While these are discussed in more detail in chapter 7 below,[92] some mention needs to be made of them here. In terms of s 99(2) any amendment or repeal of s 89 (which guarantees the equality of the two official languages) or of s 99(2) itself can be effected only by a two-thirds majority of each of the three houses of Parliament, while in terms of s 99(3) a large number of other sections can be repealed or amended by only a simple majority of each house, with no referral to the President's Council being allowed.[93] Parliament's adherence to

---

[90] 1982 (3) SA 638 (C).
[91] For a discussion of this see J D van der Vyver (1986) 103 *SALJ* 236.
[92] See 165 below.
[93] Normally, if there is disagreement among the three houses over general affairs legislation it is referred to the President's Council for a decision in terms of s 32(1). This procedure is discussed at 162 below.

these provisions (and indeed to all procedures contained in the Constitution) is secured by s 34(2) which provides as follows:

'(2)(*a*) Any division of the Supreme Court of South Africa shall, subject to the provisions of section 18, be competent to inquire into and pronounce upon the question as to whether the provisions of this Act were complied with in connection with any law which is expressed to be enacted by the State President and Parliament or by the State President and any House.

(*b*) Rules and orders of a House and joint rules and orders of the Houses shall not be regarded as provisions of this Act for the purposes of paragraph (*a*).'[94]

As is clear from the wording of s 34(2)(*a*), the framers of the Constitution intended that Parliament should be bound by all procedural restraints, whether entrenched or not, and to that extent the subsection represents a vindication of the views expressed by Van den Heever J in *Cowburn's*[95] case. The provisions of s 34 came under judicial scrutiny in *Savvas v Government of the Republic of South Africa*,[96] in which the applicant argued that the Regional Services Councils Act 109 of 1985 was invalid because it had been passed in a manner inconsistent with the provisions of s 99(3). Although finding that the Act had not in fact been passed in contravention of the Constitution,[97] Van der Walt J went further, and stated as a general proposition[98] that

'the Court has no jurisdiction to test the validity of an Act of Parliament by an assessment of its subject-matter and the possible effect it may have [on existing Acts]'.

With respect, this cannot be correct: By what means other than examining the subject-matter of an enactment, and its effect on existing legislation—and on the Constitution in particular—can a court determine whether that enactment is valid? For example, were an Act purporting to declare that Afrikaans was no longer an official language to be passed by a simple majority of all three houses, a court would have no means of testing its validity other than by noting its subject-matter and, because it dealt with the official languages, inquiring whether it had been passed in accordance with s 99(2). To say that the court was unable to engage in such inquiries would be to hold that it could not declare such an enactment invalid, and that

---

[94] The provisions of s 34(2)(*b*) are, strictly speaking, unnecessary in that in terms of the common law, the courts never had the power to enquire whether Parliament had adhered to its own internal rules of procedure. Perhaps the subsection was included to guard against the argument that Parliament's internal rules had become incorporated into the Constitution (and were thus justiciable in terms of s 34(2)(*a*)) by virtue of s 88, which states that existing constitutional and Parliamentary conventions continue to exist, and s 63 which delegates to the Houses of Parliament the power to make internal procedural rules.

[95] Note 88.

[96] 1988 (2) SA 327 (T).

[97] This aspect of the case is discussed at 161–2 below.

[98] At 333D–F and 333J–334A.

because the enactment had been passed in contravention of ss 89 and 99(2), it had presumably had the effect of impliedly repealing them! As noted above, the purpose of s 34 is to ensure adherence to the procedural requirements of the Constitution, and it is clear that that purpose would be frustrated were Parliament able impliedly to repeal the procedural restraints by legislating contrary to them. For a court to deny that it has the power to inquire into the effect one enactment has upon another would be to deprive s 34 of all force and effect.

Section 34(2) is stated to be subject to the provisions of s 18, which are as follows:

> '**18.** (1) Any division of the Supreme Court of South Africa shall be competent to inquire into and pronounce upon the question as to whether the provisions of section 17(2) were complied with in connection with a decision of the State President contemplated in those provisions.
>
> (2) Save as provided in subsection (1), no court of law shall be competent to inquire into or pronounce upon the validity of a decision on the State President that matters mentioned in the decision are own affairs of a population group, or are not own affairs of a population group, as the case may be.
>
> (3) . . . .'

This section is designed to exclude judicial review of the substance of the State President's decision on the question of whether a Bill deals with own or general affairs,[99] and to confine the courts' review powers to the issue of whether the State President has consulted the Speaker of Parliament and the chairmen of the various houses as he is required to do in terms of s 17(2). Whether this section is effective is a moot point, and depends on the rules governing the effectiveness of ouster clauses, discussed elsewhere in this book.[100] But, in our opinion, it is at least arguable that a court could use its common-law powers of administrative review[101] to inquire whether a 'decision' had in fact been taken by the State President. If the court's conclusion was that what the State President had done did not amount to a valid 'decision', then the ouster clause would be of no effect. Of course in such an instance everything would depend on the willingness of the court to accept this theory on ouster clauses, something which, unfortunately, not all courts are prepared to do—an example being the court in *Savvas's*[102] case, which held that it was precluded by s 18(2) from inquiring into the merits of such a decision by the State President. But in the absence of a decision by the Appellate Division the issue remains an open one.

VII SUMMARY

The dominant theme of South African constitutional history has been

---

[99] Own and general affairs are discussed at 158–60 below.

[100] See 295–8 below.

[101] The State President's classification of a Bill is an administrative rather than a legislative act, though it is part of the legislative process.

[102] Note 96.

the supremacy of Parliament. A brief summary of the most important rules regarding this doctrine is as follows:

1. Parliament is omnicompetent and can legislate on any subject-matter and in any terms it chooses. No court can declare an Act of Parliament to be invalid because of its subject-matter.
2. Parliament cannot pass an Act binding future Parliaments with regard to the subject-matter of legislation. Such a purported restriction could be expressly repealed by a subsequent Parliament or could be impliedly repealed simply by legislating in contravention of it. Sovereignty is thus said to reside in Parliament as a 'continuing institution'.
3. The legislative competence of Parliament can, however, be restricted by an enactment that prescribes a special procedure for legislation on a particular topic, and entrenchment of that provision effectively places it beyond the reach of Parliament unless Parliament adheres to the special procedure itself when amending or repealing it.
4. Even if unentrenched, a procedural restraint is still binding on Parliament and cannot be impliedly repealed by legislation passed in contravention of it.
5. If it were desired to enact a Bill of Rights that would effectively prevent Parliament from legislating contrary to its provisions this could be done by Parliament 'committing suicide' and being replaced by a new Parliament which was subordinate to a Constitution drafted by a constitutional convention. A less radical means of achieving this end would be for Parliament to enact an entrenched Bill of Rights requiring so large a majority to be amended (say the assent of all members of Parliament) as to make it immutable for all practical purposes.
6. Provisions which purport to oust the jurisdiction of the courts to enquire into the validity of legislation are of limited effectiveness.[103]

---

[103] See 295–8 below.

7 The 1983 Constitution

This chapter deals with the Republic of South Africa Constitution Act 110 of 1983. Before examining its provisions in detail, it is necessary to understand the events leading up to its enactment.[1]

I THE GENESIS OF THE 1983 CONSTITUTION

Why did South Africa obtain a new Constitution Act in 1983? The answer to this question is that the decision to implement a new Constitution was a political one, taken by the government in an attempt to increase its legitimacy and, it was hoped, to improve the political and economic climate of the country. The need for political reform was first mentioned by the Theron Commission, which was established to investigate the position of the coloured population. In its report, published in 1976, the commission recommended, first, that coloureds be given a direct say at all levels of government, secondly, that a committee of experts be appointed to investigate how to give effect to the first recommendation, and thirdly, that South Africa abandon the Westminster model of Constitution which, in the commissioners' opinion, was unsuited to South Africa's 'plural' society. This last recommendation became a fundamental principle from which the government would not deviate during the succeeding seven years of debate on a new Constitution: in the government's opinion, were South Africa to embark upon constitutional reform the 'one man, one vote' Westminster system would have to be abandoned.[2] Although the ostensible reason for this was that given the heterogeneous nature of South African society, the Westminster system would lead to minorities being dominated by majorities, the real reason was that the introduction of universal franchise for a common legislature would lead to the repeal of the legislative foundations[3] upon which apartheid, and thus white supremacy, rests. Thus although the government was willing to effect a degree of constitutional reform which would give some political rights to members of other races, this willingness was coupled with a refusal to deprive the white population of ultimate political control. It is therefore unsurprising that the government favoured a Constitution embodying a degree of power-sharing among racially

[1] The history of the 1983 Constitution is recounted in detail by L J Boulle *South Africa and the Consociational Option* (1984) 149–91.
[2] Writers differ on the degree to which the pre-1983 Constitution can be described as being of the Westminster type. Certainly vital elements of the Westminster model, such as universal franchise and the Rule of Law, were missing. Yet it is true to say that there were Westminster features of the new Constitution, and that some of these were omitted from the Constitution of 1983.
[3] Examples of such enactments are the Black Land Act 27 of 1913, the Population Registration Act 30 of 1950 and the Group Areas Act 36 of 1966.

defined communities, and opposed a broadening of the franchise to include other races in the existing majoritarian Westminster system.

In accordance with the Theron Commission's second recommendation, the government appointed a cabinet committee to devise a set of constitutional proposals, and these were presented for comment in 1977. Many features which appear in the 1983 Constitution can be traced back to the 1977 proposals. These include the tricameral legislature, with separate Parliaments for whites, coloureds and Indians[4] (each Parliament having its own Prime Minister and cabinet), an electoral college drawn from the three Parliaments to elect an executive State President, and a council of cabinets headed by the State President, which would draw its membership from members of the three parliamentary cabinets. The white, coloured and Indian Parliaments would have memberships in the ratio 4:2:1, which ratio was derived from the 1976 census. The racial composition of the electoral college would also be in accordance with this ratio, while the composition of the council of cabinets would come very close to it. Each Parliament would legislate for the community which elected it and in respect of matters which were of exclusive concern to that community. The council of cabinets would have executive authority in respect of matters of common concern to all three communities, and would initiate legislation on common affairs to be passed by all three houses. The council of cabinets would be assisted by an advisory presidential council elected by the three Parliaments. The 1977 draft was also similar to the final product of 1983 in that both documents were advertised as embodying consociationalism.[5] But while the 1977 Constitution (and subsequent drafts) did have some consociational characteristics, it is clear that the government used consociational language while omitting the substance of consociationalism, as will be made clear in the analysis of the final 1983 product below.[6]

The 1977 proposals were followed by a draft Bill, published in 1979, which was submitted for consideration to the Schlebusch Commission. In its interim report, issued in 1980, the commission endorsed the idea of moving away from the Westminster system, the creation of a tricameral legislature, and the abolition of the Senate— something that had been implicit in the 1977 proposals and the 1979 Bill. It further proposed that a nominated President's Council be established to advise the State President on various matters, and that a Vice-State President be elected to serve as chairman of the President's Council. The government moved quickly to implement these recommendations: the Senate was abolished,[7] care being taken

---

[4] Note that the 1977 proposals envisaged three separate and equal Parliaments, rather than a single tricameral Parliament as exists under the 1983 Constitution.

[5] Boulle op cit n 1 at 150–1.

[6] See 167–71 below.

[7] In terms of the Republic of South Africa Constitution Fifth Amendment Act 101 of 1980.

to pass legislation (by the prescribed unicameral procedure) to amend the entrenched provisions so as to permit them to be changed in future by the House of Assembly and President alone. Act 101 of 1980 also established the President's Council and the office of Vice-State President. The President could appoint any white, Indian, coloured or Chinese South African to the Council. The President's Council, which had sixty members,[8] was first convened in 1981. Although it could advise the State President on any matter, and was divided into several standing committees for this purpose, in practice the Council's most important function was to investigate the drafting of a new Constitution. Mr A L Schlebusch, who had headed the constitutional commission of 1979, was elected to the post of Vice-State President by the House of Assembly, and assumed the chairmanship of the President's Council.

The President's Council presented its first report on the Constitution in May 1982. The report endorsed the view of the government and the Schlebusch Commission that majoritarianism was not suitable for South Africa, and advocated a constitutional order which would combine 'consociational democracy' for non-blacks with a continuation of the policy of partition and independence for blacks. The President's Council did not justify this statement but, having made it, used it as the basis for its recommendations which mirrored the proposals made by the cabinet committee in 1977.

The government's response to the Council's first report was contained in the 'Bloemfontein guidelines'—a policy statement made by the Prime Minister at the federal congress of the National Party in Bloemfontein in June 1982. This statement influenced the Council's second report, issued in November 1982, which in turn formed the basis of the draft Republic of South Africa Constitution Bill, introduced into Parliament in May 1983. Most provisions of the Bill were not debated, thanks to a guillotine motion[9] which received the support of the governing party, and the Bill was passed in September. Approval by the white electorate was obtained in a referendum held in November 1983, and the Republic of South Africa Constitution Act 110 of 1983 came into force in September 1984.

Although the above may give the impression that the 1983 Constitution was the product of the recommendations of the various bodies commissioned to investigate South African constitutional affairs from 1977 to 1982, in reality the final draft, while incorporating features which were common to several of the earlier drafts, was not an exact copy of any one of them. In short, the government was eclectic in its drafting of the new Constitution, and the final document was as much a product of the immediate political objectives of the governing party as of the recommendations of the

---

[8] 43 whites, 12 coloureds, 4 Indians and 1 Chinese.
[9] That is, a motion put to Parliament that debate on a particular measure should end within a certain period of time.

various bodies which had considered proposals for a new Constitution over the preceding seven years.

II THE REPUBLIC OF SOUTH AFRICA CONSTITUTION ACT 110 OF 1983

The provisions of the 1983 Constitution are examined under eight separate headings.

A Franchise

Section 52 provides that every white, coloured and Indian over the age of 18 years who is a South African citizen, and not disqualified in terms of the Electoral Act 45 of 1979, may register as a voter for the House of Assembly, House of Representatives or House of Delegates respectively. In terms of s 53, a person wishing to stand for election to a particular house must be eligible to vote for candidates for that house, and must additionally have resided in South Africa for at least five years. Perhaps the most important feature of the franchise provisions is their denial of the franchise to black South Africans, something which had negative implications for the legitimacy of the new Constitution.

B Conventions

Section 88 preserves all constitutional and parliamentary conventions that were in existence before the Act came into force, except in so far as they are inconsistent with its provisions. It is not clear why it was felt necessary to include s 88: the conventions which existed before the new Constitution would have continued in existence even in the absence of this section, along with the common law of our Constitution. Moreover, it cannot be suggested that the effect of s 88 was to enact all constitutional conventions into law. Apart from conferring purely formal recognition on conventions, the function of s 88 therefore seems obscure.

Certain conventions were, however, enacted into law. The convention that the executive must enjoy the support of the legislature, which is fundamental to the doctrine of responsible government, has been enacted in s 21(2), which provides that a person appointed as chairman of a ministers' council must, at the time of his appointment, enjoy the support of the house of which he is a member. Similarly, the convention that the head of state must assent to Bills passed by the legislature is embodied in s 33(1), which obliges the State President to assent to legislation, unless he believes that it was not in accordance with the provisions of the Constitution. The convention that Parliament should be summoned at least once a year has been transformed into law by s 38(2), which requires that not more than thirteen months intervene between the commencement of one session and the commencement of the next.

It is to be expected that new conventions will develop around the 1983 Constitution.

C The State President and the executive

The State President has been given a prominent place in the executive branch in terms of the 1983 Constitution. This section will deal simultaneously with his office and with executive power in general.

The State President is elected by an electoral college of 88 members (s 7(1)), who are drawn from the three houses of Parliament in a ratio of 4:2:1 (50 from the House of Assembly, 25 from the House of Representatives, and 13 from the House of Delegates). As each house elects its delegates by simple majority vote, the majority party in the House of Assembly effectively decides who will be State President. Anyone who is qualified to become a member of one of the houses of Parliament is entitled to stand for election as State President (s 7(5)). This provision effectively excludes blacks from acceding to the office. The requirement contained in s 7(6) that a person elected to the office of State President must resign any public office in terms of which he receives remuneration, implies that a member of one of the houses who was elected as State President would have to resign his seat, as indeed happened when the first State President was elected in terms of the new Constitution. The State President may, however, sit and speak (but not vote) in any of the three houses of Parliament (s 65). Section 9(1) provides that the State President's term of office coincides with that of the Parliament. This section also provides that the State President is eligible for re-election.

A notable feature of the Constitution is the weakness of the controls to which the State President is subject. The only circumstances in which the Constitution requires the State President to vacate office are if he becomes ineligible in terms of s 7(5) to serve as a member of Parliament (s 9(2)), or if he is removed by the electoral college on grounds of misconduct or inability to perform his duties (s 9(3)). A possible way of forcing the State President to resign is for all three houses of Parliament to pass a motion of no confidence in the cabinet, or reject a money Bill relating to a general affairs department. In such circumstances, s 39(2)(*b*) gives the State President the option of resigning *or* of dissolving all three houses (in the latter case his term comes to an end in terms of s 9(1)). It is obvious from this that should the three houses of Parliament bring s 39(2)(*b*) into play, they expose themselves to the risk that the State President will not simply resign, but will take the option of dissolving Parliament and forcing its members to fight an election. It is therefore only in circumstances where the members of Parliament are confident of electoral support that they will be in a position to oust the State President by this means. Finally on the responsibility of the State President, it appears that although he has inherited many of the powers formerly enjoyed by the Prime Minister, he is not subject to the convention that the Prime Minister should resign if ousted as leader of the dominant party in the legislature.[10] The rationale for this is that the State President is appointed by the electoral college rather than by Parliament, but this reasoning is rather artificial given that the electoral college is controlled by the majority party in the House of Assembly, and that the State President will therefore be chosen on the basis that he is the person that that party wishes to appoint as State President. The political difficulties that arise when the State President is replaced as leader of the dominant party in the House of Assembly were vividly illustrated in 1989, when P W Botha refused to resign from the post of State President, even though he had been replaced as leader of the National Party by F W de Klerk. In such circumstances it is difficult to discover where ultimate political authority lies.

Executive power is conferred upon the State President by various provisions of the Constitution. The State President is head of state (s 6(1)), and commander-in-chief of the defence force (s 6(2)). Section 6(3) lists certain prerogatives which are exercisable by the State President, including those of conferring honours, entering into treaties, declaring peace and war, pardoning offenders and making appointments. Furthermore, s 6(4) contains a general provision that the State President shall also have all other prerogative powers which were exercised by his predecessor—in other words, the State President under the 1983 Constitution has inherited all the powers of the titular State President of the 1961 Constitution (although, as we shall see, the 'new' State President also wields many of the powers formerly exercised by the Prime Minister). The nature of the State President's prerogative powers was elucidated by the court in *Boesak v Minister of Home Affairs*,[11] where a distinction was drawn between the prerogative powers and those powers exercised by the State President in terms of s 19(1): While the latter are exercisable by the State President in consultation with the cabinet or on the advice of a ministers' council (depending on whether they relate to general or own affairs),[12] prerogative powers are not classifiable either as general or as own affairs, but are powers sui generis, most of which, by convention, are exercisable not by the State President personally, but by the appropriate government minister.[13] Thus, while s 19 regulates the exercise of those of the State President's powers which the pre-1983 titular State President never enjoyed,[14] the section does not apply to the prerogative powers which *were* exercised by the 'old' non-executive State President. These latter continue to be exercised

[10] An example of this occurred in Rhodesia in 1964, when Winston Field resigned after having lost the support of the caucus of the ruling party, and was replaced as Prime Minister by Ian Douglas Smith.

[11] 1987 (3) SA 665 (C).

[12] See 156 below.

[13] Not all prerogative powers are exercised by a government minister. Some, such as the power to address any of the houses of Parliament and the power to make appointments to the cabinet, are exercised by the State President himself.

[14] These powers were exercised by the Prime Minister.

in terms of the conventions which existed prior to the 1983 Constitution.[15]

Aside from the prerogative, the exercise of executive authority is governed by s 19 of the Constitution: In relation to the own affairs of any population group, executive authority vests in the State President acting 'on the advice of' the ministers' council in question (s 19(1)(*a*)), while executive authority in relation to general affairs vests in the State President acting 'in consultation with' the cabinet (s 19(1)(*b*)). The difference between the terms 'on the advice of' and 'in consultation with' is significant. Conventionally, where the head of the executive exercises a power 'on the advice of' a minister, it is understood that the effective power lies with the minister, and that the head of the executive acts in a purely formal capacity.[16] There is no question, in such circumstances, of power being wielded other than in accordance with the minister's advice. On the other hand, where the State President is required only to consult with the cabinet, it can be inferred that the real decision-making power lies with him, and he is under no obligation to comply with cabinet sentiments . The conclusion to be drawn is that in his relations with the ministers' councils, the State President plays a role similar to that which the titular State President played under the 1961 Constitution, but that in his relations with the cabinet, the State President wields real executive power, similar to that wielded by the Prime Minister under the old Constitution or, as is frequently pointed out, to that wielded by an executive President, as in the United States.

Section 19(2) provides that except where expressly stated or necessarily implied, any reference to the State President in the Constitution means the State President acting in terms of s 19(1) (that is, in consultation with the cabinet or on the advice of a ministers' council). Section 19(2) also enumerates certain sections which confer power on the State President but to which s 19(1) is *not* applicable — in other words, when the State President exercises power in terms of one of these sections, he does so at his own discretion. Two examples of such powers are the appointment of ministers (s 24) and assent to legislation (s 33). It must not be thought, however, that the exercise of power in terms of these sections is entirely unchecked: a person appointed as minister of a department of state for own affairs must, at the time of his appointment, enjoy the support of the relevant house of Parliament (s 24(3)(*b*)(ii)), and the State President may withhold assent to legislation only if satisfied that the Bill has not been dealt with in accordance with the Act (s 33(1)).

The power to summon and prorogue Parliament is conferred upon the State President by s 38(1). Section 66 further grants him the power to summon one house on its own. He may also call a joint sitting of all three houses if he so desires, and must do so where all

---

[15] See 176 below.
[16] See *Boesak v Minister of Home Affairs* 1987 (3) SA 665 (C) at 675I.

three houses request it (s 67(2)). The usefulness of a joint sitting is, however, limited, in view of s 67(5), which prohibits the adoption of any resolution at a joint sitting. The dissolution of Parliament is governed by s 39. Section 39(2)(*a*) gives the State President the power to dissolve Parliament (that is, all three houses) at any time he chooses, while s 39(2)(*b*) *obliges* him to dissolve Parliament *or* resign himself if all three houses pass a motion of no confidence in the cabinet, or reject a money Bill relating to a general affairs department. Section 39(3)(*a*) empowers the State President to dissolve any individual house that passes a motion of no confidence in the cabinet, rejects a general affairs money Bill or is boycotted in the manner contemplated by s 37(2). Section 39(3)(*b*) *compels* the State President to dissolve a house or reconstitute its ministers' council if it expresses lack of confidence in its ministers' council or rejects an own affairs money Bill.

One of the State President's most important functions is that of classifying Bills relating to own or general affairs. This is dealt with in a section of its own.[17]

Apart from the State President, who is undoubtedly the most important member of the executive branch, the other major executive institutions are the cabinet and the ministers' councils.

The cabinet consists of the State President, those ministers appointed by him to oversee government departments administering general affairs matters, ministers appointed without portfolio, and anyone else who is a member of a ministers' council and whom the State President chooses to appoint (s 20). The chief function of the cabinet is to control the administration of general affairs—that is anything that falls outside the scope of the relatively limited number of matters classified as own affairs.[18] It would, therefore, be true to say that most executive power in South Africa rests in the hands of the cabinet members. Persons appointed to the cabinet must become members of a house within twelve months (s 24(3)(*a*)), but there is no requirement that they must enjoy the support of that house. It is not even certain whether convention requires that they should enjoy such support. It is difficult to answer the questions of to whom individual cabinet members owe responsibility, and what role collective cabinet responsibility has to play in terms of the Constitution. Although the new Constitution is commonly said to have heralded the era of an executive presidency and to have marked the demise of the Westminster system of government, the Westminster institution of responsible government continues to exist, at least to some extent. For although those individuals whom the State President appoints to the cabinet need not enjoy the support of the houses to which they belong (indeed, there is nothing to prevent the appointment of members of opposition parties in the houses), the

[17] See 158–60 below.
[18] See n 23 below.

cabinet as a whole must retain the support of Parliament, for in terms of s 39(3)(*b*), if all three houses pass a motion of no confidence in the cabinet, then either the State President must resign (with his successor choosing a new cabinet), or Parliament must be dissolved (in which case the State President's term also comes to an end in terms of s 9(1)(*b*)). Thus it is true to say that members of the cabinet are to some degree responsible to Parliament.[19] On the other hand, the doctrine of collective cabinet responsibility enjoys only a limited scope of operation under the 1983 Constitution. This is, first, because it may be a multi-party cabinet, and secondly, because of problems that might arise where an individual who is a member of a ministers' council is appointed to the cabinet. The doctrine of collective responsibility would require such an individual to give his full support to the policies of both the cabinet and the ministers' council. If the cabinet adopted policies which were contrary to those of the ministers' council, his position would become politically untenable. This happened in the case of the Reverend Allan Hendrickse, who resigned from the cabinet in 1987 because of the conflict that existed between its policies and those of the ministers' council of the house of Representatives, of which he was chairman. Finally, as far as cabinet members are concerned, a member of the cabinet may sit and speak in any house, but may vote only in that house of which he is a member (s 65(1)).

The chief function of the ministers' councils is to administer the own affairs departments of the various population groups (s 21(1)), although some members of the ministers' councils may be appointed without portfolio. A person appointed to a ministers' council by the State President must not only be a member of the appropriate population group (in terms of s 21(1) as read with s 24(3)(*b*)(i)), but must also become a member of the appropriate house if he is not one already (s 24(3)(*a*)). Furthermore, s 24(3)(*b*)(ii) requires that any minister who holds a portfolio in respect of any department of State administering own affairs must, at the time of his appointment, have the support of a majority in the appropriate house. Similarly, s 21(2) provides that when the State President selects one of the members of a ministers' council to be chairman of the ministers' council, he must be of the opinion that the appointee has the support of the majority of the house in question. Thus the doctrine of responsible government remains a feature of the 1983 Constitution in so far as the ministers' councils are concerned.

D   Own and general affairs

The distinction between own and general affairs is of fundamental importance to the 1983 Constitution, and none of its institutions can

---

[19] The usefulness of the doctrine of cabinet responsibility is much diminished in South Africa, where ministers frequently refuse to answer questions regarding the activities of their departments on the ground that to disclose the required information would not be in the interests of state security.

be properly understood without reference to it. Section 14(1) defines own affairs as 'matters which specially or differentially affect a population group in relation to the maintenance of its identity, and the upholding and furtherance of its way of life, culture, traditions and customs'. Section 14(2) states that those matters listed in Schedule 1 of the Constitution are own affairs. These include health, social welfare, education, culture, community development and water supply. However, it is important to note that even those matters listed in Schedule 1 are, in some cases, stated to be own affairs 'subject to any general law' on such matters. For example, it is clear from the provisions of paragraph 6 of Schedule 1 that, although local government is an own affair, own affairs legislation on this matter may be overridden by general affairs legislation on local government. This tends to limit the effective scope of own affairs and, as noted by Van der Walt J in *Savvas v Government of the Republic of South Africa*,[20] to obscure the distinction between them and general affairs.[21] It should also be noted that the provisions of s 14(1) and (2) are both expressly made subject to s 16 which, as explained below, gives the State President the power to decide whether a particular matter is an own or a general affair. In other words, even a matter which is stated in terms of s 14(1) or Schedule 1 to be an own affair could effectively be 'reclassified' as a general affair by the State President. Thus both Schedule 1 and s 16 diminish the concept of own affairs by making it possible for general legislation to be passed on what are nominally own affairs matters.

In terms of s 15, all matters which are not own affairs of a population group in terms of s 14 are general affairs. It is interesting to note that item 11 of Schedule 1 specifically excludes the levying of taxes and the raising of loans from the ambit of own affairs, and that s 84 expressly classifies as a general affair the payment of any money from the state revenue fund. These two provisions serve to deny the three population groups control of their own financial resources— something which indicates how little autonomy they are intended to enjoy in terms of the tricameral system.

The State President plays an important role in the classification of issues as own or general affairs. Section 16(1)(a) provides that in the event of a dispute over the classification of an issue, the State President[22] shall decide whether the issue is an own or a general affair and, as stated above, it seems that the State President's discretion is wide enough for him to be able to classify an issue as a general affair even though it is mentioned in Schedule 1 as being an

[20] 1988 (2) SA 327 (T) at 330A–F.
[21] The overlap between s 14(1) and Schedule 1 also has implications for the legislative process. See 161–2 below.
[22] As s 16(2) provides that the question of whether an issue is an own or general affair is itself a general affair, this reference to the State President must, in terms of s 19(1)(b), be interpreted as the State President acting in consultation with the cabinet.

own affair. Section 17(1) provides that the State President may refer such an issue of classification to the President's Council for its advice. There is, however, nothing to suggest that that advice is binding on the State President.

As far as legislation is concerned, s 31(1) provides that only if a Bill is certified by the State President as concerning own affairs may it be dealt with by a single house.[23] Before making such a decision, the State President must consult with the Speaker of Parliament as a whole and with the chairmen of the three houses (s 17(2)). However, the term 'consult' indicates that the State President is under no obligation to pay heed to the advice he receives from such consultations. In terms of s 18(1) the Supreme Court is competent to inquire whether the procedure prescribed in s 17(2) has been adhered to. But non-compliance with the s 17(2) procedure is the only ground upon which a decision by the State President may be invalidated—s 18(2) excludes the competence of the courts to test the validity of the decision on any other ground. There is room to doubt the effectiveness of provisions designed to oust the jurisdiction of the courts,[24] but if s 18(2) does have this effect, it would mean that the courts are prohibited from inquiring into the merits of the State President's decision, and that for all intents and purposes his power in regard to the classification of Bills is unlimited. Although this conclusion was indeed reached in *Savvas's*[25] case, the subsection has yet to be interpreted by the Appellate Division.

E Legislative power

Legislative power vests in the State President and Parliament (s 30). In terms of s 37(1) Parliament consists of three houses—the House of Assembly (178 members), the House of Representatives (85 members) and the House of Delegates (45 members). Each house consists of directly elected members with a fixed number of legislators elected by the electorate of each province, members elected by the directly elected members on a proportional basis, and other members appointed by the State President. Thus, in terms of s 41, the House of Assembly consists of 166 directly elected members (56 from the Cape, 20 from Natal, 14 from the Orange Free State and 76 from the Transvaal), as well as 8 indirectly elected members and 4 appointed members. In terms of s 58(1) the same electoral college which elects the State President must elect a member of one of the houses as Speaker of Parliament. The Speaker is entitled to preside over any house, and s 60(1) provides that each house must elect a chairman from among its members; it is the chairmen who preside over their

---

[23] In practice, only a very small proportion of Bills are classified as own affairs legislation—of 221 Bills presented to Parliament in 1985 and 1986, only 24 were so classified.

[24] Ouster clauses are dealt with at 295–8 below. On s 18(2) see also 148 above and 166 below.

[25] Note 20, at 333D.

respective houses in the normal course of events. The person presiding over a house keeps order, and regulates debate.

The requirements for the enactment of legislation differ depending on whether the legislation deals with own or general affairs. Section 31(1) provides that a Bill certified by the State President as relating to the own affairs of a population group may be dealt with by one house acting alone. However, s 31(2) provides that if an own affairs Bill is amended in such a way as to change its provisions so that it becomes a general affairs matter, the State President may table a certificate to that effect in the house concerned, and the Bill may not be presented to him for assent unless the offending amendment has been removed, or has been altered so as to bring the Bill once more into the category of own affairs. Section 31(3) provides that a Bill passed in terms of s 31(1) or after alteration in terms of s 31(2) may then be sent to the State President for his assent, and must be accompanied by a certificate from the chairman of the relevant house stating that it has been passed in accordance with the provisions of s 31.

All legislation which has not been certified as relating to own affairs must be passed by Parliament as a whole (s 30). Although Parliament is defined in s 37(1) as consisting of three houses, the Constitution does make provision for the continued functioning of the legislature in the event of the inability of one or two of the houses to perform their functions. Where a house is unable to perform its functions because it fails to meet, or because it has insufficient members to form a quorum (which may occur if no one stands in elections for the house, if members resign, or if members boycott the house when it is in session), then Parliament shall consist of the house or houses that are able to perform its, or their, functions (s 37(2)). In other words, if two of the houses were unable to function because their proceedings were boycotted by the members, then the sole functioning house would constitute Parliament for all purposes, including that of passing general affairs legislation. However, a single house could not amend the Constitution—s 99(3) specifically provides that amendments must be passed by a majority of all the members of every house. The use of the term 'every house', rather than 'Parliament' suggests that s 37(2) is not applicable where constitutional amendments are concerned.

A problem arises from the fact that although a particular matter may fall into the category of own affairs in terms of s 14(1), that same subject may, in terms of Schedule 1, be classified as an own affair *subject to* any general legislation on that topic. In other words, Schedule 1 clearly contemplates the enactment of general legislation on subject-matter classified as own affairs by s 14(1). But, as we have just seen, different legislative procedures are used depending on whether the subject-matter of the legislation falls into the category of own or general affairs, and thus the overlap between s 14(1) and Schedule 1 means that according to Schedule 1 (but not according to s 14(1)) it is permissible to use general affairs procedures to legislate on subject-matter falling into the category of own affairs. Is such legislation valid? This question was answered in the affirmative by Van der Walt J in *Savvas's*[26] case on the ground that whenever a Bill is introduced into Parliament unaccompanied by a certificate from the State President that it is an own affairs Bill, it is deemed, in terms of s 18(3), to have been classified as a general affair by virtue of a decision of the State President. The Bill would therefore validly be dealt with in terms of general affairs procedures.

Given that general affairs legislation must, in the normal course of events, be passed by all three houses, it is possible that conflicts might arise among the three houses. What happens in the event of such conflicts? Section 32(1) defines the situations in which a conflict is said to exist. These are when one or two houses approve a Bill and the other(s) rejects or is deemed to have rejected it; where two houses pass different versions of a Bill and the other rejects or is deemed to have rejected it; where two of the houses adopt one version of a Bill and the third adopts another; or where all three houses adopt different versions of a Bill. Section 32(2) provides that a house is 'deemed to have rejected' a Bill if the Bill has already been dealt with by at least one of the other houses, the State President has called upon the house in question to deal with it by a certain date, and the house has failed to do so. This provision is designed to prevent a house from using delaying tactics to prevent the enactment of general affairs legislation. In the event of a conflict arising in any of the ways stipulated above, s 32(1) empowers the State President to refer the Bill, or the different versions thereof, to the President's Council, which will then decide whether the Bill, or which version thereof, should become law.[27] The State President is not *obliged* to refer legislation to the President's Council; furthermore, he may withdraw legislation from the Council at any time before it has made a decision. Legislation which is not referred to the Council or which is withdrawn from it simply lapses. Once the President's Council has made its decision on legislation referred to it, the legislation is deemed to have been passed by Parliament and can be presented to the State President for his assent (s 34(2)). Thus it is possible for general affairs legislation to be enacted into law having been passed by just one house and the President's Council. In such circumstances the State President and the President's Council effectively assume the status of the two houses that have failed to pass the legislation in question. This constitutes an unwarranted intrusion by the executive into the legislative function, and in our opinion causes a severe imbalance (in favour of the executive) in the distribution of power between the branches of government.

[26] Note 20.

[27] Examples of this are provided by the Internal Security Amendment Act 66 of 1986, the Free Settlement Areas Act 102 of 1988, and the 1989 appropriation Bill for the Department of Constitutional Affairs and Development, all of which failed to secure the assent of the three houses, but were assented to by the Council.

Both own and general affairs legislation must receive the assent of the State President to become law. Section 33 indicates that the giving of his assent by the State President is a purely formal act, and that he may refuse his assent only if satisfied that the legislation in question has not been dealt with in terms of the Constitution, or if he is of the opinion that an own affairs Bill has been amended in such a way as to take it out of the category of own affairs, and he sends it back to the house in question with a certificate to that effect.

As far as the passing of a Bill is concerned, the procedure for passing own affairs legislation is very similar to that which was used before the enactment of the 1983 Constitution.[28] The first stage is called the first reading. This involves a request to the house by the person introducing the Bill, usually a minister (but otherwise a private member in the case of a 'private member's Bill') that the house agree to consider the Bill. If this motion is successful, the members of the house vote (without any debate) on whether to pass the Bill for the first time. If it is passed, a date is set for the second reading. It is important to note that the text of the Bill is not orally 'read out' at the first or any other reading—at the first reading the members have a copy of the 'long title' of the Bill (wherein are stated the objectives it is meant to achieve), while at subsequent readings each member simply consults the printed copy of the Bill distributed to him. At the second reading a debate takes place on the general principles of the Bill. The house is then asked to decide whether the Bill should be read (that is, passed) for a second time, and, if the house votes in the affirmative, then the 'short title' of the Bill is formally read out. The next step is the 'committee stage', when the house converts into a 'committee of the whole house', and debates the Bill clause by clause. No debate on the general principles takes place, as this has already occurred during the second reading. Amendments on the details of the Bill can, however, be introduced during the committee stage, and if they are passed by the house in committee, they are deemed to have been approved by the house. At the end of the committee stage, the house reverts to its normal mode of operation and hears a report from the member who acted as chairman during the committee stage, in which he details the decisions which were made on the Bill. This is called the report stage. Finally, the house proceeds to the third reading. Little debate takes place at this stage, as all major amendments have been considered, although the house may agree to minor changes to the Bill. Once it has been passed for the third time, it is sent to the State President for assent.

The procedure for passing general affairs legislation is complicated by the fact that such legislation must receive the assent of all three houses. Space does not permit a full description of all aspects of the

[28] See Gretchen Carpenter *An Introduction to South African Constitutional Law* (1987) 248–52 for a full explanation of this procedure.

process.[29] However, the enactment of legislation has been simplified by the establishment of joint standing committees of the three houses. In terms of s 64, the joint rules and orders of the houses may provide for the creation of standing committees to deal with general affairs legislation. These committees may function even when Parliament is in recess. There is a standing committee for each general affairs portfolio, as well as several other standing committees dealing with such things as accounts, private members' motions and domestic parliamentary affairs. Each joint standing committee consists of the members of three standing select committees, one from each house. The Houses of Assembly, Representatives and Delegates have select committees of eleven, seven and five members respectively, and so each joint standing committee has twenty-three members. Each standing select committee is elected from its particular house, with political parties being represented on it in proportion to their numerical strength in the house. The select committees can function on their own as well as together. When they function together (that is, as a joint standing committee) decisions are made by concurrent majority. In other words, a majority within each of the three components of the joint committee acting separately must agree to a particular decision. There is thus no possibility of the members of the opposition parties in the three houses 'ganging up' against the joint committee members representing the majority party in the House of Assembly. The importance of the joint standing committees is that once a Bill has been presented to each house and has been formally read for the first time, it is automatically referred to the appropriate joint standing committee. The committee examines both the principle and the detail of the Bill and may amend it. It has been suggested that the framers of the Constitution hoped that committee meetings (which are not public) would provide an opportunity for the various houses to resolve their differences over legislation and achieve consensus *before* the second reading stage, thus avoiding contentious public debate and obviating the necessity to have recourse to the s 32 'conflict procedure'.[30] Passage of legislation through the houses after this would be a formality. Whether consensus is achieved by it or not, the standing committee reports back to the houses, and the Bill is read for the second time. How much debate and amendment occurs during this stage depends on how many issues were left resolved by the standing committee— the greater the degree of consensus achieved in committee, the less likely the Bill is to be amended by the houses, and the less likely it is that the houses will pass different versions of the Bill. If all three houses pass the same version of a Bill for a second time it is sent directly to the State President for signature—the traditional committee stage and third reading are dispensed with, unless at least two of

[29] Ibid 340–7.
[30] Boulle 201.

the houses pass motions that the Bill should be referred back to the joint standing committee, or to a committee of the whole house for further debate and possible amendment. If such a referral takes place, and the Bill is amended, then it must be passed for a third time by each house before being sent to the State President. If no amendments are passed, then the Bill is submitted to the State President without a third reading taking place. Money Bills are treated slightly differently from other legislation, but essentially in terms of the same procedure.

F Constitutional amendment

Special procedures govern constitutional amendment. Section 99(3) provides that all sections of any significance,[31] as well as s 99(3) itself, may be amended only by a majority of *all* the members of each of the three houses. Section 99(2) provides that s 89 (which confers equal status on the two official languages), and s 99(2) itself, may not be amended except by a two-thirds majority of all the members of each of the three houses. The use of the phrase 'has been agreed to in every house' in s 99(2) and (3) indicates that all three houses *must* function for constitutional amendment to take place—s 37(2), which makes provision for the passage of legislation where one or more houses are not functioning, is not applicable in such cases. Furthermore, s 99(4) provides that any constitutional amendment of s 99(2) or (3) or of s 99(4) itself must receive the assent of all three houses—the general affairs 'conflict procedure' prescribed by s 32 is also not applicable to Bills embodying constitutional amendments. Section 99(1) provides that those sections of the Constitution not covered by s 99(2) or (3) may be amended by means of the normal general affairs procedures (including those provided for in ss 32 and 37(2)).

G Validity of Acts

Section 32(2)(*a*) confers upon the Supreme Court the competence to inquire whether an Act of Parliament is formally valid—that is, whether it has been enacted in accordance with the procedures prescribed by the Constitution. This subsection is, however, subject to s 18(2), the purpose of which is to deny the Supreme Court the power to inquire into the validity of the State President's decision on the classification of any matter as being an own or general affair.[32] Furthermore, s 34(2)(*b*) excludes the internal rules and orders of the houses from the definition of procedures prescribed by the Constitution for the purposes of s 34(2)(*a*). However, it is gratifying to note that s 34(2)(*a*) has settled the dispute over whether the courts are entitled to inquire whether what is before them is an Act of Parliament in favour of the courts, and that the view of parliamentary

[31] See Carpenter op cit n 28 at 351–2.
[32] See 160 above.

sovereignty expressed by Van den Heever J in *Cowburn v Nasopie (Edms) Bpk*[33] has thereby been vindicated.

In *Savvas's*[34] case the question arose whether legislation passed in accordance with the general affairs procedure, but on subject-matter which fell into the category of own affairs, had had the effect of impliedly repealing s 99(3). The legislation in question had not been passed by a majority of the total number of members of each house, and it was argued that by using general affairs procedures to legislate on an own affairs matter, Parliament had legislated contrary to, and had thus impliedly repealed, s 14(1) which states what are own and general affairs. It was further argued that by impliedly repealing s 14(1) without securing a majority of the total number of members of each house, Parliament had purported to legislate contrary to (and thus impliedly repeal) s 99(3) which mandates such majorities if it is sought to repeal or amend s 14 or s 99(3) itself. The court found against the applicant, holding that the legislation in question had become a general affairs matter by virtue of a decision of the State President in terms of s 18(3),[35] and that it was therefore permissible to use the general affairs procedure. The court also stated that in terms of s 18(2) it was precluded from pronouncing upon the validity of the State President's decision regarding own and general affairs. Whether this is in fact the case is open to dispute.[36] But, with respect, we cannot agree with the court's finding[37] that in any event it lacked the competence to declare invalid Acts which, because of their subject-matter, had the purported effect of impliedly repealing s 99(3). If, for example, Parliament purported to pass an Act repealing s 14, and did so without obtaining a majority of all the members of each house, it is in our opinion beyond question that s 34(2)(*a*) would empower a court to inquire into the subject-matter of the Act, and to strike it down if it found that the Act had been passed in a manner inconsistent with s 99(3) and that if allowed to stand, the Act would have the effect of impliedly repealing s 99(3). To hold otherwise would be to confer validity on something which did not meet the definition of an 'Act of Parliament' in terms of the Constitution, and which the drafters of s 34(2)(*a*) intended the courts to strike down.

Finally, it should be noted that in terms of s 35 the official copies of an Act (one in English and one in Afrikaans) that are lodged with the Registrar of the Appellate Division constitute conclusive proof of the contents of the Act, and that in the event of a conflict between the English and Afrikaans versions, the version signed by the State President prevails. In practice the State President alternates in signing the English and Afrikaans versions of Acts.

---

[33] 1980 (2) SA 540 (NC). This case and the approach to the doctrine of parliamentary sovereignty taken in it are discussed at 145–6 above.
[34] Note 20.
[35] See 162 above.
[36] See 148, 160 above and 295–8 below.
[37] At 333E–F and 333J–334A.

H The President's Council

The composition of the President's Council is regulated by s 70(1). Of the 60 members, 35 are elected on a majority basis[38] by the members of the three houses of Parliament: 20 by the House of Assembly, 10 by the House of Representatives and 5 by the House of Delegates. The remaining 25 are nominated by the State President. Of these, 15 are appointed by him at his own discretion, while the remaining 10, although formally appointed by the State President, are in fact elected in terms of s 70(2) on a proportional basis by the members of the opposition parties in the three houses—6 by the House of Assembly, 3 by the House of Representatives, and 1 by the House of Delegates. One cannot be a member of the President's Council and of Parliament at the same time. Simple arithmetic shows that as the State President in practice appoints supporters of the majority party in the House of Assembly to 'his' 15 seats in the Council, that party effectively controls the council: 15 nominees of the State President plus 20 members elected on a majority basis by the Assembly making a total of 35 out of 60.

According to s 78(1), the function of the President's Council is to advise the State President on any matter which he refers to it, and on any other matter (excluding draft legislation) which it believes to be of public interest. But the Council's most important function is to advise the State President on legislative matters referred to it. In terms of s 17(1) the State President may refer to the Council the question of whether a Bill falls into the category of own or general affairs. The advice given by the Council is not binding on the State President. Of more significance is the power given to the Council by s 78(5) to decide whether a Bill (or which version thereof, if there is more than one) should be signed by the State President in the event of a conflict between the houses over general affairs legislation. It should, however, be noted that s 32(1), which gives the State President the option of referring a Bill to the Council, also empowers him to withdraw the Bill from the Council at any time before it has made a decision on it, in which case the legislation in question simply lapses.

III THE 1983 CONSTITUTION—AN EVALUATION

The 1983 Constitution has been advertised as heralding a new era in South African constitutional history in that it replaced a Westminster system with a consociational one. This claim can be challenged on two grounds. First, the pre-1983 Constitution was an imperfect example of the Westminster model. As has been pointed out,[39] certain characteristics which are fundamental to the Westminster system were missing from the South African Constitution: There was no universal franchise, the Constitution was not colour-blind, the

---

[38] In other words, by the dominant party in each house.
[39] Boulle at 17–18, 77, 98–9.

Rule of Law and the conventions associated therewith were not adhered to, the country was partitioned, constituency boundaries were distorted to give undue weight to the rural vote, and the legislature was unicameral from 1980 onwards. In short, before 1983, South Africa can be described as having had only a 'quasi-Westminster' Constitution. In the second place, the 1983 Constitution can by no means be said to be fully consociational, as many Westminster institutions survive. Thus the majoritarian electoral system has been retained, and little use is made of proportional representation. The ministers' councils operate as one-party majoritarian executives rather than as coalitions embracing all parties represented in their respective houses. Similarly the cabinet has never contained more than a couple of members who did not belong to the majority party in the House of Assembly.[40] In addition, some link continues to exist between the legislature and the head of the executive, as Parliament elects the electoral college which in turn elects the State President. The absence of a justiciable Bill of Rights is also characteristic of the Westminster system.

But aside from the presence of these Westminster features, the 1983 Constitution is not truly consociational simply because it incorporates few of the fundamental features of consociationalism. As has been stated elsewhere in this book,[41] there are four basic elements of consociationalism: (i) power-sharing (which includes the concept of 'grand coalition'), (ii) mutual veto, (iii) proportionality and (iv) segmental autonomy. To what extent has each of these elements been incorporated into the 1983 Constitution?

A Power-sharing

One of the most striking features of the 1983 Constitution is the dominant position of the majority party in the House of Assembly. It controls the composition of the electoral college, and hence has the decisive say in who is elected State President. Moreover, in the event of a boycott by either or both of the other houses, or in the event of a dispute between the houses over general affairs legislation, the will of the majority party in the House of Assembly is bound to prevail, given that it controls the composition of the President's Council, which is given the power to validate legislation in such circumstances. Thus it has happened that general affairs legislation which has received the assent only of the House of Assembly has become law, after being referred to the President's Council and receiving that body's assent.[42] There is thus no genuine sharing of power between the three houses, and the achievement of consensus between them is not a prerequisite for the passage of legislation. This stands in contrast to consociational theory, which places much emphasis on

---

[40] At date of publication there were no non-white members of the cabinet, and no members who were not members of the majority party in the House of Assembly.
[41] See 54 above.
[42] See the examples mentioned in n 27 above.

the use of consensus to solve political problems, and which also requires that legislation should be the product of compromise between all significant political interest groups, rather than the product of the will of that political or racial group which has secured dominance over the others. The dominance of the House of Assembly over the other houses of Parliament also means that there is, in effect, one site of political competition which is more important than any other. This too is incompatible with consociationalism, which seeks to diffuse power and authority among several sites of political competition, rather than to concentrate it in one decisive site.

As far as the executive is concerned, the consociational principle of power-sharing dictates that the cabinet should take the form of a 'grand coalition' of political interest groups. In other words, a consociational executive should contain representatives of all shades of political opinion, and every significant political interest group in society should take part in the decision-making process. In no way could the cabinet established by the 1983 Constitution be said to be a 'grand coalition'. The State President has a free hand in relation to whom to appoint to it, and although he might therefore appoint persons of diverse opinion, there is no requirement that he should do so—there are at the moment no non-white cabinet members.

The President's Council is to some extent a 'grand coalition' in that it contains representatives of all three houses, including members of opposition parties. However, the various political interest groups are not proportionately represented in the President's Council—the certainty that supporters of the majority party in the House of Assembly will be in the majority in the Council and the absence of a mutual veto make this 'grand coalition' a very unequal one.

B Mutual veto

In view of the fact that all general affairs legislation (with the sole exception of constitutional amendments) can be passed by just one house of Parliament assisted by the President's Council, it is evident that the concept of mutual veto (that is, that each politically significant group should have the right to veto executive or legislative actions which pose a threat to its essential interests) is accorded very little recognition by the 1983 Constitution. The possibility that one group can legislate for the whole population is clearly incompatible with this element of consociationalism, as is the absence of any veto over decisions taken by the cabinet. The only circumstance in which a veto is exercisable is when legislation is considered by a parliamentary joint committee—the rules of Parliament requiring that decisions be made by a concurrent majority of the three components of the committee.

C Proportionality

The only element of proportionality in the 1983 Constitution is the 4:2:1 ratio[43] used to determine the number of seats allocated to the legislative chamber of each population group. This ratio also determines the number of representatives each house of Parliament sends to parliamentary joint committees, the President's Council and the electoral college. However, it must be remembered that each house chooses its representatives by majority vote—in other words, the dominant party in each house chooses all the representatives of that house on the bodies[44] mentioned above. Elections to the three houses are conducted by the 'first past the post' method in single-member constituencies. The State President has a free hand in deciding whom to appoint to the cabinet, there being no requirement that the composition of the cabinet should reflect the electoral support of political parties. Nor is there any requirement that the 'spoils of government' be proportionately allocated to members of the various communities. The only concession to proportionality is contained in the provision that the representatives of opposition parties in the President's Council be chosen on a proportional basis so as to reflect the number of members they have in the respective houses.

D Segmental autonomy

Perhaps the only element of consociationalism to be incorporated into the 1983 Constitution to any significant degree is that of segmental autonomy, as each house can legislate on the own affairs matters of their respective communities. However, even this right of communal autonomy is subject to the State President's power to decide what is an own affair,[45] and also by the financial constraint imposed by s 84, which classifies as a general affair the payment of money from the state revenue fund.

Furthermore, there are fundamental reasons why the 1983 Constitution cannot be said to be consociational: Group identity is imposed on subordinate groups by the dominant white group,[46] something that is contrary to consociationalism, which is predicated upon the *voluntary* formation of groups by individuals. More important than this is the exclusion of the majority of the population from participation in institutionalised political life—the denial of political rights being as incompatible with consociational democracy as it is with the Westminster system.

---

[43] This ratio reflected the relative sizes of the white, Indian and coloured populations as shown by the census of 1976.

[44] The only exception to this is in the case of the President's Council, where members of opposition parties are represented.

[45] A very small proportion of legislation is classified as pertaining to own affairs—see n 23.

[46] In terms of s 100 of the 1983 Constitution, which defines people in terms of the Population Registration Act 30 of 1950.

What conclusions can be drawn from the above? First it appears that the drafters of the Constitution were selective both in their elimination of Westminster institutions and in their adoption of consociational ones, as certain Westminster institutions were retained, while the elements of consociationalism were incorporated in only a very attenuated form. An analysis of how the features of each system were treated indicates that the desired political object of the drafters of the Constitution was to establish a system which embodied formal power-sharing between the white, coloured and Indian communities, but which would not deprive the white community of ultimate political control. Thus those elements of the Westminster system which served to maintain white control were retained, while those features of consociationalism which would have rendered the whites equal rather than dominant partners in the sharing of power were not incorporated. Coloureds and Indians were in reality to become junior partners in the continued exercise of power by whites and, it was hoped, would increase the legitimacy of the government by sharing not only its power but also *responsibility* for its actions.

The result was that South Africa obtained a Constitution which does not fit into any of the conventional categories which are used to classify Constitutions, but which is rather a 'hybrid' Constitution, incorporating elements of both the Westminster and consociational systems. It is unfortunate that the opportunity was not taken to enact a truly reformist Constitution in 1983, but as has been noted earlier, the government's programme of constitutional reform was at all times subordinate to the ruling party's determination to protect the political supremacy of the white population. For this reason, the inclusion of the black majority in the political process was never even contemplated, with the result that the new Constitution was denied legitimacy from the outset.

8 The Executive

In the previous chapter we discussed the supremacy of the legislature in South African constitutional history. The subject of this chapter is the executive, the branch of government that puts into force the laws made by Parliament and which also exercises some inherent powers of its own.

I THE ORIGIN AND SCOPE OF EXECUTIVE POWER

All members of the executive branch of government, from the State President down to the lowest official, exercise power which derives from either one of two sources—Parliament or the executive prerogative.[1]

A Delegated power

The power which derives from Parliament, called 'statutory' or 'delegated' power, is exercised by virtue of an authorisation contained in an Act. Such an authorisation derives from a provision empowering a member of the executive (usually but by no means always a cabinet minister) to make a decision. Thus, for example, s 28 of the Internal Security Act 74 of 1982 provides as follows:

'(1) Notwithstanding anything to the contrary in any law or the common law contained, the Minister may—. . . [here follow three circumstances in which the Minister may exercise his power] by a written notice signed by him and addressed to a member of the Prisons Service . . . who is in charge of a prison . . . direct that the said person be detained in that prison.'

Because the power is delegated, the common law provides that its exercise may be reviewed by the courts on the various grounds established in administrative law.[2] Statutes frequently attempt to exclude this common-law power of review. Thus, to take a further example from the Internal Security Act, while s 29(1) of the Act empowers any commissioned officer in the police of or above the rank of lieutenant-colonel to detain persons for interrogation, s 29(6) provides that

'no court of law shall have jurisdiction to pronounce upon the validity of any action taken in terms of this section, or to order the release of any person detained in terms of the provisions of this section'.

Whether such clauses purporting to oust the jurisdiction of the courts are effective is disputed, and is discussed elsewhere,[3] but where a court does hold such a clause to be effective it obviously has fatal

---

[1] Custom and estoppel are also sources of authority (see 11 above and 308–9) but are of limited importance for our purposes.
[2] See chapters 14 and 15 below.
[3] See 295–8 below.

consequences for the case of any party contending that the discretion delegated to the executive by Parliament was exercised unlawfully.

Apart from delegating the power to exercise a discretion, Parliament may even confer upon a member of the executive the power to make statute law in the form of regulations. Thus, in terms of s 3(1) of the Public Safety Act 3 of 1953, the State President may

'in any area in which the existence of a state of emergency has been declared under section *two*, and for as long as the proclamation declaring the existence of such emergency regulations remains in force, by proclamation in the *Gazette*, make such regulations as appear to him to be necessary or expedient for providing for the safety of the public. . . .'.

Such regulations are called 'subordinate' legislation in that they are invalid if they conflict with an Act of Parliament. They are also called 'delegated' legislation in that the authority (such as a government minister) making the legislation does not derive legislative power direct from the Constitution as does Parliament (which is thus said to enjoy 'original' legislative power) but rather derives the power from Parliament—in other words there is an intermediary (namely Parliament) between the authority making the delegated legislation and the Constitution. But notwithstanding their inferior status, regulations have the same force of law as do Acts of Parliament. This being the case, it is important to ask whether Parliament has any control over the executive in the latter's exercise of legislative power. The answer is that for the most part Parliamentary control is very weak. Although under the common law Parliament can by simple resolution annul any delegated legislation, in terms of s 17 of the Interpretation Act 33 of 1957 it is only required that a *list* of such enactments issued by the State President, a minister or a provincial Administrator should be tabled in Parliament within a certain time—the section does not require that copies of the actual *text* of the regulations be laid before the legislature. Nevertheless, some Acts do require that copies of regulations made in terms of them be laid before Parliament—for example, s 3(5) of the Public Safety Act requires that any regulation made in terms of s 3(1) must be tabled before Parliament. However, it is important to note that, as was held by M T Steyn J in *Bloem v State President of the RSA*,[4] failure to comply with s 17 of the Interpretation Act, or with a requirement such as that contained in s 3(5) of the Public Safety Act, does not invalidate the regulations concerned. Thus, the power of Parliament to annul delegated legislation is of little value, given that the sanction of invalidity does not attach to a failure to make Parliament aware of what delegated legislation has been created. The huge volume of delegated legislation that is produced every year makes it very difficult for MPs to keep abreast of it if it is not tabled. A far greater degree of control would exist if the enabling legislation provided that any subordinate legislation made in terms of it would not come into

[4] 1986 (4) SA 1064 (O) at 1091D.

effect until it had received the assent of Parliament, or that it would lapse unless it received that assent within a specified period, but unfortunately only a few statutes contain such provisions.[5]

A far more effective means of controlling the executive in its exercise of delegated legislative powers is through judicial review. For although delegated legislation has the same effect as an Act of Parliament, it differs in that *because* it is delegated it is subject to the testing power of the courts,[6] which may strike it down if it was enacted contrary to the statute delegating legislative power[7] *or if its contents are 'unreasonable'*.[8] Of course, as in the case of judicial review of administrative action, Parliament often attempts to oust the jurisdiction of the courts to inquire into the validity of delegated legislation. The ouster may be contained in the delegated legislation or in the enabling Act, but the ouster is obviously more effective in the latter instance, because if the ouster clause is put into the delegated legislation it could itself be declared invalid on grounds of unreasonableness.[9]

Before leaving the topic of delegated legislation it is necessary to clarify the status of provincial legislation, as this has changed since the coming into force of the Provincial Government Act 69 of 1986. Prior to this Act, Provincial Councils enjoyed original, not delegated, legislative power, in that like Parliament they obtained their authority direct from the Constitution;[10] it was not delegated to them by some other person or body who had received his or their power from Parliament. For this reason, ordinances produced by Provincial Councils had the same status as Acts of Parliament, and could *not* be reviewed on grounds of their subject-matter by the courts. However, ordinances differed from Acts of Parliament in the following respects:

(i)   in terms of s 89 of the Constitution, ordinances came into force only if approved by the State President, it being clear from that

---

[5] Section 48(6) of the Customs and Excise Act 91 of 1964 provides that regulations not assented to will lapse.

[6] Both the Supreme Court and the magistrates' courts enjoy this power, the only difference being that s 110 of the Magistrates' Courts Act 32 of 1944 prohibits magistrates' courts from pronouncing upon the validity of proclamations issued by the State President. See 133 above.

[7] In other words, if it was not enacted in accordance with the correct procedure, or if it was ultra vires in that it dealt with subject-matter on which the statute conferring legislative power did not intend the delegatee to legislate.

[8] 'Unreasonable' is here used in the broad sense in which it is used in administrative law. See 340–60 below.

[9] See 351–3 below.

[10] Power was conferred on the Provincial Councils by s 84 of the Republic of South Africa Constitution Act 32 of 1961. Most of the provisions of that Act were repealed by the Republic of South Africa Constitution Act 110 of 1983, which also gave the old Constitution a new title, that of the Provincial Government Act 32 of 1961. Finally, all remaining sections of the Provincial Government Act of 1961, with the exception of s 84, were repealed by the Provincial Government Act 69 of 1986, which conferred upon provincial Administrators the powers formerly exercised by the Provincial Councils in terms of s 84.

section that the State President was entitled to withhold his assent;

(ii) the Supreme Court[11] could declare ordinances invalid on grounds of ultra vires if they purported to deal with matters lying outside the limited list of subjects which were stated by s 84 of the Constitution to lie within the legislative competence of the Provincial Councils; and

(iii) although they were not classed as *delegated* legislation, ordinances were still examples of *subordinate* legislation, and thus in terms of s 85 of the Constitution, an ordinance would be of no force or effect to the extent that its provisions were repugnant to those of any Act of Parliament.

All this changed with the passing of the Provincial Government Act 69 of 1986, which abolished Provincial Councils and conferred on the Administrator of each province the legislative powers formerly entrusted to the Provincial Councils. In terms of s 14 of the Provincial Government Act, Administrators have the power to amend, replace or repeal any existing ordinance. Section 14 also confers upon Administrators the power to issue new provincial legislation, now called 'proclamations', subject to the proviso that such proclamations deal only with the subjects listed in s 84 of the old Provincial Government Act 32 of 1961.[12] What is most significant, however, is that when an Administrator performs a legislative function in terms of s 14 he does so as a member of the executive exercising delegated legislative authority, as he does not obtain his power direct from the Constitution but rather through delegation by Parliament. The position, therefore, is that while old provincial ordinances were subordinate but not delegated legislation, any new provincial legislation is both subordinate and delegated, and so while old provincial ordinances continue to enjoy immunity from judicial review, any proclamation issued in terms of s 14 (be it one amending or replacing an old ordinance or enacting new legislation) is subject to review by the Supreme Court and the magistrates' courts on both procedural *and* substantive grounds, just like any other delegated legislation produced by the executive.[13]

B Prerogative power[14]

Apart from those powers delegated to it by Parliament, the executive possesses 'inherent' power—that is, power which under the common law belongs to the executive simply because it is the executive, and which it does not receive from anyone else. This inherent power is usually referred to as the 'executive prerogative'.

[11] But not the magistrates' courts, see 133 above.
[12] The only surviving section of the Republic of South Africa Constitution Act 32 of 1961.
[13] This view is supported by Lourens M du Plessis and H J Erasmus (1988) 105 *SALJ* 763.
[14] Prerogative power is also discussed at 70 above and 175–82 below.

The prerogative has undoubtedly decreased in significance over past decades in view of the wide discretionary powers which Parliament has conferred on the executive by means of statute (the so-called 'statutory prerogative'). Nevertheless a number of important executive acts are still performed by virtue of prerogative powers. The most significant rule regarding the executive prerogative used to be that the manner of its exercise was not subject to judicial review, unlike power which had been delegated to the executive by Parliament. However, since the case of *Boesak v Minister of Home Affairs*,[15] this rule has been thrown into doubt. Before dealing with changes in the law, we must examine what prerogative powers are and the common-law rules regarding them that are still in force.

1   The origin and nature of prerogative power

It is clear that the prerogative powers enjoyed by the executive in South Africa are the same as those exercised by the British monarch: In terms of s 6(4) of the Republic of South Africa Constitution Act 110 of 1983 the State President inherited all prerogative powers enjoyed by his predecessor under the 1961 Constitution, and in terms of s 7(4) of that document (the Republic of South Africa Constitution Act 32 of 1961) the State President was stated as having

'such powers and functions as were immediately prior to the commencement of this Act possessed by the Queen by way of prerogative'.

It follows that the common-law rules governing crown prerogative in British law apply to the executive prerogative as it exists in South Africa.[16]

Prerogatives have traditionally been classified under three headings—as immunities, privileges and powers. Examples of these are as follows:

(a)   Immunities

The state is not bound by a statute unless the statute expressly provides that it is applicable to the state. Thus state property is exempt from rates and taxes, and in theory a vehicle driven by a member of the executive branch is not subject to the speed limit![17] In Britain the monarch is immune (in her personal capacity) from criminal or civil suit, although it is a moot point whether this aspect of the prerogative has been inherited by the State President as head of state.

---

[15] 1987 (3) SA 665 (C).
[16] A further reason for this is that English common law forms an important component of the common law of the South African Constitution, particularly in so far as relationships between the various organs of government are concerned.
[17] In *Cooper v Hawkins* [1904] 2 KB 164 it was held that a servant of the Crown who had exceeded the statutorily prescribed speed limit (of 2 miles per hour!) in an urban area while on government business could not be convicted of exceeding the speed limit. Subsequent road traffic legislation was expressly made binding on the Crown.

(b) Privileges

The most important example of privilege is that the state is preferred creditor and so, for example, claims made by the Receiver of Revenue must be satisfied before other creditors of an insolvent or deceased estate receive anything they are owed.

(c) Powers

These are by far the most important aspect of the prerogative. In Britain the powers of the monarch are extensive, and include the power to assent to legislation, dissolve Parliament, dismiss a government, appoint the Prime Minister and other ministers, stop prosecutions, bestow honours, pardon criminals and declare peace and war, to name the most important. However, by convention, almost all prerogative powers, with the exception of the conferral of a few honours, are exercised by the monarch only on the advice of someone else. Thus ministers are appointed on the advice of the Prime Minister, war is declared on the advice of the cabinet, prosecutions are declined on the advice of the Attorney-General, and criminals are pardoned on the advice of the Home Secretary. Similarly, the monarch conventionally does not refuse assent to legislation, does not dissolve Parliament unless requested to do so by the Prime Minister, and is bound to choose as Prime Minister whoever has the support of a majority of members of Parliament. Thus while the *formal* position is that the monarch enjoys wide prerogative powers, the power of the cabinet has increased at the expense of the monarch over the past three hundred years, and this has given rise to a convention that *real* decision-making power rests with the queen's ministers acting in her name.

The position in South Africa is a little more complex. In terms of the 1961 Constitution South Africa had a purely titular State President who, like the British monarch, enjoyed only a few real powers, and who usually exercised his prerogatives on the advice of the cabinet. But, as has been noted above,[18] South Africa now has a State President who wields real executive powers along with the purely formal ones attaching to the office of head of state. As was explained by Friedman J in *Boesak v Minister of Home Affairs*,[19] the manner in which a particular power is exercised depends on its nature: when acting in his executive capacity the State President exercises his power (with a few stated exceptions) in terms of s 19(1)—that is, on the advice of the relevant ministers' council in the case of own affairs, and in consultation with the cabinet in the case of general affairs. But, as was emphasised by Friedman J,[20] the prerogative powers mentioned in s 6(3) and (4) are not classifiable as either own or general affairs, and when the State President wields

---

[18] See 155–6 above.
[19] 1987 (3) SA 665 (C) at 674A–678B.
[20] At 677G.

them he does so in the 'figure-head' capacity he inherited from his predecessor under the 1961 Constitution. As has been mentioned above, most of these powers are exercised by the State President in name only, with the real power conventionally being wielded by a cabinet minister. A prime example of such a power is that of granting or withdrawing passports, which is nominally done by the State President but which is in fact done by the Minister of Home Affairs. Of course, not *all* prerogative powers are wielded by someone else on the State President's behalf—some (such as addressing Parliament or conferring honours) are, because of their nature, exercised by him personally.

2 Common-law rules governing the prerogative

Irrespective of whether a prerogative is exercised by the State President or by someone acting on his behalf, certain common-law rules (inherited from English law) are applicable:

(a) Existence and scope

The existence and scope of a prerogative is determined by the common law, and can therefore be tested by the courts as they discharge their function of expounding the common law. This was established by two cases decided in England in the early seventeenth century. In the *Case of Prohibitions*,[21] decided in 1607, King James I had claimed that it was part of his prerogative to hear law suits himself, and that he could therefore prohibit the courts from hearing a case until he had decided whether or not he should dispose of it himself. The great English jurist Coke CJ held that in terms of the common law, it was *not* part of the royal prerogative to dispense justice, and that the judiciary had the exclusive right to hear and determine all cases. In the *Case of Proclamations*,[22] decided in 1611, the King had purported to make a law forbidding the construction of new buildings in London and imposing penalties on anyone who did so. The court reaffirmed that the existence and scope of a prerogative (that is, whether something was a prerogative, and if so how far it extended) was determined by the common law, and that it was therefore up to the courts to interpret the common law and to decide whether a particular power claimed by the Crown was part of the prerogative. Furthermore, the court held that since the common law determined what was and what was not a prerogative, it followed that the prerogative was subordinate to the common law, and could therefore not be used for the purpose of changing the common law. The court thus held that the royal prerogative did not include the power to make law, and so the prohibition against construction of buildings was declared invalid.

[21] (1607) 12 Co Rep 63, 77 ER 1342.
[22] (1611) 12 Co Rep 74, 77 ER 1352.

(b) Common-law conditions

The prerogative may be subject to conditions or limitations in terms of the common law. The case of *Burmah Oil Co Ltd v Lord Advocate*[23] arose out of military action during World War II. In 1942 the British army blew up oil installations in Burma to prevent them falling into the hands of the Japanese. After the war, the government refused to compensate the Burmah Oil Co Ltd for the £31 million in damages they had suffered, arguing that Crown prerogative permitted the destruction of civilian property where this was necessary for the defence of the realm. The court, while agreeing that the prerogative did permit such destruction, held that where such destruction took place off the actual battlefield (as this had done) the common law imposed the condition that compensation be paid, and on this basis awarded the oil company damages.[24]

(c) Statutory conditions

In accordance with the doctrine of parliamentary sovereignty, the legislature can abolish a prerogative. However, should legislation be passed which, while not abolishing the prerogative, deals with an area of law governed by it, then the prerogative must in future be exercised in accordance with the rules laid down by the legislature rather than in accordance with the pre-existing common-law rules. This is well illustrated by the case of *Attorney-General v De Keyser's Royal Hotel Limited*.[25] During World War I the government had requisitioned the hotel for use by the army. After the war the government resisted a claim for compensation for the use of the hotel, claiming that it had acted in terms of common-law prerogative powers, and that under the common law no compensation was payable for the use of civilian property. The court did not decide the issue of whether the common law imposes a duty of compensation (in fact it does),[26] but decided the case on the basis that the Defence Act of 1842 governed the requisitioning of property by the armed forces, and because that statute required that compensation be paid, the government was liable. The court held that where a statute regulates the same subject-matter as the prerogative, the prerogative is in abeyance so long as the statute is in force, and the executive can no longer act in terms of the old common-law rules.

(d) Judicial review

As mentioned above, the most important common-law rule regarding the prerogative used to be that although the courts could inquire

---

[23] [1965] AC 75.

[24] An interesting sequel was that in order to avoid this claim and others like it, the government passed the War Damages Act 1965 which provided, with retroactive effect to World War II, that such damage was not compensable!

[25] [1920] AC 508.

[26] The British government had to pay a substantial amount in compensation to the owners of the ocean liners *Queen Elizabeth II* and *Canberra* used as troopships during the Falklands war in 1982.

into the existence and scope of a prerogative, they could not inquire into the manner of the exercise of prerogative powers—in other words, when the executive wielded such powers (as opposed to statutorily delegated powers) it could do as it pleased. There would, for example, be no remedy available to a person who could show that the withdrawal of his passport had been effected with an improper motive. Recent decisions in England and South Africa have changed the law in this regard. In *Council of Civil Service Unions & others v Minister for the Civil Service*[27] (the 'CCSU' case) the House of Lords heard a case in which the Minister (who was also the Prime Minister) had issued an order in terms of the executive prerogative that civil servants at the Government Communications Headquarters could henceforth not belong to a trade union. This order was issued without consultation and on the ground that to permit union activity at an installation that was responsible for handling secret military communications would endanger national security. The union sought to have the order struck down on review. A majority of the Law Lords deciding the case[28] held that in their opinion it was archaic to maintain that simply because a power wielded by the executive derived from the prerogative it should therefore be immune from judicial review. All executive powers, whether emanating from the common-law prerogative or from statute are, the Law Lords held, reviewable on the usual administrative-law grounds. The only reason why a particular prerogative might be exempt from this new general rule would be because it was of such a nature as to make review inappropriate. Examples of such prerogatives adduced by Lord Roskill[29] were the making of treaties, the defence of the realm, the prerogative of mercy, the granting of honours, the dissolution of Parliament and the appointment of ministers. These prerogatives are obviously of so 'political' a nature as to make review ridiculous—for example, one could not imagine any court entertaining an application by an aggrieved party who claimed to be entitled to a medal for heroism or to a place in the cabinet! In view of the above, the court held that the Prime Minister's order was reviewable and concluded that failure to consult with the union would normally have constituted a procedural impropriety invalidating the order. However, the court further held that in this case, considerations of national security entitled the executive to issue the order without prior consultation, as warning the union might have precipitated a strike, thereby endangering the handling of vital military communications.

The decision in the *CCSU* case was found to be persuasive in the South African case of *Boesak v Minister of Home Affairs*[30] in which the

---

[27] [1984] 3 All ER 935 (HL).
[28] See Lord Scarman at 948*j*, Lord Diplock at 950*g–j* and Lord Roskill at 956*b–*957*c*.
[29] At 956*d–e*.
[30] Note 19.

applicant sought to have overturned the withdrawal of his passport by the Minister of Home Affairs. In delivering judgment Friedman J noted[31] that while earlier decisions had declared prerogative powers to be exempt from judicial review, the *CCSU* decision had reversed this position, and in deciding the case before him chose to follow this line of reasoning, and so assumed[32] that the withdrawal of a passport was subject to review on the usual administrative-law grounds. Neither the Appellate Division nor any other division of the Supreme Court has yet pronounced upon the reviewability of actions taken in terms of the executive prerogative, but the judgment in *Boesak's* case gives one hope that South African courts will be receptive to this new development. There is after all no good reason why any executive act should be immune from judicial review solely on account of its origin—certainly an arbitrary rule which provides that a power is immune simply because it has its source in the common law rather than in a statute can find no justification. The most equitable rule in our opinion is the one adopted by Lord Roskill in the *CCSU* case: that all executive acts are subject to judicial review save for a few 'political' prerogatives which by their nature ought not to be reviewable. It is interesting to note that on this formulation most prerogative powers (except for Acts of State mentioned below) which are exercised by someone on the State President's behalf (or by him but on their advice) would be reviewable, whereas those few powers that the President exercises himself fall into the category of 'political' powers that would be immune from review. Examples of the latter would be the power to address Parliament, to confer honours, and to make cabinet and other appointments.

3 Acts of State

Mention must finally be made of the special rules that govern a particular class of prerogatives known as 'Acts of State'. Although some uncertainty exists regarding the precise nature of an 'Act of State', the clearest definition (and one which distinguishes Acts of State from other exercises of prerogative power) was that expressed by Dumbutshena CJ in *Patriotic Front-ZAPU v Minister of Justice, Legal and Parliamentary Affairs*[33] where it was held that

'"acts of State" are prerogative acts connected and concerned with external affairs or, more specifically, with foreign States and their subjects'.

LAWSA provides another useful definition,[34] stating that

'An act of the executive performed as a matter of policy in relation to another State or a subject of another State is termed an "act of State" '.

It is apparent, then, that the distinguishing feature of an Act of State is that it is an exercise of the executive prerogative *in the field of*

[31] At 680H–J.
[32] At 681E.
[33] 1986 (1) SA 532 (ZSC) at 539C.
[34] W A Joubert (ed) *The Law of South Africa* (1978) vol 5 para 44.

foreign affairs. Acts of State are treated differently from other prerogative acts in that the former are automatically immune from administrative-law review, and no damages will be awarded to a plaintiff who claims that he has suffered loss as a result of an Act of State. The rationale for these rules is that the expeditious conduct of foreign affairs would become almost impossible if the executive were fettered by the procedural requirements of administrative law, and would become prohibitively expensive if it were faced with claims for damages every time people suffered pecuniary loss as a result of changes brought about in relations with foreign countries. It is, however, important to note that the executive can raise the plea of Act of State as a defence to an action for damages only in cases where it has performed an act *against a foreign citizen resident outside its own territory* or *against a foreign country*. Four situations can be used as examples illustrating the operation of these rules. The first two demonstrate situations in which the defence of Act of State is available (because the state's actions are directed against a non-resident foreigner and against a foreign country respectively) while the second two exemplify instances in which the defence is unavailable (because the actions are directed against a resident alien and a citizen respectively).

(i) If a warship belonging to country X destroys a vessel belonging to a person who is neither a citizen of X nor resident inside the territory of X, then that foreigner could not claim damages in the courts of country X, and would instead have to rely on diplomatic remedies obtained for him by the country of which he is a citizen.

(ii) If the government of country X declares trade sanctions against country Y, a company (even if it is registered in country X) will not be able to claim damages for loss of profits from a contract concluded with someone in country Y.

(iii) If, however, the government of country X damages the property of a citizen of country Y who is resident in country X, the defence of Act of State would not avail, as a foreigner resident in a country is entitled to the same protection from that country's government as it affords to its own citizens.

(iv) If the government of country X performs an act against one of its own citizens the defence of Act of State would again not be available, irrespective of whether the citizen was resident at home (obviously) *or* abroad.

II STATE LIABILITY

One of the most important maxims governing the legal position of the British monarch was 'the King can do no wrong', in other words that no civil or criminal liability could attach to the monarch for anything he might do either as a private person or in his official capacity.[35] Although the personal immunity of the monarch (which she still enjoys) raised no legal problems, immunity for the official acts of the Crown had serious implications because it extended to *servants* of the Crown. The consequence of this was that no damages could be recovered from the state for any wrongful act performed by a public official acting in his capacity as such. This rule was incorporated into South African law along with the rest of the royal prerogative, and so in *Binda v Colonial Government*[36] the court held that the plaintiff could not recover damages from the government for the wrongful seizure of his cattle by one of its tax collectors. The obvious inequity of this situation led to the enactment in the Cape Colony of the Crown Liabilities Act 37 of 1888, and of similar legislation in all the other colonies by 1903. This legislation made the Crown liable for delicts committed by its servants when acting within the scope of their employment. State liability is now governed by the State Liability Act 20 of 1957, s 1 of which provides as follows:

> 'Any claim against the State which would, if that claim had arisen against a person, be the ground of an action in any competent court, shall be cognizable by such court, whether the claim arises out of any contract lawfully entered into on behalf of the State or out of any wrong committed by any servant of the State acting in his capacity and within the scope of his authority as such servant.'

The device employed by the colonial legislatures and the South African Parliament to make the state liable for the misdeeds of its servants was the delictual doctrine of 'vicarious liability'—that is liability by one person for a wrong committed by another. Although vicarious liability has been used by claimants against the state with a great deal of success, the fact that it originates in private law has meant that its adoption into public law has not been free from difficulty.[37]

The doctrine of vicarious liability was conceived as a means of giving recourse to third parties against an employer whose employee had committed a delict while about his master's business. Given that validity hinged upon the employer–employee relationship, it became crucial for a plaintiff to establish that the perpetrator of the delict was an employee, and that he was acting within the scope of his duties when he committed the delict. Failure to prove either of these two facts was (and still is) fatal to a delictual suit brought by the plaintiff against the employer. How have these requirements operated in the field of state liability? We will answer this question with particular reference to cases involving the police, as a large proportion of state liability cases arises out of delicts committed by them.

---

[35] The rationale for this rule is that it would be inappropriate to bring the monarch before her own courts.

[36] (1887) 5 SC 284 at 290.

[37] See Lawrence Baxter *Administrative Law* (1984) 622–32.

A The employer–employee relationship

The requirement that a plaintiff prove that the harm he has suffered was caused by a servant of the state has become easier to fulfil over the past decade or so, due primarily to enlightened court decisions. Whereas it used to be the case that a plaintiff had to prove that the defendant was exercising 'control' over, or at least had a 'right to control', the person who caused the harm, the position as laid down by the Appellate Division in *Smit v Workmen's Compensation Commissioner*[38] is that one must simply have regard to the 'dominant impression' given by the relationship between the employer and the causer of the harm. In deciding whether this 'dominant impression' indicates that an employer–employee relationship exists, the element of 'control' is just one of many factors that must be considered. Determining who is a servant of the state is a relatively simple matter in cases where the person concerned is in the full-time employment of the state, but difficulties arise where, for example, a person is employed by a parastatal—that is, an organisation which is not part of the 'government' but which is state-owned. So far as policemen are concerned the position as laid down in *Minister van Polisie v Gamble*[39] is that a policeman is prima facie acting in his capacity as a servant of the state, and so the state is liable for any delicts he commits, provided that it be shown that they were committed in the course and scope of his employment.

B Course and scope of employment

It is the second requirement (that the plaintiff prove that the person who caused the harm was acting within the scope of his employment)[40] that has given rise to the greatest difficulty. As was emphasised by Smuts AJA in *Minister of Police v Mbilini*,[41] it does not follow that because a policeman is prima facie a servant of the state, the state is liable for any delict that policemen might commit—an onus rests upon the plaintiff to prove that the act allegedly giving rise to liability was one which fell within the category of 'police work' and was not performed while the policeman was engaged on a 'frolic of his own'. What types of act have been held by the courts to fall within the scope of employment of policemen? In *Mhlongo v Minister of Police*[42] it was held that the use of a weapon in effecting an arrest fell within the scope of police work, and that the state was therefore liable to pay damages in compensation for the death of a bystander

[38] 1979 (1) SA 51 (A) at 62F–63B.
[39] 1979 (4) SA 759 (A) at 765H.
[40] As is pointed out by Baxter op cit n 37 above at 629, employers rarely 'authorise' the commission of delicts by their servants, and so the phrase 'within the scope of the servant's authority' is interpreted by the courts as meaning 'within the scope of the servant's employment'. This is true even in the case of the State Liability Act, which uses the words 'scope of his authority'—see *Minister van Polisie v Gamble* 1979 (4) SA 759 (A) at 765E–G.
[41] 1983 (3) SA 705 (A) at 710E–712A.
[42] 1978 (2) SA 551 (A).

killed by a policeman firing at a fleeing suspect. Damages were also recoverable in *Minister van Polisie v Gamble*[43] for the unlawful arrest and detention of a suspect by the police. Similarly, the state was held liable for assaults inflicted by policemen on suspects they had lawfully arrested (*Sibiya v Swart NO*,[44] *Bennet v Minister of Police*[45]), and upon a person being interrogated during a criminal investigation (*Dladla v Minister of Police*).[46] In *Minister of Police v Mbilini*[47] the court was even willing to affix liability to the state for an insult spoken to a person two days after she had been interrogated by the security police—the court held that the insult lay within the course and scope of the employment of the policemen involved because it was merely supplementary to a threat to detain the respondent which had been uttered during the preceding interrogation.

The courts have sometimes strained the 'course and scope' concept in order to give plaintiffs a remedy. In *African Guarantee and Indemnity Co Ltd v Minister of Justice*[48] the Appellate Division held that two constables who were engaged in a race with another vehicle while on duty in their patrol van had *not* departed from their duties to such an extent for it to be said that they were engaged in a frolic of their own! Although this decision may seem startling, it is not inconsistent with the trend made manifest by the most recent police case, that of *Minister of Police v Rabie*.[49] In an horrific train of events, an off-duty sergeant in the South African Police, named Van der Westhuizen, (who was employed as a mechanic, and whose job it was to repair police vehicles) assaulted an innocent passer-by early one morning first by hitting him with a spanner, and then by trapping his arms in a car window and driving the car down the street, dragging the respondent alongside it. Van der Westhuizen then arrested the respondent, and laid a false charge of attempted housebreaking against him, which resulted in his spending 16 days in prison before being released on bail and finally acquitted. In dismissing an appeal against the decision of the court a quo, which had awarded damages against the Minister of Police, Jansen JA held that although Van der Westhuizen had acted in pursuit of his private interests throughout the various stages of committing the delict against the respondent, he had ostensibly acted in his capacity as a policeman in that he had identified himself as a policeman to the respondent at the time of the assault, and had used his police powers to arrest and charge the respondent. In holding the Minister vicariously liable, the court applied the theory of 'risk liability', first

[43] 1979 (4) SA 749 (A).
[44] 1950 (4) SA 515 (A).
[45] 1980 (3) SA 24 (C).
[46] 1973 (2) SA 714 (W).
[47] 1983 (3) SA 705 (A).
[48] 1959 (2) SA 437 (A).
[49] 1986 (1) SA 117 (A).

mentioned by Watermeyer JA in *Feldman (Pty) Ltd v Mall*.[50]
According to this theory, where a master empowers a servant to
discharge certain functions the former must bear the risk (a risk that
he has created) that the servant might abuse those powers while
engaged in his own private affairs. Thus, although the court in
Minister of Police v Rabie[51] found that Van der Westhuizen had not
been engaged in police work at the time of the delict,[52] the state was
still liable because, in the words of Jansen JA,[53]

> 'By appointing van der Westhuizen as a member of the Force, and thus
> clothing him with all the powers involved, the State created the risk of
> harm to others, viz the risk that Van der Westhuizen could be
> untrustworthy and could abuse or misuse those powers for his purposes
> or otherwise, by way of unjustified arrest, excess of force constituting
> assault and unfounded prosecution. Van der Westhuizen's acts fall within
> this purview and in the light of the actual events it is evident that his
> appointment was conducive to the wrongs he committed.'

The courts have yet to define the parameters of 'risk liability', but it
appears that the doctrine will prove useful in affixing liability to the
state in those cases where the facts indicate that it would be equitable
to do so and yet where it is difficult to satisfy the 'course and scope'
requirement.

C Statutory requirements

In terms of s 32(1) of the Police Act 7 of 1958, any civil action against
the state arising out of anything done in terms of the Act must
commence within six months of the date upon which the cause of
action arose. The subsection further provides that a month's notice
must be given to the defendant (that is the state) before the action
commences. In practice this means that plaintiffs wishing to sue the
state for damages caused by members of the police force have only
five months within which to give notice that they intend bringing an
action, and only one month after that within which to commence
proceedings (that is to issue summons). The courts have made an
exception to this rule in the case of persons who are held in detention
and are prohibited from having access to their legal representatives.
In *Montsisi v Minister van Polisie*[54] it was held that in accordance with
the maxim lex non cogit ad impossibilia (the law does not compel
that which is impossible) the period mentioned in s 32(1) will not run
against a person who is, by virtue of the restrictions placed upon him
as a detainee, unable to give the required notice or commence
proceedings within the required time.

D Unsuitability of vicarious liability

Although enlightened court decisions in recent years have in practice

[50] 1945 AD 733 at 741.
[51] Note 49.
[52] At 134B.
[53] At 134J–135B.
[54] 1984 (1) SA 619 (A).

made it far easier for plaintiffs to recover damages from the state than it was only a decade ago, it must be noted that from a theoretical standpoint the doctrine of vicarious liability is not wholly satisfactory as a mechanism for dealing with state liability. Baxter[55] gives three reasons for this. In the first place the criterion of 'control', which remains one of the facts to be considered in deciding whether an employment relationship exists, is of no use in the case of public officials exercising a discretion in terms of statutory power. Indeed, if a superior interfered with an official in the latter's exercise of his discretion he would be doing something illegal. Second, as we have already seen, the term 'scope of authority' has to be read as 'scope of employment' in vicarious liability cases, as the state could never incur liability from the acts of an official who was acting within the 'scope of his authority' because his acts would always be lawful. Finally, when officials exercise statutory (as opposed to prerogative) powers they do not act as servants of the executive, *they are in fact the executive themselves*, exercising power delegated to them by the legislature.

A far more satisfactory basis upon which to found state liability would be for Parliament to enact a statute which stated simply that the public treasury would be liable for any claims arising out of any wrong committed by any person acting in the course and scope of any employment for which he is paid from the treasury. This formulation would eliminate the problems discussed in this paragraph, and would also leave the way clear for the courts to develop the 'risk liability' doctrine used in *Minister van Polisie v Rabie* to determine which acts fell within the 'course and scope' of the wrongdoer's employment.

III STATE CONTRACTS

The state frequently uses its power to enter into contracts as a means of implementing its policies, and of 'subcontracting' the implementation of its policies to the private sector.[56] The liability of the state for its contracts is therefore a matter of some importance.

Although s 1 of the State Liability Act 20 of 1957 makes the state liable for contracts entered into on its behalf, this is subject to the requirement that the contracts have been entered into 'lawfully'. The requirement of 'lawfulness' has a special meaning in the context of state contracts because, apart from the usual common-law rules of contract, contracts entered into by the state are void ab initio if they purport to fetter the state's discretion in the exercise of its powers or, if initially valid, they may be terminated by the state if some new power is conferred upon it, and the contract impedes the exercise of

[55] At 631–2.
[56] An example of this is the introduction of the system of toll roads, which enables private companies to purchase from the state the right to charge motorists for the use of certain roads which the companies have undertaken to maintain.

that power.[57] The reason for this rule (which applies in respect of both prerogative and statutory powers) is one of public policy— given that the executive is meant to wield its powers for the public good, it is impermissible for the state to commit itself in advance to exercise its powers in a particular way or not to exercise them at all. The clearest example of the operation of this rule is provided by the case of *Rederiaktiebolaget Amphitrite v R,*[58] in which a Swedish shipping company had obtained an undertaking from the British government during World War I that if they sent one of their ships to a British port carrying a stipulated cargo it would be allowed to leave once the cargo was off-loaded. However, the British government detained the ship, and the owners sued for damages for breach of contract. In dismissing the claim, Rowlatt J held as follows:[59]

> '. . . it is not competent for the Government to fetter its future executive action, which must necessarily be determined by the needs of the community when the question arises. It cannot by contract hamper its freedom of action in matters which concern the welfare of the State.'

Although there are very few South African cases dealing with this area of the law, the Appellate Division decision in *Fellner v Minister of Interior*[60] is relevant. In this case the appellant sought an order compelling the respondent to renew her passport. She based her case on the wording of the passport regulations which stated that passports were renewable upon payment of a fee. In rejecting the appeal Centlivres CJ held[61] that:

> '. . . the Crown cannot by contract fetter its future executive action. The granting of a renewal of a passport is, in my opinion, an executive act on the part of the Queen. Consequently even if the Crown had professed to fetter its future executive action by entering into a contract with the holder of a passport and agreed that the holder should have the right to require the Crown to renew his passport, such an agreement would not be binding on the Crown.'

An example involving statutory powers is provided by *Waterfalls Town Management Board v Minister of Housing.*[62] In this case the applicant sought, first, to restrain the Minister from building houses within a strip of land separating a white residential area from a black residential area and, secondly, an order compelling him to demolish any houses that had already been built in the area concerned. The applicant's case was based on a written agreement previously entered into by the Minister with the board that no such housing

---

[57] It should however be noted that where the state does terminate a contract, it may not in so doing encroach upon rights conferred upon the other party by *statute*. For example, where the state seeks to dismiss a servant, it must comply with the procedures prescribed in the relevant Act governing the conditions of service of public employees.

[58] [1921] 3 KB 500.

[59] At 503.

[60] 1954 (4) SA 523 (A).

[61] At 536D.

[62] 1957 (1) SA 336 (SR).

would be built. However the court dismissed the application, holding that as s 34 of the Land Apportionment Act 11 of 1941 conferred upon the government a discretion to use certain land (including the land in question) for the purpose of constructing houses for blacks, any agreement in terms of which the Minister purported to fetter the exercise of these discretionary administrative powers was not binding.

The inability of the state to bind itself contractually extends also to the doctrine of estoppel. This means that the courts will not hold the state to be bound to act or refrain from acting in a certain way because of representations it has made. So, for example, were a public official to give an assurance to an applicant for a licence that the licence would be granted, there would be no question of the licensing authority being obliged to exercise its discretion in favour of the applicant.

Although the above rules are well established in the law, it is obvious that their unqualified operation would make untenable the position of those entering into contracts with the state. The state enters into contracts for the supply of goods and services every day, and it would be absurd to suggest that agreements such as these are of no force and effect. The problem is how to distinguish between those contracts which do pose a threat to the free exercise of discretion and those which do not. Attempts to distinguish between 'commercial' and 'non-commercial' contracts have been unsuccessful, and so (unfortunately) it cannot be said that there is a class of purely 'commercial' contracts which are innocuous as far as administrative discretion is concerned. The best solution in our opinion is to recognise that in each case the test should be whether the contract would fetter administrative power in such a manner as would conflict with the very purpose for which the power has been conferred. In other words, as Baxter indicates,[63] the court will have to decide in each instance whether the agreement in fact *furthers* the purpose for which the power was conferred (as would be the case where, for example, the Minister of Education entered into a contract for the construction of schools), or whether it has the impermissible effect of prejudicing the common good by *depriving* the executive of the opportunity to exercise a discretion conferred on it (for example where the Minister of Education purported to agree with a particular community that its educational requirements will be given priority over those of all other communities). Admittedly this solution might be difficult to apply in particular cases, but no practical alternative presents itself.

The rule on estoppel is also not applied in all its rigour. In particular the courts have frequently interpreted an indication by a public authority of how it will exercise its discretion as an actual *decision* and not merely as a *representation*. In such circumstances

---

[63] At 422–3.

there is in fact need to have recourse to estoppel in order to compel the public authority to act in the manner it has indicated—the public authority is in fact held to have made the decision already and is thus functus officio. An example of this is *In re 56 Denton Road, Twickenham*[64] in which the owner of a house claimed compensation from the War Damage Commission for damage suffered during World War II. A preliminary determination of the damage had been that it was a 'total loss', but by a subsequent letter it was indicated to the claimant that her case had been reviewed and that if she agreed, the damage would be classified as 'not total loss' (the practical effect of which was that a greater sum would be paid in compensation). The plaintiff did agree to the proposal. Some months later another letter was sent, stating that it had been decided to revert to the preliminary determination of a 'total loss'. In finding for the claimant the court held that the indication made to her in the letter had in fact amounted to a *decision* by the War Damage Commission, and that it was therefore not open to them to revert to the preliminary determination.

There will, of course, be cases where contracts are declared void and where estoppel does fail to operate. If the contract is void from the outset or if, in cases of estoppel, the person has not yet acted on the representation to his or her detriment, no harm will have been caused. But in those cases where a contract is terminated after performance has begun (that is if it was not apparent at the outset that the contract was void, or a new power incompatible with the contract has been conferred upon the state), or where a representation has led a person to act to their detriment, financial loss would be suffered. South African law provides no remedy for those whose contracts are frustrated by the operation of law—all they are entitled to is the return of any performance they have already rendered, if that is possible.[65] Baxter's proposed solution (which he advocates in cases of both contract and estoppel)[66] is that courts should take notice of the *moral* obligation which, according to our common-law writers, rests on the state to pay compensation where its actions render unenforceable contractual rights that would otherwise avail against it. Were the courts, in pursuance of equity, to elevate this moral obligation to the status of a legal one, we believe that a satisfactory solution would have been found to the problems posed by the unenforceability of state contracts.

IV   THE EXECUTIVE IN SOUTH AFRICA

A   The structure of the executive

In chapter 7 we discussed the different branches into which the executive is divided in South Africa (that is the national cabinet and

---

[64] [1953] Ch 51.
[65] See for example *Bayley v Harwood* 1954 (3) SA 498 (A).
[66] At 423–4, 426.

Figure 1

EXECUTIVE AUTHORITY AND EXECUTIVE INSTITUTIONS FOR OWN AND GENERAL AFFAIRS

STATE PRESIDENT	
CABINET	
State President's Office Secretarial Services Advisory and Liaison Services Protocol and Legal Services Household Services	**MINISTER OF TRADE AND INDUSTRY** **Department of Trade and Industry** Industrial Affairs Strategic Supplies Affairs Trade Affairs
MINISTER OF TRANSPORT AFFAIRS **SA Transport Services** Railway and Road Transport Services Harbours and Pipelines Airways **Department of Transport** Road Transport Affairs Civil Aviation and Shipping Oil Pollution	**MINISTER OF JUSTICE** **Department of Justice** Legal Services Security Legislation Prisons
MINISTER OF CONSTITUTIONAL DEVELOPMENT **AND PLANNING** **Department of Constitutional Development and Planning** Physical Planning Constitutional Affairs General Local Government Affairs	**MINISTER OF AGRICULTURAL ECONOMICS** **AND OF WATER AFFAIRS** **Department of Agricultural Economics and Marketing** Agricultural Economics Advisory Services Agricultural Produce Quality Control Veterinary Services Soil Conservation **Department of Water Affairs** Water Conservation and Supply
MINISTER OF FOREIGN AFFAIRS **Department of Foreign Affairs** Diplomatic Services Information Services (Exterior) International Development Aid	**MINISTER OF MINERAL AND ENERGY AFFAIRS** **Department of Mineral and Energy Affairs** Mining Geological Survey Energy Affairs
MINISTER OF NATIONAL EDUCATION/Chairman: Ministers' **Council of the House of Assembly and Minister of the** **Budget Department of National Education** General Education Policy Language, Library and Archives Services Sport and General Cultural Affairs Science Planning	**MINISTER OF FINANCE** **Department of Finance** Inland Revenue Customs and Excise Public Finance Financial Control **Office of the Auditor General** Public Auditing
MINISTER OF LAW AND ORDER **SA Police** Police Affairs	**MINISTER OF ENVIRONMENT AFFAIRS AND TOURISM** **Department of Environment Affairs** Forestry Affairs Environment Conservation Marine Affairs Weather Services
MINISTER OF COMMUNICATIONS AND OF PUBLIC WORKS **Department of Posts and Telecommunications** Postal Services Telecommunication Services Savings Bank Services **Department of Public Works and Land Affairs** State Accommodation and Land Affairs Macro Housing Affairs Deeds Registration Survey and Mapping Services Government Printing Works	**MINISTER OF HOME AFFAIRS** **Department of Home Affairs** Civic Services Migration Affairs Media Control
MINISTER OF EDUCATION AND DEVELOPMENT AID **Department of Development Aid** Community Development Agriculture and Works Budgetary Affairs **Department of Education and Training** Education and Training	**MINISTER FOR ADMINISTRATION AND ECONOMIC** **ADVISORY SERVICES IN THE OFFICE OF** **THE STATE PRESIDENT** **Office of the Commission for Administration** Public Service Personnel Administration Management Systems Development Promotion of Efficiency Government Co-ordination Statistical Services
MINISTER OF DEFENCE **SA Defence Force** Defence Force Affairs **MINISTER OF MANPOWER** **Department of Manpower** Labour Affairs Unemployment Insurance Workmen's Compensation Industrial Training	**MINISTER OF NATIONAL HEALTH AND POPULATION** **DEVELOPMENT** **Department of National Health and Population Development** Disease Prevention Patient Care Civil and Military Pensions Social Welfare Co-ordination Social Planning
Chairman Ministers' Council of the House of Representatives	**DEPUTY MINISTER OF INFORMATION** **Bureau for Information** Information Services (Interior)
National Intelligence Service Intelligence Services Co-ordination of Security Information	**Chairman** Ministers' Council of the House of Delegates

(Reproduced from *State Departments of Southern Africa 1988*, Randburg: Dictum (1987), with the kind permission of Penrose Holdings Limited, Johannesburg.)

Figure 2
MINISTERS' COUNCILS

STATE PRESIDENT

MINISTERS' COUNCIL OF THE HOUSE OF ASSEMBLY	MINISTERS' COUNCIL OF THE HOUSE OF REPRESENTATIVES	MINISTERS' COUNCIL OF THE HOUSE OF DELEGATES
CHAIRMAN/MINISTER OF THE BUDGET **Administration: House of Assembly**	**CHAIRMAN** **Administration: House of Representatives**	**CHAIRMAN** **Administration: House of Delegates**
Department of Budgetary and Auxiliary Services Management Services Financial Administration Personnel Administration Civic Services Secretarial Services	**MINISTER OF THE BUDGET** **Department of Budgetary and Auxiliary Services** Management Services Financial Administration Personnel Administration Civic Services Secretarial Services	**Department of Budgetary and Auxiliary Services** Management Services Financial Administration Personnel Administration Civic Services Secretarial Services
MINISTER OF AGRICULTURE AND WATER SUPPLY **Department of Agriculture and Water Supply** Agricultural Services Water Supply Financial Assistance	**MINISTER OF EDUCATION AND CULTURE** **Department of Education and Culture** Education Promotion of Culture	**MINISTER OF LOCAL GOVERNMENT, HOUSING AND AGRICULTURE** **Department of Local Government, Housing and Works** Local Government Services Community Services Works Agriculture
MINISTER OF LOCAL GOVERNMENT, HOUSING AND WORKS **Department of Local Government, Housing and Works** Local Government Services Community Services Works	**MINISTER OF LOCAL GOVERNMENT, HOUSING AND AGRICULTURE** **Department of Local Government, Housing and Works** Local Government Services Community Services Works Agriculture	**MINISTER OF EDUCATION AND CULTURE** **Department of Education and Culture** Education Promotion of Culture
MINISTER OF HEALTH SERVICES AND WELFARE **Department of Health Services and Welfare** Health Services Social Welfare	**MINISTER OF HEALTH SERVICES AND WELFARE** **Department of Health Services** Health Services Social Welfare	**MINISTER OF HEALTH SERVICES AND WELFARE** **Department of Health Services and Welfare** Health Services Social Welfare
MINISTER OF EDUCATION AND CULTURE **Department of Education and Culture** Education Promotion of Culture		

(Reproduced from *State Departments of Southern Africa 1988*, Randburg: Dictum (1987), with the kind permission of Penrose Holdings Limited, Johannesburg.)

the three ministers' councils), and their interaction with each other and with the legislature. This section is concerned with how the executive is divided into administrative bodies (called ministries and departments) and who controls them.

Strictly speaking, a distinction ought to be drawn between the 'executive' and the 'administration', as the former refers to all the institutions and people which form the executive branch of government, while the latter refers to the executive branch of government minus the cabinet.[67] Thus although the cabinet and the administration together comprise the executive, the members of the cabinet *control* the administration in that they formulate the policy which is implemented by the civil servants who make up the latter. The structure of the national (that is 'general affairs') executive is represented by figure 1. Note that although all those cabinet members represented on the diagram are appointed 'with portfolio' that is, in charge of a government department, s 20 does empower the State President to appoint cabinet ministers 'without portfolio', in other words without being allocated the responsibility of running a department. Some ministers are assisted by deputy ministers. These deputies are not members of the cabinet. It should also be noted that some ministers are in charge of more than one department, and that departments are sometimes transferred from one minister to another with an appropriate change in the ministers' titles. There would therefore be nothing unusual in responsibility for the Department of Water Affairs being transferred from the Minister of Agricultural Economics and of Water Affairs to the Minister of Trade and Industry, the new title of the latter becoming the 'Minister of Trade and Industry and of Water Affairs'. Although who is in charge of government departments changes according to the fluctuating fortunes of the politicians who hold ministerial appointments, the personnel who staff the administration tend to remain stable. Many career civil servants spend their whole lives in the same government department, hoping eventually to reach the handsomely remunerated level of Director-General, who is the most senior person in a government department and is second only to the minister who formulates the policies which the department executes.

Figure 2 illustrates the structure of the three own affairs executives. The similarities with the structure of the national administration are evident, the only difference being that a lesser number of ministries is required for the administration of the limited number of functions defined as own affairs. Note that in terms of s 21(1)(c) deputy ministers appointed to assist own affairs ministers are members of the ministers' council (contrast this with the position of deputies to cabinet ministers).

[67] Baxter 98–9.

B   Parastatal organisations

Mention must be made of organisations which, although not forming part of the administration, are defined as 'public organisations' by virtue of the fact that they owe their origin to statutes, and that government controls or has a financial interest in them.[68] The reach of these 'parastatal' organisations is truly awesome. They include entrepreneurial bodies (such as ESKOM and ISCOR which supply electricity and produce iron and steel respectively), regulatory bodies (such as the various boards, for example the Maize Board, established to regulate the output of agricultural produce), and even institutions engaged in academic research (such as the Human Sciences Research Council). Universities also fall into this category, as they are publicly financed statutory bodies.[69] Virtually all these bodies are statutory, and they all rely on taxpayer's money—whether directly or indirectly—for their operation. It is this latter fact which gives importance to the question of what means of control exist to regulate their actions.[70]

Although nominal political responsibility for the activity of parastatals is often given to government departments, the fact that the parastatals are said to be 'autonomous' enables the relevant ministers to evade complete responsibility for what they do. Judicial review has far greater potential as a means of controlling parastatals. This is because in much that they do parastatals employ coercive administrative powers which affect private rights and interests. This is true even in cases where such bodies have ostensibly only entered into a contract, for very often what are in fact administrative acts take place in a contractual context.[71] The importance of judicial review on administrative-law grounds is demonstrated by the number of administrative-law cases involving parastatals—and in particular regulatory bodies such as licensing boards and adjudicatory bodies such as appeals tribunals.

Finally, it is important to note that in addition to organisations in which the state is involved, there are many *private* organisations which, although not publicly financed or controlled by the government, are statutory, and exercise powers affecting private rights and interests. For this reason, their actions are reviewable in terms of administrative law. An example of such organisations is the Medical and Dental Council,[72] which regulates admission to the medical

---

[68] See Baxter 159–86 for a comprehensive discussion of parastatals and non-government authorities.

[69] For example Rhodes University, which was established in terms of the Rhodes University (Private) Act 15 of 1949.

[70] The issue of control is also important in view of the fact that many parastatals enjoy extensive (and even repressive) powers which enable them to make gross inroads on the economic freedom of individuals by maintaining state monopolies or by setting prices.

[71] See 249 below.

[72] Established in terms of the Medical, Dental and Supplementary Health Service Professions Act 56 of 1974.

profession and which has disciplinary power over medical practitioners.

C The State Security Council—a shadow executive?

Although the establishment of ad hoc committees of a small number of cabinet members to deal with particular issues is a well-known feature of government, special mention needs to be made of the four standing (that is, permanent) cabinet committees that exist in South Africa, and in particular of one of them, the State Security Council. The four standing cabinet committees deal with constitutional, economic, social welfare and national security matters respectively.

Of the first three little needs to be said, other than that they serve to co-ordinate government policy in the specified areas on a permanent basis. But much attention has in recent years been focused on the State Security Council, which is the only cabinet committee to have been established by statute (the Security Intelligence and State Security Council Act 64 of 1972). According to s 5 of the Act, the function of the council is to advise the government with regard to the formulation of policies in the field of national security and intelligence. The composition of the council is specified by s 4 of the Act, and is as follows: the State President (who is chairman), the most senior cabinet minister, the Ministers of Defence, Foreign Affairs, Justice and Law and Order, any other minister co-opted by the State President, the Directors-General of the Departments of Foreign Affairs and Justice along with the Director-General of the National Intelligence Service, the Chief of the South African Defence Force, the Commissioner of the South African Police, and any other heads of government departments co-opted by the State President.

Much attention has been focused on the State Security Council in recent years,[73] due chiefly to its changing role and the vastly increased significance it has assumed. Prior to the election of Mr P W Botha as Prime Minister in 1978, the council met only once or twice a year to review matters of state security. However, over the past decade it has become virtually an 'inner cabinet', consisting of a select circle of ministers and security service chiefs, who meet frequently and regularly to consider the security implications of *the whole range* of government policies. Many commentators see this as indicative of an increase in influence over government policy of the security forces at the expense of civilian members of the cabinet, most of whom are not members of this 'inner circle'.[74] But even more striking than the enlarged field of interest of the council is the way in which it has changed its role from that of an advisory body to one which actually makes policy decisions. This development, which has taken place despite the clear wording to the contrary in s 5 of the Act

---

[73] See Dion Basson and Henning Viljoen *South African Constitutional Law* (1988) 68–75 and the references cited there.
[74] See P Berger and S Godsell *A Future South Africa* (1988) 32–5, 44–6.

(which gives the council a mandate only to offer advice to government) is evidenced by a number of statements made in government documents[75] which indicate that the council takes *decisions* that are then simply given formal *confirmation* by the larger cabinet. As Basson and Viljoen[76] point out, this development is most disturbing from a legal point of view, because it suggests that an executive body has, over an extended period, been able successfully to transgress the boundaries set to its operations by Parliament, and this despite the supremacy enjoyed by Parliament in terms of the common law! Further cause for concern is the fact that so many of the members of the council are military officers who, unlike civilian cabinet members, are not responsible to Parliament for the decisions they take.

The final (and most recent) development involving the State Security Council is the establishment of what is called the National Security Management System (NSMS).[77] The NSMS can be likened to a pyramid (see figure 3), at the apex of which is the State Security Council assisted by a work committee (which arranges its agenda), several interdepartmental committees (consisting of representatives from a wide range of government departments who provide assistance to the council), and a secretariat. Beneath these are eleven joint management centres[78] (one for each army command of the Defence Force), sixty sub-JMCs, and four hundred and fifty mini-JMCs, each reporting up the chain, with information from local level eventually reaching the State Security Council. Each mini-JMC is staffed by local security chiefs and representatives of those organs of both central and local government providing social services in the area. It is an important element of the task of the mini-JMCs to foster close links with the local community, hence their concern not only with security matters but also with the economic development of the community and the solution of local problems. Although lacking a budget of their own, the fact that mini-JMCs are able to use the channel of communication provided by the NSMS ensures that the State Security Council is alerted to the needs of their particular areas and can recommend to the cabinet that the appropriate government departments spend money to satisfy these needs. The NSMS was established in order to prevent unrest by co-ordinating security-force activities and by dealing with local grievances, and according to its sponsors it has met with a substantial degree of success. However, given that a high proportion of NSMS personnel are drawn from the military and police, and that the whole system forms a chain of command which is separate from other government departments and which extends to the highest levels of the executive, there is a real

---

[75] Quoted in Basson and Viljoen op cit n 73 above at 72–3.
[76] Ibid.
[77] See M Kotze and E Lourens in D J van Vuuren, N E Wiehahn, N J Rhoodie and M Wiechers (eds) *South Africa: The Challenge of Reform* (1988) 193–4, 412–14.
[78] Usually called 'JMCs'.

danger that the NSMS may develop into an autonomous 'shadow' government, existing parallel to and independent of the civilian administration, and usurping both its functions and its authority.

Figure 3

NATIONAL SECURITY MANAGEMENT SYSTEM

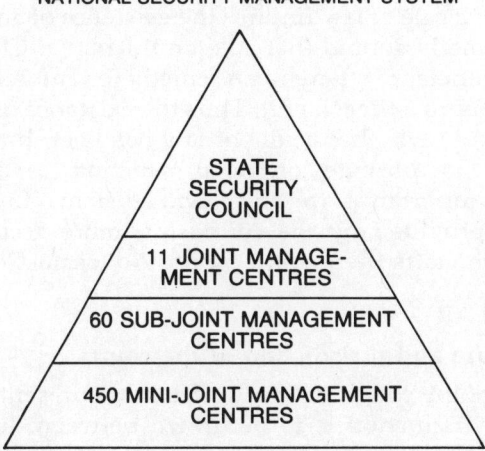

9 The Judiciary and the Advocate-General

One of the most important maxims of our law is ubi ius, ibi remedium—where there is a right there is a remedy. This means that the existence of a rule of law implies the existence of an authority that will grant a remedy should that rule be infringed. Clearly, a rule of law is vitally deficient if there is no remedy for enforcing it and if no sanction attaches to a breach of it. Thus the existence of an institution which will decide whether a rule of law has been broken, and if so what remedy to provide or what sanction to impose, is of fundamental importance to any legal system. In South Africa remedies are provided by the courts (or, more accurately, by the judiciary which staffs them), and by the Advocate-General.

I THE JUDICIARY

A The structure and jurisdiction of the courts

The structure of the courts in South Africa is represented by figure 4. An important distinction is to be drawn between the lower courts (the magistrates' courts) and the superior courts (the Supreme Court in its various divisions, including the Appellate Division). While the lower courts are creatures of the statute which created them[1] and have no jurisdiction (that is, sphere of competence or power) other than that which the statute has conferred on them, the superior courts have 'inherent jurisdiction' in terms of the common law, which means that they have jurisdiction to hear all matters other than those specifically removed from their jurisdiction by statute.[2]

All courts in South Africa are bound to follow precedents set by the Appellate Division. A decision by a full bench of a provincial or local division is binding on a single judge of the same provincial or local division, and upon the regional and district magistrates sitting in that provincial or local division. Decisions by single judges are binding on magistrates in the same division.[3] A decision by the Supreme Court in one provincial division has no binding effect on any court (be it a full bench, single judge, or magistrate's court) in any other provincial division; but a full bench decision of a provincial division binds a single judge of its satellite local division and vice versa. Thus, for example, a full bench decision of the Durban and Coast Local Division will bind a single judge of the Natal Provincial Division. This hierarchy of courts is significant not only in relation to the doctrine of precedent, but also with respect to appeals. Although the detailed rules governing appeals from a judgment and

---

[1] The Magistrates' Courts Act 32 of 1944.
[2] See Jérold Taitz The Inherent Jurisdiction of the Supreme Court (1985).
[3] It should, however, be noted that magistrates do not follow precedents set by their fellows, even in the same province.

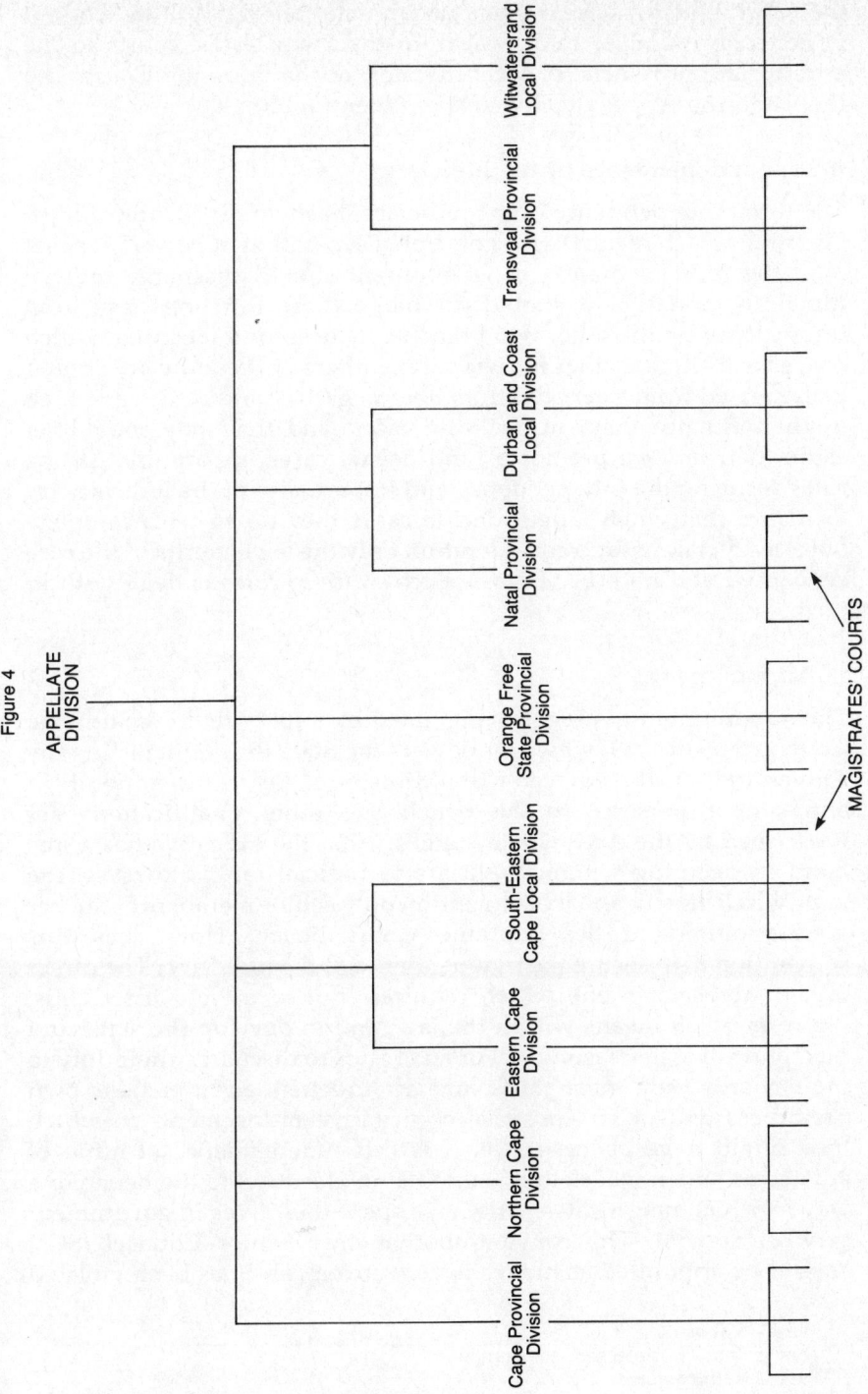

Figure 4

APPELLATE DIVISION

Cape Provincial Division

Northern Cape Division

Eastern Cape Division

South-Eastern Cape Local Division

Orange Free State Provincial Division

Natal Provincial Division

Durban and Coast Local Division

Transvaal Provincial Division

Witwatersrand Local Division

MAGISTRATES' COURTS

the court which will hear the appeal are not relevant to this work, it is generally possible to appeal from the magistrates' courts to the appropriate provincial or local division of the Supreme Court, and thence to the Appellate Division in Bloemfontein.

B The independence of the judiciary

The term 'independence of the judiciary' has two distinct meanings. The first, which relates to the concept of separation of powers,[4] is that only the judicial branch of government should discharge judicial functions, and that it should discharge those functions free from interference by the other two branches. The second meaning, which concerns us here, is that individual members of the judiciary should be insulated from *external* factors both negative[5] and positive[6] which might influence them in deciding cases, and that they should set aside their *internal* prejudices and decide cases impartially. All the rules securing the independence and impartiality of the judiciary try to insure that when judges decide cases they do so with complete objectivity, taking into consideration only the legal merits of the case concerned and no other factors. Each of these rules is dealt with in turn.

1 Appointment

The appointment of judges is regulated by s 10(1)(*a*) of the Supreme Court Act 59 of 1959, which empowers the State President (acting, by convention, on the advice of the Minister of Justice) to appoint 'fit and proper persons' to the bench. No other qualifications are prescribed by the Act,[7] which suggests that the executive has a free hand in deciding whom to elevate to judicial rank. However, the reality is different, and by convention only senior members of the bar are appointed to the Supreme Court bench. How does this convention help secure the independence of the judiciary? The career of the advocate is one which requires him to uphold his clients' interests by all means within the law, and to develop the skills and discipline of legal reasoning. For advocates to discharge their duty to their clients they must think and act independently of their own prejudices and of any positive or negative inducements to which they might have been subject. It is this independence of mind of advocates which makes them suitable for elevation to the bench in a way in which magistrates, who have spent their lives in government service, are not. The convention that only Senior Counsel (SCs) should be appointed as judges is very strong, and has been violated

---

[4] See 43–5 above.

[5] That is, fear of unpleasant consequences.

[6] That is, inducements.

[7] With the exception of s 10(5), which requires that anyone appointed as Chief Justice or as judge of appeal must have served as a Supreme Court judge.

in only a few instances.[8] The most famous of these was the case of L C Steyn, who was not only made a judge after a career as government law adviser (an appointment which led to an unprecedented protest by the Johannesburg bar),[9] but was swiftly elevated to the Appellate Division, and was then appointed Chief Justice ahead of more senior colleagues.

2 The judicial oath

Upon appointment a judge must take the oath prescribed by s 10(2)(a) of the Act, in terms of which he assumes the obligation to 'administer justice to all persons alike without fear, favour or prejudice, and . . . in accordance with the law . . .'. The oath requires the judge to decide any case that comes before him on its legal merits and without showing either favour or disfavour to the litigants. In short, the judge swears to decide all cases independently.

3 Security of tenure

A judge would not be completely independent if he was concerned that should he make a decision adverse to the interests of the executive branch, he might be dismissed from office. For this reason, a judge enjoys security of tenure, which means that only in exceptional circumstances may he be dismissed from office. Until 1989, the only way in which a judge could be removed was in accordance with the provisions of s 10(7) of the Supreme Court Act, which state that a judge may be dismissed by the State President only if all three houses of Parliament have called for dismissal, which they may do only on grounds of misbehaviour or incapacity. However, since the enactment of the Judges' Remuneration and Conditions of Employment Act 88 of 1989, the State President has had the power to dismiss a judge who has been afflicted by a permanent infirmity of mind or body which prevents him from discharging his duties.[10] In view of the power which Parliament has to secure the dismissal of judges who have become incapacitated, the purpose of this new provision is unclear. It is also unfortunate that the executive should be able to dismiss a judge without the concurrence of the legislature.

Although the Supreme Court Act empowers the State President[11]

---

[8] Statistics are unavailable for the provincial and local divisions of the Supreme Court, but it is known that of all the judges of appeal appointed since the Appellate Division was established in 1919, only Steyn CJ (appointed in 1955) and Botha JA (appointed in 1961) had never practised privately at the Bar.

[9] See C F Forsyth *In Danger for their Talents* (1985) 14. This book, along with Hugh Corder *Judges at Work* (1984) provides an interesting insight into the judiciary. The subject is treated from a somewhat different perspective by Adrienne van Blerk *Judge and be Judged* (1988).

[10] Section 3(1)(c).

[11] Section 10(4) empowers the Minister of Justice to appoint someone as acting judge, but for no longer than one month.

to appoint an acting judge[12] for a defined period (s 10(3)), after which the judge ceases to hold office, it must be remembered that the protection afforded by s 10(7) extends to acting judges as well as to judges, and that the former also enjoy security of tenure until their term of office expires.

No South African judge has ever been removed from office and so, in the normal course of events, a judge will end his career by retiring. The retirement of judges is regulated by the Judges' Remuneration and Conditions of Employment Act, which provides that a judge retires from 'active' (that is, full-time) service at the age of 70, or after completing 10 years' service, whichever comes later.[13] Such a judge has the option of carrying on in active service until he has served a total of 15 years or has reached the age of 75, whichever comes sooner, at which stage he must retire from active service.[14] But retirement from active service does not necessarily mark the end of a judicial career:[15] those judges who have not reached the age of 75 may be called upon to perform three months' service per annum, and may volunteer to perform more than three months' service if they wish.[16]

4 Financial security

Fear of reduction in salary constitutes as great a threat to judicial independence as does fear of dismissal, and for that reason judges enjoy financial security. Thus, the Supreme Court Act provides that a judge's remuneration shall not be reduced during office (s 10(1)(*a*)).[17]

The remuneration of judges is regulated by the Judges' Remuneration and Conditions of Employment Act 88 of 1989. In terms of s 2 of the Act, judicial salaries (which are not taxable)[18] are determined by the State President, and announced by him in the *Government Gazette*.[19] Judges continue to receive remuneration even after

[12] Chief Justice Rabie was appointed Acting Chief Justice after having reached retirement age. This appointment met with criticism—see Edwin Cameron (1987) 3 *SAJHR* 338 at 343.

[13] Section 3(1)(*a*). Section 3(1)(*b*) provides that judges who have reached the age of 65 and who have served for at least 15 years may retire if they wish to.

[14] Section 4.

[15] Nor does it mean the cessation of the judicial salary, see n 20 below.

[16] Section 7(1).

[17] This is subject to the proviso that the salary of a judge who fails to render three months' service as required by s 7(1) of the Judges' Remuneration and Conditions of Employment Act 88 of 1989 may be reduced to a limited extent. Of course, there would be nothing to stop Parliament from using its sovereign powers to reduce judicial salaries any time it pleased.

[18] Section 2(4). This provision perhaps constitutes long overdue vindication of the argument presented by an optimistic judge, but rejected by the Appellate Division in *Krause v Commissioner for Inland Revenue* 1929 AD 286, that the levying of income tax on judicial salaries constituted an unlawful reduction of remuneration.

[19] Section 2(1). In terms of s 2(3)(*b*) the State President's proclamation will be invalidated if all three houses of Parliament pass a resolution to that effect during the same session in which the proclamation is tabled. However, this would be

discharge from active service,[20] and receive an additional salary[21] while performing their annual three months' post-retirement service. Judges' salaries are not included in the allocation to any government department, but are paid directly from the state revenue fund.[22] At the time of publication, the salary of a provincial or local division judge was R115 000 per annum, while that of the Chief Justice was R137 500 per annum.

5 Limitation of civil liability

In order to discharge his function a judge must be secure in the knowledge that he will incur no civil liability for what he says or does in the line of duty. For example, the freedom which a judge must enjoy to deliver judgment against someone would be severely prejudiced if he could be sued in delict for delivering a judgment which was not in accordance with the law, but which the judge in good faith believed was in accordance with the law when he delivered it. Thus in *Penrice v Dickenson*,[23] it was held that delictual damages will not be awarded against a judicial officer (whether a judge or magistrate) unless it is shown that he acted with malice. This principle was applied in *May v Udwin*[24] where it was held that a judicial officer can raise the defence of qualified privilege to a defamation action, and will be liable for defamatory statements only if the plaintiff can prove that the judicial officer was malicious in what he said—that is, that he was actuated by personal spite, ill-will or an improper, unlawful or ulterior motive. The reason for this rule is obvious—the judicial task would be made impossible if a judge could be sued for defamation every time he expressed unfavourable views about a litigant while delivering judgment, or made an adverse finding regarding the credibility of a witness.[25]

Section 25(1) of the Supreme Court Act affords judges a different kind of immunity. In terms of this section, no civil summons or subpoena can be issued against a judge without the permission of the court out of which the process is to be served.[26] The reason why such permission is needed is not entirely clear: possibly to protect

highly unusual, and so for practical purposes it can be accepted that an increase in judicial salaries takes effect upon promulgation of the State President's proclamation, and cannot thereafter be reduced except by Parliament.

[20] This remuneration is calculated in accordance with a formula prescribed by s 5 and is substantial, amounting in the case of judges who have served for 15 years to 100 % of their pre-retirement salary.

[21] Section 7(3).

[22] Section 14.

[23] 1945 AD 6.

[24] 1981 (1) SA 1 (A).

[25] It is interesting to note that in terms of the rules of parliamentary privilege, the law grants *complete* immunity to MPs who make defamatory statements in Parliament. This rule is meant to ensure the absolute freedom of parliamentary debate.

[26] If it is sought to serve process out of a magistrate's court, then the prior permission of that division of the Supreme Court which has appeal jurisdiction over the magistrate's court in question must be obtained.

judges from becoming the victims of frivolous proceedings, or it is to prevent a disruption of the work of the courts. Support is provided for the latter view by s 25(2) of the Act, which states that where process has been issued against a judge, the date upon which he has to appear in court must, in the case of an Appellate Division judge, be determined in consultation with the Chief Justice, and in the case of a Provincial or Local Division judge, in consultation with the Judge President of the Division.

6 The rule against bias

The concept of judicial independence includes the principle that a judicial officer[27] should have no interest in the outcome of a case before him, a principle which is often expressed in the form of the maxim nemo iudex in sua causa.[28] The practical implications of this principle are as follows: Where a judge (or a member of his immediate family) has any financial interest, however slight, in the outcome of a case, he must recuse himself. This was explicitly stated in *Dimes v Grand Junction Control Properties*,[29] where a decision by the Lord Chancellor was set aside on the ground that he owned shares in the canal company in whose favour he had given judgment. It made no difference to the case that the value of the shareholding had been minute, or that the judge was unaware of the fact that he owned the shares at the time he heard the case. The only exceptions to the rule that a judge who has a financial interest in a case must recuse himself are where both parties consent to his sitting as judge notwithstanding his interest, or where the judge's financial interest relates to the payment of tax. The reason for the latter exception is self-evident—since everyone pays tax,[30] it would be impossible to find a disinterested person to try cases wherein the Receiver of Revenue was a litigant.

So far as non-financial interests are concerned, the rule as formulated in *R v St. Edmondsbury Borough Council*[31] is that a judge must recuse himself where there is a real likelihood of bias on his part or, expressed differently, where a reasonable man would suspect that the judge might be biased. Thus, to take an obvious example, it would be impermissible for a judge to sit on a case where he was a close friend of one of the litigants or witnesses, or where he (the judge) had made statements outside court expressing prejudice against one of the litigants. But the list of circumstances in which a judge might have to recuse himself for bias is not closed. Everything depends on the facts of the particular case and whether they give rise to a reasonable suspicion of bias—or in other words, to a suspicion

[27] This rule applies to anyone exercising a judicial or quasi-judicial function.
[28] No one shall be judge in his own cause.
[29] (1852) 3 HLC 759, 10 ER 301.
[30] Judges, although exempt from income tax (see 202 above) pay indirect taxes such as sales tax.
[31] [1985] 1 WLR 1168.

that the judge has not set aside his personal prejudices, and has not decided a case objectively. Thus in *S v Herbst*,[32] Eksteen J held that a reasonable suspicion of bias did exist in the case of a magistrate who had embarked upon a powerful cross-examination of an accused appearing before him, and that the magistrate ought to have recused himself. Similarly, in *S v Tyebela*,[33] the Appellate Division set aside the proceedings of the court a quo on the ground that hostile and sarcastic interventions by the judge had given the impression that he had not been fair and unbiased in his conduct of the case.

Much research has been conducted in recent times into the appointment of South African judges, their social background and the decisions they make, in an attempt to discover first whether the executive is biased in whom it appoints to the bench, and second whether judges are subject to a significant (albeit subconscious) bias because of their personal and political background. Particular controversy surrounded the appointment of six additional judges of appeal to the Appellate Division by the National Party government during the constitutional crisis of the 1950s, and the elevation of L C Steyn to the office of Chief Justice a few years later. Both events have been cited as examples of the executive appointing to the appeal court judges sharing its political philosophy.[34] It is more difficult to find examples of judges who allow personal beliefs to colour their activities on the bench, and notwithstanding the often justified suspicion that the government selects judges on a 'political' basis, the conduct of judges once they have been appointed is generally held to be beyond reproach, and the judiciary is legitimately stated as having a tradition of acting without bias or favour. Of course the essence of the judicial function is to give judgment as dispassionately and objectively as possible, and for that reason judges are aware of the necessity for eliminating the influence of any personal bias on their judicial activities. Whether it is possible to do so completely is open to dispute, and there are studies which suggest that a statistical analysis of Appellate Division decisions reveals a 'pro-executive' bias on the part of some judges,[35] that some decisions reveal a trend of racial disparity in sentencing,[36] and that politically partisan statements have been made from the bench.[37] But it should also be remembered that the legislature has increasingly restricted the scope within which the judiciary can act,[38] with the result that South Africa has a generally independent judiciary whose effectiveness has been

---

[32] 1980 (3) SA 1026 (E).
[33] 1989 (2) SA 22 (A).
[34] See for example Edwin Cameron (1982) 99 *SALJ* 38.
[35] See the comprehensive studies in the works by Hugh Corder and C F Forsyth cited in n 9.
[36] See Barend van Niekerk (1979) 3 *South African Journal of Criminal Law and Criminology* 151.
[37] See Edwin Cameron (1987) 3 *SAJHR* 338 at 340, and D M Davis (1987) 3 *SAJHR* 229.
[38] See 295–99 below.

reduced because of its diminished jurisdiction to inquire into the legality of governmental action.

Finally, it is necessary to mention that judges must not only be impartial but must be seen to be impartial. For this reason a person who impugns the integrity of a judge, thereby diminishing the standing of the judiciary and public respect for the courts, may be held criminally liable for contempt of court. This does not, of course, prevent people from criticising judicial actions in good faith[39]—only if they impute improper motives, partiality or unfairness to a judge will they be liable for contempt.

7　Offices of profit

A further rule securing the independence of the judiciary is contained in s 11 of the Supreme Court Act, which prohibits a judge from holding any other office of profit or receiving any other remuneration in respect of services provided, apart from the salary he earns as a judge. In order to be completely independent it is thought necessary that a judge should be in no one else's employ, and should not be bound to perform services for gain, as this might affect his ability to decide cases in a wholly objective manner.

8　Political non-involvement

By convention, judges do not engage in politics. The reason for this is obvious: the impartiality of a judge would be called into question were he to make public statements on political issues which might become relevant in court proceedings,[40] or identify himself with a particular political party.

C　The judiciary and commissions of inquiry

It frequently occurs that when an issue of public importance arises the State President exercises the power given by s 1 of the Commissions Act 8 of 1947 to appoint a commission of inquiry to conduct an investigation into, and to present a report on, the issue concerned. Very often such commissions of inquiry are headed by a judge, and for that reason are termed 'judicial commissions of inquiry'. However, this terminology should not lead one to think that a commission of inquiry is in any way a 'judicial' body, or that a judge who presides over a commission discharges a 'judicial' function. A commission of inquiry is an ad hoc body established by the *executive* to assist the latter in the discharge of its functions by providing it with a report on a specified matter of public interest. A commission of inquiry cannot make a finding regarding civil or criminal liability, nor can it impose punishments. The only way in

---

[39] Thus an academic does not (it is hoped!) run the risk of imprisonment should he or she write an article on a case arguing that a judge took a mistaken view of the law, or imposed too heavy a sentence.

[40] Judges sometimes refuse to give judgments in student moot competitions on the ground that they might have to decide a similar case in real proceedings!

which a commission resembles a court of law is that a commission may subpoena witnesses to give evidence before it,[41] and may punish those who are guilty of contempt towards it.[42]

Given that commissions of inquiry are not judicial bodies, strong (and we believe cogent) criticism has been voiced against the practice of using judges to chair them.[43] Firstly, it is thought inappropriate that members of the judiciary should preside over executive bodies, as this is incompatible with the doctrine of the separation of powers. Secondly, while many commissions deal with relatively innocuous matters,[44] some are established to inquire into matters which are potentially controversial. An example of such a commission was that chaired in 1949 by Mr Justice F P van den Heever, which was established to inquire into the riots that had recently taken place in Durban. Its findings were extensively debated in the press, and this inevitably led to the judge becoming embroiled in political controversy. The same applied to the Rabie Commission[45] which issued a report on security legislation in 1981. Such an occurrence cannot but harm the judiciary, as it compromises the aloofness which judges must maintain from current political disputes. The position of members of the judiciary is made even more difficult if the findings of commissions of inquiry which they have chaired lead to legal proceedings in which they have to participate in their judicial capacity, hearing much of the same evidence again. Anyone who appears before a court ought to be confident of obtaining a fair hearing. This confidence could be undermined by the not unreasonable belief that the bench might be influenced by findings of fact contained in a commission report authored by a judge. Finally, the point has often been made that it is precisely because the judiciary is held in such esteem that its members are requested by the executive to chair commissions of inquiry. This has given rise to a suspicion that the executive exploits the reputation of the judiciary by giving to it the task of making findings on politically sensitive public issues, which the government can then adopt as policy. Any subsequent criticism of the policy can be met with the response that the government has simply followed the recommendations of a judicial commission of inquiry. This should not lead one to think that a reprehensible attempt to link the prestige of the judiciary with government policy lies behind the appointment of every judicial commission of inquiry; but it does show why judges must be careful in deciding which commission appointments to accept.

---

[41] Section 3.

[42] Section 1 as read with ss 5 and 6.

[43] See Ellison Kahn 1980 *De Jure* 188 and Raymond Suttner (1986) 14 *Journal of the Sociology of Law* 47 at 60–1.

[44] For example the commission chaired by Judge Margo to investigate the crash of the SAA airliner *Helderberg* in 1987.

[45] Chaired by Mr Justice P J Rabie, who became Chief Justice in 1982.

D Magistrates and judges compared

Apart from the lesser jurisdiction enjoyed by magistrates,[46] there are further significant differences between them and judges. Magistrates are civil servants, employed by the Department of Justice, who achieve promotion to the bench once they have passed the relevant examination.[47] As civil servants, they are subject to directions from their departmental superiors, upon whom they are reliant for promotion. They therefore do not enjoy the same degree of independence as the judiciary. Of the factors securing the independence of the judiciary only the oath, the nemo iudex in sua causa principle and the limitation of civil liability are applicable to magistrates.

1 The magistrate's oath

In terms of s 9(2)(a) of the Magistrates' Courts Act, magistrates must swear that they will 'administer justice to all persons alike without fear, favour or prejudice and . . . in accordance with the law'. By this oath a magistrate undertakes to decide cases on their merits and without succumbing to external pressures or inducements that might be brought to bear.

2 The rule against bias

Independence requires not only that a magistrate decide cases free from outside influence, but that he himself have no interest in the outcome of cases. For this reason a magistrate must adhere to the nemo iudex in sua causa rule, and the failure of a magistrate who has an interest in a case (or who is biased in some other way) to recuse himself constitutes a ground for review by the Supreme Court.[48]

3 Limitation of civil liability

The principles governing the limitation of civil liability of magistrates and judges have already been discussed.[49]

Because magistrates do not enjoy as protected a position as do judges, they are in a relatively weak position vis-à-vis the executive branch of government, and that is why they are said to enjoy less independence than judges. They are also at a disadvantage in that few of them have had the benefit of the training provided by a career in private practice.[50] Of course all this does not mean that magistrates deliberately act subjectively—they strive to act impartially just as

---

[46] Discussed at 198 above.
[47] In terms of s 9(1)(b) of the Magistrates' Courts Act, regional magistrates must have an LL.B degree or have passed the Public Service Senior Law Examination or its equivalent, while in terms of s 10(a) district magistrates must have passed the civil service lower law examination or its equivalent.
[48] Section 24(1)(b) of the Supreme Court Act 59 of 1959.
[49] See 203 above.
[50] They also decided cases unassisted by precedents set by fellow magistrates—see n 3.

judges do. It is simply that their profession is structured in such a way that they are not given as great a degree of independence by the law as are judges.

II THE ADVOCATE-GENERAL

A The ombudsman

The office of the ombudsman, which in South Africa is to some extent paralleled by that of the Advocate-General, has long existed in foreign legal systems, and the ombudsman will be discussed before his South African equivalent is examined.

The term ombudsman originated in Sweden in the early 18th century and means 'representative'. This gives a clue to his function, which is to protect the citizen from maladministration. The way in which the ombudsman does this evolved gradually over two centuries, and it is now generally accepted that it is the ombudsman's task to receive complaints of executive misbehaviour from citizens, to investigate those complaints, and then to make a report to the legislature. Thus, the International Bar Association's definition of the office of ombudsman[51] is

> 'a high-level public official who is responsible to the legislature or parliament, who receives complaints from aggrieved persons against government agencies, officials and employees or who acts on his own motion, and who has the power to investigate, recommend corrective action, and issue reports'.

In 1962 New Zealand became the first English-speaking country to appoint an ombudsman, and in 1967 the first Parliamentary Commissioner for Administration, who performs the same functions as an ombudsman, was appointed in Britain.[52] The Parliamentary Commissioner has jurisdiction to investigate claims by citizens that they have suffered injustice as a result of maladministration by a government department. It is important to note that it is the Commissioner's primary function to deal with cases where the conduct of the government department has not been *unlawful* even though it may have been *unjust*. Where the conduct has been unlawful, the complainant must avail him- or herself of the appropriate remedy provided by a tribunal or the courts. It is precisely where there is no existing remedy (because the conduct complained of was not strictly unlawful) that the Commissioner comes into his own. Only where he thinks that the complainant

---

[51] As quoted by Harold Rudolph in (1983) 100 *SALJ* 92 at 92. This article contains a wealth of information on the office of ombudsman and its South African equivalent, the Advocate-General. Also of interest is Lawrence Baxter *Administrative Law* (1984) 287–92.

[52] The role of the Parliamentary Commissioner is comprehensively dealt with by the following sources: S A de Smith *Constitutional and Administrative Law* 5 ed (1985) 646–53, A W Bradley *Constitutional and Administrative Law* 10 ed (1985) 721–7, and O Hood-Phillips and Paul Jackson *O Hood-Phillips' Constitutional and Administrative Law* 7 ed (1987) 653–60.

could not reasonably be expected to pursue an existing remedy (for example where the expense would be prohibitive or the delay too long) can the Commissioner investigate an otherwise remediable case.

The Commissioner may not, in terms of the statute governing his office, act on his own initiative—he may act only after having received a complaint. Furthermore, such a complaint may not be made to the Commissioner directly, but must in the first instance be directed by the complainant to a member of Parliament who will then decide whether to forward the complaint to the Commissioner. It is then up to the Commissioner to decide whether to investigate, and his decision is not justiciable. Whether he decides to launch an investigation or not, he must report his decision to the member of Parliament. The Commissioner has a wide jurisdiction, and may investigate the activities of most central government departments. He is, however, prohibited from investigating a number of governmental activities, including the conduct of foreign affairs, matters relating to state security, civil or criminal proceedings commenced before any court, matters relating to contractual or other commercial transactions on the part of the government, and personnel matters in the civil service and armed forces. The Commissioner may also not investigate the conduct of the police, whose activities in any event fall under the control of local rather than central government. However, although the Commissioner's jurisdiction is somewhat circumscribed, he has extremely wide powers so far as the conduct of his investigations is concerned. Once he has decided to investigate a complaint, the Commissioner has the power to subpoena witnesses to give evidence or produce documents, failure to do so being punishable just as it would be by a court of law. Neither the rules relating to Crown privilege nor the Official Secrets Act may be used to prevent the giving of evidence to the Commissioner, though *publication* of this evidence by him can be prevented by a government minister. The Commissioner must give the head of the government department against which the complaint has been made, as well as any specific individual mentioned in the complaint, an opportunity to comment on the allegations.

Once he has completed his investigation, the Commissioner must report to the member of Parliament who forwarded the complaint, and to the head of the government department which was the subject of the investigation. Furthermore, if the Commissioner thinks that an injustice has taken place and that it is unlikely that the responsible government department will remedy it, he may lay a special report before Parliament. The threat of such adverse publicity is usually enough to ensure that injustices are remedied. Thus, although the Commissioner lacks any power to provide remedies, he has sufficient power to embarrass the executive into taking corrective measures itself. It is this power, plus the fact that his office provides for cheaper, accessible and more expeditious assistance than do the courts, that makes convenient the service offered by Britain's Parliamentary Commissioner.

There are ombudsman-like institutions closer to home. Bophuthatswana has had an ombudsman since 1981,[53] and it is instructive briefly to examine his jurisdiction and power. In terms of s 9(1) of the Ombudsman Act 9 of 1986, the ombudsman may investigate any government department if he has reason to suspect that the department is guilty of inefficiency, irregularity, dishonesty or fraud, or if an act or omission by a department constituted a violation of Bophuthatswana's Bill of Rights, was unreasonable, unjust, or oppressive, was based on a mistake of fact or law, or was simply wrong. The ombudsman may investigate on his own initiative or upon receipt of a complaint. The ombudsman has the power to subpoena witnesses to give evidence or produce documents.[54] The extremely wide jurisdiction of the Bophuthatswana's ombudsman has made him an effective citizens' representative, as is evidenced by the rapid increase in the number of cases handled by his office since 1981.[55]

B The Advocate-General

Despite frequent pleas by parliamentarians, academics, and the legal profession, an ombudsman has yet to be created in South Africa. No satisfactory reason why the office of ombudsman should not be established has been provided by the government.[56] The closest the country has come to the establishment of such an office[57] was the creation in 1979 of the post of Advocate-General, established in the wake of the 'information scandal' of 1978 in which it was revealed that a number of cabinet members had authorised the unlawful expenditure of public money. But, as will become evident, the Advocate-General occupies a position with much more limited jurisdiction and fewer powers than does a true ombudsman.

---

[53] Known as the Control Commissioner until 1986. Zimbabwe also has an ombudsman, whose office was created by s 107 of the Zimbabwe Constitution.

[54] However, s 12(4) of the Act states that the normal rules of privilege with regard to the giving of evidence apply; and thus state privilege can be used to prevent evidence from being presented to the Ombudsman.

[55] According to the 5th Report of the Bophuthatswana Ombudsman, 1209 cases were dealt with during 1986. In 200 of these no investigation ensued, either because the matter lay outside the jurisdiction of the ombudsman or the complainant did not pursue the case. 594 complaints were found to be unjustified, while the other 415 were found to be justified.

[56] See, for example, the spurious reasons given in Parliament in 1973 for the non-establishment of an office of ombudsman, quoted by Rudolph op cit n 51 at 99. Were an ombudsman to be appointed, he would doubtless receive an avalanche of complaints of mistreatment on grounds of race and by the security forces; but if these two areas of the law were excluded from his jurisdiction, there would be little point in creating the office.

[57] Apart from the establishment of the South African Defence Force Complaints Office, which acts as a military ombudsman.

1 Appointment

In terms of the Advocate-General Act 118 of 1979, the State President must appoint as Advocate-General a person who is entitled to practise as an advocate, and who has practised law for at least ten years since becoming so entitled (s 2(1)). The Act empowers the State President to dismiss the Advocate-General only on grounds of misconduct or inability to carry out his duties (s 6(*a*)). The State President must inform Parliament of such a dismissal (s 6(*b*)), the dismissal being effective unless the houses of Parliament present a joint address calling for his reinstatement (s 6(*c*)). Parliament may itself compel the State President to dismiss the Advocate-General by passing a motion calling for his dismissal on grounds of misconduct or inability to discharge his duties (s 7). The present Advocate-General is a former judge.

2 Jurisdiction

The jurisdiction of the Advocate-General is governed by s 4(1) of the Act. In essence the section provides that a complaint may be laid before[58] the Advocate-General for investigation by any person who has reasonable grounds to suspect (i) that public money has been or is being dealt with in a dishonest manner, or (ii) that any person is being or has been enriched, or has received an advantage in an unlawful or improper manner, as a result of any act or omission by any body to which public money accrues, by any employee of such a body, or at the expense of such a body. An attempt to do either (i) or (ii) may also be investigated. Section 4(1) is undoubtedly the most significant section in the Act, as it serves to distinguish the Advocate-General's role from that normally fulfilled by an ombudsman: while the latter protects the individual from maladministration by the State, s 4(1) suggests that the former serves mainly to protect the State from suffering financial prejudice at the hands of the individual! This is an astonishing reversal of functions, but it becomes explicable when one considers that the Advocate-General Act was passed in the aftermath of the 'information scandal', which involved the misuse of large amounts of public money. No one denies the seriousness of corruption in general, and the misappropriation of public money or the abuse of public office in particular, but it surely cannot be maintained that the number of instances in which the public funds need protection even approaches the number of instances in which the citizen needs protection from unfair treatment by the State. Given that the modern State invades the life of the individual to an ever-increasing extent, the provisions of s 4 of the Advocate-General Act are clearly inadequate, and ought to be expanded so as to confer upon this official the jurisdiction appropriate to an ombudsman.

[58] Although s 5(5) empowers the Advocate-General to initiate an investigation on his own initiative.

3 Procedure

Complaints to the Advocate-General must be made on affidavit (s 4(2)). Once he has received a complaint, the Advocate-General must investigate whether the allegations are well-founded. In terms of s 7(1) as read with s 7(2) the Advocate-General has the power to subpoena witnesses to give evidence or produce documents, failure to do so constituting a criminal offence. This power is however subject to the rules of state privilege, codified in s 66 of the Internal Security Act 74 of 1982, which empowers any minister to prevent a person giving evidence or producing a document if, in his opinion, this would be prejudicial to state security. Such a decision is not reviewable by the courts. This presents a stark contrast with the position in Britain, where a government minister may rely on Crown privilege only to prevent the *publication* of evidence, and not its presentation to the Parliamentary Commissioner. Should it appear to the Advocate-General that any person is being 'implicated' in the matter being inquired into, he must be afforded an opportunity to present a defence to the allegations made (s 7(6)(*a*)).

Once he has completed his investigations, the Advocate-General must convey to Parliament a report on his findings and any recommendations he may wish to make (s 5(1)), and these must in due course be tabled. However, if the Advocate-General is of the opinion that publication of his report would not be in the interests of state security, he must recommend that the report not be tabled and that it be considered instead by a select committee of Parliament. If the Advocate-General believes that the evidence received indicates that a criminal offence may have been committed, he may refer the matter to the appropriate prosecuting authority (s 5(4)).

4 The Advocate-General—an evaluation

As was stated earlier in this section,[59] the reason for the success enjoyed by the Parliamentary Commissioner in Britain is that he provides aggrieved citizens with a relatively accessible and cheap means of securing redress against the executive. How does the office of Advocate-General compare? In the first place, the requirement that complaints must be made to the Advocate-General on affidavit severely limits his accessibility in a country with a large number of illiterate persons. Moreover, the lack of publicity that has been given to the Advocate-General means that he has not become generally known as someone to whom a citizen can turn when in need of assistance.[60] But the most significant factor that prevents one from classifying the Advocate-General as a true ombudsman is the narrowness of his jurisdiction—of the 18 complaints received by the Advocate-General during the two-year period covered by his latest

[59] See 210–11 above.
[60] According to Advocate-General report No 10, only 18 complaints were received during the period March 1985 to February 1987!

report[61] only 6 fell within the provisions of s 4(1)! The best that can be said is that South Africa has a 'specialist ombudsman'[62] who performs just one of the vast range of functions which should be performed by such an official. To give the Advocate-General his due, he does appear to have given a wide interpretation to s 4(1), and even where it has not been possible to bring a complaint within his jurisdiction in this manner, he has investigated it nonetheless.[63] However, this is not really a long-term solution, and it is submitted that what is needed is either a radical extension of the Advocate-General's jurisdiction, or the establishment of a separate post with an incumbent who has the jurisdiction and powers of a full ombudsman.

[61] Advocate-General report No 10 of 27 July 1987.
[62] This is the conclusion reached by Baxter op cit n 51 at 291–2.
[63] Rudolph op cit n 51 at 104–6.

10 Sub-national and Independent Authorities

Apart from the central legislature and executive, a number of other governments exist within South Africa's borders, and they are the subject of this chapter.

I THE PROVINCES

A The provincial system

In terms of the South Africa Act of 1909[1] the Union of South Africa was divided into four provinces, each with its own Provincial Council. The election and composition of the councils were governed by discriminatory legislation: Except in the Cape and Natal, non-whites could not stand for election and did not enjoy the franchise. Section 85 of the Act conferred original legislative powers on the Provincial Councils,[2] and enumerated those areas on which they would be competent to pass provincial ordinances.[3] Provincial executive powers were vested in an Administrator appointed by the Governor-General. The Administrator performed a dual function. In the first place he represented the central government, and had the responsibility of implementing government policy in his particular province. In so doing he wielded such powers as had been assigned to him by the cabinet in terms of s 84 of the South Africa Act. His second function was that of administering provincial affairs in his capacity as chairman of the executive committee of the province, the other four members of which were elected by the Provincial Council. The committee reached its decisions by majority vote, with the Administrator having a casting vote in cases of deadlock. Members of the executive committee could be members of the Provincial Council, but did not have to be. It is interesting to note that in performing their task of running the provincial administration and of executing ordinances passed by the Provincial Council,[4] the executive committee was not responsible to the council, and could therefore govern the province in opposition to the wishes of the council. However, the fact that the committee (with the exception of the Administrator) was elected by the council diminished the possibility that committee and council would be political antagonists.

Although the provincial system was established in deference to the sentiments of those who had urged that the Union of South Africa be given a federal constitution, it fell far short of creating a federal

---

[1] 9 Edw 7, c 9.
[2] See 173 above on the difference between original and delegated legislative power.
[3] Examples of these were education, hospitals and roads.
[4] Like the Administrators, the provincial executive councils also on occasion exercised power delegated to them by central government. See Lawrence Baxter *Administrative Law* (1984) 127–8.

system. Section 90 provided that provincial ordinances would not come into force unless assented to by the Governor-General, while s 86 (the so-called 'repugnancy clause') provided that ordinances would be of no force or effect should their provisions conflict with those of any existing or future Act of Parliament. Furthermore, it was always open to Parliament to use its supreme legislative authority to amend s 85 of the Constitution and thereby to abridge the legislative power of the provinces. This power was used when Parliament took control of black education away from the provinces,[5] when it abridged the Provincial Councils' powers to pass ordinances regarding local government,[6] and when it removed areas of land from provincial control by giving independence to the various homelands.[7] All these enactments were in theory invalid, because Parliament had not received a petition from the various Provincial Councils prior to abridging their powers, as was required by s 149 of the South Africa Act[8] and subsequently by s 114 of the Republic of South Africa Constitution Act 32 of 1961. However, this legislation was not challenged,[9] and it was thought necessary to legalise only those enactments which had had the effect of changing provincial boundaries. This was done (with retroactive effect to 1961) by the Republic of South Africa Constitution Second Amendment Act 101 of 1981. These changes aside, the provincial system put in place by the South Africa Act was preserved in its essence until 1986.[10]

The introduction of the 1983 Constitution and the change in the locus of power at central government caused the abolition of the independent legislative power of the provinces. For although the provincial system continued to function until 1986, the concentration of power in the hands of the State President at the expense of Parliament made it likely that, in accordance with this trend, power would be transferred from the legislature to the executive at provincial level as well. It has already been noted that the Administrators and executive committees exercised some powers on behalf of the central government, and that even in the exercise of 'provincial' powers they were not responsible to the Provincial Councils. The effect of the re-ordering of provincial government in 1986 was drastically to increase the powers of the provincial executives and to abolish the Provincial Councils altogether. The introduction of the concept of own and general affairs in 1983 also had an impact on provincial powers: Many matters that formerly lay within the sphere of competence of the Provincial Councils were

[5] In terms of the Black Education Act 47 of 1953.
[6] In terms of the Group Areas Amendment Act 49 of 1962.
[7] For example, in the case of Bophuthatswana, by means of the Status of Bophuthatswana Act 89 of 1977.
[8] As amended by s 1 of the South Africa Act Amendment Act 45 of 1934.
[9] With the exception of the legislation giving independence to Bophuthatswana and Ciskei, see 143–6 above.
[10] For a description of the old provincial system, see Baxter op cit n 4 at 124–30.

classified as own affairs by Schedule 1 of the 1983 Constitution, and were therefore to be legislated on at Parliamentary level by the different communities, rather than by the Provincial Councils.[11]

Provincial government is now regulated by the Provincial Government Act 69 of 1986.[12] The most important effect of the Act was to terminate the existence of the Provincial Councils,[13] although all .provincial ordinances remained in force.[14] A further radical departure brought about by the Act was to confer on the State President (acting on the advice of a joint committee of Parliament) the power to change provincial boundaries by proclamation, and even to create new provinces out of the old ones.[15] But it was in the redistribution of power within the provinces that the most far-reaching changes took place. The most important political figure in each province is now the Administrator who, along with his executive committee, is appointed by the State President,[16] and who holds office during the State President's pleasure.[17] The powers of the Administrator and his executive committee (in whom executive authority in the province is collectively[18] vested) are enumerated in s 14 of the Act. The section is badly drafted in that it does not adequately distinguish between legislative and executive functions. However, the following essential provisions can be deduced from its terms:

1 Legislative power

In terms of s 14(1)(*a*) all legislative powers formerly enjoyed by the Provincial Councils are now exercised by the Administrator, and the Administrator is now empowered to amend or repeal any existing ordinance and to make new ordinances by proclamation in the *Government Gazette*.[19] Such proclamations come into force once they receive the approval of a standing committee of Parliament. The only difference between enactments by the Administrator and ordinances passed by the old Provincial Councils is that while the latter were classified as 'original' legislation and were thus immune from

---

[11] A prime example of this is local government, mentioned in s 6 of Schedule 1.

[12] For a discussion of the Act see Dion Basson and Henning Viljoen *South African Constitutional Law* (1988) 289–93, and Gretchen Carpenter *Introduction to South African Constitutional Law* (1987) 428–32.

[13] Which was brought about by s 2 of the Act, and which took effect on 1 July 1986.

[14] Sec 4.

[15] This power is conferred by s 5, which simply requires the State President to consult with the Administrators concerned.

[16] Sec 7. Note that blacks have been appointed to the executive committees—see Basson and Viljoen op cit n 12 at 285–6.

[17] Sec 11(1).

[18] Sec 7(2). Note that, in terms of s 13, decisions of the executive committee are taken by the Administrator, and that in terms of s 1 this means the Administrator acting 'in consultation with' the other members of the executive committee of which he is chairman. The use of the phrase 'in consultation with' in preference to 'on the advice of' suggests that the Administrator does not have to have the support of the other members of the committee for any decision he might take.

[19] Sec 14(2)(*a*).

judicial review on all grounds except that of ultra vires, proclamations by the Administrator (whether they are new legislation or are simply amendments of existing ordinances) are examples of delegated legislation and are therefore reviewable.[20] The matters over which the Administrator has legislative power are stipulated in s 84 of the Provincial Government Act 32 of 1961—that is, those matters previously lying within the competence of the Provincial Councils.

2   Executive power

Section 14(1)(*a*) also deals with executive power, and provides that the Administrator has inherited those powers previously entrusted to the old executive committee and that he also exercises any other powers defined by the State President as being 'provincial' in nature. In addition to these powers, other powers are conferred upon the Administrator in his executive capacity, but because of the poor standard of draughtsmanship evident in the Act, it is unclear what powers these are. Section 14(2)(*b*) entitles the Administrator to 'perform any functions on behalf of any department of State'. This absurdly wide phraseology could, if literally interpreted, mean that the Administrator has the discretion to conduct foreign affairs or take decisions pertaining to national defence. Clearly this cannot be the case, but in the absence of any limitations on the scope of the subsection, its meaning remains unclear. The only sensible interpretation is that s 14(2)(*b*) refers to those instances in which the Administrator acts as representative of central government, implementing its policies in the province. But if this be the case, it is difficult to see the necessity for the subsection—s 14(3) specifically states that with respect to all matters over which the executive committee of a province has no powers,[21] the Administrator shall act on behalf of the State President when required to do so, and may act without consulting with the executive committee. One cannot imagine any circumstance in which the Administrator would perform an action on behalf of a department of state without having been authorised to do so by the State President, and so s 14(2)(*b*) seems to be redundant as well as cryptic.

In terms of s 15(1) of the Act the State President can assign to an Administrator a function normally performed by a cabinet minister, while s 15(1B) empowers any minister belonging to a ministers' council to assign any of his functions to an Administrator.[22]

---

[20] For a full discussion of the status of provincial legislation, see 174–5 above. See also Lourens M du Plessis and H J Erasmus (1988) 105 *SALJ* 763.

[21] Presumably matters which are not 'provincial' in nature.

[22] An example of Administrators being assigned a power normally exercised by a cabinet minister is provided by the notice in *GG* 10565 of 2 January 1988, which assigned the power to issue exemption permits in terms of s 21 of the Group Areas Act 36 of 1966 (normally exercised by the Minister of Constitutional Development and Planning) to provincial Administrators.

Section 15(3) in turn empowers an Administrator further to delegate any such function[23] to any provincial official.

It needs to be emphasised that the main political effect of the Provincial Government Act 69 of 1986 has been to remove legislative power from a deliberative body elected by the white inhabitants of the provinces and to confer it on officials appointed by central government. This is indicative of trends which have become increasingly important over recent years: a concentration of power in the hands of the executive at the expense of the legislature, and a concentration of power in the organs of central government at the expense of sub-national institutions. So far as executive power is concerned, although provincial executives continue to supervise the administration of provincial affairs, the execution of central government policy now comprises an increasing part of their function, with the result that in many instances they have simply become the agents of central government. Moreover even those powers that are purely 'provincial' are constantly being eroded by parliamentary legislation which removes them from the provinces and transfers them to Pretoria.[24]

B Joint executive authorities

Section 17 of the Provincial Government Act provides for the establishment of a joint executive authority upon the recommendation of any provincial Administrator and the Chief Minister or Ministers of any one or more homelands. The function of such an authority would be to undertake the joint exercise of certain powers normally exercised separately by the province and the government or governments of the self-governing territories concerned. The only areas of South Africa for which such an authority has been established are KwaZulu and Natal. During 1986 negotiations (known as the KwaZulu–Natal Indaba) took place between the government of KwaZulu, the Natal Provincial Administration and other interested parties with the aim of drafting a constitution for the region. At time of publication, the government has yet to make a formal response to the constitutional proposals eventually agreed upon.[25] However, the government did respond to an agreement reached earlier in 1986 by participants in the Indaba that a joint executive authority (JEA) should be set up for the region as an interim measure. The result was the enactment of the Joint Executive Authority for KwaZulu and Natal Act 80 of 1986.

The Act empowered the State President to establish by proclamation a joint authority for Natal and KwaZulu (s 5). This he did by

---

[23] With the exception of the power to issue proclamations or make regulations.

[24] For example, although s 84(1)(*h*) of the Provincial Government Act 32 of 1961 gave legislative power over roads to the provinces, s 20 of the National Roads Act 54 of 1971 gives the Minister of Transport the power to make regulations governing roads.

[25] The full text of the proposals, assented to on 28 November 1986, is contained in the KwaZulu–Natal Indaba Constitutional Proposals and Memoranda.

means of Proclamation 119 of 1987[26] which brought the authority into being on 7 August 1987. In terms of the proclamation, the JEA consists of ten members—five each from the Natal Provincial Administration and the KwaZulu government. The powers of the JEA are stipulated in s 6 of the Act, and simply stated are to co-ordinate the administration of any matter in which the governments of the province and the self-governing territory have an interest. The JEA may also perform any function assigned to it by the State President in terms of s 7 of the Act. Although the Act authorises co-operation only at executive level, a positive response to the Indaba proposals from the government would pave the way for the unification of Natal and KwaZulu and the establishment of a joint legislature as well.

II THIRD-TIER GOVERNMENT

A Local authorities

If central government is considered to be the first tier in the hierarchy of governmental structures, and the provinces the second tier, then the third tier comprises those institutions collectively referred to as local authorities. There is no uniform system of local authorities in South Africa. Each province and each racial group has its own local authorities, which makes this topic difficult to analyse.[27]

1 Black local authorities

In contrast to local authorities for whites, coloureds and Indians which are established by provincial authorities in accordance with the powers conferred on them by the Provincial Government Act 32 of 1961,[28] all local authorities operating in urban areas inhabited by blacks owe their existence to various Acts of Parliament dealing with black local government as a class of its own. Although provincial Administrators have the power to establish local authorities for blacks,[29] and exercise day-to-day supervision over black local government, ultimate control is exercised by the Department of Constitutional Development and Planning.[30] Originally, urban areas designated for residence by blacks were administered by non-elected Administration Boards established in terms of the Black Affairs Administration Act 45 of 1971. However, the unpopularity of these boards, which were responsible for the administration of repressive

---

[26] *GG* 10858 of 7 August 1987.
[27] For other analyses see Baxter 138–58, Basson and Viljoen 296–306 and Carpenter op cit n 12 at 432–4.
[28] See 222–5 below.
[29] In terms of s 2(1) of the Black Local Authorities Act 102 of 1982.
[30] In terms of s 17A of the Promotion of Local Government Affairs Act 91 of 1983, when Administrators establish new local authorities they must do so in accordance with any directives issued by the Minister of Constitutional Development and Planning.

legislation such as that dealing with influx control,[31] led to an attempt to increase the legitimacy of black local authorities by the enactment of the Community Councils Act 125 of 1977. This Act established a number of elected councils which took over some of the functions of the administration boards. Once again, lack of legitimacy thwarted the success of the system, with very low percentage polls being recorded in elections for the councils. The next attempt to put black local administration on a firmer foundation was the Black Local Authorities Act 102 of 1982, which repealed the Community Councils Act[32] and which replaced community councils with elected city councils, town councils, town committees and local authority committees (depending on their size) similar to local authorities which exist in 'white' South Africa.[33] Section 2(1) of the Act empowers provincial Administrators to establish such local authorities in townships newly opened for black residence.[34] Like local authorities in white areas, the bodies established in terms of the Black Local Authorities Act may enact by-laws and regulations, although these are subject to the approval of the provincial Administrator in whose area the local authority is situated.[35]

Although the result of the legislative developments discussed above is that black urban areas are now governed by elected local authorities which are structurally the same as those which exist in white areas, it is important to note that these local authorities enjoy powers that are considerably less extensive than those enjoyed by their white counterparts. Indeed, s 23(1)(*l*) of the Act makes it clear that only city councils enjoy powers to deal with the limited range of matters specified in the Schedule to the Act, and that all other types of local authority must have power specifically conferred upon them by the provincial Administrator, subject to any conditions he may impose in terms of s 25(1). Moreover, the powers formerly wielded by the Administration Boards are still in existence (even though the boards themselves have been abolished),[36] and are now stated (in terms of s 5(1) of the Abolition of Development Bodies Act 75 of 1986) to vest in the provincial Administrators.[37] The power that local authorities have to make by-laws is subject to the approval of those by-laws by the Administrator,[38] and the Administrator may himself make by-laws on any matter on which the local authority may make

[31] The boards were finally abolished by s 3(1)(*d*) of the Black Communities Development Act 4 of 1984.
[32] Sec 56A.
[33] Sec 2(3).
[34] But see n 30.
[35] Sec 27.
[36] See n 31.
[37] Subject to the Minister of Constitutional Development and Planning transferring them to any other public authority.
[38] Sec 27(1).

by-laws (this last provision presumably having been enacted to thwart boycotts).[39]

Local government in rural areas inhabited by blacks was originally regulated by the Black Authorities Act 68 of 1951.[40] In terms of s 2(1) of the Act, the State President may establish black tribal, community, regional and territorial authorities (in ascending order of importance) in black rural areas. These authorities need not necessarily be elected—s 3(3) provides that their members are either elected or are selected in terms of the regulations governing their establishment. The most developed of these authorities (the territorial authorities) have the power to make by-laws on a variety of local government matters[41] which might be assigned to them by the State President, although such by-laws come into force only once they have received his approval.[42] Such authorities also have the power to levy taxes.[43] Although the Black Authorities Act remains on the statute books, it seems to have fallen into desuetude, and its chief importance now is in relation to the granting of independence to black states within South Africa (discussed in section III below), because the establishment of a black territorial authority is the first stage in that process. The Act would therefore have to be used should the government wish to grant independence to any other black area of South Africa.

Nowadays black local government in rural areas is governed by the Black Administration Act 38 of 1927. Section 30 of this Act empowers the Minister of Education and Development Aid to establish local authorities in black rural areas. These local authorities have such powers as are assigned to them by the Minister, which may even include the powers enjoyed by black urban authorities.[44] Section 30A provides that authorities established in terms of s 30 shall have the power to pass by-laws, subject to the Minister's approval.

Undoubtedly the greatest handicap faced by all black local authorities is their lack of legitimacy, which derives from their association with the policy of racial segregation of governmental institutions.

2   Coloured and Indian local authorities

In terms of s 28 of the Group Areas Act 36 of 1966, the Minister of Constitutional Development and Planning is empowered to establish advisory committees for coloured and Indian areas. Their function is to advise the white local authority under the jurisdiction of which they fall on matters affecting the interests of the local coloured or Indian community. However, most of these committees were

---

[39] Sec 27(2A).
[40] See Baxter 142, Basson and Viljoen 309–10 and Carpenter 403–4.
[41] These are listed in s 5(1)(b) and include things such as roads, hospitals and education.
[42] Sec 7(1)(g) as read with s 5(2).
[43] Sec 7(6).
[44] In terms of the Black Local Authorities Act 102 of 1982.

established by provincial Administrators[45]—for example, s 306 of Natal's Local Authorities Ordinance 25 of 1974 provides that in the absence of the establishment of a committee by a minister in a particular area, the Administrator could establish such a committee (called local affairs committees in Natal) for the area. Other provinces have similar ordinances. Although these advisory committees are elective bodies, their lack of financial independence means that they are powerless should the relevant white local authority refuse to heed their advice. Hence these institutions lack support among the populations they were designed to serve. Somewhat more successful have been the fully fledged local authorities (enjoying exactly the same status as white city councils and town councils discussed below) which have been established by Administrators acting on the instructions of the Minister[46] or on their own initiative.[47] Only a limited number of advisory committees have been upgraded to local authority status. Moreover, it is necessary to note that since the enactment of s 17A of the Promotion of Local Government Affairs Act 91 of 1983, whenever an Administrator establishes, dissolves or alters the jurisdiction of *any* local authority,[48] he must do so in accordance with any directives issued by the Minister of Constitutional Development and Planning.

Finally, it is worth mentioning the existence of boards of management for rural areas inhabited by coloured people, although these are few in number. The election of these boards is regulated by the Minister of Local Government, Housing and Agriculture of the House of Representatives in terms of s 23 of the Rural Areas Act (House of Representatives) 9 of 1987. Section 26 of the Act confers extensive powers of local government on these boards of management,[49] while s 27 confers upon them the power to make regulations, subject to the Minister's approval. The power to levy rates on immovable property is conferred by s 31. In terms of these provisions the boards enjoy much the same status as do those local authorities which have been established in coloured urban areas.

3 White local authorities

White local authorities have always fallen under the jurisdiction of provincial rather than central government, with Administrators having the power to establish local authorities in terms of s 84(1)(*f*) of the Provincial Government Act 32 of 1961.[50] It is therefore unsurprising that the nomenclature of local authorities differs slightly from province to province, but in general one finds the

---

[45] Acting in terms of s 84(1)(*b*) of the Provincial Government Act 32 of 1961, which empowers Administrators to establish local government bodies.

[46] In terms of s 29 of the Group Areas Act 36 of 1966.

[47] For example, in the case of Natal, in terms of s 307 of the Local Authorities Ordinance No 25 of 1974.

[48] Be it one for blacks, whites, Indians or coloureds, or even an RSC.

[49] Sec 55 gives the Minister the authority to grant such boards additional powers.

[50] However, see n 30.

following institutions of local government in white urban areas (ranked in size from largest to smallest): city councils, town councils, village councils and local boards. All these bodies are elective in nature. By contrast, local government in rural areas is conducted by boards appointed by the provincial Administrators (with the exception of the Cape Province, where elected divisional councils govern rural areas).

The most important (and most interesting) feature of local government in urban areas is that although they are subordinate bodies in that their powers are delegated to them by the provincial government, they are not subordinate to the provincial government in the exercise of those powers. They must exercise them in accordance with the democratically expressed wishes of the local inhabitants. It is thus the elective nature of local authorities that is their most significant characteristic. Elections for local authorities are held in a manner very similar to those for Parliament, with the area of each local authority being divided into wards, which are the equivalent of parliamentary constituencies. After local elections have been held, the councillors elect a mayor and deputy mayor from among their number. The council appoints a town clerk, who is the chief administrative officer of the authority and is in charge of its 'civil service'. Control over this municipal civil service may be effected in either one of two ways: in some councils all administrative functions are delegated to a single standing committee of particular councillors, leaving other council members free to formulate policy (this is the 'management committee' system), while other local authorities operate through a number of committees each charged with a single administrative function, which means that all councillors are involved in the workings of at least one of these committees (this is the 'multiple committee' system).[51]

One of the most important powers of local authorities is that of making legislation, called by-laws or regulations. Because they are the product of a body to whom power has been delegated, by-laws are fully subject to judicial review, and as subordinate legislation, by-laws may not conflict with provincial ordinances or Acts of Parliament. In addition, by-laws do not come into force until they have received the approval of the provincial Administrator.[52] Finally, as Baxter points out,[53] local authorities have been able to achieve a greater degree of financial autonomy than did provincial authorities. This is chiefly because local authorities derive about 50 % of their revenue from rates charged on immovable property, and rely for only about 4 % of their income on grants from central and provincial government. This is to be contrasted with the provincial govern-

---

[51] The two systems are explained in Johan Meyer *Local Government Law. Volume I—General Principles* (1978) 66–7.
[52] See, for example, s 268(4) of the Natal Local Authorities Ordinance 25 of 1974.
[53] At 152.

ments which, at the time of the demise of the Provincial Councils, relied for about 85% of their income on grants from central government.[54]

B Regional Services Councils

The most recent development pertaining to local government is the establishment of Regional Services Councils. Prior to the enactment of the Regional Services Councils Act 109 of 1985, local government in South Africa was conducted on the strictly segregated lines discussed in the preceding pages. Thus the councils, which are 'multi-racial' bodies designed to take over some of the functions of the different 'racial' local authorities, represent a departure from previous government policy.

The first stage in the establishment of a Regional Services Council ('RSC') is the delimitation of the area over which it will have authority. In terms of s 2 of the Act this is done by the provincial Administrator acting with the concurrence of the Minister of Constitutional Development and Planning, the Minister of Finance, the minister in charge of black local government, and the ministers of local government in the three ministers' councils. Section 2(2)(*b*) also obliges the Administrator to 'consult' with the local authorities in the area of the proposed RSC, but s 2(A) makes it clear that he can establish an RSC without their co-operation. Once the area of jurisdiction of the RSC has been determined, the Administrator may then formally establish it by proclamation in terms of s 3 of the Act. The matters for which the new RSC will be responsible are also stipulated by the Administrator, who has the power to select which of the functions listed in Schedule 2 of the Act the RSC may perform. Examples of those are the supply of water and electricity; the supply of passenger transport; the provision of ambulance, fire brigade and health services; and the running of libraries and museums. It should be noted that Schedule 2 is not exhaustive, and the Administrator may assign any 'other regional functions' to the RSC. Once a particular function has been placed under the RSC's authority it is vested with the powers formerly exercised by the local authorities in their discharge of that function, and the latter not only lose their power to deal with that particular matter,[55] but are also prohibited from having it dealt with by any institution other than the RSC.[56]

In terms of s 6 of the Act each RSC consists of a chairman[57] appointed by the Administrator plus representatives of each local body operating within its jurisdiction. The great majority of the local bodies will of course be the black, coloured, Indian and white local authorities and advisory committees described earlier in the chapter, but s 1 of the Act, as read with s 6, does provide for other

[54] See Basson and Viljoen 289.
[55] Sec 3(2).
[56] Sec 5.
[57] Who has no vote; see s 11(1).

'representative bodies' to nominate members to sit on RSCs. Examples of these are organisations such as farmers' unions which are elective, which use the services provided by the RSC, and which are entitled to send representatives to the RSC because to some extent they represent the interests of rural communities whose inhabitants are not represented on any local authority.[58] The number of nominees which a local body may send to the RSC varies in proportion to the voting strength assigned to each body, subject to the entitlement of each local body to have at least one, but no more than five, representatives on the RSC.[59] The apportionment of votes on RSCs is governed by s 9(1) of the Act, which provides that the voting strength of each local body represented on an RSC shall be in proportion to the amount of revenue it contributes to the RSC. The only exceptions to this principle are that no body represented on the council may cast more than 50 % of the votes (even if it contributes more than 50 % of the council's revenue)[60] and that each body will have at least one vote.[61] Section 11 of the Act provides that a two-thirds majority of votes is required for decisions to be taken by an RSC. If, after a reconsideration by the RSC, a motion still fails to get a two-thirds majority, it is referred to an appeal board[62] consisting of the Administrator (replaced by the Minister of Finance if a financial matter is at issue), the minister responsible for black local government, and the ministers in charge of local government on the three ministers' councils. The assent of at least four of the five appeal board members is required for any decision to be taken.[63] If a body represented on the RSC is dissatisfied with a decision taken by the RSC s 11(4) provides a limited number of grounds upon which it may refer the decision to the appeal board for final determination. Although RSCs are prohibited from raising money by means of rates on immovable property,[64] they are entitled to charge fees for the provision of services and, in terms of s 12, are entitled to the proceeds of a 'regional services levy' imposed upon employers and a 'regional establishment levy' imposed upon other persons carrying on an enterprise in the region.

Several comments can be made about the RSC system. RSCs were conceived by the government as a mechanism for providing a limited degree of power-sharing at the third tier of government. Many services that were previously provided by the racially separate local authorities are now under the control of regional bodies on which all communities living in the region are represented. To this extent, the

---

[58] As mentioned at 224 above, many rural areas (except in the Cape) are governed by non-elective boards.
[59] Sec 6(2).
[60] Sec 9(2).
[61] Sec 9(4) provides that the allocation of votes must be revised annually.
[62] Sec 11(3).
[63] Sec 11(7).
[64] Sec 4(1)(*a*).

establishment of RSCs is a positive development. RSCs have, however, proved to be politically controversial, and have encountered opposition both from whites who are unwilling to participate in multi-racial structures and from blacks who consider RSCs to be contaminated by the fact that they still form part of a structure based on racial differentiation. Indeed, such opposition was anticipated by the government, as is indicated by sections in the Act which permit the establishment of RSCs without the support of the subordinate local authorities,[65] and which compel local authorities to use services provided by the RSCs.[66] Finally, RSCs do have the advantage of making available to all races in a particular region services that were previously reserved for whites, and which were often of a higher quality than those provided for other race groups. However, against this must be set the fact that control of RSCs is effectively retained in the hands of the representatives of the white local authorities, given that votes are allocated in proportion to revenue generated rather than in proportion to population—although this domination is tempered somewhat by the rules that no local authority may control more than 50 % of the votes[67] and that decisions must be taken by a two-thirds majority.[68]

III INDEPENDENT STATES

In accordance with the policy of 'grand apartheid', the black inhabitants of South Africa were to lose their South African citizenship and become citizens of 'homelands' to which South Africa would eventually grant independence. This section deals with the process involved in the granting of independence and with the implications it has for the citizenship rights of blacks. Although it might at first seem strange to deal with the Constitutions of independent states in a textbook on South African constitutional law, it is of cardinal importance to remember first that no country (apart from South Africa herself) recognises the 'independence' of the homelands and that in terms of public international law they therefore do not exist; and second that despite their supposed political independence, these states remain economically dependent on South Africa, where most of their citizens live and work. In addition, the homeland governments are heavily subsidised by the South African government.

A The independence process

Four stages can be identified in the process of granting independence to black areas.

---

[65] Sec 2A.
[66] Sec 5.
[67] Sec 9(2).
[68] Sec 11. Additional protection is provided by the rule that in cases of deadlock decisions must be taken by an appeal board. The composition of this board is such that it could contain a maximum of only three whites, whereas decisions must be taken by at least four of its members. See s 11(3) and s 11(7).

1   Creation of a black territorial authority

The first stage is the establishment of a black territorial authority in terms of the Black Authorities Act 68 of 1951. The provisions of this Act have already been discussed.[69] Here it is simply necessary to note that the highest rung on the ladder of rural black local government also serves as the lowest rung on the ladder to independence, and that in the normal course of events, only those areas which achieve territorial authority status proceed further along the road of constitutional development.

2   Establishment of a non-self-governing national state

In terms of s 1(1) of the National States Constitution Act 21 of 1971, the State President may establish a legislative assembly for an area governed by a black territorial authority. The area then becomes what can be called a 'non-self-governing' national state, and its territorial authority is automatically dissolved.[70] The legislative assembly may, but need not necessarily, be elective in nature,[71] and has legislative power as prescribed in s 3 of the Act. In terms of this section, the assembly may enact laws on those topics[72] listed in Schedule 1 of the Act, which in practice means that it has roughly the same legislative powers as does a provincial Administrator. Laws passed by the assembly enjoy the status of original rather than delegated legislation[73] and, with the prior approval of the State President, may even be applicable to citizens of the national state living outside its borders but within South Africa.[74] Although the assembly may repeal existing laws governing matters listed in Schedule 1, it may not repeal Acts of the South African Parliament.[75] Moreover, laws passed by such a legislative assembly do not come into effect until they receive the approval of the State President.[76] Finally, the power to legislate on certain matters (such as defence, foreign affairs, the police, currency and communications) is specifically withheld from legislative assemblies of non-self-governing national states.[77]

Executive power is regulated by s 5, which provides for the establishment of an executive council, whose composition is determined by the State President, but whose members must be drawn from the legislative assembly—in other words s 5 provides for responsible government. All national states have passed through this phase of development.

---

[69] At 222 above.
[70] Sec 13.
[71] Sec 2.
[72] Which includes the power of taxation—see s 15 of the Schedule.
[73] Baxter 132.
[74] Sec 3(1)(c).
[75] Sec 3(1)(b).
[76] Sec 3(2).
[77] Sec 4.

3 Conferral of self-government

The third stage on the road to independence is the conferral upon a national state of self-government. At the moment all six non-independent national states[78] enjoy this status. In terms of s 26 of the National States Constitution Act, the State President may declare any existing national state to be a self-governing national state, complete with flag[79] and national anthem.[80] The legislative assembly of a self-governing state enjoys the power to legislate on those matters specified in Schedule 1, and in addition may repeal or amend any Acts of the South African Parliament dealing with such matters.[81] Furthermore, South African Acts passed after the conferral of self-government and dealing with matters referred to in Schedule 1 do not apply in the national state, unless expressly stated to do so.[82] In terms of s 30(2) laws made by a national state's assembly will automatically apply to its citizens living anywhere in South Africa, and although a national state's legislation must receive the assent of the State President, s 31(2) makes it clear that the State President cannot withhold his assent unless he is satisfied that the enactment contravenes the National States Constitution Act, or is ultra vires in terms of Schedule 1. Responsible government is a feature of self-governing national states, s 29(1) providing that executive power vests in a cabinet consisting of a Chief Minister and other ministers drawn from the legislative assembly. The South African government is represented in each of the six national states by a commissioner-general.

In terms of s 30(4) of the Act, the State President retains the very important power he enjoys in terms of s 25(1) of the Black Administration Act 38 of 1927 to legislate by proclamation for black rural areas. However, this power is limited in that s 30(4) of the National States Constitution Act permits the State President to pass laws only on those matters not falling within the legislative competence of the national state assemblies.[83] Furthermore, as was held by Rabie CJ in *Government of the Republic of South Africa v Government of KwaZulu*,[84] certain of the State President's powers in terms of s 25(1) of the Black Administration Act are inconsistent with the provisions of the National States Constitution Act, and must therefore be taken to have been repealed by the later Act. On this basis, the court held that a purported excision of part of the territory of KwaZulu by the State President in terms of s 25(1) of the Black Administration Act was invalid because there had been no prior consultation with the KwaZulu cabinet in accordance with s 1(2) of

[78] KwaZulu, Lebowa, Gazankulu, Qwaqwa, KaNgwane and KwaNdebele.
[79] Sec 27.
[80] Sec 28.
[81] Sec 30(1)(*b*).
[82] Sec 30(3).
[83] That is, the matters listed in Schedule 1 of the Act.
[84] 1983 (1) SA 164 (A).

the National States Constitution Act, which mandates such consultation where the State President seeks to change the boundaries of a national state. This case is also important in that the court held that although one organ of the state cannot sue another organ of the state, and although KwaZulu was, as a national state, not entirely separate from the South African state, still KwaZulu enjoyed a sufficient degree of autonomy from South Africa to give it locus standi to sue the South African government.

The State President's power to change national state boundaries is subject to the requirement that he exercise the power for the purposes for which it was conferred.[85] In *Mathebe v Regering van die Republiek van Suid-Afrika*[86] the Appellate Division held that the dominant purpose which the legislature had sought to achieve in passing the Act was the promotion of 'national association', and that the purported incorporation of the Moutse district into KwaNdebele in terms of s 1(2) had been null and void, because it had been done for reasons of administrative convenience, rather than in order to further that purpose. Similarly, the court in *Lefuo v Staatspresident*[87] held that the incorporation of Botshabelo into QwaQwa was void because it had not been done in order to promote the political development of the inhabitants of Botshabelo in terms of 'national association'.

4 The granting of independence

The final stage is the granting of full independence to a self-governing national state. The taking of this final step is politically controversial—first, because many see it as an implicit endorsement of apartheid and, secondly, because of the serious ramifications it has for the citizenship rights of black South Africans.[88] Thus the KwaZulu government has refused to proceed to full independence, and severe political strife arose in KwaNdebele over the issue resulting in this state also deciding to remain a self-governing territory. However, four states (Transkei, Ciskei, Venda and Bophuthatswana) have achieved independence, and this subsection focuses on them.

The granting of independence to the national states involved two steps. First, the South African Parliament had to surrender sovereignty over the territories concerned. This was done in terms of the 'Status Acts',[89] which provided that these territories would no longer be part of the Republic of South Africa and that South Africa would cease to have any authority within them. The legislatures of the territories were given unlimited legislative competence. South

---

[85] See 309 below.
[86] 1988 (3) SA 667 (A).
[87] 1989 (3) SA 924 (O).
[88] See Budlender (1985) 1 *SAJHR* 210.
[89] The Status of Transkei Act 100 of 1976, the Status of Bophuthatswana Act 89 of 1977, the Status of Venda Act 107 of 1979 and the Status of Ciskei Act 110 of 1981.

African laws in force at the date of independence would remain in force until amended or repealed by the independent legislatures.[90] No South African legislation (including amendments to existing South African statutes) passed subsequent to independence would apply in the new states. Once South Africa had passed the relevant Status Acts, the independent states were free to proceed to the second step in the process—the enactment of their own Constitutions. Space does not permit a detailed analysis of these Constitutions,[91] and so only their most basic characteristics will be mentioned.

The Transkeian Constitution follows the Westminster model, providing for a titular President acting on the advice of a Prime Minister who has the support of the legislature. By contrast the Constitution of Bophuthatswana deviates from the Westminster system in that it combines the characteristics of the presidential and the parliamentary executive systems, by providing for an executive President, who is elected by the legislature and who, along with the members of his cabinet, must be a member of the legislature. The Constitution is also inflexible, and contains a justiciable Bill of Rights. The Constitution of Venda is similar to that of Bophu-thatswana—the President (who is elected by the legislature) and his cabinet must be members of the legislature. The Constitution is entirely flexible and there is no Bill of Rights. Finally, the Ciskeian Constitution provides for a President elected by the legislature and an executive council whose members (along with the President) must be members of the legislature. The Constitution includes a compre-hensive Bill of Rights, but its effect is rendered nugatory by a specific denial of any testing right to the courts.

The constitutional history of the independent states has by no means been smooth: Venda is now a one-party state, Transkei is under military rule after a coup, there was an attempted coup in Bophuthatswana, and civil strife has occurred in the Ciskei, whose relations with the Transkei have been strained. Moreover, none of the states has received international recognition, and all remain heavily dependent on South Africa financially. But perhaps the greatest problem facing the governments of those states is the limited popular support they enjoy, due largely to the fact that they owe their existence to the policy of apartheid.

[90] Controversy arose in the case of the Bophuthatswana Constitution. Section 93(1) of this document enacted into Bophuthatswanan law a provision that, subject to the Constitution, all laws in force at the time of independence would remain valid until amended or repealed. The Constitution contains a Bill of Rights which was inconsistent with certain security legislation 'inherited' from South Africa, and the question arose as to whether this legislation remained in force. In *S v Marwane* 1982 (3) SA 717 (A) it was held that because the provision that all existing laws remained in force was 'subject to' the provisions of the Constitution, and because the Bill of Rights was part of the Constitution, the security legislation was no longer valid in Bophuthatswana.

[91] See M P Vorster, Marinus Wiechers, D J van Vuuran (eds) *The Constitutions of Transkei, Bophuthatswana, Venda and Ciskei* (1985).

B   Citizenship

The process of granting independence to the homelands had serious implications for the citizenship rights of black South Africans. Although, as Basson and Viljoen point out,[92] black South African citizens enjoy what amounts only to a titular or 'bare' citizenship in view of the denial to them of so many rights normally attaching to citizenship,[93] still the compulsory deprivation of citizenship constituted a serious infringement of their personal rights. The reason for the removal of South African citizenship from blacks and the connection between this and the homeland policy is not hard to discover: In terms of the policy of apartheid, all black South Africans were allocated the citizenship of an ethnic homeland (irrespective of whether they lived in the area assigned to that ethnic homeland), and were eventually to lose their South African citizenship once that homeland was granted full independence. In theory that stage would be reached when all blacks living and working in South Africa would become aliens, whose continued presence in South Africa would depend on the pleasure of the South African government, and in particular on the requirements of the South African labour market. Blacks would never enjoy political rights in South Africa, but would be expected to exercise these by voting for the governments of their respective homelands, even though they might neither have been born nor have set foot in them. Quite apart from the manifest injustice involved in stripping people of South African citizenship, and of foisting upon them the citizenship of an artificial entity with which they might have felt no identity, the system paid no regard to economic realities. The black and white populations of South Africa are inextricably interlinked, and economic forces dictate that the majority of black South Africans will be born, live and work in 'white' South Africa, as there is simply insufficient economic activity in the homelands to support them. It was primarily for this reason that legislation was passed in 1986 restoring South African citizenship to some of the people who had previously been deprived of it.[94] But many continue to be denied their citizenship rights, and this section deals with the effect upon them of citizenship laws at both the pre- and post-independence stages of national state development.

1   Citizenship of a national state

Section 2(1) of the National States Citizenship Act 26 of 1970 creates a citizenship of every black territorial authority established in terms of the Black Authorities Act 68 of 1951, and of every national state established in terms of the National States Constitution Act 21 of 1971. Every black person in South Africa who is not a citizen of one

[92] At 330–1.
[93] For example, to live where they please and to vote.
[94] The Restoration of South African Citizenship Act 73 of 1986.

of the four independent states, and who has not had South African citizenship restored to him in terms of the Restoration of South African Citizenship Act 73 of 1986, is automatically held to be a citizen of one of the territorial authorities or national states,[95] and enjoys political rights there.[96] Such a person does not, however, lose his South African citizenship[97]—indeed, as Basson and Viljoen[98] and Carpenter[99] point out, such persons cannot be considered to be anything other than South African citizens, because citizenship can only be held in relation to an independent state. The manner in which it is decided of which national state a person is a citizen is regulated by s 3(1). This section provides several 'connecting factors'[100] which will make a person a citizen of a particular national state. Of course the vagueness of some of these criteria makes it quite possible that a person could be a citizen of more than one national state, hence the provision in s 9 of a right of appeal in disputed cases to the Minister of Constitutional Development and Planning, whose decision is final.

2 Citizenship of an independent state

The conferral of independence upon a national state had further consequences for the citizenship rights of its inhabitants. All four of the Status Acts which gave independence to Transkei, Bophuthatswana, Venda and Ciskei contained identical provisions[101] making certain prescribed categories[102] of person citizens of the independent state and depriving them of their South African citizenship. Here again the vagueness of the criteria leaves wide scope for doubt, and each Status Act provides that in such cases citizenship matters are to be determined by a board established jointly between the government of the independent state and that of South Africa—a rather unusual way of deciding issues of citizenship and nationality![103]

---

[95] Sec 2(2).

[96] Sec 2(3).

[97] Sec 2(4).

[98] At 341.

[99] At 392.

[100] Such as birth, lawful domicile, ability to speak the language of the area, relationship with a member of the area's population, or even identification or association with the population.

[101] See s 6 of each of the Status Acts listed in n 89. The only exception was Bophuthatswana—in terms of s 6(3) of its Status Act the possibility was created for people to renounce Bophuthatswanan citizenship.

[102] The prescribed categories were listed in Schedule B of each of the Acts, and embraced the following persons: all existing citizens of the independent state, persons one of whose parents were at the time of their birth citizens of the independent state, and South African citizens who were not citizens of another national state within South Africa and who (i) spoke the language of the state being granted independence, or (ii) were related to a member of the population of the national state, or (iii) identified or associated themselves with that population.

[103] Carpenter 391.

3 Consequences of deprivation of South African citizenship

Notwithstanding the deprivation of South African citizenship caused by the granting of independence (frequently referred to as 'denationalisation'),[104] each Status Act provided that citizens of the newly independent states who were lawfully resident in South Africa at the time of independence would not, by reason only of the deprivation of their South African citizenship, lose other rights and privileges they might enjoy in South Africa. In other words, those who were entitled to live and work in South Africa would not automatically lose such rights simply by virtue of the fact that their 'homeland' had been granted independence. However, there would, of course, be nothing to prevent the South African government from withdrawing those rights at some later stage if it felt that the presence of these non-citizens in South Africa was no longer desirable. Indeed, the existence of this possibility was fundamental to the success of the apartheid policy.

But even the tenuous protection of existing rights by the Status Acts was of varying usefulness, with much depending on the attitude of the courts. In *Ex parte Moseneke*[105] the applicant, who was born in South Africa, but who had lost his South African citizenship in terms of the Status of Bophuthatswana Act 89 of 1977, sought admission as an attorney. One of the requirements for admission as an attorney was citizenship of, or lawful admission for permanent residence in, South Africa. The applicant, who was already resident in South Africa, was for certain reasons statutorily precluded from applying for permanent residence. However, Boshoff AJP held that as s 6(4) of the Status of Bophuthatswana Act 89 of 1977 had preserved all rights the applicant had enjoyed as a citizen (apart from citizenship itself) and as residence was one of those rights, the applicant was not required to apply for admission as a permanent resident, and thus should be enrolled as an attorney. However, this uncomplicated explanation of residence rights of denationalised persons failed to find favour with the majority of the court in *Tshwete v Minister of Home Affairs (RSA)*.[106] In this case Joubert JA held[107] that the 'rights-preserving' section (s 6(3)) of the Status of Ciskei Act 110 of 1981 had *not* had the effect of preserving the right to permanent residence. This conclusion was reached on the basis that as the rights-preserving section expressly provides that persons will not forfeit rights by virtue *only of the Status Act*, it follows that it does not preserve rights that might be lost by virtue of the provisions of any *other* legislation. Since the right of permanent residence is dependent on the provisions of the Aliens Act 1 of 1937 and the Admission of

---

[104] For a full discussion of denationalisation, see Dugard (1980) 10 *Denver Journal of International Law & Policy* 11. See also A J Rycroft in A J Rycroft (ed) *Race and the Law in South Africa* (1987) 217–20.

[105] 1979 (4) SA 884 (T).

[106] 1988 (4) SA 586 (A).

[107] At 607B–H.

Persons to the Republic Regulation Act 59 of 1972, and not on the holding of South African citizenship, Joubert JA concluded that the rights-preserving section does not absolve those wishing permanently to reside in South Africa from complying with the aforementioned Acts. Luckily for the appellant, the court found that because he had acquired a *domicile* in South Africa prior to deprivation of citizenship, he fell within the ambit of s 12(1)(*a*) of the Aliens Act, which meant that he could reside in the country without a permit. But, hard as it may be to believe, this did not mean that the appellant had an unrestricted right to *enter* South Africa, because in terms of s 40(1) of the Admission of Persons to the Republic Regulation Act, only those claiming to be South African citizens by birth or descent are entitled to enter the country without a visa! The appellant was thus left in the bizarre position of being entitled to live in South Africa but not to enter it! The last word clearly remains to be said on the residence rights in terms of the Status Act. Not only does Joubert JA's decision deprive the rights-preserving sections of all meaning,[108] but the position has been further complicated by legislation[109] (enacted in the light of *Tshwete's* case) preventing denationalised persons from relying on domicile to retain residence rights, and the fact that the *restoration* of South African citizenship is dependent upon the restoree possessing residence rights.[110] In short, and with due respect, the decision in *Tshwete's* case raises more questions than it answers, and makes indeterminate the legal position of hundreds of thousands of citizens of independent states living in South Africa.[111]

Misfortune also attended the respondents in *South African Television Manufacturing Co (Pty) Ltd v Jubati*,[112] who were in the process of launching an action for wrongful dismissal against the applicant, when the latter gave notice that it required the respondents to furnish security for costs. This it did on the basis that when Ciskei became independent, the respondents had become peregrini (that is, foreigners) from whom the applicant as an incola (that is, inhabitant within the court's jurisdiction) could demand such security. The respondents lived in Ciskei, but commuted daily to work in South Africa. In upholding the application for security for costs, Kannemeyer J adopted a narrow interpretation of the rights-preserving section.[113] This he did by holding that the section

---

[108] Given that only citizenship rights are affected by the Status Acts, and that, in Joubert JA's opinion, the rights-preserving sections protect only those rights (other than citizenship itself) touched upon by the Status Acts (and *only* the Status Acts) one is left with the position that the rights-preserving sections protect a vacuum!

[109] The Matters concerning Admission to and Residence in the Republic Amendment Act 53 of 1986.

[110] See 236–7 below.

[111] For a critical analysis of *Tshwete's* case and a valiant attempt to discern possible paths through this statutory minefield see Geoff Budlender (1989) 5 *SAJHR* 37.

[112] 1983 (2) SA 14 (E).

[113] Sec 6(3) of the Status of Ciskei Act 110 of 1981.

applied only to those 'resident in the Republic at the commencement of' the Act, and that because the respondents had always resided in what became the Ciskei, and because Ciskei had ceased to be part of South Africa the moment the Act came into force, the respondents had been resident in Ciskei and not South Africa at that commencement! The respondents had thus not had their rights preserved by the Status of Ciskei Act, and could be classed as peregrini. The judgment is also notable for the court's refusal[114] to take cognisance of the fact that the granting of independence to Ciskei had a negative impact on the rights of its inhabitants, or to see this as a special circumstance warranting the use of the court's discretion to refuse an application that security be provided.[115] Surely involuntary deprivation of citizenship was itself a violation of rights amounting to a special circumstance?

Finally, it is interesting to note that although deprivation of citizenship may cause one to lose rights in a country, it will not necessarily absolve one from obligations towards that country. For example, it is possible to find a person guilty of treason towards a country of which he is not a citizen, because in terms of the common law[116] a person ordinarily resident in a country owes loyalty to it, irrespective of whether he is a citizen. Thus, in *S v Tsotsobe*[117] the court found that an accused who had been deprived of South African citizenship could nevertheless be found guilty of treason because he was ordinarily resident in the Republic, while in *S v Magxwalisa*[118] it was held that the reason why the accused could not be found guilty of treason was not because he had been deprived of South African citizenship, but because he was not resident in South Africa.

4 Restoration of South African citizenship

As mentioned above, the impracticality of the homeland policy led to a partial retreat by the South African government on the question of citizenship, and the enactment of the Restoration of South African Citizenship Act 73 of 1986. Space does not permit a detailed discussion of the provisions of the Act,[119] but its basic features are as follows: Persons who lost their South African citizenship in terms of any of the Status Acts can have it restored in one of four possible ways—by birth, descent, registration or naturalisation. The key to regaining citizenship by birth[120] is that the person concerned must have been born in South Africa and have been lawfully resident there at the time the Restoration Act was passed. Similarly, a person born outside South Africa who seeks to gain South African citizenship on

---

[114] At 16F–G.
[115] At 19E.
[116] See, for example, Voet *Commentarius ad Pandectas* 48.4.4.
[117] 1983 (1) SA 856 (A).
[118] 1984 (2) SA 310 (N).
[119] See Basson and Viljoen 342–6 and Carpenter 388–9.
[120] Sec 2.

grounds of descent[121] must be the minor child of a person who regained his or her citizenship on grounds of birth, and must also have been granted lawful residence in South Africa before the commencement of the Restoration Act. Much obviously hinges in both instances on the requirement of lawful residence. The same applies with regard to restoration of citizenship by registration[122] or naturalisation:[123] In both cases applicants must have been lawfully resident in the Republic for a prescribed period. In other words, all those seeking restoration of South African citizenship must prove that they were lawfully resident in South Africa at the appropriate time. This means they must show that they fulfilled the requirements imposed by s 10 of the Blacks (Urban Areas) Consolidation Act 25 of 1945 (which governed residence rights up to June 1986), or the Abolition of Influx Control Act 68 of 1986 and the Prevention of Illegal Squatting Act 52 of 1951 (which have governed residence rights of blacks since June 1986). The continued relevance of statutes designed to implement the policy of restricting the right of black persons to live in South Africa, which was an integral element of apartheid, has justifiably led commentators[124] to conclude that the citizenship reform is not as far-reaching as it might seem to be. It is, however, encouraging to note that persons to whom citizenship has been restored are not compulsorily made citizens of one of the national states,[125] but simply remain South African citizens. Basson and Viljoen[126] regard this as possibly indicating an intention on the part of the government to create a single citizenship for all South Africans at some stage in the future.

[121] Sec 3.
[122] Sec 4.
[123] Sec 5.
[124] See, for example, A J Rycroft op cit n 104 at 220–4.
[125] See s 2(3) of the National States Citizenship Act 26 of 1970.
[126] At 345–6.

Part III

Administrative Law in the Courts

11 Judicial Review of Administrative Action

Public authorities are not at liberty to do as they please. With one exception,[1] they have no inherent powers. They may do only what Parliament expressly or impliedly authorises them to do, and they must act in accordance with minimum standards which the law imposes on them. In short, they must comply with the requirements of 'legality'. When public authorities (collectively though inaccurately[2] 'the administration') go beyond their statutory powers, fail to perform statutory duties or otherwise breach the standards imposed on them by law, aggrieved persons may challenge their actions and decisions in the Supreme Court by means of an application for judicial review. Judicial review, then, is a process concerned with identifying and curing illegalities committed by the administration. Its purpose is to ensure that the requirements of legality are met and to provide complainants with remedies when legality is breached.

As we explain in chapter 13,[3] there is a special procedure in our law for challenging administrative action in the Supreme Court by way of application. But one of the most interesting characteristics of judicial review is that it does not always take this conventional form; there are various ways in which a party in an ordinary civil or criminal case may invoke judicial review indirectly. The reason for this is that almost any case involving statutory powers or duties could conceivably involve the principles of legality, the substance of administrative law in the courts. Take, for instance, a criminal trial in which the accused is charged with contravening a regulation made by the Minister of Law and Order under the Public Safety Act 3 of 1953. As a defence to the charge, the accused might well argue that the regulation is illegal (or 'ultra vires') because in phrasing it too widely the Minister went beyond the lawmaking powers conferred on him by the Act. By raising this defence, the accused has successfully invoked an indirect form of judicial review in what is apparently a criminal case. The same sort of thing can happen in private law, typically in contract cases where one of the parties is a public authority. If it can be shown, for example, that the public authority was contracting in pursuance of a statutory power or duty, it may be possible to imply into the contract a duty on the authority

---

[1] The inherent prerogative power of the executive head of state; see above, 175–82 and below, 248–9.
[2] Not all public authorities form part of the administration; see above, 11 and 16.
[3] Below, 284–6.

to comply with the principles of legality.[4] Judicial review is a potential 'back-door' remedy whenever a statute is present.

I JUDGES AND JUDICIAL REVIEW

The adjective 'judicial' is doubly appropriate. It suggests not only the obvious, that judges are the officials who have jurisdiction to review administrative decisions in this way, but also a less obvious fact: that it is the judges who actually make most of the rules relating to review. While the powers and duties of public authorities are generally statutory in origin, the law relating to the review of their actions is largely to be found in the law reports. It is 'judge-made' law.

The power of our judges to shape the rules of administrative law is easily apparent throughout Part III of this book. In chapter 12, we see that the courts themselves decide who may apply for judicial review and in what circumstances they may do so. The remedies discussed in chapter 13 depend to a great extent on judicial creation and maintenance; and in chapters 14 and 15 we try to show that the judges have it in their power to alter the standards of legality applicable in cases of judicial review by adding to the list of standards, shortening the list, or by increasing or decreasing the scope of a particular standard. This is not to say that Parliament never intervenes; it does, sometimes so drastically as to exclude the court's jurisdiction. But until such time as Parliament codifies[5] the rules relating to judicial review of administrative action, they are likely to retain their characteristic common-law flavour. It is arguable that even codification is incapable of changing the strong 'judicial' character of administrative-law review, since there is no area of statutory law which is completely immune from the effects of judicial interpretation and judicial creativity—or the lack of it. Ultimately, the role of our courts is (and is likely to remain) something controlled by them, and not by Parliament. This has repeatedly been demonstrated in the many cases where our courts have refused to implement the clear intention of Parliament to oust their jurisdiction or to limit it.[6] However, this power of interpretation and creation is one which many lawyers (including judges) are reluctant to recognise. Because there are such hotly contested views as to the proper role of the judiciary in relation to the other two arms of government, the proper extent of judicial control over the review of illegalities is the most controversial issue of our administrative law. The 'justiciability' of administrative issues—the extent to which adjudication is regarded as an appropriate and feasible method of

---

[4] For an actual (albeit unsuccessful) attempt to do exactly that, see the case of *Scholtz v Cape Divisional Council* 1987 (1) SA 68 (C), discussed at 249 below.

[5] The possibility of codification is being investigated by the South African Law Commission; see *Working Paper 15*, Project 24 (1986) and the fledgling Judicial Review Bill appended to it.

[6] See 295–8 below.

dealing with them—depends to a large extent on the prevailing 'judicial ideology', the theory of what the division of power in government should be.

A Justiciability and theories of adjudication

At one end of the spectrum is the orthodox theory, which sees the courts' function as that of a politically impartial watchdog over the rest of government, and especially over its executive arm. This view has a great deal in common with the principle of the Rule of Law as propounded by Dicey,[7] and is sometimes referred to as the 'Rule of Law' model. It treats law as being elevated above politics, depicts judges as independent and impartial arbiters, and stresses their function of guarding against arbitrariness in government—that is, against the use of powers without the authorisation of law. This watchdog or 'red-light'[8] model of the judicial role is also in keeping with the notion of a clear separation of governmental powers into legislative, executive (including administrative) and judicial arms, with the corresponding functions of *making law, making or implementing policy decisions* and *stating the law*. And this division in turn lends support to a 'phonographic' theory of adjudication. Judges, it is said, do not make law; they interpret the will of Parliament and they 'declare' the law. They are the 'mouthpiece' of Parliament.

A more radical, 'green-light'[9] view tends to blur the separation of governmental functions by supporting a much more interventionist and bureaucratic form of government—a government which increasingly regulates what are traditionally 'private' activities, such as commerce—and a much less antagonistic judiciary: a judiciary which *assists* the state in implementing its policies instead of placing obstacles in its way, or, to put it crudely, behaves more like a lap-dog than a watchdog. Here legislation and administrative action are given priority over judicial scrutiny and judicial rule-making as being far more efficient and certainly more democratic ways of running a country. In this interventionist model, policy is given priority over law, and internal controls on the administration are preferred to the more traditional external control by the judiciary, whose orthodox, rule-bound, dispute-solving role is regarded as inappropriate to the flexible demands of modern, 'responsive'[10] government.

This is not a model which has gained much favour amongst South African lawyers, though for obvious reasons it might well be preferred by the government. One of the reasons for lawyers' hostility to it is our system of legal education, which has tended to perpetuate the liberal Rule of Law view. Another lies in the

[7] A V Dicey *The Law of the Constitution* 10 ed (1959) 183–205.
[8] See above, 80ff.
[9] See above, 81.
[10] See n 11 below.

undemocratic nature of the South African political process and the racial oppression associated with it.

In this country interventionist government is all too easily associated with *repressive* government rather than *responsive* government,[11] and the amount of politically oppressive legislation promulgated by our Parliament tends to ensure that faith in the interventionist model will be slow to emerge. In fact, some South African writers[12] reject both the interventionist model and the outdated watchdog model, and argue instead for a more interventionist and creative *judiciary* in order to soften the blows of repressive government. In view of the fact that judges are unelected officials, more or less overt judicial lawmaking may be regarded as an illegitimate exercise of power; but objections of this kind have a very hollow ring when one considers that the lawmakers themselves are not democratically elected.[13]

B Theory and reality

It is undoubtedly true to say that a version of the watchdog or red-light model underpins most of the principles of our administrative law as it is argued in the courts and portrayed in the textbooks. Indeed, the liberal notions of the Rule of Law, parliamentary sovereignty and the separation of powers underlie the very first principle of judicial review—that public authorities may do only what Parliament empowers them to do. This is not surprising, since we inherited most of our administrative-law principles from English law at a time when watchdog theories dominated in that country, and these continue to be fostered by our legal education. A glance at the administrative-law curricula of South African law schools will confirm that, even in recent years, the more radical theories have been given scant attention or none at all. What is surprising is that there are lawyers who still believe in the watchdog's counterpart, the naïve theory of phonography. The myth that judges merely declare pre-existing law and never make policy decisions or new law was thoroughly discredited by the American legal realists half a century ago, and it has since been the butt of a great deal of mockery, some

---

[11] These terms are used by Phillipe Nonet and Philip Selznick in their useful analysis of evolutionary forms of law in society, *Law and Society in Transition: Towards Responsive Law* (1978). These writers identify three main types of law: 'repressive', 'autonomous' and 'responsive'. The repressive model envisages a governing power which 'gives short shrift to the interests of the governed . . . when it is disposed to disregard those interests or deny their legitimacy' (ibid 29). It is succeeded by the autonomous (or Rule of Law) model, where 'the legal order becomes a resource for *taming* repression' by means of its commitment to procedural justice (at 53). Finally, the responsive model recognises that 'good law should offer something more than procedural justice. It should be competent as well as fair; it should help define the public interest and be committed to the achievement of substantive justice' (at 73–4).

[12] See Cora Hoexter (1987) 104 *SALJ* 436 at 437ff and the works cited there.

[13] See Laurence Boulle (1987) 104 *SALJ* 104, especially at 111.

of it coming from judges themselves.[14] But it is a strangely tenacious myth. In almost every volume of the South African Law Reports one can read judicial statements affirming that judges are not politicians: that the role of the judge is to declare, not make, law; to give effect to, and not make, policy. In short, the traditional game of separating the powers continues to be played with every appearance of seriousness.

The trouble with this is that the liberal Rule of Law model and its phonographic accompaniment seem to provide an increasingly unhelpful and unrealistic theoretical framework for our administrative law. Admittedly it has been an inappropriate framework from the start, since this country has never practised the most basic liberal principle of equal political rights; but in the acute political crisis of the last decade it has become more obviously inaccurate and uninformative. On one hand, it does not account for the strong evidence[15] of judicial activism and creativity in security and other 'political'[16] cases over the past few years; evidence which is abundant in administrative law, a subject which lends itself to perceptions of direct antagonism between the individual and the government. On the other hand, it does not explain the countervailing trends of extreme judicial conservatism or restraint: cases in which the judiciary has allegedly abandoned its impartial watchdog role and has taken up what is sometimes called a 'pro-executive' stance.[17] These fluctuations are undoubtedly linked to political events, most obviously the various states of emergency, and to shifting judicial attitudes towards the judges' own role; so that it is perhaps to political and social reality that we must look for the real explanations and underpinnings of the case law, and not outdated theories of adjudication.

Since it is still possible to cling to the orthodox model of adjudication in the less politicised areas of administrative law— licensing, agricultural and economic regulation, and the like—one may prefer to regard 'security' and 'apartheid' cases as sui generis, exceptional or aberrant. This is a tempting option, if only because it

[14] A useful account appears in Lord Lloyd and M D A Freeman *Lloyd's Introduction to Jurisprudence* 5 ed (1985) chapter 12, especially at 1129ff.

[15] See, for example, Dion Basson (1987) 3 *SAJHR* 28; Hoexter op cit n 12, especially at 446ff.

[16] 'Political' has a special shade of meaning for South African lawyers, who commonly use the word to describe cases involving apartheid and security legislation. Here we use the word in a still looser sense to include not only these subjects, but any areas in which the interests of the government and those of the majority of the people may be perceived to conflict.

[17] 'Restraint' is a commonly used term in this context, but a misleading one: it suggests a lack of activism, whereas executive-mindedness is, of course, activism of a different kind. For examples of allegations of executive-mindedness, judicial conservatism and/or abstentionism, see Edwin Cameron (1982) 99 *SALJ* 38 and (1987) 3 *SAJHR* 223; D M Davies (sic) (1987) 3 *SAJHR* 96 and (1987) 3 *SAJHR* 229; the various writers who contribute to the 'Focus on *Omar*' in (1987) 3 *SAJHR* 295–337; Dennis Davis and Hugh Corder (1988) 4 *SAJHR* 281; Nicholas Haysom and Clive Plasket (1988) 4 *SAJHR* 303; Christopher Forsyth (1988) 105 *SALJ* 679; Hugh Corder (1989) 5 *SAJHR* 1; Etienne Mureinik (1989) 5 *SAJHR* 60.

explains away the many recent cases in which fundamental liberal principles of our common law have been cast aside in the face of repressive legislative measures.[18] But this approach can lead one to ignore two important considerations. The first is that repressive legislation is pervasive in this country. The catalogue of legislative inroads on the basic rights assumed in our common law is so long as to make it doubtful whether these excesses can be dismissed as exceptional occurrences.[19] It must be remembered, too, that South Africa is not in its first, but in its *fourth* year of emergency rule in this decade.[20] The second is that while judicial attitudes are perhaps thrown into their sharpest relief in the political cases, their importance is not confined to those cases. The entire field of administrative law is 'political' in the sense that it is characterised by a continuous tension between two opposing ideals: the ideal of governmental freedom of action, and the ideal of judicial control. Whether a dispute relates to a trading licence or a banning order, its outcome depends at least partly on the judge's willingness to interfere.

II   THE BOUNDARIES OF JUDICIAL REVIEW

The most popular description of judicial review of administrative action is probably one made more than eighty years ago by Innes CJ in *Johannesburg Consolidated Investment Co v Johannesburg Town Council*:[21]

> 'Whenever a public body has a duty imposed on it by statute, and disregards important provisions of the statute, or is guilty of gross irregularity or clear illegality in the performance of the duty, this Court may be asked to review the proceedings complained of and set aside or correct them. This is no special machinery created by the Legislature; it is a right inherent in the Court. . . .'

This statement, though dated, still pinpoints some of the most salient features of judicial review. Others no longer hold true for modern administrative law, and it is misleading to cite the dictum without qualification (as is sometimes done in the cases). The most important points are listed below.[22]

A   'Public body'

As a general rule, the doings of private individuals and organisations

---

[18] To mention only a few, *Omar v Minister of Law and Order* 1987 (3) SA 859 (A) (discussed below, 353); *Minister of Law and Order v Dempsey* 1988 (3) SA 19 (A) (below, 317–8); *Staatspresident v United Democratic Front* 1988 (4) SA 830 (A) (below, 261ff; 297–8; 304–5; 355–7). For more thorough surveys, see Davis and Corder op cit n 17; Haysom and Plasket op cit n 17.

[19] For recent accounts of the impact of security and apartheid legislation on the daily lives of citizens, see Anthony S Mathews *Freedom, State Security and the Rule of Law* (1986); A J Rycroft (ed) *Race and the Law in South Africa* (1987).

[20] The state of emergency was renewed by the State President on 9 June 1989 (*GG* 11945 R85, 1989).

[21] 1903 TS 111 at 115.

[22] See also the cogent account of Etienne Mureinik (1985) 102 *SALJ* 434.

are not reviewable by courts of law, while those of 'public' bodies are. This corresponds with the notion that public bodies, because they exercise public powers, are subject to a sort of public trust which imposes special standards and duties on them. Most fundamentally, the law requires them to exercise their powers in the public interest, and not arbitrarily or for their own advantage; and more generally, they are subject both to the statutory terms on which their powers are conferred and to the common-law rules imposed on them by the courts. By contrast, private bodies and individuals acting in terms of their private rights have far more freedom to do as they please. The difference is neatly described in a dictum of Schreiner JA in *Mustapha v Receiver of Revenue, Lichtenburg*:[23]

> 'For no reason or the worst of reasons the private owner can exclude whom he wills from his property or eject anyone to whom he has merely given precarious permission to be there. But the Minister has no such free hand. He receives his powers from the statute alone and can only act within its limitations, express and implied. If the exercise of his powers is challenged the Courts must interpret the provision, including its implications and any lawfully made regulations, in order to decide whether the powers have been duly exercised.'

Most governmental institutions, such as ministers and departments of state, provincial and local authorities, are easily identified as having a public character. But it is not always so easy to tell whether a particular body is public or private; in particular, the demands of modern government have made it common for public bodies to undertake activities traditionally associated with the private sector.[24] Writers on the subject[25] agree that affirmative answers to any of the following questions will point towards a public agency, though not decisively so:

● is the body created or controlled by statute?
● is public money one of the body's sources of funding?
● does the body fall under the control of a recognised public authority?

Baxter[26] proposes a more crucial question: is the agency under a duty to *act in the public interest*? If so, it can be regarded as 'public' for the purposes of judicial review. The 'public interest' test can beg the question, since the conclusion that a body is under such a duty may well be based on the fact that it has already been recognised as a public body! Nevertheless, the test was used successfully in *Dawnlaan Beleggings (Edms) Bpk v Johannesburg Stock Exchange*,[27] where a decision of the JSE, a non-statutory body, was held to be reviewable on the ground that the JSE was under a statutory duty to

---

[23] 1958 (3) SA 343 (A) at 347.
[24] See above, 4.
[25] See Marinus Wiechers *Administrative Law* (1985) 67–70; Lawrence Baxter *Administrative Law* (1984) 100.
[26] Baxter op cit n 25 at 100.
[27] 1983 (3) SA 344 (W). See also Mureinik op cit n 22.

act in the public interest. Such a duty will not necessarily be obvious on the face of the statute; it may have to be inferred from all the circumstances, *including* the statute.

There are a number of exceptions to the general rule that only the actions and decisions of public bodies are reviewable. In *Turner v Jockey Club of South Africa*,[28] for instance, the Appellate Division held that the club, a private body, had acted illegally in taking disciplinary action against a jockey without giving him a fair hearing. The fact that the contract between the parties said nothing about fairness could not excuse the club's failure to give him an adequate opportunity of defending himself, since the requirement of a fair hearing, although part of administrative law and not private law, was held to have been implied into the contract. There are many other cases in which private bodies wielding (contractual) coercive or disciplinary powers have been made to conform to the principles of natural justice.[29] In these cases, the coercive nature of the power (rather than the nature of the organ exercising it) seems to be the factor which justifies[30] the courts' interference. For the sake of convenience we refer throughout Part III of this book to 'public' bodies and 'public' authorities, but it should be borne in mind that private bodies are not always immune from judicial review.

B 'Statutory duty'

This term is quite misleading. While it remains true that public bodies can be made to comply with statutory duties (provisions which *require* something to be done), the existence of a statutory *power* (a provision which *enables* someone to do something) is sufficient to ensure that an administrative agency is subject to review. Furthermore, the power need not necessarily be a statutory one. As cases like *Turner*[31] show, even private (usually contractual) powers may be subject to judicial control where they have a coercive character; and prerogative powers,[32] the inherent powers of the head of state, are not exempt from judicial review. For many years the rule was that the courts could enquire as to the existence and scope of a prerogative power, but that they could not pronounce on the way in which it was exercised.[33] That rule has been thrown into doubt by the case of *Boesak v Minister of Home Affairs*,[34] where Friedman J, following the English example, was prepared to assume that certain prerogatives are reviewable on the grounds of 'illegality, irrationality

---

[28] 1974 (3) SA 633 (A).
[29] See *Theron v Ring van Wellington van die NG Sendingkerk in Suid-Afrika* 1976 (2) SA 1 (A) and the discussion at 335ff below.
[30] On justification, see 262ff below.
[31] 1974 (3) SA 633 (A).
[32] See further above, 175ff.
[33] *Sachs v Dönges NO* 1950 (2) SA 265 (A).
[34] 1987 (3) SA 665 (C).

and procedural impropriety'.[35] This approach has not yet received the approval of the Appellate Division, but it is consistent with the modern view that judicial control over the abuse of power should not depend solely on the *source* of the power.[36]

Though the reviewability of statutory powers has been settled for some considerable time,[37] the principle is not always recognised in the cases. A recent instance is *Scholtz v Cape Divisional Council*,[38] a case of 'back-door' review which involved a contract of lease entered into between the appellant and the council—a public body—in pursuance of its powers to provide accommodation for indigent persons under the Housing Act 4 of 1966. When the appellant was suddenly evicted from his low-rent cottage, he argued that it was an implied term of the contract that the council could not exercise its contractual power of eviction 'arbitrarily or capriciously', but that, since it received its contractual powers from the Housing Act, the council had to act in accordance with the requirements of legality. The failure of this argument was at least partly due to the court's insistence on a statutory *duty* to provide cheap housing. Van den Heever J (Baker J concurring) found that there was no such duty on the council,[39] and that the lease was therefore an 'ordinary commercial contract'—meaning that the council could evict the appellant for any reason or none, provided of course that the eviction did not breach the express terms of the contract. This approach is unfortunate, since it ignores not only important case authority, but also the fundamental principle that public powers are always accompanied by implicit duties: a general duty to act in the public interest, and a more specific duty to act in accordance with the purposes of the particular statute.[40] In other words, there are strong grounds for arguing that the council would in fact have been acting illegally if it evicted a tenant for a reason not contemplated by the Housing Act.[41]

C 'Gross irregularity or clear illegality'

This is a very broad description of the occasions on which a court will interfere with administrative action. Those occasions are generally referred to as the *grounds of review*, though the list of grounds is rather more detailed than is suggested by the two heads above. The grounds are specific manifestations of a larger concept known as the

---

[35] At 681E, relying on the judgment of Lord Diplock in *Council of Civil Service Unions v Minister for the Civil Service* [1984] 3 All ER 935 (HL).

[36] For example, Baxter points out that it is 'purely an accident of history' that some prerogative powers are not statutory (Baxter 332). See also the strong views of Dumbutshena CJ in *Patriotic Front-ZAPU v Minister of Justice, Legal and Parliamentary Affairs* 1986 (1) SA 532 (ZS); and see below, 262.

[37] See the judgment of Corbett J in *Harnaker v Minister of the Interior* 1965 (1) SA 372 (C) at 377B–H and the authorities cited there.

[38] 1987 (1) SA 68 (C).

[39] At 70I–71I.

[40] See below, 309; 343ff.

[41] See Bede Harris and Cora Hoexter (1987) 104 *SALJ* 557.

principle of *legality*; the notion of government according to law. Legality is discussed in detail later on in this chapter,[42] together with its counterpart, the ultra vires doctrine, and the particular grounds of review to which they give rise. For the moment it is necessary only to note that neither of the adjectives used by Innes CJ is particularly apt. It is very seldom that the 'grossness' of maladministration need be established before a court will quash it;[43] and maladministration will not escape scrutiny merely because it is not a 'clear' case of maladministration. Judicial review exists precisely in order to let judges scrutinise conduct which might—or might not—turn out to be illegal:

> '[T]o decline jurisdiction simply because the illegality is not clear would be to confer a margin of immunity from judicial review in borderline cases to which the administration, in the absence of statutory authority, is not entitled.'[44]

D 'Set aside or correct'

'Review' really has two meanings: scrutiny, and the granting of a remedy. The Supreme Court thus has dual jurisdiction to *review* (scrutinise) administrative action and to *grant an appropriate remedy*. As far as the second sort of jurisdiction is concerned, the 'or' should not be read disjunctively, since the court may both set aside *and* correct administrative action in appropriate cases.

In many instances setting aside (or 'quashing') will be a sufficient remedy. But where setting aside or correction would not cure the damage caused by the illegality, or even damage threatened, the court may be asked for a more appropriate remedy such as an award of damages or a mandatory interdict.[45] While applications for special remedies like these may or may not be coupled with an application for review in the sense of *setting aside*, they usually do entail indirect judicial review in the sense of *scrutiny*. This feature is discussed more fully in chapter 13.

E 'Inherent'

This is perhaps the most crucial of all the points raised in the dictum of Innes CJ, and it remains entirely valid. While *appeals* to both administrative agencies and to courts of law are made possible only by specific statutory provision, the jurisdiction of the Supreme Court to *review* decisions of the administration requires no such authority; it is inherent in the Supreme Court. This inherent review jurisdiction, a feature which we have in common with the English legal system, was recognised as part of our law in the earliest days of the

---

[42] Below, 255ff.
[43] An important dictum of Stratford JA in *Union Government v Union Steel Corporation* 1928 AD 220 at 236–7 refers to 'gross' unreasonableness; but see below, 341–3.
[44] Mureinik op cit n 22 at 434–5.
[45] See below, 284.

old Cape Supreme Court.[46] It is quite distinct from the various types of statutory review in our law (see below).

There are many other important points of distinction between appeal and review. Some of these are discussed in the next section of this chapter.

III REVIEW AND APPEAL

A right of appeal may be thought of as a second chance: an opportunity to have one's case heard a second time by a new decision-maker, with the possibility of a different decision being reached. Appeal is concerned with the merits of the case, which is to say that the second decision-maker is entitled to express the view that the decision reached by the first was *right* or *wrong*. A simple example is a criminal case in which a lower court finds the accused guilty and the appeal court comes to the opposite conclusion on the same facts.

Review is not concerned with the question whether the decision was right or wrong, but whether the decision was *reached* in an acceptable way. Review looks at the decision-making process rather than at the decision itself; in theory,[47] a court of review is not entitled to concern itself with the merits of the decision (though the converse is not always true—there are some appellate bodies which may exercise review powers as well). An example of review is the case where a court quashes the decision of a lower court or tribunal on the ground that the latter took completely irrelevant evidence into consideration when coming to its decision. That decision would be set aside *even if the review court felt that the same decision would have been reached on relevant evidence*. This indicates that, unlike appeal, the focus is really not on the decision itself, but on the way in which it was reached.

While the orthodox approach in the cases is to preserve a rigid distinction between the focus of appeal and that of review, the distinction is not necessarily as clear as it is made to seem. It may be argued, for instance, that the grounds of review relating to the unreasonableness of administrative action involve an enquiry as to the substantive *merits* of the decision as well as the legality of the decision-making process. The problem of substantive judgments is discussed in the last chapter of this book.[48]

---

[46] On this and other forms of inherent jurisdiction, see Jérold Taitz *The Inherent Jurisdiction of the Supreme Court* (1985) especially at 28–36. See also Baxter 303–5. At 304 Baxter notes that 'inherent' in this context means *logically inherent* rather than *inherited*: the courts' jurisdiction to review illegalities is a logical consequence of their duty to apply the law enacted by Parliament. This idea is expressed in the 'ultra vires doctrine' which we discuss at 259 below.

[47] In practice, the decision may be so obviously wrong that it alerts the court to a flaw in the decision-making process. The two issues, merits and process, are not always capable of clear separation.

[48] Below, 341–3.

A   Types of review

Apart from instances where the word 'review' is used (infuriatingly) to mean 'appeal',[49] there are three main sorts of review jurisdiction enjoyed by the Supreme Court: automatic review, ordinary review of civil and criminal cases, and inherent jurisdiction to review the decisions of administrative authorities.

1   Automatic review

The Criminal Procedure Act 51 of 1977 provides for the automatic review by judges of certain sentences imposed by magistrates.[50] Other instances of automatic review occur in relation to orders made under such statutes as the Mental Health Act 18 of 1973 and the Prisons Act 8 of 1959.

2   Review of proceedings of inferior courts

Provincial divisions may be asked to review the proceedings of inferior courts in both civil and criminal cases on certain grounds, which are set out in the Supreme Court Act 59 of 1959.[51] These include absence of jurisdiction, bias or corruption on the part of the presiding officer, and the admission of inadmissible evidence.

3   Inherent jurisdiction to review administrative decisions

This is the 'administrative-law review' or 'common-law review' jurisdiction with which this chapter is mainly concerned. While its scope is sometimes altered or limited by legislation, it does not depend on legislation for its existence.

B   Types of appeal

Broadly speaking, there are two types of appeal in South African law: appeals from lower courts of law to higher courts of law, and administrative appeals, which might be heard by administrative officials, tribunals or by ordinary courts. But all appeals in our law have one characteristic in common: they are provided for by statute. It is not possible to appeal against any decision, whether of a court or of an administrative official, unless a right of appeal is created by legislation.

1   Appeals from lower courts to higher courts of law

Appeals of this kind are provided for in the Magistrates' Courts Act 32 of 1944, the Supreme Court Act[52] and the Criminal Procedure Act, and include civil and criminal appeals from magistrates' courts to

---

[49] Parliament sometimes gives the courts special statutory powers of 'review' which are wider than their inherent jurisdiction, and which allow the court to pronounce on the merits of the case; see below, 293.
[50] Section 302(1)(*a*).
[51] Section 24(1).
[52] Sections 19 and 20.

provincial divisions and from provincial divisions to the Appellate Division of the Supreme Court.

2 Administrative appeals

This type of appeal is the one primarily to be contrasted with judicial review of administrative action, because in the administrative-law scheme of things it is a complementary and yet quite different way of achieving reconsideration of decisions and decision-making. First, the power to review administrative action is inherent in the Supreme Court, whereas administrative appeals must be specially provided for by statute. Second, an appeal focuses on the merits of the decision, whereas review focuses on the manner in which the decision was reached; and third, while judicial review is an external safeguard against maladministration, administrative appeals are *internal* to the administrative process. This last point is discussed under the next heading of this chapter.

C Administrative appeals

Appeals from one administrative body to another constitute a major internal or 'domestic' safeguard against bad decision-making in government. The reasoning behind the administrative appeal structure is threefold. First, administrative authorities are thought to be the best judges of decisions made by other administrative authorities: they have the necessary specialist expertise, and they are likely to have a thorough grasp of the relevant policy considerations. Secondly, they are very often cheaper and more efficient than courts of law. Thirdly, the theory of the separation of powers holds that it would be wrong for courts of law to exercise the political function of pronouncing on the merits of administrative matters. As it is frequently stated in the cases,[53] to do so would be to usurp the function of another arm of government. However, it should not be supposed that the administrative appeals system necessarily *excludes* the possibility of judicial review. On the contrary, it is always theoretically open to an aggrieved individual to take the decision of an administrative authority on review to the Supreme Court, though there is usually a duty to exhaust one's domestic remedies[54] (such as internal appeal itself) before applying for review, and there are various other constraints (such as the requirement of standing)[55] which may see to it that the possibility remains theoretical.

---

[53] See, for instance, *African Realty Trust Ltd v Johannesburg Municipality* 1906 TH 179 at 182 (Bristowe J); *Crossley v Durban Town Council* 1934 NPD 226 at 248 (Lansdown J); *Jivan v Louw NO* 1950 (4) SA 129 (T) at 131 (Blackwell J); *Anchor Publishing Co (Pty) Ltd v Publications Appeal Board* 1987 (4) SA 708 (N) at 728–9 and the judicial statements reproduced there (Booysen J).

[54] See chapter 13.

[55] See chapter 12.

Unlike some common-law jurisdictions with comparable systems,[56] South Africa has no central body (administrative appeals tribunal) to which all administrative appeals are sent; instead, there are scores of different appellate bodies in the administration, ranging from single officials to administrative tribunals. There is no uniformity in the composition of these appellate bodies, and some have much wider jurisdiction than others. Some tribunals resemble courts of law very closely, often having as their presiding officers legally trained persons (for instance, the industrial court and licensing appeal boards), or even judges, as is the case with the patents, tax and water courts. Other appellate bodies are less like courts of law and appear to fulfil policy-making functions as well as adjudicative functions, be they high-ranking government officials such as ministers or tribunals like the rent control board. To add to the confusion created by the sheer variety[57] of appellate bodies, the terminology used in the legislation is often totally misleading: it is not unusual to find that a body described as a 'review board' is actually an *appeal* board in terms of its powers![58]

There is a strong argument for the creation of a single controlling body (like the Australian Administrative Appeals Tribunal) with jurisdiction to hear all (or most) administrative appeals. Certainly, such a tribunal would be infinitely preferable to the haphazard, incoherent and complex appeal structure which exists at present. However, the South African Law Commission has so far rejected the possibility. Its rather mysterious reasoning is that it would be constitutionally undesirable to allow a special 'administrative' division of the Supreme Court to exercise administrative functions.[59] The Law Commission seems in fact to have missed the point of the Australian experience quoted in it, since the Australian Tribunal was created *outside* the system of ordinary courts for this very reason.

D Does appeal include review?

In *Tikly v Johannes NO*[60] Trollip J drew a distinction between two types of appeal. Appeal in the wide sense, or *wide appeal*, refers to a complete rehearing and redetermination on the merits of a case with or without additional evidence or information. This means that the appellate body is not confined to the record of the authority a quo. In an *ordinary* appeal, on the other hand, the rehearing on the merits is limited to the evidence on which the decision was originally given; that is, restricted to the record of the authority a quo.

The distinction becomes significant when the question arises

---

[56] See *Working Paper 15* at 56ff.
[57] A list of administrative appeals appears in chapter 6 of the South African Law Commission's *Working Paper 15* op cit n 5. The list is not exhaustive, but nevertheless illustrates the diversity of the various appellate bodies.
[58] See n 49 above.
[59] *Working Paper 15* at 97–102. On administrative courts in general, see above, 92ff; and on the Australian AAT, see 93–4 above.
[60] 1963 (2) SA 588 (T) at 590F–591A.

whether an appellate body is entitled to correct illegalities committed by the authority a quo (that is, whether the appellate body is allowed to *review* the decision as well as pronounce on the merits), since a body confined to the original record will not usually be in a position to do this effectively. The reason for this, as Baxter[61] points out, is that the record itself may be distorted by the illegality. If, for instance, there was a failure to observe natural justice, this would probably not be apparent on the face of the record; and an ordinary appellate body would not be entitled to adduce fresh evidence to establish a breach of natural justice. The logical answer, then, is that only bodies exercising wide jurisdiction (not confined to the original record) may scrutinise alleged illegalities.

The trouble is that it is not usually apparent from the legislation which form of appeal is intended. Sometimes the legislation expressly states that the appellate body may perform review functions, but more often than not it simply invites the appellate body to 'confirm, vary or set aside' the original decision. Baxter[62] offers the following pointers to the existence of wide appellate jurisdiction:

● Lack of a record: If there is no provision for the keeping of a record, the appeal jurisdiction will almost certainly be wide.[63]

● Procedural powers: There is a strong indication of wide jurisdiction where the powers of enquiry are identical to those of the authority a quo.

● Decisional powers: A wide appellate jurisdiction is indicated where the decision of the appellate body is deemed in the legislation to be that of the authority a quo.

There is, however, no closed list of factors which might indicate a wide appeal. In *Tikly's* case,[64] for instance, Trollip J took into account the revision court's 'elaborate procedure for a trial hearing of an essentially judicial character' which, he said, could not have been designed merely for an ordinary appeal.[65]

IV THE HEART OF REVIEW: LEGALITY AND ULTRA VIRES

A Legality

When a court is asked to review an administrative action for correctness, it will generally frame its enquiry in terms of *grounds of* (or for) *review*. As is apparent from the dictum of Innes CJ in the *JCI* case,[66] the presence of one or more of these grounds enables the court to interfere, and to set aside or correct the action taken. But the specific grounds of review are merely the detailed version of a much

[61] Baxter 258–9.
[62] Ibid 261–3.
[63] See also *National Union of Textile Workers v Textile Workers Industrial Union (SA)* 1988 (1) SA 943 (A) at 941–2.
[64] Note 60 above.
[65] At 592–593A.
[66] Above, 246.

more general concept which is the very core of judicial review: that of *legality*. The task of the court is in fact to decide whether the action in question is *legal*: whether it meets the requirements of legality, or government according to law. The notion of legality, then, is the source of all the various grounds of review. In administrative law, legality embraces at least one of the legs of the Rule of Law as conceived by Dicey—the notion of government *authorised* and *regulated* by law, otherwise stated as the absence of arbitrary power in government.[67]

1 The sources of legality

The most fundamental requirement of legality is that statutory powers must always be exercised strictly in accordance with the terms on which they were conferred by Parliament to the executive. But this is not as simple as it sounds, for while some of those terms emerge more or less clearly from the actual legislation which confers the power, most of them are, strictly speaking, not terms laid down by Parliament at all; they are 'principles of good administration',[68] the product of judicial creation and interpretation over many years, and are implied into the law in much the same way as terms are implied into some contracts. This means that the concept of legality is rather wider than it might at first appear. It contains not only the express provisions enacted by Parliament, but also judicially created principles—the judges' notions of what would be enacted by an 'ideal' legislature.[69]

This may be illustrated by means of the following example. The wording of a university statute may indicate that the council of the university is the only body which has the power to expel students, so that it is reasonably clear that anyone else who purports to expel a student in terms of that law is acting contrary to Parliament's intention. A purported expulsion by any other body or person, even the chancellor himself, would be regarded as invalid—illegal—by a court of law. On the other hand, the empowering legislation may say nothing at all about giving the unfortunate student a hearing before her expulsion, but this will not prevent a court from finding that the student was illegally expelled by council on the ground that it failed to give her a fair hearing before making the decision to expel her. Exactly the same concept of legality is at work in each of these instances, but the rule about giving the student a hearing is a judge-made standard of good administration which does not appear obvious on the face of the statute. The interpretive device which allows judges to impose standards like this is the (common-law) principle that, where there is doubt as to the meaning of a statute, it should be construed so as to do the least harm to the liberty of the individual: 'if Parliament had intended a student to be expelled

---

[67] Dicey op cit n 7 at 188.
[68] D J Galligan (1982) 2 *Oxford Journal of Legal Studies* 257 at 261.
[69] Wiechers op cit n 25 at 176.

without the benefit of a hearing, it would certainly have said so'. Thus, though Parliament sets the basic limits of legality in every case, it is left to the courts to impose further common-law standards on the relevant administrative activity. As the example above illustrates, this is generally done by reference to the 'intention of Parliament'.[70] Cynics will notice that the converse ('if Parliament had wanted a hearing it would have said so') is also available for use by judges who wish to come to the opposite conclusion!

The distinction between the 'express' (statutory) and 'implied' (judge-made) requirements of legality is important to one's understanding of judicial review, but it cannot be taken too far. In a sense, *all* the requirements of legality are judge-made, because they all require judicial recognition and interpretation. To use the university example again, a court might well find that the chancellor *impliedly* has the power to expel students—even though the council is the only body with the *express* power to do so.[71] The requirements of legality are never self-defining, and they are always at the mercy of judicial interpretation and choice.[72]

2 Legality, legitimacy and justiciability

As has already been suggested, judicial choice is shaped and guided by the judicial 'ideology' or 'policy'[73] of the courts—the judges' view of their role in relation to the two other arms of government. Thus, a judge's willingness to interfere in administrative disputes will depend partly on his view of the amount of freedom which the executive and legislature may legitimately enjoy, and the legitimate extent of judicial control over legislative and executive acts. The tension between these two elements produces questions of *justiciability*: Which issues should be controlled by the courts, and which left to the other arms of government? How far should judicial control extend? When is judicial interference justified? What makes a dispute amenable to adjudication? These questions and their answers seldom receive explicit recognition in judgments. Instead, judges use a special vocabulary of justiciability, a sort of code whereby they explain and justify the scope of their interference in governmental action. Thus, a judge will establish the boundaries of the judicial preserve by referring to the difference between *appeal* and *review*, *process* and *merits*; he will justify his restraint or activism by typifying the power in question as *wide* or *narrow*, *discretionary* or *mechanical*, framed in *subjective* or *objective* language; and he will certainly be sensitive to the nature of the dispute—whether it is dominated by issues of *policy* or questions of *law*, and whether it relates to a matter of *private right* or *public interest*. All these classifications and categories help to shape the justiciability of the

[70] But see below, 262–4.
[71] On express and implied powers, see further below, 300–1.
[72] See further below, 357.
[73] On the idea of judicial policy, see further Cora Hoexter op cit n 12.

dispute, and therefore the requirements of legality which apply to it. For instance, an issue characterised by its policy content or by wide administrative discretion will tend to be less susceptible to judicial review. The requirements of legality which apply to it will be correspondingly weak.

Perhaps the most important terminology of all is that of the 'classification of functions', a technique whereby administrative activity is divided up to correspond with the three basic functions of government: *legislative*, *judicial* and *administrative*. The division (discussed at some length in Part I of this book)[74] is important to one's understanding of the kinds of tasks performed by the administration, and can be a helpful analytical tool when used with discretion. Unfortunately, the process of classification seems to have acquired a magical significance in our administrative law. Once a particular administrative action has been classified, the requirements of legality in relation to it are supposedly fixed and certain; so, in order to find the legal answer to a problem, all a judge has to do is classify the administrative action which gave rise to the problem. This means that the content of legality actually changes according to the 'type' of administrative action involved. The artificiality of this process of classification (for *all* the functions of the administration are by definition 'administrative'), and its grand insensitivity to the natural variety of administrative functions, have caused judges to resort to further subclassifications: 'purely administrative', 'quasi-judicial' and the like.

The consequences of functional classification should not be underestimated. To revert to our example of the expelled student, she is accorded the right to be heard on the basis that a decision to expel someone is a particular *type* of function. One cannot, therefore, assume that a fair hearing is a requirement in all types of administrative action. On the contrary, our courts are always saying (however reluctantly) that the maxim audi alteram partem, or 'hear the other side' applies only to quasi-judicial acts of the administration, and not to purely administrative or legislative ones.[75] As we shall see, this rigid classification of functions bedevils other principles of legality in administrative law. The requirement of reasonableness, for instance, applies with differing rigour to legislative, administrative and purely judicial activity.[76]

3   The requirements of legality

The requirements of legality are subject to constant change and development by judicial interpretation. The audi alteram partem principle, for example, was not always applied only in cases of a quasi-judicial nature; there are older cases which show that its

[74] Above, 85–90.
[75] See below, 330ff.
[76] Below, 340ff.

application has been much wider than this in the past.[77] And in recent years there have been judicial statements which suggest that the maxim represents nothing more than a common-sense notion of fairness, and that 'fairness' applies to *all* administrative acts![78]

The flexible nature of the concept makes it impossible to state concisely the precise requirements of the principle of legality in every case; these details (the grounds of review) are the subject-matter of the last two chapters of this book. However, it is possible to state the broad requirements of legality for most types of administrative action, and they are as follows:

(a) The principles of authority and regularity

The principle of authority entails that every act must be duly authorised by Parliament or its nominees, and that the official performing the action must be the one who is duly empowered. The principle of regularity means that the formalities and other prescriptions of the empowering legislation must be complied with. These requirements tend to be expressly stated in the enabling legislation and to apply uniformly to *all* kinds of administrative action. They are discussed in chapter 14.

(b) The principles of fairness and reasonableness

The standards of reasonableness and fairness are more complex because they tend to vary according to their classification as a particular type of administrative action. They are sometimes expressly stated in legislation, but more often they are implied into legislation by the courts. They are dealt with in chapter 15.

B Ultra vires

The concept of legality is a frequent source of confusion to students, since it is not a term used with any regularity in the reported cases. Instead, a court which finds that the requirements of legality have not been met will usually set the action aside as ultra vires—'beyond the powers' of the administrative authority concerned. Similarly, textbook writers make frequent reference to the *ultra vires doctrine* when discussing the courts' jurisdiction to scrutinise administrative action. This doctrine is tied to the theory of the separation of powers and the sovereignty of Parliament. Its essence is that Parliament, in conferring powers or 'vires' on public authorities, sets statutory boundaries for the exercise of those powers. Parliament is the sovereign lawmaker, while the function of the courts is to apply the law made by Parliament; therefore the courts are required to see that the intention of Parliament is carried out, and that public bodies act

---

[77] On ancient and English law, see H W R Wade *Administrative Law* 6 ed (1988) 499ff; on the older South African cases, see Baxter 575.

[78] Below, 339–40. This corresponds with the trend in English law, where a rigid classification of functions has been eroded by such cases as *Ridge v Baldwin* [1964] AC 40.

intra vires—that they remain within the boundaries of their powers. Conversely, the courts are entitled to set aside administrative action which is ultra vires the powers of public authorities.

Broadly speaking, there are two theories of ultra vires in our law, a wide theory and a narrow one. The wide or orthodox theory has dominated South African law (and its English parent) ever since administrative law received recognition as an independent branch of the law. It is epitomised in a dictum of Milne AJ in *Estate Geekie v Union Government*:[79]

> 'In considering whether the proceedings of any tribunal should be set aside on the ground of illegality or irregularity, the question appears always to resolve itself into whether the tribunal acted *ultra vires* or not.'

Professor Baxter,[80] a strong proponent of the wide theory of ultra vires, isolates three of its fundamental characteristics. First, it is a doctrine: a justificatory doctrine for the existence of judicial review. Second, it is comprehensive: any administrative action which fails to comply with *any* of the principles of legality is ultra vires. It does not matter whether public bodies *exceed* the limits of their powers or *abuse* those powers; in either case, the public body concerned will have acted contrary to the legislature's intention, for Parliament does not intend powers to be abused any more than it intends the powers conferred to be exceeded. Third, it is a negative statement (or the 'obverse facet'[81]) of the positive requirements of legality. Thus the terms 'illegality' and 'ultra vires' are synonymous in the language of the wide theory, as are 'legality' and 'intra vires'. This simple and elegant explanation receives clear, though tacit, support from the vast majority of decided cases in our law. It partly explains the courts' traditional reluctance to give effect to ouster clauses; the ultra vires doctrine *justifies* the court in exercising its inherent jurisdiction to determine whether legality has been breached, and no ouster clause on earth can do away with that justification.[82]

A number of writers have argued for a more literal, narrower conception of ultra vires, sometimes called 'procedural' ultra vires. The most notable proponent of the narrow view is Professor Wiechers,[83] who states that the idea of ultra vires is relevant only to the purely formal grounds of review; that is, those grounds which have to do with exceeding the limits of express powers, or with failing to comply with express statutory prerequisites. According to Wiechers, the courts' jurisdiction to control abuses of power as well as excesses is due to the wider principle of legality, which requires that

> 'an administrative act must not only be performed within the scope of the conferred powers and the requirements embodied in the empowering

[79] 1948 (2) SA 494 (N) at 502.
[80] Baxter 307–12 and 301–5.
[81] Ibid 301.
[82] See below, 295ff.
[83] Wiechers 174–9.

statute, but must also be in accord with those rules and prescripts of the common law which postulate the intention of the ideal legislature . . .'.[84]

Thus for Wiechers, the concept of legality—and not ultra vires—is the justification for the courts' interference in all but the formal grounds of review. Since ultra vires is not a *doctrine of justification* for the narrow school, 'ultra vires doctrine' will refer only to the wide school in the discussion below.

With one or two exceptions,[85] South African case law has always adhered to the wide view, and our judges have therefore referred to *any* kind of illegal action as 'ultra vires'. This view has, however, been discarded by the majority of the Appellate Division in the recent case of *Staatspresident v United Democratic Front*.[86] Here the court was concerned with scrutiny of emergency regulations made by the State President under the Public Safety Act 53 of 1953. The court found that some of these regulations were vague and uncertain, which would ordinarily mean that the State President had acted ultra vires his powers under the Public Safety Act (our courts having always reasoned that Parliament does not intend lawmaking powers to be abused in this way). However, the majority of the court decided that the State President could *not* in fact be said to have acted 'ultra vires'. This was because he had not *literally* exceeded his powers: the empowering legislation simply allowed him to make regulations, and did not expressly prevent him from making vague regulations.[87]

The court's rejection of the ultra vires doctrine has important consequences both for the rule against vagueness and for ouster clauses, and these are dealt with under the relevant headings in later chapters.[88] In the discussion that follows, we examine the implications of this revolutionary approach in the light of two crucial propositions which inform the judgment of Hefer JA:[89] first, that the ultra vires doctrine is undesirable because of its artificial and strained nature, its 'konseptualisme'; and second, that South African

---

[84] Ibid 176.

[85] The most famous is *Lipschitz v Wattruss NO* 1980 (1) SA 662 (T); for criticism of this case, see Baxter 311–12 and (1980) 43 *THRHR* 324.

[86] 1988 (4) SA 830 (A) per Rabie ACJ (in whose judgment Hefer and Vivier JJA concurred); Hefer JA (in whose separate judgment Vivier JA concurred); Grosskopf JA (in whose separate judgment Hefer and Vivier JJA concurred), Van Heerden JA dissenting. The court reversed the decision of the court a quo in 1987 (3) SA 296 (N) where Page and Galgut JJ rejected an argument based on a narrow conception of ultra vires. A similar argument was rejected in *Natal Newspapers v State President of the RSA* 1986 (4) SA 1109 (N), where a full bench of the Natal Provincial Division (Leon, Kumleben and Nienaber JJ) refused to draw a distinction between ultra vires 'in the broad sense' and 'narrow' ultra vires. In the opinion of this court, there was 'no difference in principle between the one species of ultra vires and another' (at 118H).

[87] See the judgment of Rabie ACJ at 853D–F.

[88] In relation to ouster clauses, see below, 297–8; in relation to vagueness and other abuses of discretion, see below, 355–7.

[89] At 868D–E. Though Rabie ACJ and Hefer JA reach the same conclusions, the latter's judgment is more fully reasoned and substantiated, and therefore more amenable to analysis.

courts have no need of a comprehensive principle ('allesomvattende grondreël') to explain their review jurisdiction. While the first of these propositions has some justification, the second would seem to hold alarming implications for South African administrative law.

1 The artificiality of the wide ultra vires doctrine

There is no doubt that the ultra vires doctrine is a highly strained and artificial framework for modern judicial review. Wade (whose views are reproduced in the judgment of Hefer JA)[90] calls the doctrine a 'bed of Procrustes'[91] because every instance of administrative malpractice, from obvious failure to comply with the terms of the statute to subtle forms of unreasonableness and unfairness, must somehow be fitted into it:

> 'The technique by which the Courts have constructed their system for the judicial control of powers has been by stretching the doctrine of *ultra vires* ... they can make the doctrine mean almost anything they wish by finding implied limitations in Acts of Parliament, as they do when they hold that the exercise of a statutory power to revoke a licence is void unless done in accordance with the principles of natural justice. Realising that their task is to protect the citizen against unfairness and abuse of power, they build up a body of rules of administrative law which they presume that Parliament wishes them to enforce.'[92]

But worse still—and Hefer JA does not mention this—the ultra vires doctrine is firmly tied to legislative intention, and therefore to statutes. Because of this, it fails to justify the many non-statutory features of modern judicial review. It fails, for instance, to account for the reviewability of prerogative power; and it cannot explain why some of the decisions of private, non-statutory bodies should be reviewable, or why cases involving purely contractual powers should be subject to the courts' scrutiny. As Oliver[93] has pointed out, the ultra vires doctrine is an incomplete explanation of why courts interfere in areas where there is no question of legislative intention, and no question of vires whose bounds have been laid down by Parliament. The truth is that the ultra vires doctrine is a legal fiction which we have—at least to some extent—outgrown. It is time we gave explicit recognition to the fact that the courts impose their own standards of legality on public authorities as a matter of common law, and that the relationship between common-law standards and Parliament's intention is often an uneasy one.

2 The need to justify judicial interference

The second of Hefer JA's two propositions is that the courts do not

[90] At 867H–868D.
[91] Wade op cit n 77 at 42. Procrustes is a legendary robber with the ghastly habit of stretching his victims or trimming them down in order to fit them into the same bed.
[92] Wade 41–2.
[93] Dawn Oliver (1987) *Public Law* 543. Oliver suggests that judicial review in English law has 'moved on from the ultra vires rule to a concern for the protection of individuals, and for the control of *power*, rather than *powers*, or *vires*' (at 543).

need the ultra vires doctrine or, for that matter, any other comprehensive principle to justify their review jurisdiction. According to this judge of appeal, there is no reason why common-law rules of good administration have to be related to the intention of the legislature at all; legislative intention becomes relevant only when a particular rule or standard has expressly been excluded.[94] Thus, in the case of a vague regulation, there would be no need to resort to the familiar formula: 'Parliament could not have intended this official to make laws which are hopelessly vague and uncertain'; the vagueness itself would be a sufficient justification for the court's interference.[95] Though this reasoning seems to flow logically from the recognition that the ultra vires doctrine is a highly strained legal fiction, it is in fact a much more startling claim. It is tantamount to a rejection of the accepted constitutional relationship between the legislature and the judiciary; for, as Wade says, the courts

'. . . have only one weapon, the doctrine of *ultra vires*. This is because they have no constitutional right to interfere with action which is within the powers granted (*intra vires*): if it is within jurisdiction, and therefore authorised by Parliament, the Court has no right to treat it as unlawful.'

This suggests that it would be fatal for the English courts to do away with the ultra vires doctrine, for they would be left without a constitutional justification for their intervention. As Baxter has argued, the courts' inherent review jurisdiction is not *inherited*, but *logically* inherent: as long as the courts continue to apply the laws made by the sovereign Parliament, they have a logical reason for striking down action which violates Parliament's intention, express or implied.[96] Since the South African version of parliamentary sovereignty is no weaker than the English brand, a rejection of the wide doctrine would seem to be equally fatal for our courts. And yet our Appellate Division has taken this fatal step, which—if Wade and Baxter are right in their reasoning—has effectively stripped the courts of their inherent jurisdiction to review administrative action *except in a minority of cases where express legislative provisions have been violated*. Legality, a judge-made concept which postulates the 'ideal legislature',[97] cannot provide the necessary justificatory link with Parliament's intention. It might, however, be possible to fill the gap with statutory jurisdiction, such as a Judicial Review Act.[98]

Meanwhile, administrative lawyers may well decide that a strained and artificial reason for interfering is better than no reason at all: at

---

[94] At 870H–J and 872E. This seems to imply that the making of vague regulations is 'authorised' by Parliament unless it expressly prohibits such an abuse of power. It is difficult to believe that this result was intended by Hefer JA, since it would also mean that presumptions of statutory interpretation generally have no significance!
[95] At 867A.
[96] See n 46 above.
[97] Wiechers 176.
[98] So far, the South African Law Commission has produced a draft Bill which is appended to its *Working Paper 15*.

least one court has held, in *Natal Indian Congress v State President*,[99] that the *UDF* principle applies not only when regulations are challenged on the ground of vagueness, but also when they are challenged on the ground of unreasonableness. There is no doubt that the regret expressed by Friedman J in that case[100] will be shared by many.[101]

V THE LIMITED ROLE OF JUDICIAL REVIEW

In the preface we suggested that there is a tendency in common-law texts on administrative law to highlight the role played by judicial review in the administrative system, and consequently to downplay other, equally significant, controls on government power. So far we have tried to avoid this pitfall by discussing the other forms of control in Parts I and II of this book; but here we attempt to redress the balance in a more direct way by exposing the essentially limited role of judicial review. In this regard, the point has already been made[102] that the 'justiciability' of legal issues in administrative law depends to a considerable extent on the judges' attitudes to their position in government. These attitudes affect the judges' willingness to strike down administrative action as illegal, and are thus capable of limiting (or, of course, expanding) the contents of legality. The technique of classifying administrative functions,[103] for instance, can be regarded as evidence of a judicial reluctance to encroach too freely on the 'proper' preserve of the executive. Similarly, the tendency to see disputes in terms of *private right* rather than *public interest*[104] suggests that the judge's 'proper' function is to resolve the concrete disputes of individuals, and not to make policy. Besides these rather nebulous constraints, there are many other potential stumbling-blocks to a successful challenge of administrative action, both of a practical and a legal nature. Their existence makes judicial review a rather random and contingent safeguard, since its invocation depends largely on factors which have little or nothing to do with the cogency of the applicant's case.

A Legal constraints

Some of these are imposed by the courts themselves, and some by Parliament. Of the former, the rules of standing must constitute one of the most formidable obstacles to review. Any applicant for judicial review must have 'locus standi' to go to court, and, as we shall see in the next chapter, many deserving cases fall by the wayside because the complainant cannot satisfy the judge-made requirements of

[99] 1989 (3) SA 588 (D).
[100] At 594H–595B.
[101] For criticism of this case, see Haysom and Plasket op cit n 17; Mureinik op cit n 17; John Grogan (1989) 106 *SALJ* 14.
[102] Above, 242–3; 246.
[103] Above, 258; and see below, 322ff.
[104] See below, 267ff; above, 95.

standing. The availablity of remedies is another limiting factor. Many of the remedies are discretionary—that is, not available as of right. While this fact does not prevent judicial review from taking place, it may certainly discourage complainants from bringing cases of maladministration to court.

Of the latter, ouster clauses and limitation clauses are probably the most obvious constraints. These clauses are intended to preclude judicial review of specified administrative action or to limit it, though it is true that they do not achieve this aim in every case. Subjectively phrased clauses—wording which confers a very wide discretion—are another significant limitation on the courts' ability to scrutinise administrative action. These and other constraints are discussed in more detail in chapter 13.

B Practical considerations

Not everyone has the time, energy and, above all, the financial resources demanded by litigation. We do not know how many potential applicants for judicial review are prevented by these constraints from challenging administrative action, but it seems entirely likely that only a small proportion of possible claims actually end up in court. This means that many instances of maladministration may never come to light at all.

A final question relates not so much to the availability of review as to its effectiveness in changing administrative practices and attitudes: do administrators learn from the case law?[105] A negative answer would further lessen the possible value of judicial review as a promoter of good administration and a safeguard against bad administration.

---

[105] Carol Harlow and Richard Rawlings explore this question in the British context: *Law and Administration* (1984) at 256ff.

12 Standing

In order to sue in South African courts, every litigant must have 'locus standi in judicio'. Locus standi, or more simply 'standing', refers partly to a person's capacity to litigate and partly to his or her interest in the case. The requirement of capacity is uncontroversial, and will not be discussed here since it holds little interest for administrative lawyers.[1] The requirement of a legally recognised interest, on the other hand, is a particularly important one in the context of administrative law review. It is the subject-matter of this chapter.[2]

I THE NEED FOR AN INTEREST

Strange though it may seem, it is not enough that the applicant for review is able to demonstrate that a public authority has been acting illegally. The applicant, if challenged, must also be able to show that he or she has a *sufficient, personal and direct interest* in the case; a legally recognised reason, as it were, for claiming the court's attention. The issue of standing is one to be decided 'in limine', that is, before the substance of the case is presented. The significance of this is that even an obvious illegality will evade the court's scrutiny if the applicant is found to lack standing. Lack of standing, though not logically linked to the substance of the applicant's case, is fatal to it.

The interest required by the law is not a subjective one: the court is not concerned with the intensity of the applicant's feelings of indignation at the alleged illegal action, but with an objectively defined interest.[3] More important, the citizen's concern with the legality of governmental action is not regarded as an interest which is worth protecting in itself. Because of the way in which personal interest has come to be defined, the complainant must be able to point to something *beyond* a mere concern with legality—typically, though not necessarily, a financial or proprietary interest. Our law recognises no actio popularis or class action whereby an individual (or a group) not personally affected may vindicate the public interest by exposing an illegality.

---

[1] On the capacity of public authorities to litigate, see Lawrence Baxter *Administrative Law* (1984) at 649–50.

[2] The requirements for standing may vary according to the remedy applied for. Apart from one instance (see 275 below), we have found it convenient to deal with these variations in chapter 13.

[3] This interest may, however, be accompanied by sentimental considerations; see *Mweuhanga v Cabinet of Interim Government of SWA* 1989 (1) SA 976 (SWA).

A considerable range of actiones populares were known in Roman law,[4] including actions to put an end to public nuisances, to prevent the violation of sacred places and things, and various possessory interdicts. The actiones were largely created by that inventive Roman official, the praetor, who developed special rules of procedure for these remedies.[5] Most importantly, the actiones were designed by him to serve the *public* interest: the plaintiff or applicant did not have to be personally affected by the offending conduct in order to bring an action. (In accordance with great Roman tradition, minors and women did not have the benefit of this rule!) In Roman-Dutch law, however, the actiones fell into disuse,[6] quite possibly as a result of the praetor's practice, whenever there were a number of potential plaintiffs, of choosing the one who had the most personal interest in the case.[7] The only exception to this obsolescence was the interdictum de libero homine exhibendo, a remedy whereby a free man could be liberated from slavery. From the start, our law of standing appears to have been modelled on the Roman-Dutch law.[8] Thus, with the one exception referred to, South African law holds that

'the *actiones populares* generally have become obsolete in the sense that a person is not entitled "to protect the rights of the public" or "champion the cause of the people" '.[9]

This means that a complainant is not entitled to defend someone else's interest, even if that interest would qualify the injured person to bring a complaint. The general rule, then, is that one cannot act on behalf of others, irrespective of the type of interest possessed by those others. It is important to appreciate that if one's only interest is in the legality of administrative action, then one is regarded as attempting to act on behalf of the general public.

The administrative law context does little to change the 'private law' flavour of the South African rules of standing, with their emphasis on personal—as opposed to public—interest. As a result, the standing requirements are curiously at odds with the idea of legality, which focuses on the illegitimacy of illegal administrative action rather than on the position of the applicant. Indeed, there would seem to be no logical link at all between the concept of administrative legality and the position of the applicant for review; yet, if the applicant is unable to show the necessary personal interest,

[4] On the position in Roman and Roman-Dutch law, see J A van der Vyver (1978) *AJ* 191, especially at 192–4.
[5] Digest 47.23. See Van der Vyver op cit n 4 at 192.
[6] Ibid 193, where the Roman-Dutch authorities are reviewed.
[7] See further below, 280n83.
[8] See, for instance, *Bagnall v Colonial Government* (1907) 24 SC 470; *Dalrymple v Colonial Treasurer* 1910 TS 372; *Director of Education, Transvaal v McCagie* 1918 AD 616.
[9] Per Rumpff CJ in *Wood v Ondangwa Tribal Authority* 1975 (2) SA 294 (A) at 310F.

the court will decline to exercise its review jurisdiction.[10] Such an applicant can only trust to luck: there would seem to be applications which have succeeded on review in spite of an apparent lack of standing simply because the respondent chose not to raise the point and the court did not question it![11]

II RESTRICTING ACCESS TO JUDICIAL REVIEW

The rules of standing constitute one of the major ways in which the law restricts the number and controls the nature of cases going to court. Since the rules are largely 'judge-made', they enable the courts themselves to decide which applicants are deserving of judicial review and which are not; which interests are worthy of protection and which are not.

This feature of judicial choice raises an interesting question of legitimacy which was touched on in the last chapter: is it appropriate for judges, unelected officials, to wield such considerable power?[12] After all, it is always open to Parliament to make whatever rules it considers necessary to restrict access to the courts. On what ground, then, do judges—who are not responsible to Parliament—claim the political jurisdiction to make their own rules about access?

The question is not, of course, confined to this country; it is a source of concern to lawyers in various jurisdictions, most obviously in England. However, (as has already been suggested in more general terms)[13] there are at least two possible justifications for ignoring the apparent illegitimacy in its present South African context. The first is that the illegitimacy is indeed apparent, not real: because Parliament is not itself democratically elected, it seems ridiculous to worry about the legitimacy of our judges' powers. The second may be that South African lawyers have become so accustomed to regarding the judiciary as the sole surviving bastion of individual freedom in the welter of oppressive legislation passed by Parliament that the legitimacy of its jurisdiction has become an almost irrelevant consideration. For this reason, lawyers who care about liberal values may be only too eager to allow the judicial arm of government all the rule-making jurisdiction it claims—though, as we will see, there is no guarantee that the judiciary will come up with a rule that serves those values!

Some academic writers[14] in this country have expressed considerable dissatisfaction with the way in which our judges have exercised their power to refuse an applicant judicial review for want of

---

[10] The exceptions to the usual requirements are discussed below, 275–8.
[11] For three possible examples, see Cheryl Loots (1987) (3) *SAJHR* 66 at 71.
[12] Above, 242ff.
[13] Above, 244.
[14] For instance, C F Eckard *Die Locus Standi van Aansoekers by die Geregtelike Hersiening van Administratiewe Handelinge* unpublished LLD thesis, UNISA (1975); André Rabie and Cor Eckard (1976) 9 *CILSA* 139; Loots op cit n 11; Baxter op cit n 1 at 666–7 and the works cited there.

standing, though criticisms have tended to focus on the restrictive effects of the standing rules rather than on the legitimacy of the judges' actions. The South African Law Commission may or may not be aware of these critical opinions; so far, it is hard to tell whether they are being given serious attention, and whether the commission's ultimate proposals for reform (if any) will aim to alter the common law to any appreciable extent.[15] It is doubtful, in any event, whether legislative reform can ever entirely replace or oust the role of the courts. If a reform effort is needed, it is primarily to be directed at the attitudes of our judges, whose interpretative control might be increased rather than diminished by codification of the rules.

III THE REQUIREMENTS FOR STANDING

The way in which our courts have developed the requirements for standing reveals a strong inclination to extend the use of private law language into the field of public law[16] and to refuse to recognise a 'public law' interest in legality. The cases discussed below illustrate the practical application of the requirements.

A Sufficient interest

As far as the type of interest is concerned, it must be one which arises out of a legal right (such as a person's right to liberty) or which has a factual basis in money, property or some other benefit. An example of a legal right giving rise to an interest appears from the Appellate Division decision in *Ngcwane v Terblanche NO*,[17] where it was held that de jure members of a school board had a right to have strangers or irregularly appointed de facto members excluded from the board's meetings. The invasion of this right gave them standing to apply to court to have the appointment of the third respondent set aside.

The case of *Director of Education, Transvaal v McCagie*[18] was concerned with a factual benefit. Here the Appellate Division held that applicants for a vacant post who were properly qualified had standing to ask the court to set aside the appointment of an unqualified person; their prospects of success were prejudiced by the failure to observe the statutory provisions relating to the qualifications of appointees.

The distinction between rights and factual benefits is not necessarily an easy one, and there is an area of overlap between them: presumably we could say that the applicants in *McCagie*[19] had a 'right' once the court had recognised the sufficiency of the benefit. In any event, the private-law orientation of the standing rules is apparent in both of these cases. The *illegality* of the irregular

---

[15] See below, 283.
[16] See generally Baxter 644ff.
[17] 1977 (3) SA 796 (A).
[18] 1918 AD 616.
[19] Note 18 above.

appointments is treated as entirely secondary to the personal injury suffered by the applicant. The bias towards private law would also seem to rule out more remote factual interests such as the benefit in *Davies v Bekker NO and Smit*,[20] another case concerning an allegedly illegal appointment to a government post. Here the competitors for the post were held not to have standing because it was not sufficiently certain that the allegedly illegal appointment had prejudiced them at all. To grant standing in such a case would come uncomfortably close to recognising an interest in legality, and that is something our courts have steadfastly avoided.

B Personal

The determination not to recognise injury of a public kind has also led the courts to evolve a requirement that the interest be 'personal' to the applicant. However, there is a major controversy in the cases as to what this means. There are two approaches: a wide construction, which holds that the personal interest may be shared by others provided the applicant can show that it is also personal to him or her; and a stricter construction which holds that the interest must be unique to the applicant. On this second approach, if the applicant belongs to a class of people (the general public, for instance) who are all sufficiently injured in some way by the alleged illegality, the applicant will have to show 'special damage' which is greater than that of the rest of the class.

The more lenient construction is well (though not uniquely)[21] illustrated by the case of *Bamford v Minister of Community Development and State Auxiliary Services*,[22] where the complainant applied for an urgent interdict to prevent the government from building illegally on the Groote Schuur Estate, a public preserve. His interest in having continued access to the Estate was held to be personal to him even though it was shared by every member of the public. Watermeyer JP did not in fact pursue the question whether every member of the public would have locus standi to restrain the respondents; he expressly based his judgment 'solely on an unlawful interference with the applicant's right of access to the park'.[23] However, it seems clear that any member of the public who could establish an invasion of his rights to access would have had standing to do so. This approach has the distinct virtue of recognising that if someone's interest has been invaded, the fact that others have suffered the same damage does not mysteriously make it less of an invasion vis-à-vis that individual![24] But there is nothing especially startling about

---

[20] 1934 TPD 384.
[21] See n 24 below.
[22] 1981 (3) SA 1054 (C).
[23] At 1060C.
[24] This logic receives support from the case of *Roberts v Chairman, Local Road Transportation Board (1)* 1980 (2) SA 472 (C).

Bamford,[25] and it cannot be said to resurrect the actio popularis: the requirement of legally recognised personal damage prevents unaffected people from taking up the cudgels on behalf of others.

The *Bamford* approach conflicts with a number of cases[26] which refer to the need for a 'special' interest, ie injury over and above that suffered by the general public or some other class. The source of this requirement is the well-worn dictum of Pollock CB in the English case of *Chamberlaine v Chester and Birkenhead Railway Co*,[27] where the judge declares that a complainant must show

> 'some special damage—some peculiar injury beyond that which he may be supposed to sustain in common with the Queen's subjects by an infringement of the law'.

This dictum was quoted with apparent approval by Solomon J in the early South African case of *Patz v Greene & Co*,[28] and the notion of special damage was thus introduced into our law. It is unfortunate that the term 'special' continues to be employed, since not only logic but also the weight of authority is against its use. Professor Baxter[29] has argued convincingly that it is wrongly thought to be part of our law, and he points to no fewer than five strong Appellate Division statements which support him in this view. In the case of *Roodepoort-Maraisburg Town Council v Eastern Properties (Prop) Ltd*,[30] for instance, Wessels CJ emphasised that in our law, any person possessing a direct interest will have standing to go to court 'whether he suffers special damage or not'.[31]

It could also be argued that the definition of special damage quoted by Solomon J was not intended by him to mean *unique* damage in the sense in which our courts have interpreted it, but simply to indicate that there is no recognised interest in *legality*. Injury beyond that suffered by the general public 'by an infringement of the law' may in fact have been intended to refer merely to public indignation roused by the illegality, and nothing more; in which case personal injury to the applicant, even if it is shared by others, would certainly qualify as 'beyond' that suffered by every citizen. That Solomon J actually intended this lesser meaning is suggested by his own statement of the law, where he approves the standing of 'any member of the public who can prove that he has sustained damage'[32] (rather than

---

[25] Note 22 above.
[26] A good example is *Von Moltke v Costa Areosa (Pty) Ltd* 1975 (1) SA 255 (C). For criticism of this case, see Baxter 657–8. See also *South African Optometric Association v Frames Distributors (Pty) Ltd T/A Frames Unlimited* 1985 (3) SA 100 (O), discussed at 272ff below; and *Noll v Alberton Frames (Pty) Ltd* 1989 (1) SA 730 (T) at 738B.
[27] 1 EX 870, 154 ER 371 at 374.
[28] 1907 TS 427 at 433.
[29] See Baxter 655–8, especially at 656.
[30] 1933 AD 87.
[31] At 101. See also the judgment of Beyers JA at 103, where he is at pains to point out that the English law on the subject is not part of South African law.
[32] At 433.

'special' damage). If this interpretation of *Patz v Greene*[33] is correct, then the cases which refer to the need for 'special' damage are entirely without foundation. Even if not, the *Bamford*[34] approach—though hardly revolutionary—is preferable for the reasons given above.

It is ironic that the judgment in *Patz v Greene*, which is responsible for so much restrictive reasoning, should also have introduced an important presumption of personal injury whenever a statutory prohibition is enacted for the protection of a particular person rather than in the interests of the general public. In such a case, 'the Court will presume that he is damnified'.[35] This presumption has been extended to include legislation (wholly or partly) enacted for the protection of a class of persons,[36] though not of course a class as large as the general public. It applies to virtually any form[37] of legislative provision enacted in the interests of that class, and not just prohibitions—presumably on the basis that statutory requirements or duties count as 'prohibitions' against non-compliance. The presumption in *Patz v Greene* is frequently used in the modern cases, as will appear from the cases discussed in the next section.

C Direct

It is well established in our law that the interest must be 'direct'. However, this may merely be another way of expressing the need for a personal interest; certainly the terms could be treated as synonymous in many cases. Baxter, though presenting the requirement of directness as a separate issue, states that it aims to ensure 'a *personal* nexus between the complainant and the act complained of',[38] and it is arguable that if one is personally but too indirectly affected, one is not personally affected at all for the purposes of the law of standing. Whatever the case, the courts have used the requirement of directness to great effect in maintaining the strong private-law bias which we have already identified. Organisations attempting to represent their members[39] frequently fall foul of the requirement, as happened in *South African Optometric Association v Frames Distributors (Pty) Ltd t/a Frames Unlimited*.[40] Here the

---

[33] Note 28 above.

[34] Note 22 above.

[35] Per Solomon J at 433.

[36] See *Roodepoort-Maraisburg Town Council v Eastern Properties (Prop) Ltd* 1933 AD 87 at 96; *BEF (Pty) Ltd v Cape Town Municipality* 1983 (2) SA 387 (C) at 400.

[37] For instance, in the *BEF* case (n 36 above) the presumption was used to allow the applicant to enforce a town-planning scheme; and in *Dawnlaan Beleggings (Edms) Bpk v Johannesburg Stock Exchange* 1983 (3) SA 344 (W), the presumption enabled shareholders to force the exchange to comply with its published rules and requirements.

[38] Baxter 654; our italics.

[39] See further below, 277.

[40] 1985 (3) SA 100 (O). The decision was followed in *Noll v Alberton Frames (Pty) Ltd* 1989 (1) SA 730 (T), another case concerning the illegal sale of spectacle frames. Here

association's interest in preventing the respondent from selling spectacle frames illegally was found not to be 'direct and substantial'; although some of the association's members stood to lose profits by virtue of having to compete with the respondent, the association was itself a non-profit organisation, so that its interest was 'at best, merely an indirect interest'.[41] The association had failed to prove that it had suffered damage,[42] and therefore lacked the necessary standing to bring the application.

An advocate of more liberal rules of standing would find much to criticise in this case. As to the directness of the financial interest, there would seem to be nothing in logic to prevent a non-profit organisation from taking a legitimate and direct (or personal) interest in the general well-being of its members. Why should financial well-being not form part of that general well-being? It seems unnecessarily formalistic to non-suit the organisation for indirectness simply because the financial interest lies *most* directly with its individual members.

Since the applicant could not prove personal damage other than the indirect financial loss, its last resort was to gain the advantage of the *Patz v Greene*[43] presumption by showing that the statute which had been breached was enacted for its especial benefit (as part of the optometrical profession). The court found, however, that while the Medical, Dental and Supplementary Health Service Professions Act[44] contains provisions which 'operate to protect qualified persons from unqualified persons',[45] that protection is not one of the aims of the Act, and is merely incidental to its aims. Nor could the Act be said to have been passed 'in the interests of any particular class or classes of persons whose qualifications come within the purview of the Act';[46] rather, it was enacted in the public interest.

This last finding is to be contrasted with the more magnanimous view taken by the court in *Veriava v President, SA Medical and Dental Council*.[47] This case arose out of the death in police custody of the

---

Goldstone J found that two of the plaintiffs, non-profit associations, lacked the required standing (at 737–8).

[41] Per Lichtenberg J at 104E.

[42] Lichtenberg J uses the term 'special damage' (the term used also by counsel for the respondent) at 105F, but at 106A he refers to 'any damage'. It is not clear, therefore, whether his judgment gives support to a requirement of unique damage or whether it is in accordance with the ordinary requirement of *personal* damage; but see *Noll*'s case (above, n 40): '. . . in order to establish *locus standi*, each of the plaintiffs would have to allege that he or it has suffered special damage' (per Goldstone J at 738B).

[43] Note 28 above.

[44] Act 56 of 1974.

[45] At 105G–H.

[46] At 105H.

[47] 1985 (2) SA 293 (T). In *Noll v Alberton Frames (Pty) Ltd* (n 40 above) Goldstone J distinguished *Veriava*'s case on the basis that '. . . the interest in question was conferred expressly by the relevant statute upon the medical council' (at 737I–J). With respect, this is open to doubt; Boshoff JP does refer in *Veriava* to 'the manifest object of the Act' (at 316F), but 'manifest' is not necessarily the same as 'express'.

activist Steve Biko and concerned the conduct of two registered medical practitioners who attended him in their capacities as district surgeons. The applicants, medical practitioners, were judged to have the necessary standing to challenge the legality of the respondents' actions in failing properly to deal with complaints and evidence lodged with the Council.

The court accepted that since the application was based on an alleged failure to carry out statutory duties, the applicants had to show either injury to themselves (a difficult task, no doubt) or that the Act in question—the very statute at issue in *Frames Distributors*[48]—had been passed in the interests of the medical profession. Boshoff JP, O'Donovan J concurring, found that the statute had indeed been so enacted. It created a Council which was '. . . the guardian of the prestige, status and dignity of the profession',[49] and could clearly be regarded as protecting not only members of the public but also members of the profession itself.

Which of these two conflicting approaches to the same statute is correct? There seems little point in denouncing the techniques of construction used in *Frames Distributors* (such as Lichtenberg J's emphasis on aims as opposed to provisions) as less efficient; on the contrary, one suspects that the extraction from a statute of benefits to a particular class is such a subjective exercise that two judges using identical rules of construction might come to different conclusions. But given Lichtenberg J's suggestion that individual optometrists affected by the illegal sale of spectacle frames would be accorded standing on the basis of a direct personal interest in financial loss, we are faced with the following anomaly: that members of the medical or optometrical professions have standing to challenge the breach of a statute while an optometric *association* which exists to protect the interests of its members is denied it. The inability of organisations to represent the interests of their members in private law[50] is regrettable; in public law it is also inappropriate because in direct conflict with the public interest in legality. Boshoff JP's more liberal interpretation of the Act avoids the anomaly, and is to be preferred on that basis at least.[51]

In any event, the issue in *Veriava*'a case was not whether the Council had the required standing, but whether medical practitioners qualified for it.

[48] Note 40 above.

[49] At 316E–F.

[50] See, for instance, *Ahmadiyya Anjuman Ishaati-Islam Lahore (South Africa) v Muslim Judicial Council (Cape)* 1983 (4) SA 855 (C), which illustrates the effect of the requirement of directness in the context of a delictual action.

[51] For a similarly practical approach, see *Society for the Prevention of Cruelty to Animals, Standerton v Nel* 1988 (4) SA 42 (W), in which the applicants successfully interdicted the respondents from committing acts of cruelty to animals. In deciding that the SPCA qualifies 'as an organisation entitled to seek an interdict . . . where harm, injury or cruelty is apprehended', Gordon AJ took into account the fact that it 'has, over the years, become well established and fully recognised as the authoritative voice in the protection of injury or cruelty to animals from whatever source . . .' (at 47B–E).

D Exceptions to the requirements

1 The interdict de libero homine exhibendo

This mandatory interdict, also known as habeas corpus,[52] is the sole survivor of the actiones populares which existed in Roman law.[53] It is used to challenge the unlawful deprivation of a person's liberty. An effect of the remedy is that the deprived (usually detained)[54] person is produced in court 'to be seen and touched'; however, production of the detained person is no longer common practice in our courts.[55] Since the detainee whose rights are at stake is generally unable to bring the application himself, the requirements of standing for an application involving this remedy have been relaxed to allow others to do so. In *Katofa v Administrator-General for South West Africa*,[56] Levy J remarked that 'virtually any relation, or for that matter any person with an interest'[57] can apply for this remedy. So, for instance, in *Bozzoli v Station Commander, John Vorster Square, Johannesburg*,[58] the court accepted that the Principal of the University of the Witwatersrand had 'a special interest'[59] in the welfare of his students; on that basis, he had the necessary standing to apply for the release of students who had been detained.

In the famous case of *Wood v Ondangwa Tribal Authority*,[60] this relaxation was extended to allow the members of a political and a church organisation to seek an interdict *prohibiting* the detention of their members, who (though not yet detained) were unable themselves to go to court. In a judgment widely praised for its generous approach, Rumpff CJ saw the interest in the liberty of another as arising not only out of a family relationship or a personal friendship, but also out of common membership of 'a partnership, or a society, or a church, or a political party'.[61] But the Chief Justice also made it clear that this liberal approach should not be regarded as anything but a clear exception to the usual requirements, an exception justified by the evil of illegal deprivation of liberty and by

[52] Since the case of *Tussentydse Regering vir Suidwes-Afrika v Katofa* 1987 (1) SA 695 (A) it is doubtful whether 'habeas corpus' may be used as a synonym for the interdict; see the judgment of Rabie CJ at 722ff.

[53] Above, 267. On mandatory interdicts in South African law, see further below, 290.

[54] In *National Education Crisis Committee v State President of the Republic of South Africa* WLD 9 September 1986 Case No 16736/86 (unreported) an attempt to include the right to receive education within the definition of 'liberty' met with a singular lack of success; see Loots at 66–9.

[55] Writing in 1962, Kentridge noted that an order to produce the person in court 'is an established and almost invariable feature of South African orders of *habeas corpus*'; S Kentridge (1962) 79 *SALJ* 283 at 285. Today, however, production of the person is an exceptional occurrence, and is in any event precluded by legislation in many cases; see further below, 290.

[56] 1985 (4) SA 211 (SWA). This remark went unchallenged in the appeal court (n 52 above).

[57] At 216D–E.

[58] 1972 (3) SA 934 (W).

[59] Per Snyman J at 935F–H.

[60] 1975 (2) SA 294 (A).

[61] At 312G.

the inability of the detainee to bring the application himself. And far from introducing an interest in legality or an actio popularis, Rumpff CJ likened the position of the applicant to that of the negotiorum gestor or the curator ad litem. As Baxter[62] points out, this is yet another demonstration of the private-law orientation of our rules of standing.

2   Presumption of injury

As already mentioned, the case of *Patz v Greene*[63] provides a presumption of personal damage where legislation has been enacted for the protection of a particular class of which the applicant forms part. This is a useful presumption, but of course it is not always possible to show that the statute has been enacted in the interests of a particular class; more usually, statutes are enacted in the interests of the general public. In such cases (and in the absence of proof of personal injury to the applicant) our courts' determination not to resurrect the actio popularis has sometimes resulted in cases where blatant illegalities have gone unchecked.

3   Ratepayers

Ratepayers are presumed to have a legitimate interest in the legality of action taken by their local authorities. Unfortunately, though not surprisingly, the courts have been unwilling to apply this reasoning to the relationship between taxpayers and the administration; in *Bamford*'s case,[64] for instance, the court refused to grant standing on this basis. Another example is *Dalrymple v Colonial Treasurer*,[65] where members of the old Transvaal Legislative Council sought an interdict to prevent the Colonial Treasurer from paying members of the Transvaal Parliament excessive salaries. Since they were unable to show personal injury, their claims to standing failed—despite their being both taxpayers and members of the legislative council.

4   Local authorities

Some statutes expressly confer standing on local authorities for specific purposes. But failing such an express grant, there are nevertheless cases which recognise the standing of local authorities to defend the public interest in administrative areas falling within their powers, such as town planning schemes and any other matters affecting their ratepayers.[66]

---

[62] Baxter 662.
[63] Above, n 28.
[64] Above, n 22.
[65] 1910 TS 372.
[66] See *Madrassa Anjuman Islamia v Johannesburg Municipality* 1917 AD 718; *Roodepoort-Maraisburg Town Council v Eastern Properties (Prop) Ltd* (n 30 above).

5 Representative organisations

In the absence of an express or implied provision[67] enabling them to represent their members, organisations[68] purporting to do so are frequently denied standing because it cannot be shown that the injury has been suffered by the organisation itself (as opposed to its members). Where the association is unincorporated, it may be possible for the members to sue in the name of the organisation in terms of Supreme Court rule 14; but incorporated associations, because of their separate legal personality, are denied this concession.[69] However, there are a number of cases which go against the trend of requiring damage to the organisation apart from that suffered by its members. One of these is *Transvaal Indian Congress v Land Tenure Advisory Board*,[70] where De Wet J allowed the standing of the congress to challenge a decision of the Board even though the former was representing the interests of its members:

'It seems to me that a body like the applicant represents all its members, its interests are the same as the interests of its members as a whole, and not only has it *locus standi* to represent its members but it is very desirable that a body like this should be able to represent its members rather than that all its members should appear individually at an enquiry of this sort with which the court is concerned.'[71]

It is difficult to reconcile the approach of De Wet J with the orthodox view as illustrated in cases like *Frames Distributors*.[72] Why, for instance, are the interests of the members and the organisation representing all of them not always presumed to be identical? It may be that purely practical considerations were what really decided this case. They seem also to have been decisive in *Ex parte Natal Bottle*

---

[67] In order to imply a power to sue, it must be incidental to the express powers, that is, 'absolutely requisite for the due carrying out of the express objects of the association' (per King AJ in *Bantu Callies Football Club v Motlhamme* 1978 (4) SA 486 (T) at 490A).

[68] Including unions; see, for instance, *P E Bosman Transport Works Committee v Piet Bosman Transport (Pty) Ltd* 1980 (4) SA 801 (T); *National Union of Mineworkers v Free State Consolidated Gold Mines (Operations) Ltd* 1989 (1) SA 409 (O).

[69] Rule 14(2) states that '[a] partnership, a firm or an association may sue or be sued in its own name'. Rule 14(1) defines an association as 'any unincorporated body of persons, not being a partnership'. Incorporated organisations are thus excluded from the ambit of the Rule. It has been held that subrule (2) is merely a procedural aid, and that if an association has no power under its constitution to sue, then this procedural aid cannot render lawful the unconstitutional act of suing (King AJ in *Bantu Callies Football Club v Motlhamme*, n 67 above, at 490A). However, at common law an unincorporated association having the characteristics of a *universitas personam* (in particular, perpetual succession and the ability to acquire certain rights, such as property rights, apart from the rights of the members themselves) may be able to sue in its own name even if there is no provision to that effect in its constitution. For a recent example, see *Motlotlegi v President of Bophuthatswana* 1989 (3) SA 119 (B), where Friedman J noted that rule 14 operated to fortify the standing of a *universitas personam* (at 126J).

[70] 1955 (1) SA 85 (W).

[71] At 90A–B.

[72] Above, n 40.

Store-Keeping and Off-Sales Licensees Association,[73] where Henochsberg J pointed out that the court would be overburdened if all 89 licensees being represented by the Association were to bring their own applications.

These cases and others involving organisations whose standing has not been questioned[74] exemplify a willingness on the part of some judges to recognise that it is appropriate and convenient for classes of persons to be represented by a body who is prepared to defend their interests. As Loots[75] asks, what possible advantage is there to be gained from forcing reluctant or penniless individuals to bring their own applications, or from the use of nominal applicants?

6   A 'relator' action

As the Crown's legal representative, the English Attorney-General has standing to defend the public interest either on his own initiative or, in a 'relator' action, at the instance of an individual complainant who lacks the requisite standing. He may, however, refuse to lend his name to such a complainant. While South African law knows no relator action as such, Baxter[76] suggests that the Minister of Justice may well have inherited this special form of standing from the four colonial Attorneys-General at the time of Union; and, alternatively, that it might be possible for the State President to delegate to the present Attorneys-General his prerogative power to do so. So far, however, these have remained purely theoretical exceptions to the standing requirements.

IV   JUSTIFICATION AND REFORM

Though the exceptions listed above offer some relief from the harsh effects of the ordinary standing requirements, they are limited in their scope; they come nowhere near recognising an interest in legality per se, and do not begin to threaten the supremacy of the private-law model of dispute-settling. Nor do they present a particularly coherent pattern. For instance, it seems illogical to allow ratepayers locus standi in relation to their local authorities while refusing taxpayers standing in relation to the executive as a whole; and why should the presumption of injury not apply to members of the general public if the statute in question has been passed in the interests of the general public?

---

[73] 1962 (4) SA 273 (D) at 276C.
[74] See Loots at 71 for a discussion of some of these. Another possible example is *East London Western Districts Farmers' Association v Minister of Education and Development Aid* 1989 (2) SA 63 (A), where the Association (one of a number of appellants) was described simply as 'representing the interests of its members' (at 78D in the dissenting judgment of Viljoen JA); and as 'a voluntary association representing the interests of organised agriculture and farmers in the region' (at 66D in the majority judgment of Hoexter JA).
[75] Loots 70.
[76] Baxter 662–3.

Given the difficulties associated with the process of litigation—the drains on resources such as time and money—it might well strike one as odd that the law further seeks to limit access to the courts by means of the standing requirements. If this is so in private law, where one is dealing only with the rights and interests of individuals, it is even stranger in the case of judicial review. Review exists essentially in order to keep public authorities within the bounds of their powers. By that token, it is of great interest to the public at large, and it would seem desirable to allow any member of the public to vindicate that interest by means of an actio popularis or class action of some kind. As things stand, there is no logical (or other satisfactory) relationship between the purpose of review and the effect of the rules of standing. The two have nothing to do with each other. In crude terms this means that some perfectly good causes—blatant breaches of statute, for instance—fail to be remedied because the complainant is not the person or body who 'ought', in terms of the judge-made rules, to bring the case. Worse still, there may be illegalities in respect of which *no one* has the required interest. The reason for the requirement of capacity is fairly obvious; it prevents the chaos which would ensue if litigants were unable, through youth or some other handicap, to understand the nature of the proceedings. But the traditional justifications of the requirement of an interest in the case are less obvious and often unconvincing.

A Justification of the requirements

A reason frequently advanced is that the requirements prevent vexatious or frivolous litigation; but this 'floodgates' reasoning has been so thoroughly discredited[77] that it hardly merits serious consideration. And even if the floodgates were opened wide, one might well ask whether a potential litigant who is prepared to go to the trouble and expense of a court action should not be permitted to do so even if others find his claim ill-founded—all the more in public law, where a citizen's vindication of the public interest or the testing of the bounds of legality might be regarded as something of a public service.

A related rationale, one which assumes the validity of the floodgates argument, is the financial cost to the state of doing away with the existing requirements. But even if one allows the assumption, this is an equally dubious claim. Craig[78] has suggested that penal costs could be awarded in the unlikely event of a vexatious claim, thus discouraging silly litigation; and Baxter has pointed out that costs would be awarded against the state only if the decision or action of the public authority were found to be unlawful: '. . . surely a price which must be borne in order to ensure lawful admini-

---

[77] See Baxter 666, especially n 149.
[78] Craig *Administrative Law* (1983) at 451 n 58.

stration'.[79] It may be that the wasted costs incurred by litigating on the question of standing far outweigh any advantage to the state of the present requirement.[80] In any event, the prevention of frivolous lawsuits—if that is indeed the effect of the rules—is frequently achieved at the expense of perfectly good causes and valid claims. The price of 'serious' litigation seems indeed to be frivolously high.

Another strand in the floodgates argument is the great inconvenience to the administration which would be caused if the actio popularis were reintroduced. In *Dalrymple v Colonial Treasurer*,[81] Innes CJ advances this as a reason why taxpayers should not be permitted to sue for breaches of statutes which regulate the allocation of revenue. He reasons as follows: if the government decided, as an emergency measure and in the public interest, to exceed the amount it was legally entitled to spend, and if any taxpayer could apply for an interdict to stop the expenditure, this would hamper the government's freedom to act in the public interest; and, of course, the public interest would suffer. But this ignores the fact that a taxpayer *with a personal interest* would be capable of wreaking precisely the same havoc with the government's freedom of action. In other words, it is not so much an argument against liberalised standing as an argument in favour of making emergency measures non-justiciable in courts of law. It is easy to confuse the two issues, but (as is suggested later on in this chapter)[82] there is a strong case for keeping them separate.

A rationale which deserves more serious attention argues that the requirements ensure that the litigant is the person or body best qualified to make the claim. The reasoning here is that 'unqualified' litigants are more likely to bring weak or half-baked actions. If a litigant brought a weak *class* action, this would create a bad precedent, which would cause prejudice to the rest of the class. It would be better, in other words, to let 'qualified' litigants bring solid cases to court, since a favourable finding would be more likely; and this would create a good precedent, which would then be followed by other courts.[83] But this rationale, even if sound, is not necessarily borne out by the case law: our courts would grant standing to members of a professional organising body where the body itself—the guardian of its profession and the protector of its members' interests—has been denied it.[84] Is it so likely that the individual members are better 'qualified' to bring the action than their organisation?

---

[79] Baxter 666.

[80] Van Dijk *Judicial Review of Governmental Action and the Requirements of an Interest to Sue* (1980) 233–4.

[81] 1910 TS 372 at 386–7.

[82] Below, 282.

[83] This seems to have been the reason for the Roman praetor's choice of the 'best' plaintiff from a number of potential plaintiffs, and may well explain why the actiones populares became obsolete in Roman-Dutch law.

[84] The *Frames Distributors* case discussed above at 272ff.

B Other possible explanations

The real function of the standing requirements may have little to do with the practical arguments which have been outlined above. Certainly the rules have the effect of limiting access to the courts, and thereby limiting access to judicial review of alleged illegalities and to the various remedies, but the traditional reasons for this rationing of the courts' attention are not compelling. Can there be other, more convincing explanations?

One possible explanation is that the rationales are just a smoke-screen for a hidden judicial agenda which allows the judges to choose which interests they want to protect. At its crudest, such an agenda might be overtly political: one might try, for instance, to show that judges exercise political restraint by tending to apply the rules of standing more strictly in high-policy areas with a strong political flavour, such as national security, and that they are prepared to relax the rules in 'apolitical' cases where government policy is not directly at issue. In fact there do not seem to be any particularly obvious links of this kind. To continue with our example, it would not be difficult to find security (or other 'political')[85] cases in which applicants have been denied standing; but one would also have to take account of the fact that most of the direct legislative attempts to preclude judicial review by means of ousters have been made in relation to that very area, and it is precisely here that the judges have been quick to resist the interference. Indeed, the most celebrated[86] relaxation of the standing requirements took place in an application for the interdict de libero homine exhibendo, a remedy sought almost exclusively in security cases.

A more subtle version of this sort of explanation agrees that judges choose the interests which in their view deserve protection, but does not argue for a simple correlation between a particular type of case and judicial activism or restraint. Rather, it suggests that judges have a particular conception of their role in relation to the other two arms of government, and it argues that they tend to use the standing requirements to enforce that model in a variety of legal contexts. It recognises that judicial restraint and activism need not be equated with pro- or anti-government attitudes, but that these terms can refer to a broader concept of justiciability in terms of which judges reinforce (or, in the case of activism, abandon) established notions of the legitimate function of judges.

In our opinion this is a more convincing way of accounting for the existence and scope of our standing requirements than any of the more traditional rationales, and a more telling one than the crude party-political equation offered above. Certainly, the private-law ideology which permeates the rules of standing (and the concomitant

---

[85] For an example, see n 54. The word 'political' is used in the broad sense referred to at 245n16.

[86] *Wood v Ondangwa Tribal Authority* 1975 (2) SA 294 (A).

unwillingness of our courts to recognise an interest in legality) may be seen as giving support to the orthodox 'watchdog' model of the judicial function which we identified in the previous chapter.[87] As Peter Cane has pointed out, a treatment of standing in terms of 'private legal right' reinforces the idea that

> 'the function of the courts is to enforce the law, and of the legislature and the executive to make it and in so doing to consider and give effect to the public interest ... [t]he courts are there to adjudicate individuals' disputes, not to decide issues of policy'.[88]

This sort of attitude may well underlie the general tendency in our law to insist on *private* injury in its applicants, to typify a dispute as one between 'individuals' rather than recognise it as a matter affecting the policy-ridden concept of 'public interest'. By way of solution, Cane advocates separating the question of standing (is this applicant entitled to come to court?) from the question of justiciability (is *any* applicant so entitled?)[89] so as to clarify both the rules of standing and the judges' definition of their 'proper' role.[90] Instead of hiding behind the rules of standing, judges would overtly state that certain matters were 'non-justiciable' and would refuse to exercise their jurisdiction on that basis.

Though Cane's is an extremely attractive proposal, it might not solve the essential problem of what *ought* to be regarded as justiciable! Certainly, there is no reason to suppose that judges will rapidly change their views about their proper role merely as a result of being forced to articulate those views. In other words, the courts could simply go on declining to exercise their jurisdiction, though they would now have a new basis for doing so. If this is true, then arguments for liberalising the rules of standing still hold good.

C   Opening the floodgates

One compelling argument for abandoning the rules has already been mentioned, and this is that the position of the applicant for review is logically irrelevant to the question of administrative legality. The recognition of an interest in legality would bring the law into line with the focus of judicial review, which is on the legitimacy of administrative action—a matter of public interest—and not on the private right of the complainant. Another obvious factor to take into account is the increased subjection of administrative action to judicial scrutiny, which is the first function of judicial review. But there are many other possible advantages to be gained by doing away with the rules of standing: amongst others, the advantages of clarity, convenience and coherence. Clarity, because impenetrable

[87] Above, 243.
[88] Cane (1980) *Public Law* 303 at 307.
[89] Or, more simply, 'is this a proper matter for adjudication, or should it be left to the other arms of government?'
[90] Cane op cit n 88 at 327.

problems of interpretation[91] would disappear; convenience, because subjective and 'natural' interests would coincide with legal ones; and coherence because the success of an application would depend on its merits and not on the applicant—or, for that matter, on luck! If abandonment is felt to be too sweeping a change, it should nevertheless be remembered that the South African test for sufficiency of interest is especially stringent when compared with those of some common-law jurisdictions. In the absence of convincing reasons for its continued existence, the more lenient approaches of the English and American courts provide appropriate and accessible examples of what our law on standing might become.[92]

As things are, the traditional rationales for the rules of standing provide easy explanations for any refusal to grant standing to a particular applicant, and thereby help to obscure what may well be a significant 'hidden agenda': the issue of justiciability. If the judges' view of their function explains their reluctance to recognise an interest in legality, the key to change would seem to lie in altering the judicial attitude rather than in legislative reform—unless that reform were truly revolutionary. So far, the Law Commission's proposals can hardly be described as such. The Draft Bill appended to its Working Paper[93] refers to applications by any person 'who is aggrieved by' an administrative decision or, as an alternative, 'whose interests are affected by' such a decision, and mention is made throughout the report to applications 'by any interested person'. In the absence of a clear and unambiguous legislative intention to change the common law and to welcome the dreaded flood, there is little reason to suppose that our courts would interpret these terms differently from the present requirements.

---

[91] See the discussion at 274 above.
[92] For a brief description of English and American law on the subject, see Carol Harlow and Richard Rawlings *Law and Administration* (1984) chapter 10, especially at 297ff. For a comparative survey, see Bernard Schwartz *Lions Over the Throne* (1987) chapter 4.
[93] *Working Paper 15*, Project 24 (1986) at 107–10.

13 Remedies

The Supreme Court has inherent jurisdiction in terms of the common law both to review (or scrutinise) the offending decision *and* to set aside or to correct it.[1] This built-in remedial jurisdiction is the most obvious source of relief for the victims of unlawful administrative action. However, there are many cases in which the damage cannot be undone by the mere setting aside or correction of the illegality, or in which review would otherwise be an inadequate or inappropriate solution to the complainant's problem. Here are some examples:

- Where the illegality has brought about a state of affairs which requires specific remedial action on the part of the public authority, the complainant might apply for a mandatory interdict which would force the authority to take the necessary action.
- Where the illegality has caused financial loss, the litigant would do best to sue for damages in delict or contract.
- Where apparently illegal action is threatened but has not yet come into existence, a prohibitory interdict or a declaratory order will be the appropriate remedy.
- Where special statutory review is provided for, the applicant may be confined to that remedy to the exclusion of inherent review.

While applications for these alternative remedies do not necessarily involve judicial review in the sense of *setting aside or correction*, they usually entail indirect judicial review, in the sense of *scrutiny*. As we have tried to emphasise in the main headings of this chapter, review in this sense is inevitably a feature of every case in which the legality of the actions of public authorities is at issue.

I DIRECT REVIEW: REVIEW TO SET ASIDE OR CORRECT

A Procedure and Rule 53[2]

Civil proceedings in the Supreme Court can be divided into *actions* and *applications*. Actions are instituted either by writ or by summons, and are conducted as oral trials, whereas applications are launched by means of a notice of motion supported by an affidavit—a written document which sets out all the evidence on which the applicant bases his or her case. While the legal argument

---

[1] This is expressed in a dictum of Innes CJ in *Johannesburg Consolidated Investment Co v Johannesburg Town Council* 1903 TS 111 at 115; see further above, 246ff.

[2] A full discussion of civil procedure is beyond the scope of this book. For detailed treatments, see *LAWSA* vol 3, especially pars 433–444; Herbstein and Van Winsen *The Civil Practice of the Superior Courts in South Africa* 3 ed by L de V van Winsen, J P G Eksteen and A C Cilliers (1979) chapter 41; Nathan, Barnett and Brink *Uniform Rules of Court* 3 ed by C J M Nathan and M Barnett (1984); Lawrence Baxter *Administrative Law* (1984) chapter 17.

in an application is oral, the *evidence* is written; it is seldom that oral evidence is called for. Because of this, motion proceedings tend to be speedier and cheaper than actions, but they are inappropriate whenever there is a 'real dispute of fact'[3] between the parties.

Applications for the review of decisions of inferior courts, tribunals, boards and officers 'performing judicial, quasi-judicial or administrative functions'[4] are governed by Supreme Court Rule 53, which sets out a compulsory form of motion procedure for the purpose. According to subrule (2), the notice of motion must set out the decision or proceedings sought to be reviewed, and must be supported by an affidavit setting out the grounds, facts and circumstances on which the applicant relies. The notice must call upon the relevant magistrate, officer, chairman or presiding officer whose decision or proceedings will be brought under review, and all other parties affected, to show cause why the decision (or proceedings) should not be reviewed and corrected or set aside.[5] It must also call upon the officer concerned to send a record of the offending proceedings to the registrar within fourteen days of receiving the notice, together with any reasons which the officer wishes to give or which the law requires him to give, and to notify the applicant that he has done so.[6] Subrule (4) allows the applicant seven days from receipt of the record to amend the notice of motion and supplement his affidavit. If the officer wishes to oppose the application, subrule (5) provides that he must inform the applicant of his intention within fourteen days of receipt of the notice (or amended notice), and deliver his answering affidavits within21 days.

1 Failure to comply with Rule 53

In theory, failure to comply with the requirements of Rule 53 is fatal unless the court is prepared to condone the lapse. But in practice the Rule 53 procedure is confined to a relatively small proportion of cases involving review, either because the Rule has been held not to apply to the public authority involved,[7] or as a result of the phenomenon of indirect review. As has already been mentioned, there are many cases which do not start as applications for review, but in which the legality of administrative decisions happens to be thrown into doubt; and so, in spite of the compulsory nature of Rule 53, the Supreme Court frequently exercises its review jurisdiction in both criminal trials and in a variety of civil contexts which have nothing to do with the Rule. It is worth noting that magistrates' courts also

---

[3] *Room Hire Co (Pty) Ltd v Jeppe Street Mansions (Pty) Ltd* 1949 (3) SA 1155 (T) at 1161–2 per Murray AJP.

[4] Supreme Court Rule 53. This includes the proceedings of small claims courts: *De Kock v Simon's Bak- en Spuitverfwerk (Edms) Bpk* 1989 (3) SA 189 (C).

[5] Subrule (1)(*a*).

[6] Subrule (1)(*b*).

[7] For an example, see *L F Boshoff Investments (Pty) Ltd v Cape Town Municipality* 1969 (2) SA 256 (C) at 274E–275B.

exercise indirect review jurisdiction of this kind,[8] though not by virtue of common-law powers.[9]

In the rare cases where condonation is requested, the most important consideration would seem to be fairness to both parties. This is illustrated by *Rampa v Rektor, Tschiya Onderwyskollege*.[10] The applicants in this case were students whose admissions to a teachers' training college had been revoked by the Qwaqwa Secretary for Education, and who sought to challenge the revocation on the basis that they ought to have been afforded a hearing before the action was taken. Their failure to apply in terms of the procedures set out in Rule 53 was condoned by Van Coller J on the ground that no prejudice had been caused by it. Though the Secretary (to whom notice of motion ought to have been addressed) was not before the court, his department was represented by the Minister of Education; and all the relevant facts had been placed before the court.

2 Delay

Review to set aside or correct is a discretionary remedy which may be refused if the applicant delays too long in bringing the application. Rule 53 stipulates no time period within which review proceedings must be brought, but it is well established[11] that an application for review must be brought within a reasonable time. What is reasonable depends, of course, on the circumstances. The court will condone an unreasonable delay only if the applicant can give a satisfactory explanation for it. This may be illustrated by the case of *Jeffery v President, South African Medical and Dental Council*,[12] where Berman J was faced with the fact of an 'inordinate'[13] delay of one year. In deciding to condone the delay, the judge took into account the time-consuming preparation required by the application, the fact that the delay was not attributable to the applicant's fault, and the respondent's failure to allege that the delay had caused him prejudice.[14]

B   Setting aside and correcting

1   Setting aside

An administrative action or decision, no matter how blatantly illegal it may appear to be, continues to have legal effect until such time as

[8] In criminal cases, for instance; see below, 293.
[9] Sec 110 of the Magistrates' Courts Act 32 of 1944 authorises magistrates' courts to pronounce on the validity of legislation, excluding provincial ordinances and proclamations of the State President.
[10] 1986 (1) SA 424 (O).
[11] *Wolgroeiers Afslaers (Edms) Bpk v Munisipaliteit van Kaapstad* 1978 (1) SA 13 (A).
[12] 1987 (1) SA 387 (C).
[13] At 391B.
[14] On absence of prejudice, see also *South African Transport Services v Chairman, Local Road Transportation Board, Cape Town; Unicorn Lines (Pty) Ltd v Chairman, Local Road Transportation Board, Cape Town* 1988 (1) SA 665 (C).

it is declared invalid by the court. At that point, the decision—be it a decision to expel a student, a piece of subordinate legislation or a banning order—ceases to have effect and may be treated as if it never existed. 'Setting aside' is a logical consequence of declaring the decision to be invalid, and is simply a way of saying that the decision no longer stands.

2 Correcting

'Correcting' a decision is a more complicated matter. The courts' respect for the distinction between appeal and review makes them extremely reluctant to usurp the decision-making powers which Parliament has delegated to the administration; so, as a general rule, the review court will refer back to tribunals and other public authorities a decision which has been set aside, together with an instruction to the authority to decide the matter again. One exception to the rule arises where the court decides that it is as well qualified as the original authority to make the decision. This consideration was present in *Theron v Ring van Wellington van die NG Sendingkerk in Suid-Afrika*,[15] where Jansen JA found the offending decision to be 'purely judicial' in type, and therefore one which the court was fully qualified to deal with. But there are at least three other situations in which the court will depart from the general rule, and actually 'correct' the decision itself. In the leading case of *Johannesburg City Council v Administrator, Transvaal*[16] Hiemstra J enumerated them as follows:

● Where the end result is a foregone conclusion, and it would be a waste of time to remit the decision to the original decision-maker. A recent illustration is *Hartman v Chairman, Board for Religious Objection*,[17] a case which arose out of the Board's refusal to classify the applicant, a Theravada Buddhist, as a religious objector in terms of s 72D(1) of the Defence Act 44 of 1957. Having held that Parliament must have intended 'religious convictions' to include convictions based on non-theistic religions, Smuts JP made an order granting the application for classification as a religious objector. There would be no point in remitting the decision to the Board, since it was bound to follow the court's classification, and since the applicant's bona fides had already been established to the Board's satisfaction.

● Where further delay would cause unjustifiable prejudice to the applicant. In *Reynolds Brothers Ltd v Chairman, Local Road Transportation Board, Johannesburg*,[18] Miller JA considered that the applicant's need for clarity and assurance with regard to

[15] 1976 (2) SA 1 (A).
[16] 1969 (2) SA 72 (T).
[17] 1987 (1) SA 922 (O).
[18] 1985 (2) SA 790 (A) at 805F–H. See also *Local Road Transportation Board v Durban City Council* 1965 (1) SA 586 (A).

road-carrier permits was such that the court should order the
board to issue the desired permits.

● Where the original decision-maker has exhibited bias or incom-
petence to such a degree that it would be unfair to ask the
applicant to submit to its jurisdiction again. A possible example is
Oskil Properties (Pty) Ltd v Chairman of the Rent Control Board,[19]
where none of the available evidence supported a valuation made
by the Rent Control Board. Van Rensburg J took into account the
fact that its decision was 'wholly unwarranted' in deciding to
correct the decision himself. And in *Mahlaela v De Beer NO*[20]
Stafford J took into account the 'boorish conduct' and 'vulgar and
abusive language' of the respondent, a township superintendent,
in his dealings with the applicant, who had unsuccefully applied
for a dwelling or township land to be allocated to him. In view of
the respondent's conduct and his obvious hostility to the
applicant, it was unlikely that the respondent would reconsider
the application in an unbiased and objective way, and this made
it appropriate for the court to make the allocation itself.

C   Standard and onus of proof

Generally speaking, criminal cases require facts to be proved 'beyond
reasonable doubt', whereas civil cases merely require proof 'on a
balance of probabilities' or 'on a preponderance of probability'.
Judicial review proceeds on the civil standard. The onus or burden of
proving the facts which constitute an illegality ordinarily rests on the
applicant, the person who alleges the existence of the illegality. If the
applicant is able to make out at least a prima facie case of illegality,
the respondent authority will then bear the onus of refuting it. Thus
if an applicant wishes to challenge a decision to refuse her a licence,
she must bring evidence to show that the licensing official concerned
acted illegally (that he ignored statutory provisions, for instance, or
that he acted in bad faith). On the other hand, if the applicant fails to
make an adequate challenge, the decision or action will be judged
lawful in accordance with the maxim 'omnia praesumuntur rite esse
acta'.[21] This maxim presumes, in the absence of evidence to the
contrary, that all legal requirements and formalities have been
complied with. It has very little significance, however, since the
presumption can be rebutted by evidence of an illegality, and since
the onus is initially on the applicant in any event.

The incidence of the onus of proof can vary according to the nature
of the administrative act. Where the alleged illegality takes the form

---

[19] 1985 (2) SA 234 (SE) at 247E.
[20] 1986 (4) SA 782 (T) at 794F–795F.
[21] In full, the maxim is *omnia praesumuntur rite et solemnitur esse acta, donec probetur in
contrarium.* See generally L A Rose-Innes *Judicial Review of Administrative Tribunals
in South Africa* (1963) 117–19; Baxter op cit n 2 at 738–9.

of an unlawful arrest,[22] for instance, it is well established in our common law that the applicant's initial task is merely to challenge the respondent to prove the lawfulness of the action. In such a case, the applicant will have to adduce evidence of an illegality only if the respondent succeeds in establishing a prima facie case of lawful action. Similarly, where the alleged illegality relates to a subjectively phrased statutory prerequisite or 'jurisdictional fact', the onus of proving compliance with the prerequisite rests on the respondent. Exceptions like these are often more apparent than real, however, since the crucial question is not where the onus lies but *what is required to discharge it*. This is well illustrated by cases dealing with subjectively phrased powers of detention (discussed in the next chapter), where the initial onus on the respondent official can be discharged merely by an assertion that the statutory prerequisite has been complied with.[23]

II INDIRECT REVIEW (SCRUTINY)

A Discretionary remedies

1 Interdicts

When used on its own, without a qualifying adjective, the word 'interdict' is commonly understood to be a synonym for the prohibitory interdict. The effect of this type of interdict is to stop an unlawful interference with a person's rights, or to prevent a threatened interference from taking place. The mandatory interdict—one which requires action to be taken—is not so well known, but is just as important a remedy. Both types may be brought by public bodies as well as against them.

Interdicts may be either *interlocutory* (interim) or *final*. An interlocutory interdict is a temporary measure which provisionally decides the rights of the parties 'pendente lite' (that is, when legal proceedings are pending between the parties), and which loses its effect once the court has finally decided where the rights lie. A final interdict, on the other hand, is permanent, and only a successful appeal can alter its effect. The availability of interdicts is strictly limited in our law. In the case of an interlocutory interdict,[24] the applicant must establish a prima facie[25] right, and show that irreparable harm is likely to result if the remedy is not granted, that the balance of convenience is in favour of granting the remedy, and that there is no other satisfactory remedy available. The interdict will

---

[22] *Brand v Minister of Justice* 1959 (4) SA 712 (A). See also the judgment of Rabie CJ in *Minister of Law and Order v Hurley* 1986 (3) SA 568 (A) at 587–9, especially at 589D–G, and the authorities cited there.

[23] See below, 316ff.

[24] *Setlogelo v Setlogelo* 1914 AD 221 at 227.

[25] A right 'established upon a balance of probabilities': Jones and Buckle *The Civil Practice of the Magistrates' Courts in South Africa* Vol I 8 ed by H J Erasmus and D E van Loggerenberg (1988) at 88.

not be made final until the court is satisfied that three conditions[26] have been met: that the applicant has a clear (or definite)[27] right which is being infringed; that the interference with the right has actually taken place or is reasonably apprehended; and that there is no other satisfactory remedy available to the applicant.

(a) Prohibitory interdicts

This remedy may be used to prevent the commission of threatened illegal action (such as a threatened assault by a policeman) or to put a stop to continuing illegal action (such as police harassment).

(b) Mandatory interdicts

A mandatory interdict is known as a mandamus when it is granted against a public authority. It is used to force a public authority to perform a statutory duty (to grant a licence, to consider an application) or to cure a state of affairs brought about by illegal action (to demolish a building encroaching on the applicant's land, for instance). Because mandatory interdicts require positive action to be taken, a court will take the difficulty of enforcement into account when deciding whether to grant the order.

The interdictum de libero homine exhibendo, also known as 'habeas corpus',[28] is an important and unique form of mandatory interdict. It is used to obtain judicial scrutiny of the unlawful deprivation of a person's liberty, and it is prized for one traditional feature in particular: the person who is being held or detained is produced in court 'to be seen and touched'. Though this is obviously an important safeguard of a detainee's welfare, production of detained persons is frequently prohibited by the enabling legislation,[29] and is by no means the norm in South African courts.[30] Nor is it clear whether the interdict allows for the production of detainees for the purpose of giving oral evidence.[31] However, this

---

[26] *Setlogelo v Setlogelo*, n 24 above.

[27] Jones & Buckle op cit n 25 at 85.

[28] Habeas corpus is the English law version of this remedy. The two remedies are often said to be identical, but it seems that they can no longer be regarded as such: see the judgment of Rabie CJ in *Tussentydse Regering vir Suidwes-Afrika v Katofa* 1987 (1) SA 695 (A) at 722ff.

[29] For instance, reg 3(10)(*a*) of the emergency regulations promulgated by Proc R109 in *GG* 10280 of 12 June 1986 states that 'No person, other than a Minister or a person acting by virtue of his office in service of the State, shall have access to any person detained in terms of the provisions of this regulation, except with the consent of and subject to such conditions as may be determined by the Minister or a person authorised thereto by him'.

[30] See above, 275n55.

[31] The point was raised, though not pursued, by Vivier JA in *Nkwentsha v Minister of Law and Order* 1988 (3) SA 99 (A) at 116J–117B. In this case the Minister, relying on emergency regulation 3(10) (n 29 above), defied a subpoena by refusing the detainee permission to come to court. The Appellate Division held that a person detained under emergency regulations was not precluded from giving viva voce evidence in court in spite of the provisions of reg 3(1). See also *Apleni v Minister of*

remedy is more easily available to applicants than other interdicts, not only because the standing requirements are especially liberal,[32] but also because the interdict is awarded readily once the applicant has established a prima facie case.[33] Applications are usually dealt with as matters of urgency.

2 The spoliation order

Though the spoliation order (mandament van spolie) may be classified as an interdict, it is such a distinctive remedy that it deserves to be treated separately.

The order has the effect of restoring possession of a thing to an applicant ('spoliatus') who has been dispossessed. Its rationale is said to be the prevention of self-help: people should not take the law into their own hands, even if they believe they are justified in depriving others of their possessions. In accordance with this rationale and with the maxim 'spoliatus ante omnia restituendus est', the order does not decide rights of ownership; it merely restores the position (the status quo ante) which existed before the illicit action was taken. This means that the court will not concern itself with the merits of the matter, or the lawfulness of the applicant's possession, but will simply order restoration if it is satisfied, on a balance of probabilities, that the applicant has been dispossessed without his or her consent.[34]

Since the spoliation order does not determine rights of ownership or ultimate possession, it has the appearance of an interlocutory interdict; but the order is always final in the sense that it is a decisive determination of the *immediate* right to possession, and in that there need be no legal action pending between the parties. And, unlike interdicts, the spoliation order is neither a discretionary remedy nor one which takes into account the balance of convenience. There are nevertheless orders which bear a definite resemblance to the mandamus, the best-known example being the case of *Fredericks v Stellenbosch Divisional Council*.[35] In this case the council had illegally demolished squatters' dwellings inhabited by the applicants. The court restored possession of the shanties by ordering the council to rebuild them. In a more recent case, *Vena v George Municipality*,[36] the respondent municipality was similarly ordered to restore the applicants' houses to the state they were in before the illegal demolition.

Law and Order; *Lamani v Minister of Law and Order* 1989 (1) SA 195 (A); and cf *Schermbrucker v Klindt NO* 1955 (4) SA 606 (A).

[32] See above, 275.

[33] *In re Willem Kok and Nathaniele Balie* (1879) 9 Buch 45; *In re Marechane* 1 SAR 27.

[34] *Nino Bonino v De Lange* 1906 TS 120; *Bon Quelle (Edms) Bpk v Munisipaliteit van Otavi* 1989 (1) SA 508 (A).

[35] 1977 (3) SA 113 (C). The effects of the decision were immediately wiped out by means of retrospective legislation.

[36] 1987 (4) SA 29 (C). For comment on this and other cases, see Johan Roos (1988) 4 *SAJHR* 167.

3 The declaratory order (declaration of rights)

Section 19(1)(*a*)(iii) of the Supreme Court Act 59 of 1959 states that the Supreme Court may in its discretion enquire into and determine any existing, future or contingent right or obligation at the instance of any interested person, 'notwithstanding that such person cannot claim any relief consequential upon the determination'. The leading case is *Ex parte Nell*,[37] where the Appellate Division held that the only requirements for the exercise of the court's declaratory jurisdiction are interested parties on whom the order will be binding. There is no need for an *existing* dispute; though the right or obligation in question must not be a purely speculative, abstract or intellectual one, it is clear that an order can be made even before rights have been infringed, or before illegal action has been taken. Thus in *Reinecke v Nel*,[38] the Appellate Division confirmed the correctness of an order declaring that an election candidate *who had not yet been nominated* was ineligible for nomination.

Declaratory orders are particularly useful because they allow parties to obtain a final (though appealable) determination of their rights before a dispute has arisen, and therefore before any harm has been done. The availability of these orders has, however, been thrown into some doubt by the decision of the appeal court in *Cabinet of the Transitional Government for the Territory of South West Africa v Eins*.[39] This case concerned the enactment of legislation[40] which enabled the cabinet to deport a person not born in the territory if it had reason to believe that the person concerned constituted a security risk. The applicant, who was born in Germany, challenged the validity of the section in the Supreme Court of South West Africa, and obtained an order declaring the section to be unconstitutional because contrary to the rights accorded all citizens in the Bill of Fundamental Rights. The South African appeal court overturned the decision on the ground that the applicant had no locus standi to claim the order. Refusing to regard the application as being of the kind envisaged in s 19 of the Supreme Court Act,[41] Rabie ACJ found that unless and until the cabinet should take action against the applicant under the section, the declaration would be of mere academic interest to him. Since Rabie ACJ gave no reasons for his conclusion that the order sought bore no relation to that sought in *Nell's* case,[42] it is difficult to know what effect his judgment will have on future applications of this kind, and whether the requirements of standing for the remedy have changed as a result of it. A similar (and also unsuccessful) application in *Cabinet for the Territory of South*

[37] 1963 (1) SA 754 (A).
[38] 1984 (1) SA 820 (A).
[39] 1988 (3) SA 369 (A).
[40] Section 9 of Act 33 of 1985.
[41] At 390B–F.
[42] Note 37 above.

West Africa v Chikane[43] throws little light on the issue, since the applicant in this case had in fact been issued with a deportation order under s 9, and therefore possessed the standing required in terms of the *Eins*[44] case.

B   Civil actions[45]

Public authorities are delictually liable for damage caused during the performance of their statutory functions, and are liable also for breaching their contractual obligations, but may escape liability by showing that their actions were justified by statute. Since the defence of statutory justification necessarily involves the court in an examination of the legality of the action taken, an action of this kind is an indirect way of obtaining review of the decisions of public authorities.

C   Criminal cases

Subordinate legislation is frequently used to create criminal offences. The accused who is charged with committing such an offence can plead not guilty on the basis that the legislation which creates the offence is invalid—and therefore, that whatever he or she did was not an offence. Obviously, the attack on the subordinate legislation brings judicial review into play, whether in the Supreme Court or the magistrates' courts. An example of such a case is *R v Carelse*,[46] where a magistrate had convicted a 'non-white' person of the offence of using a beach reserved for whites. Though the beach set aside for 'non-whites' was inferior to the 'white' beach, the magistrate had rejected the argument that the regulation which created the offence was invalid. This argument succeeded on appeal, however, and the conviction was set aside.[47]

III   STATUTORY REVIEW ('APPEALS')

Apart from the 'domestic' remedies (usually a form of appeal) which a statute might provide, and which do not involve courts of law, Parliament sometimes gives the courts a statutory power of review which is wider than its inherent review jurisdiction. In many cases this wider jurisdiction allows the court to pronounce on the merits to a greater or lesser extent, so that statutory reviews are often referred to as 'appeals'. As far as the scope of these reviews is concerned, the possibilities and permutations are endless. Parliament might give the court power to provide special remedies, or confine its enquiry to questions of law; and as with their domestic counterparts, the 'appeal' may incline to the wide or the narrow.

[43] 1989 (1) SA 349 (A).
[44] Note 39 above.
[45] On state liability in general, see above, 182–7.
[46] 1943 CPD 242.
[47] See further below, 351ff.

In *Madrassa Anjuman Islamia v Johannesburg Municipality*[48] it was held that, in the absence of language which clearly points to a contrary legislative intention, the provision of statutory relief does not oust common-law remedies which are ordinarily available. Moreover, it has been held that even where a statute prescribes a specific remedy for the enforcement of a new liability created by it, there is no 'initial inference' that the prescribed remedy was intended to be exclusive of ordinary remedies.[49]

IV OBSTACLES TO JUDICIAL REDRESS

The rules of standing discussed in the last chapter are not the only restriction on access to judicial review and the other remedies, though they undoubtedly constitute a very significant restriction. A number of judicially imposed obstacles have to be overcome by the successful applicant for relief, and there are statutory devices used to restrict access to the courts, or to make such access conditional, or to oust judicial redress altogether. As suggested in chapter 11,[50] the proliferation of obstacles makes a mockery of the traditional view of review as the most significant way of enforcing the legal use of government power. As it turns out, the watchdog's patrols are limited, sporadic and, to some extent, random. Where the obstacles relate primarily to the qualification of the applicant, or where (as with ouster clauses) they have nothing to do with the merits of the case, it is clear that the principle of legality is sacrificed to considerations of convenience, propriety or expediency.

A Judicial control and discretion

Like review to set aside or correct, interdicts and declaratory orders are 'discretionary' remedies, which is to say that the court may refuse to grant them if it considers that the remedy is inappropriate or that it will be ineffective; that the applicant has delayed too long before applying for the relief,[51] that the applicant has come to court prematurely,[52] or that the illegal action is unlikely to cause the applicant any prejudice. In addition, the courts have developed special limitations on the availability of interdicts.[53]

B The duty to exhaust domestic remedies

This judge-made requirement obliges the complainant to make full use of the domestic or internal remedies available before seeking

---

[48] 1917 AD 718 at 727 (Solomon JA dissenting).

[49] Per Kroon J in *Kwanobuhle Town Council v Andries* 1988 (2) SA 796 (SE) at 801 (refusing to follow cases which suggest otherwise). See also *Radebe v Eastern Transvaal Development Board* 1988 (2) SA 785 (A), where the common-law vindicatory right to reclaim possession of property was held not to be excluded by statutory remedies providing for eviction from premises in black residential areas.

[50] Above, 264–5.

[51] On undue delay in Rule 53 applications, see 286 above.

[52] The most obvious form of premature application occurs when domestic remedies have not been exhausted; see 294–5.

[53] Above, 289–91.

help from the court, and so avoids wasting the court's time with complaints which could have been settled sooner and more cheaply by officials chosen specifically for the purpose. The unsuccessful applicant for a provincial licence, for example, should go to the relevant appeal board before resorting to court proceedings; and a club member who has been expelled from her hockey club should first appeal to the special committee which exists for the purpose. Whenever there is statutory or contractual provision for domestic redress—in our examples, redress which is internal to the provincial licensing system or the hockey club—there is the possibility that the court will require those remedies to be exhausted.

In some cases it is appropriate for the court to condone a failure to pursue an available remedy, either because the remedy is inadequate or because it is tainted by the alleged illegality. In *Mahlaela v De Beer NO*,[54] for instance, the applicant had failed to make use of his statutory right of appeal to a development board from the decision of a township superintendent not to allocate him a house in the township. Stafford J found that it would be useless for the applicant to appeal to the development board because it had laid down a fixed policy that houses were not to be allocated. Similarly, in *Mathale v Secretary for Education, Gazankulu*,[55] Leveson J held that since the appellate authority, a minister, had already condoned the respondents' action, an appeal to him would have 'yielded a fruitless result'.

C Ouster clauses

Ouster (or 'privative') clauses are legislative provisions which are intended to prevent the court from exercising its review jurisdiction over specified administrative decisions. When effective, they give the administration carte blanche to act as it pleases, without regard for the standards of legality which judges set for the conduct of those in public office: authorisation, regularity, fairness and reasonableness. In South Africa, ousters are relied upon particularly heavily by the authors of security and immigration legislation, though they appear in many other contexts too. A typical example is the clause appearing in s 29(6) of the Internal Security Act 74 of 1982:

> 'No court of law shall have jurisdiction to pronounce on any action taken in terms of this section, or to order the release of any person detained in terms of the provisions of this section.'

There are a number of Appellate Division decisions in which ouster clauses have been held to be effective in preventing judicial review, most notably *Schermbrucker v Klindt NO*[56] and *Barday v Passport Control Officer*.[57] And yet there is a strong judicial antipathy towards

---

[54] Note 20 above at 790I.
[55] 1986 (4) SA 427 (T) at 431A.
[56] 1965 (4) SA 606 (A).
[57] 1967 (2) SA 346 (A).

ouster clauses. This is reflected in a long-standing presumption[58] against ousting and in the large number of cases in which the clauses have been utterly ineffective. In two early cases, *Union Government v Fakir*[59] and *Narainsamy v Principal Immigration Officer*,[60] Innes CJ found that an ouster clause would not prevent a court from interfering with a decision which showed a manifest absence of jurisdiction, fraud 'or a similar element'. Since there is nothing to suggest that by 'fraud' Innes CJ meant actual dishonesty,[61] it would seem that these three grounds between them cover *all* the gounds of review; in other words, that ouster clauses can only prevent review in those cases where there has been no illegality! This is not as odd as it sounds. Because ouster clauses typically prevent review of action taken *'in terms of'* or *'under'* a particular piece of legislation, it actually makes sense to say that illegal action is not action taken 'in terms of' or 'under' the enactment, and therefore that the ouster clause does not apply. This approach does, of course, make ouster clauses quite spurious,[62] but it has nevertheless been applied in a number of South African cases,[63] and is firmly entrenched in English law.[64] It received endorsement in the important Appellate Division decision of *Minister of Law and Order v Hurley*.[65]

The case arose out of the arrest and detention of K, a pacifist, under s 29 of the Internal Security Act. That section requires the arresting officer to have 'reason to believe' that the person to be detained has committed, or is likely to commit, one of the offences set out in s 54 of the Act, or that the person is withholding from the police information relating to the commission of such an offence. It also purports to prevent the court from 'pronouncing on any action taken in terms of this section'. In the court a quo,[66] the applicants successfully contended that the officer could not possibly have had reason to believe that K was such a person. On the basis that the arresting officer was ultra vires his powers, and relying largely on English case authority, Leon J found that the ouster clause in s 29 did not prevent him from interfering, since action which is ultra vires is action which is *not* in terms of the section. Hailed as a considerable

---

[58] In the absence of incontrovertible evidence to the contrary, it will be presumed that the legislature did not intend to oust the courts' jurisdiction: *R v Padsha* 1923 AD 281 (Innes CJ); *Minister of Law and Order v Hurley* 1986 (3) SA 568 (A) at 584A–C (Rabie CJ).

[59] 1923 AD 466 at 469–70.

[60] 1923 AD 673 at 675.

[61] On dishonesty, see further below, 345ff.

[62] See also n 67 below.

[63] For instance, *South West African Peoples Democratic United Front v Administrateur-Generaal, Suidwes-Afrika* 1983 (1) SA 411 (A); *Ngqulunga v Minister of Law and Order* 1983 (2) SA 696 (N).

[64] It was approved by the House of Lords twenty years ago in *Anisminic Ltd v Foreign Compensation Commission* [1969] 2 AC 147.

[65] 1986 (3) SA 568 (A).

[66] *Hurley v Minister of Law and Order* 1985 (4) SA 709 (D).

blow for individual freedom, this result was approved by the Appellate Division on appeal.[67]

To lawyers who thought themselves justified in the view that ousters had no teeth left at all, the majority decision in *Staatspresident v United Democratic Front*[68] has come as a rude shock.[69] In this case, the Appellate Division decided that an ouster clause contained in s 5B of the Public Safety Act effectively prevented review of an emergency regulation where challenge was based on the ground of vagueness. Though this result might appear to be a startling volte-face from *Hurley*,[70] the court found it unnecessary to overrule its previous decision or to distinguish it. Instead, the court held that the term 'ultra vires' could only be applied to decision-makers who *literally* exceeded their statutory powers or otherwise transgressed boundaries laid down by the enabling legislation. Though the State President had made vague regulations, and though the rules of administrative law do not permit delegated lawmakers to make vague regulations, he could not literally be said to be acting *beyond his powers* or ultra vires, for *the statute itself* did not contain a provision preventing him from making vague regulations.[71] If he did not act ultra vires his statutory powers, he must have acted intra vires—and therefore 'under' the legislation; and since the ouster clause prevented the court from pronouncing on the action taken 'under' the Act, the court was barred from granting the relief sought by the applicants.

The effect of ouster clauses from now on will, it seems, depend on the type of illegality with which the court is confronted. If the illegality relates to express statutory requirements which can be exceeded in a literal sense (probably requirements relating to authority or regularity),[72] the clause will be ineffective in preventing judicial scrutiny; but where there has been a breach of one of the implied, common-law or judge-made requirements, such as reasonableness,[73] the clause may well be effective. Unfortunately, the distinction between these two categories of illegality is not always clear—a fact which seems to have escaped the appeal court's

---

[67] It is interesting to note that Rabie CJ was not prepared to concede the spuriousness of ouster clauses. In his view, ouster clauses did not lack meaning because they prevented the court from pronouncing on the merits (at 586G–I). With respect, it should be pointed out that this limitation on the court's jurisdiction is secured by the distinction between appeal and review, and that the position is not affected by the presence or absence of an ouster clause.

[68] 1988 (4) SA 830 (A), Van Heerden JA dissenting.

[69] For criticism of the case, see Nicholas Haysom and Clive Plasket (1988) 4 *SAJHR* 303; Etienne Mureinik (1989) 5 *SAJHR* 60, especially at 69–72; John Grogan (1989) 106 *SALJ* 14.

[70] Note 65 above.

[71] See the judgment of Rabie ACJ at 853D–F.

[72] These are discussed in chapter 14.

[73] It has already been held, in *Natal Indian Congress v State President* 1989 (3) SA 588 (D), that an ouster clause effectively prevents a court from considering the unreasonableness of subordinate legislation. See further below, 356.

attention, and which is likely to present great practical problems in future cases. The difficulty is discussed in greater detail later on in this book.[74]

D   Limitation clauses

Limitation clauses are partial ousters which achieve their object of confining access to judicial relief by setting time limits within which applications must be brought, stipulating minimum periods of notice to the respondent authority and excluding the power of the court to award certain remedies, such as interdicts. A typical example is contained in s 32(1) of the Police Act 7 of 1958, which states that

> 'Any civil action against the State or any person in respect of anything done in pursuance of this Act, shall be commenced within six months after the cause of action arose, and notice in writing of any civil action and of the cause thereof shall be given to the defendant one month at least before the commencement hereof.'

Since limitation clauses are not intended to preclude judicial scrutiny altogether, and since their use is easily supported by reasons of practical convenience (such as the need to establish the legality of action at the earliest possible stage), they tend not to excite the indignation aroused by ousters. Even so, our courts tend to interpret them restrictively, especially where injustice would otherwise be done to a complainant who is unable to start proceedings within the time limit. Thus in *Montsisi v Minister van Polisie*[75] the Appellate Division found that it was impossible for a detainee to comply with the requirements in s 32(1) of the Police Act. Since the law does not demand the impossible (lex non cogit ad impossibilia), the period of six months would only begin to run against him from the moment of his release.

E   Indemnity clauses

It is difficult to be polite about indemnity clauses, since they are even more shameless than ousters. The most common kind, retrospective indemnities, protect public authorities from the legal consequences of unlawful acts committed in the past. Prospective indemnities are worse still. As Budlender[76] has put it,

> 'By enacting a prospective indemnity, the state effectively says that it anticipates that its officials are going to act unlawfully, but it cannot or will not do anything to prevent this. State officials must therefore be given a free hand.'

Prospective indemnities are routinely included in emergency regulations,[77] the only saving grace being that they refer to acts taken

---

[74] Below, 357.
[75] 1984 (1) SA 619 (A). See also *Mati v Minister of Justice, Police and Prisons, Ciskei* 1988 (3) SA 750 (Ck).
[76] Geoff Budlender (1988) 4 *SAJHR* 139 at 144.
[77] For instance, reg 12(1) Proc R96 of 1987; reg 16(1) Proc R109 of 1986.

'in good faith' and 'in terms of these regulations'. Though it is not clear what 'good faith' means,[78] the second phrase does leave such clauses open to circumvention in the manner of ouster clauses.[79]

F Subjective language

Parliament frequently makes use of subjectively phrased clauses to confer particularly wide discretion on certain decision-makers, thereby aiming to limit the scope of review of their decisions. Ironically enough, in the period between the *Hurley*[80] and the *United Democratic Front*[81] cases subjective language was often felt to be a greater obstacle to review than ouster clauses themselves; for while ousters could be sidestepped entirely, a discretion phrased in subjective terms was not at all easy to challenge. Even since the *UDF* decision, it may still be possible to ignore at least some ouster clauses, but subjective language remains an effective limitation on the scope of the applicant's challenge. Such clauses are discussed in more detail in the next chapter.[82]

---

[78] See Anthony S Mathews *Freedom, State Security and the Rule of Law* (1986) 205–7; and see below, 347–9.

[79] See above, 296. It was argued in *Makhasa v Minister of Law and Order, Lebowa Government* 1988 (3) SA 701 (A) that an indemnity Act should be tested most stringently because it had the effect of ousting the courts' jurisdiction. Grosskopf JA found it unnecessary to deal with the point (at 725J–726B).

[80] Note 65 above.

[81] Note 68 above.

[82] Below, 314–18.

14 Authority and Regularity

The principles of authority and regularity imply that administrative actions and decisions must be duly authorised by law and that all statutory requirements and preconditions must be complied with. The two principles overlap to a great extent: an unauthorised decision (such as a decision made by a person who has no authority to make it) can easily be described as 'irregular'; and an irregular decision (such as one made by an improperly constituted tribunal) may well be called 'unauthorised'. For the sake of convenience, the requirements of authority and regularity are discussed separately in this chapter; but it should be borne in mind that the natural overlap between the two principles is bound to make any distinction between them somewhat arbitrary.

I SOME TERMINOLOGY

Our courts have drawn some important distinctions between various kinds of power and different types of statutory provision. Much of the material in this chapter requires some understanding of these, so that it is convenient to deal with them at the outset.

A Powers and duties

The difference between powers and duties can be expressed very simply by saying that powers *enable* things to be done; duties *require* them to be done. Whether a legislative provision confers a power or imposes a duty depends to a large extent on the language used (see below). In administrative law, powers are always accompanied by some implied duties, such as a duty to act in the public interest.

B Express and implied powers

In most cases *express* powers are needed for the actions and decisions of public bodies. *Implied* powers may, however, be ancillary to the express powers, or exist as a necessary or reasonable[1] consequence of the express powers: just as the power to make omelettes must include a power to break eggs, so the power to build a dam may include the power to remove silt,[2] or perhaps to expropriate property. Factors which the court will take into account in deciding on the scope of the authorised power include:
- The language of the statute: The language used in statutes is always crucial to discovering the legislature's intention.
- The context of the provision: The Act as a whole and the purposes for which it was enacted may indicate whether further powers are

---

[1] *Johannesburg Consolidated Investment Co v Marshalls Township Syndicate Ltd* 1917 AD 662; *Randfontein Estates G M Co Ltd v Randfontein Town Council* 1943 AD 475.
[2] *Bloemfontein Town Council v Richter* 1938 AD 195.

reasonably incidental to the express authority which has been given. There is a very strong argument in favour of implying a power if, for instance, the main purpose of the statute cannot be achieved without it.[3]

● The nature of the administrative action: Where the action is coercive, oppressive[4] or is likely to have far-reaching effects, it is less likely that a court will find implied authorisation for it. A typical instance is *Lipschitz NO v SA Pharmacy Board*,[5] where the question was whether the power to regulate the 'conduct of business' and the 'tariff of fees' of pharmacists included the implied power to prohibit pharmacists from selling certain goods. Munnik JP held that it did not, particularly since it would have been a simple matter for Parliament to add 'trading activities' to the list of matters which the Minister was empowered to regulate.[6]

C Discretionary and mechanical powers

Discretionary powers are characterised by the element of choice which they confer on their holder. As Davis[7] has put it,

> '[A] public officer has discretion whenever the effective limits of his power leave him free to make a choice among possible courses of action and inaction.'

Mechanical powers, on the other hand, involve little or no choice on the part of their holder. In fact, 'purely mechanical' (or 'ministerial') powers are more in the nature of *duties*. This can be illustrated by comparing the following powers: the power to issue a dog-licence on payment of a fee, and the power to grant it 'in deserving cases'. In the first case, the purely mechanical power gives the licensing official no choice at all in the matter; and this means that official is really under a duty to issue a licence on payment of the fee. In the second, the power to identify 'deserving cases' entails a considerable degree of choice, and is therefore discretionary. Though the second power seems to involve no duty at all, it is important to realise that the holder of discretionary power never has a completely free hand. To act with discretion means to act wisely and after due reflection; and so, though discretion can be very wide, it is never completely 'free' or 'unfettered'. In the second case, then, there would be an implicit duty to act according to minimum standards of good administration. For instance, the official would not be entitled to ignore an application for a licence, or to refuse licences to everyone except his family and friends.

D Mandatory and directory provisions

The general rule is that statutory requirements are compulsory or

[3] *Johannesburg Municipality v Davies* 1925 AD 395.
[4] See, for instance, *Mokoena v Commissioner of Prisons* 1985 (1) SA 368 (W).
[5] 1985 (2) SA 702 (C).
[6] At 709B–D.
[7] Kenneth Culp Davis *Discretionary Justice* 2 ed (1971) at 4.

'mandatory': a court will not lightly assume that Parliament has used words in vain. But failure to comply strictly with the provisions (and especially the formalities) of a statute does not inevitably lead to invalidity. The following are some of the more obvious factors which a court will take into account in deciding whether a provision may be treated as merely 'directory'. None of them is decisive:

- Language: Has peremptory or permissive language been used? It should be noted that though peremptory language is seldom interpreted as being permissive, courts have been known to interpret permissive words like 'may' as meaning 'must'.[8]
- The context and importance of the provision: The provision should be construed in the light of the legislation as a whole and in relation to the purposes it seeks to achieve. If the provision is a mere technicality, there is little point in requiring strict compliance with it, and it may be asked whether Parliament would seriously have intended invalidity to result from a breach of it.
- The nature of the administrative action: The impact and importance of the action taken may provide a clue to Parliament's intention. Conversely, the urgency of the action or decision may give the court added reason to interpret the provision as merely directory.

II   AUTHORITY

The first principle of administrative law is the same as the first requirement of the Rule of Law: that the exercise of power should be authorised by law. Public bodies have no powers of their own. With the exception of the State President, who possesses some inherent prerogative powers, they are dependent on Parliament[9] for their authority. This means that an action performed without due legislative authorisation is illegal. Similarly, legislative authority given to a particular body should be exercised by that body, and not by some unauthorised official. The requirement of authority, or *authorised power*, can be translated into a number of grounds of review, to which we now turn.

A   Lack of authority

It seldom happens that public bodies purport to make decisions for which there is no authority at all; it is more usual to find that they *exceed* or *abuse* authority which they already possess, or that

---

[8] A recent example is *Veriava v President, SA Medical and Dental Council* 1985 (2) SA 293 (T), where the statute in question stated that the Council 'shall have power' to hold an inquiry on being presented with prima facie evidence of misconduct. The court held that the Council was obliged to hold an inquiry in those circumstances, thus treating a purely enabling provision as mandatory.

[9] Custom is another possible source of law, but a relatively insignificant one: see above, 14–15.

authority given to one body is wrongly exercised by another, unauthorised body.

B Authority exercised by an unauthorised body

As a general rule, power given to a public body cannot lawfully be exercised by some other (unauthorised) body. Since Parliament has chosen the State President to be the author of emergency regulations, it would be inappropriate for the Minister of Manpower to make emergency regulations. In such a case, the Minister would be acting contrary to Parliament's expressed intention by usurping the powers conferred upon the State President; and the State President, by his failure to exercise the power himself, would also be acting illegally. Whether one classifies the situation as the *usurping* of authority (by the Minister) or the *abdication* of authority (by the State President), the action remains illegal. However, it has been held that action incorrectly stated to be taken under the wrong legislation may be valid provided that authority for the action does in fact exist. This was the position in *Avenue Delicatessen v Natal Technikon*,[10] where a Minister erroneously stated that he was issuing a Government Notice under s 51 of the Rent Control Act, a section which did not, in fact, empower him to issue the Notice. The Appellate Division found that the Notice was valid on the ground that the Minister possessed the necessary power under s 2 of the same Act.

1 Unlawful delegation

When Parliament confers authority on public bodies, it *delegates* power. Because Parliament is sovereign, there is no limit on its ability to delegate powers to others; and it may, of course, stipulate that its delegees may further delegate their powers to other bodies. (To avoid the usual confusion caused by this terminology, we use the term 'delegate' to refer to delegation from Parliament, and 'subdelegate' to refer to further delegation from Parliament's delegees.) In the absence of an express statutory provision to that effect, the question often arises whether the power to subdelegate can be implied into the statute. There are strong arguments both for and against implied subdelegation. On one hand, it is a necessary feature of modern government; without it, ministers and other high-ranking officials would find it impossible to carry out the thousands of tasks entrusted to them by Parliament every year. On the other hand, Parliament no doubt has good reasons for entrusting certain tasks to hand-picked individuals: their superior qualifications, their political responsibility, and so on. The legal solution to this difficulty is a compromise in the form of a rebuttable presumption against subdelegation, which is expressed in the maxim 'delegatus delegare non potest':

> 'The maxim *delegatus delegare non potest* is based upon the assumption that, where the Legislature has delegated powers and functions to a

[10] 1986 (1) SA 853 (A).

subordinate authority, it intended that authority itself to exercise those powers and to perform those functions, and not to delegate them to someone else, and that the power delegated does not therefore include the power to delegate. It is not every delegation of delegated powers that is hit by the maxim, but only such delegations as are not, either expressly or by necessary implication, authorised by the delegated powers.' [11]

Whether the presumption can be rebutted in a particular case depends on a number of well-established considerations, to which we now turn.

(a)   The nature of the power

'Judicial' and 'quasi-judicial' powers[12] are said to be non-delegable in our law. This means that the willingness of the court to approve the subdelegation will depend partly on whether the power transferred is highly discretionary[13] or envisages special care and discernment. A 'mechanical' power, because it involves little or no discretion, may be subdelegated more readily. Thus, while a Minister would not be entitled to subdelegate the power to deem a person 'an undesirable inhabitant' of the country, he might well be entitled to subdelegate the task of informing the affected inhabitant of the Minister's decision.[14] Subjectively phrased powers usually signal the widest discretion, and are therefore badly suited for subdelegation. In a leading case, *Shidiack v Union Government*,[15] Innes CJ held that where immigrants had to complete a writing test 'to the satisfaction of the Minister', the task of evaluating the work could not be subdelegated to another official in his Department; it was a power that had to be exercised in a 'judicial spirit'.[16]

Similarly, powers which have far-reaching consequences are not as appropriate for subdelegation as powers with less impact. For this reason, law-making or 'legislative' powers are not easily subdelegable in our law. This was an important factor in the case of *Aluchem (Pty) Ltd v Minister of Mineral and Energy Affairs*,[17] where it was held that the price controller could not subdelegate to another official the discretionary power to impose conditions on the sale of coal. However, the case of *Staatspresident v United Democratic Front*[18] challenges the traditional approach of our courts in this regard, as indeed it threatens many other well-established principles of our

---

[11] Per Botha JA in *Attorney-General, OFS v Cyril Anderson Investments (Pty) Ltd* 1965 (4) SA 628 (A) at 639C–D.

[12] The classification of administrative functions is discussed in more detail above, 85–90; 258; and in chapter 15 below.

[13] *Minister of Trade and Industry v Nieuwoudt* 1985 (2) SA 1 (C) at 13.

[14] *Jeewa v Dönges NO* 1950 (3) SA 414 (A) at 420–1. Cf *SA Airways Pilots Association v Minister of Transport Affairs* 1988 (1) SA 362 (W).

[15] 1912 AD 746.

[16] At 752.

[17] 1985 (3) SA 626 (T) at 631H–632D.

[18] 1988 (4) SA 830 (A).

law.[19] This case concerned the validity of emergency regulations made by the State President; in particular, regulations making it an offence to publish or even to possess a 'subversive statement'. In one of the regulations, the State President had purported to subdelegate to the Commissioner of Police the power to determine what acts and omissions amounted to a 'subversive statement' for these purposes. Since the subdelegated power was unaccompanied by any guidelines for its exercise, the court a quo[20] found that there had been an unlawful delegation of a legislative function. In the Appellate Division, however, Rabie ACJ came to the surprising conclusion that the subdelegated power was neither legislative nor discretionary. In his view, the process of identification required of the Commissioner was quite mechanical.[21] Grosskopf JA, who found that the power was legislative, agreed with Rabie ACJ that the power was non-discretionary, since the Commissioner would merely have to identify acts and omissions which the State President had *already decided* were subversive.[22] As Haysom and Plasket[23] point out, both of these judges seem to proceed on the assumption that subversive statements are self-evident and self-defining. The dissenting judgment of Van Heerden JA is an incisive and persuasive argument against this approach, and is in any event in harmony with the established principles of our law. It is to be hoped that future courts will confine the effects of the *United Democratic Front* decision to the specific context in which it arose.

(b) The extent to which the power is transferred

The court will be more inclined to approve a subdelegation where the discretionary power is only partly transferred. This will be the position where the original delegee retains a measure of control over the exercise of the discretion, or where the subdelegee is provided with adequate guidelines for the exercise of the power. In *SA Freight Consolidators (Pty) Ltd v Chairman, National Transport Commission*,[24] Stafford J adopted Wiechers's distinction[25] between *deconcentration* of power (where the delegatus retains control and may withdraw the delegation at any time) and *decentralisation* (a total delegation of power). The court took the view that guidelines were unnecessary in a situation amounting merely to deconcentration.[26]

(c) The importance of the delegee

In a case of 'delectus personae', where the delegee appears to have

---

[19] See above, 261–4; 291–2; below, 355–7.
[20] 1987 (3) SA 296 (N).
[21] See the judgment of Rabie ACJ at 845.
[22] See the judgment of Grosskopf JA at 874I–J.
[23] Nicholas Haysom and Clive Plasket (1988) 4 *SAJHR* 303 at 313–15.
[24] 1987 (4) SA 155 (W).
[25] Marinus Wiechers *Administrative Law* (1985) 56–62.
[26] At 169B–D. It should be noted, however, that in this case the official concerned was expressly empowered to delegate such powers 'as he may deem desirable'.

been chosen for his or her special abilities or qualifications, it is very likely that the subdelegation will be disallowed. This factor was relevant in the case of *Minister of Trade and Industry v Nieuwoudt*,[27] which dealt with the question whether inspectors appointed by the Minister to investigate the affairs of a company were entitled to subdelegate to an advocate the task of questioning the company director. A full bench of the Cape Provincial Division held that they were not so entitled. Though it was possible that the advocate might turn out to be better qualified in law and accountancy than the inspectors, the court had to assume that the Minister had chosen the particular inspectors for their personal abilities and qualifications.[28] In the *Aluchem*[29] case, the court took into account the fact that the subdelegation had the effect of transferring the power from one Department (Economic Affairs) to another (Mineral and Energy Affairs), which further militated against the subdelegation.

(d) Practical necessity

Parliament's apparent intention may have to bow to necessity where it is impossible for the delegee to exercise the power personally. In this respect, a court deciding *Shidiack's* case[30] in the 1990s might well come to a different conclusion on the same facts!

2   Unlawful dictation and referral

There are at least two other ways in which a public body may abdicate its power or usurp the power of another body: unlawful dictation and unlawful referral. Because they are more covert and less official forms of delegation, these illegalities are more difficult to prove. The first describes a decision which appears to have been made by the authorised body, but which has in fact been made *at the dictation* of an unauthorised body. The second, also known as 'passing the buck', describes a decision *referred* by an authorised body to one who is unauthorised. Both of these actions flout the basic principle that the responsibility for the exercise of discretionary power rests with the authorised body and with no one else.

C   Failure to exercise authority

Powers conferred upon public bodies are always subject to a duty to exercise the power. Even the widest discretionary power is accompanied by an implied duty to exercise it. Thus, even if a licensing official has a discretion to grant or refuse a licence, the official is not entitled to ignore an application for a licence. At the very least, she must consider the application and *decide* whether to grant or refuse the licence.[31]

---

[27] 1985 (2) SA 1 (C).
[28] At 14D–15A.
[29] Note 17 above.
[30] Note 15 above.
[31] *Chotabhai v Union Government* 1911 AD 13.

1 Refusal to act or to decide

It follows that public bodies may be required by a court to exercise their powers, whether these be mechanical or discretionary. Obviously, they may also be made to comply with duties, either express or implied.

2 Unlawful fettering

In accordance with the duty to exercise authority, public bodies may not act in ways which will effectively prevent their discretionary powers from being exercised in the manner which was envisaged when the power was conferred. To put it differently, discretion may not be unduly limited or 'fettered' by its holder or by anyone else. Some of the recognised instances of fettering are listed below.

(a) Adherence to rigid policies

Public bodies are expected to develop and to implement policies, provided of course that the policies are in keeping with the empowering legislation. But blind adherence to rigid policies is unacceptable, for this may '. . . preclude the person exercising the discretion from bringing his mind to bear in a real sense on the particular circumstances of each and every individual case coming up for decision'.[32] A recent illustration of this principle is *Morelettasentrum (Edms) Bpk v Die Drankraad*,[33] which concerned a decision of the Liquor Board to refuse a bottle-store licence. The decision was set aside, one of the grounds being that the Board had allowed itself to be blinded by a policy against allowing bottle-stores in small shopping centres serving residential areas. Its mistake was to apply the policy as a hard-and-fast rule in circumstances which justified a departure from the policy.

(b) Misreading of powers or mistake of law

Not all errors of law committed by public bodies are reviewable by courts of law.[34] However, the court will be prepared to review a decision based on a misreading or misconstruction of statutory powers where the error has prevented the public body from exercising its discretion in the intended manner, has led to a failure to appreciate the nature of the discretion, or has resulted in a 'failure to apply the mind to the matter'.[35] For example, in *Reynolds Brothers Ltd v Chairman, Local Road Transportation Board, Johannesburg*[36] it was found that the Board's decision to refuse an application for private

[32] Per Marais J in *Richardson v Administrator of Transvaal* 1957 (1) SA 521 (T) at 530. See also *Britten v Pope* 1916 AD 150; *Pietermaritzburg City Council v Local Road Transportation Board* 1959 (2) SA 758 (N); *Mahlaela v De Beer NO* 1986 (4) SA 782 (T).

[33] 1987 (3) SA 405 (T).

[34] See 319–21 below.

[35] *Local Road Transportation Board v Durban City Council* 1965 (1) SA 586 (A). The ground of 'failure to apply the mind' is discussed fully below, 349–50.

[36] 1985 (2) SA 790 (A).

transport permits was based on a misunderstanding of its powers under s 18(3) of the Road Transportation Act 74 of 1977. The Board had refused the permit because it considered that the applicant could reasonably be expected to use an 'available' railway service instead, even though the nearest railway station was some considerable distance from the applicant's place of business. The Appellate Division held that the distance prevented the railway service from being an 'available' service as intended by s 18, and directed the Board to grant the permits.[37] Similarly, in *Hartman v Chairman, Board for Religious Objection*[38] the court found that the Board had wrongly concluded that the applicant, a Theravada Buddhist, was ineligible for classification as a religious objector under the Defence Act 44 of 1957. The Board's faulty interpretation of the term 'religious convictions' had prevented it from considering the merits of the applicant's claim, and thus it had failed properly to exercise its discretion.

(c) Contracting so as to fetter discretion

The exercise of public power through the medium of contract is a thorny problem, since there is an obvious clash between one of the most characteristic features of contracts—their power to *bind* both parties—and the principle that public bodies should not fetter their future freedom of discretion. A more detailed discussion of the issue is provided in Part II of this book.[39]

(d) Promises or assurances

If it is hazardous to contract with public bodies, it is even more dangerous to rely on promises and assurances as to their future actions.[40] As many taxpayers and ratepayers have found out to their dismay,[41] public bodies cannot be held to their assurances where this would have the effect of fettering the free exercise of a discretion in the future. Consequently, public bodies are virtually immune from the equitable doctrine of estoppel. This doctrine ordinarily protects those who have relied to their detriment on a representation by 'estopping' or preventing the person who made the representation from denying its truth. However, estoppel is available against public bodies only in exceptional circumstances.[42] Though this seems very

---

[37] See also *South African Transport Services v Chairman, Local Road Transportation Board, Cape Town* 1988 (1) SA 665 (C).

[38] 1987 (1) SA 922 (O).

[39] Above, 187–90.

[40] See *Collector of Customs v Cape Central Railways Ltd* (1889) 6 SC 402.

[41] See, for instance, *Commissioner for Inland Revenue v The Master* 1957 (3) SA 693 (C); *Burghersdorp Municipality v Coney* 1936 CPD 305; *Durban City Council v Glenore Supermarket and Cafe* 1981 (1) SA 470 (D).

[42] Professor Baxter suggests that the courts will be prepared to estop public authorities where a legal provision has not been violated; where the legal defect is a mere internal irregularity; and where a legal duty which has been violated is not 'mandatory' but merely 'directory'; see Lawrence Baxter *Administrative Law* (1984)

unfair on members of the public who may have planned their affairs on the basis of a promise or assurance officially made to them, there is another important reason for the immunity: if the assurance made by a public body turns out to have been unauthorised by law, the application of estoppel would have the effect of 'ratifying' decisions which the body *is not entitled to make*. This would obviously conflict with the basic principle that lawful authority is required for all the actions and decisions of public bodies.

In some cases, it may be possible to argue that the assurance actually constitutes a *decision* or the taking of *action*. This would mean that the body was 'functus officio':[43] it would not be allowed to go back on its decision or change its mind about the action that had already been taken. Another possibility is an action for damages in delict, though this would only be available in the case of a negligent misrepresentation. Failing these solutions, it has been suggested that individuals should be compensated[44] in money for the prejudice they may have suffered—though this is admittedly a suggestion which the Receiver of Revenue is unlikely to adopt in the income-tax cases!

D Unauthorised purposes

Public bodies are not entitled to deviate from the purposes for which power was conferred on them. At the most general level, this means that powers must always be exercised in the public interest, and not for the personal advantage of the officials who wield them. More specifically, the purposes envisaged in statutes and other enabling legislation are binding on officials acting in pursuance of them. These purposes will sometimes be expressly stated in the enabling legislation, but are not always obvious to the reader. Since judicial interpretation and selection play a significant part in this ground of review, and in view of the fact that it overlaps with our discussion of the requirement of reasonableness, a full discussion of it is deferred to the next chapter.[45]

E Mistaken authority

Public bodies sometimes base their authority (or 'jurisdiction') on mistaken assumptions of fact or mistaken interpretations of law. The same questions arise in both cases: can a court of review correct those mistakes? Who has the final say as to whether an interpretation is right or wrong? It is not surprising that our courts have no easy answers to these apparently simple questions, since they conceal a dilemma. On one hand, a court of review is not entitled to say that a conclusion reached by a public body is 'wrong', and the mistake may

402–3. On the distinction between mandatory and directory provisions, see above, 301–2.

[43] That is, the body would have performed its function and thereby exhausted its role in respect of that decision.

[44] Baxter op cit n 42 at 403–4.

[45] Below, 343–6.

in any event relate to a matter which Parliament has left to the subjective assessment of the public body. On the other hand, mistaken authority is surely no authority at all. How can the court allow a blatant violation of the first principle of administrative law?

The issue of mistaken authority or jurisdiction arises most obviously in the context of statutory prerequisites. For this reason, a full discussion of the problem is provided in the second part of this chapter.[46]

III REGULARITY

The principle of regularity requires that all statutory prescriptions and formalities be complied with. In accordance with the maxim omnia praesumuntur rite esse acta, the courts will presume that the public body has complied with all statutory formalities; but the presumption has little significance, since it may be rebutted by presenting evidence to the contrary. In any event, the onus of proving the existence of an illegality generally rests on the party who alleges it.[47]

A Irregular appointment and composition of bodies

Subject to what has been said about directory provisions,[48] officials and other public bodies must comply with all statutory prescriptions concerning their appointment, qualifications and composition. Thus decisions made by a licensing officer who is unqualified or improperly appointed will be illegal, as will the decisions of a tribunal sitting without the required quorum.

An interesting and rather unusual example of an allegation of improper appointment is contained in the recent case of *Lucas v Attorney-General, Cape*,[49] where the appointment of an Acting Chief Justice was challenged by a convicted murderer who had been sentenced to death. The Cape Provincial Division having refused leave to appeal, the applicant petitioned the Appellate Division for leave as provided for in s 316(6) of the Criminal Procedure Act 51 of 1977. When this proved unsuccessful, he applied in the Transvaal Provincial Division for a stay of execution. Here it was argued that since the State President had not appointed a Chief Justice, and since there was no statutory provision for the appointment of an Acting Chief Justice in the absence of an existing Chief Justice, the applicant's petition to the Appellate Division had not been properly considered by 'two Judges of the Appellate Division designated by the Chief Justice', as required by s 316(7) of the Criminal Procedure Act. Harms J dismissed the application, holding that the Supreme

---

[46] Below, 313ff.
[47] See further above, 288–9.
[48] Above, 301–2.
[49] 1988 (4) SA 639 (T).

Court Act did in fact permit the appointment of an Acting Chief Justice where a vacancy existed for the post of Chief Justice.[50]

B Are reasons required?

'The giving of reasons is one of the fundamentals of good administration.'[51] Lord Denning's words echo a common-sense perception that reasoned decisions are always preferable to unreasoned ones. For one thing, it is much less likely that an official who has to give reasons for his decision will act arbitrarily or unreasonably, and it is correspondingly much more likely that he will be found out if he does act in those ways. Common sense tells us, too, that it is fair to inform affected individuals of the reasons for the action which has been taken against them, and that citizens are more likely to have faith in a system of government which respects their interests. On the other hand, a duty to give reasons for every conceivable action or decision would place an extremely inconvenient burden on administrative bodies. Practical considerations like this have led some jurisdictions to provide that aggrieved individuals may call on administrative decision-makers to give reasons justifying their decisions.[52] This strikes a sensible balance, and it is encouraging to see that the South African Law Commission's proposals include a similar duty.[53]

At present our law contains no *general* common-law or statutory duty to give reasons. Some statutes do, however, contain such a requirement; and sometimes a court will draw an adverse inference from a failure to give reasons, notwithstanding the lack of an express duty to provide them.

1 An express duty to give reasons

When reasons are expressly required by a statute, those reasons must be properly informative. This point is nicely illustrated by the legal battle fought over s 28(3)(*b*) of the Internal Security Act 74 of 1982, which requires the Minister of Law and Order to furnish a person detained under s 28(1) of the Act with written reasons for the detention and 'so much of the information which induced the Minister (to detain the person) as can, in the opinion of the Minister, be disclosed without detriment to the public interest'. Section 28(1), in turn, empowers the Minister to detain a person (inter alia) 'if he is satisfied that the person engages in activities which endanger . . . the security of the State'. The case of *Gumede v Minister of Law and Order*[54] arose out of such a detention. In the detention notice the Minister had given as his 'reason' a statement which read: 'I am satisfied that

---

[50] At 643C–D.
[51] Lord Denning MR in *Breen v Amalgamated Engineering Union* [1971] 2 QB 175 at 191.
[52] For instance, Australian and American federal laws require written reasons to be given on request in many cases.
[53] *Working Paper 15*, Project 24 (1986) at 103ff.
[54] 1984 (4) SA 915 (N).

the said . . . engages in activities which endanger the maintenance of law and order'. The 'information' given was similarly a reiteration of the enabling section. Law J held that a mere reiteration of the wording of the enabling legislation did not constitute reasons. This decision was upheld by the Appellate Division in *Nkondo & Gumede v Minister of Law and Order*.[55] Unfortunately, the court in this case did not find it necessary to decide whether the 'information' given was sufficient for the purposes of the section.[56]

2   An implied duty to give reasons

In the absence of an express duty to give reasons, our courts have sometimes been prepared to find an implied statutory duty or to recognise a common-law duty. In the case of arrest, for instance, it is a well-established rule of our common law[57] that the reason for the arrest must be communicated to the arrested person; and in relation to emergency arrest and detention, the Appellate Division has held in *Ngqumba v Staatspresident*[58] that such a duty must be implied into reg 3(1) of the emergency regulations.

3   Adverse inferences

Even where there is no duty to give reasons for a decision, a decision-maker who fails to give reasons runs the risk that the court will draw an adverse inference from the failure which will be 'weighed together with all the other factors in the totality of the case'[59] in deciding whether there has been an illegality. If there is prima facie evidence of an illegality, the absence of reasons is likely to add considerable weight to the applicant's case. Thus in *Oskil Properties (Pty) Ltd v Chairman of the Rent Control Board*,[60] where none of the evidence supported a valuation made by the Rent Board, its failure to give reasons for the determination tended to support the inference that the evidence before it had been ignored, and that the Board had acted 'arbitrarily, irregularly and otherwise than in accordance with reason and justice'.[61] Another example is *Jeffery v*

---

[55] 1986 (2) SA 756 (A).

[56] In *Gumede v Minister of Law and Order* 1985 (2) SA 529 (N), a full bench of the Natal Provincial Division overruled the decision of Law J, holding that the Minister had given adequate reasons and information. It, in turn, was overruled by the Appellate Division, but only on the point relating to reasons.

[57] See n 58 below.

[58] *Ngqumba v Staatspresident, Damons v Staatspresident , Jooste v Staatspresident* 1988 (4) SA 224 (A). On the position at common law and under various statutes, see the judgment of Rabie ACJ at 263E–267B. See also *Minister of Law and Order v Swart* 1989 (1) SA 295 (A); *State President v Tsenoli; Kerchhoff v Minister of Law and Order* 1986 (4) SA 1150 (A).

[59] Holmes JA in *National Transport Commission v Chetty's Motor Transport (Pty) Ltd* 1972 (3) SA 726 (A) at 736F–G. See also *Control Magistrate, Durban v Azanian Peoples Organization* 1986 (3) SA 394 (A).

[60] 1985 (2) SA 234 (SE).

[61] Per Van Rensburg J at 246I–J.

President, South African Medical and Dental Council,[62] where a disciplinary committee had given no reasons for its finding that the applicant was guilty of improper conduct. Here Berman J decided that the principles of fairness dictated the need for informing the applicant of the reasons for the finding.[63] In circumstances where doubt had already been cast on the fairness of the proceedings, the absence of reasons weighed against the contention that the inquiry was a fair one.

C Problems of jurisdiction

Judicial review enables judges to decide whether public authorities have exceeded the boundaries of their 'jurisdiction'—which is simply another way of saying 'powers' or 'authority to act'. Since legislation is by far the most important source of administrative power, the setting of those boundaries generally involves judicial interpretation of the legislation in question. But the interpretation of legislation is by no means the exclusive preserve of the judiciary. Public authorities, too, are constantly engaged in similar interpretive exercises; they, too, must decide on the boundaries of their own jurisdiction and on their entitlement to act. The problem is that there are strongly opposing views as to whether the court or the public body should have the final say when it comes to the interpretation of statutory requirements. This problem arises in relation to both *factual* prerequisites and interpretations of *law*. Though it is often difficult to tell which is which, our law assumes that they are distinct from each other, and this makes it convenient to deal with them separately in the discussion that follows.

1 Factual preconditions

Take, for example, a statute which enables a policeman to arrest and detain a person 'if in his opinion' that person has committed an offence. Here, the existence of the policeman's opinion is a prerequisite for his ability to arrest and detain. On one extreme view, the policeman's jurisdiction to arrest and detain is something for him to decide; in other words, if he assures the court that he held the required opinion, then the court should accept his word and uphold his action. On the opposite extreme is the view that the court should always establish whether there were good grounds for the policeman's opinion. After all, public authorities are capable of making mistakes and of abusing their powers; why should innocent citizens suffer these wrongs? In between, there are compromise views which argue that some jurisdictional decisions should be left to the public body, and that some should be left to the court.

(a) Classifying jurisdictional facts

Our law has adopted a compromise based on a distinction between

[62] 1987 (1) SA 387 (C).
[63] At 395D–I.

two categories of jurisdictional fact which was drawn by Corbett J in *SA Defence and Aid Fund v Minister of Justice*.[64] The first category contains the type of fact or state of affairs which must exist objectively before the statutory power can validly be exercised. Here the court is entitled to enquire as to the objective existence of the fact or state of affairs. But in the second category, where 'the statute itself has entrusted to the repository of the power the sole and exclusive function of determining whether in its opinion the prerequisite fact . . . existed',[65] the court is entitled only to consider whether the opinion was in fact held. In other words, the jurisdictional fact in this second category is not whether the opinion existed in an objective sense, but merely *whether the body in question decided that it did*. This distinction can be illustrated by means of the following example. In terms of s 30 of the Internal Security Act 74 of 1982, the Attorney-General may refuse to release on bail a 'person (who has been) arrested on a charge'; the arrest on a charge is a precondition of his jurisdiction to refuse bail. When the exercise of his power is challenged, the court is entitled to enquire as to whether the required 'arrest on a charge' was present when the Attorney-General made his decision.[66] But if s 30 referred instead to 'a person who, in the opinion of the Attorney-General, has been arrested on a charge', then the jurisdictional fact is not whether the person *was in fact* arrested, but merely whether the Attorney-General *held the opinion* that he was.

(b)   Subjectively phrased clauses

As the above example shows, the classification of jurisdictional facts depends to a great extent on the language used in the legislation. In particular, prerequisites will tend to fall within the second category if they are phrased *subjectively*.[67] Since this classification imposes a great limitation on the justiciability of the jurisdictional fact, a subjectively phrased clause operates as a sort of covert ouster clause—and has, until recently, been a far more successful technique for ousting the court's jurisdiction than ouster clauses themselves![68] Nowhere has this been more apparent than in cases dealing with legislative powers of arrest and detention, the most important of which are discussed below. But it would be naïve to think that language is the only factor which shapes our courts' attitude to justiciability. Other factors, such as the prevailing political climate, the nature of the case, the judges' personal beliefs and the composition of the bench, also play a part. Since judges do not officially acknowledge the existence of such factors, one can only speculate about their precise influence in a particular case, but their

[64] 1967 (1) SA 31 (C).
[65] At 34F–H.
[66] *S v Ramgobin* 1985 (3) SA 587 (N).
[67] But see below, 318–19.
[68] See above, 295ff.

presence is difficult to deny. And where cases are marked by sharp differences in the attitudes of the court a quo and the appeal court—as are two of the cases discussed below—it is difficult to resist the conclusion that the result in each case depends more on the judicial ideology[69] of the particular bench than on the language used in the legislation.

(i) 'Has reason to believe'

The 'subjective' reputation of this clause probably stems from its close resemblance to the wording in the famous English wartime case of *Liversidge v Anderson*.[70] That case dealt with powers of the Secretary of State for Home Affairs to detain a person if he had 'reasonable cause to believe' that the person was 'of hostile origins or associations'. The majority of the House of Lords held that the court could not question the grounds for the Secretary's belief. Provided the Secretary acted honestly, his subjective satisfaction was enough for a valid detention. Only Lord Atkin dissented from this opinion. He pointed out that there is a difference between *having* reasonable cause to believe and *thinking* that one has reasonable cause to believe. Since the legislation in question required the Secretary to *have* reasonable cause, the court could enquire as to the existence of objectively reasonable grounds for the belief.

After years of vacillation[71] in our courts between the subjective and objective interpretations of 'reason to believe' and similar formulations, the question was laid to rest in *Minister of Law and Order v Hurley*.[72] This important case was concerned with s 29 of the Internal Security Act 74 of 1982, which provides that a police officer above a certain rank may arrest and detain a person for the purposes of interrogation if he has 'reason to believe' that the person has committed or intends to commit an offence referred to in s 54 of the Act, or that the person is withholding information relating to the commission of such an offence. In the court a quo[73] it was successfully argued for the applicant that no-one remotely acquainted with the detainee, a pacifist, could possibly have had the required 'reason to believe'. Since the respondent made no serious attempt to controvert this allegation, the application for the detainee's release was granted. This result was upheld in the

---

[69] That is, the judge's perception of the 'proper' judicial function; see further above, 242ff; 257–8; 281–2.

[70] [1942] AC 206.

[71] The cases in which a subjective approach was adopted include *Mnyani v Minister of Justice* 1980 (4) SA 528 (Tk) ('reason to believe'); *Mbane v Minister of Police* 1982 (1) SA 223 (Tk) ('reason to believe'); *Matroos v Coetzee* 1985 (3) SA 474 (SE) ('reason to apprehend'). The objective approach was supported in cases including *Watson v Commissioner of Customs and Excise* 1960 (3) SA 212 (N) ('reasonable cause to believe'); *Sigaba v Minister of Defence and Police* 1980 (3) SA 535 (Tk) ('reason to believe'); *Honey v Minister of Police* 1980 (3) SA 800 (Tk) ('reason to believe'); *United Democratic Front v Theron* 1984 (1) SA 315 (C) ('reason to apprehend').

[72] 1986 (3) SA 568 (A).

[73] 1985 (4) SA 709 (N) (Leon J).

Appellate Division, Rabie CJ holding that the respondent bore the onus of showing that there were objective grounds or facts which gave rise to, or formed the basis of, the officer's belief.[74] As in the court a quo, this onus was not discharged.

(ii) 'Is satisfied'

In *Hurley's* case,[75] the objective interpretation of the relevant clause was based partly on the contrast between it and the more subjective wording of a clause appearing in s 28(1)(a) of the Internal Security Act: 'if in his opinion there is reason to apprehend'.[76] It came as no great surprise, therefore, when Rabie CJ (in whose judgment Jansen JA concurred) took the view in *Tussentydse Regering v Katofa*[77] that the words 'is satisfied' appearing in Namibian legislation[78] conferred a subjective discretion on the Administrator-General to arrest and detain certain persons. Though the Administrator-General bore the onus of showing that his action was legally taken, that onus could be discharged merely by asserting that he was 'satisfied' that the detainee was a person as described in s 2 of the legislation. It would then be up to the applicant to show that the respondent had failed to apply his mind to the decision to arrest and detain, or that it was tainted with mala fides (bad faith) or ulterior motives.[79] As the Chief Justice so rightly remarked,[80] the real question is not where the onus lies, but what is required to discharge it. The applicant's onus is far more difficult to discharge; indeed, 'onus' strikes one as an inappropriate term for the respondent's easy task.

What did come as a surprise was the refusal of these judges of appeal to make anything of the legislative obligation on the Administrator-General[81] to provide the detainee with reasons and information pertaining to the arrest and detention; for Rabie CJ simply stated that this obligation did not mean that the *court* was entitled to reasons.[82] This is in marked contrast to the more liberal *Hurley*-like approach of the court a quo[83] and with the scholarly opinion of Trengove JA, in whose judgment Botha JA concurred.[84] Trengove JA found that an ipse dixit from the Administrator-General was not sufficient to discharge the onus resting on him. In addition,

---

[74] At 578–9.
[75] Note 72 above.
[76] At 578I–579D.
[77] 1987 (1) SA 695 (A).
[78] Sec 2(1) of Proc AG26 of 1978 (South West Africa).
[79] These grounds were laid down by Innes CJ as the 'circumstances in which interference (by a court) would be possible and right' where a matter has been 'left to the discretion or determination of a public officer': *Shidiack v Union Government* 1912 AD 746 at 755–6. On their content, see below, 343ff.
[80] At 730E–F.
[81] Sec 4(2) of Proc AG26 of 1978 (South West Africa).
[82] At 731B–C.
[83] *Katofa v Administrator-General for SWA* 1985 (4) SA 211 (SWA) (Berker JP and Levy J).
[84] Since the case was decided on other grounds, Van Heerden JA found it unnecessary to deal with the point of disagreement between the other judges of appeal.

he would have to persuade the court that he had 'duly and honestly applied himself to the question which has been left to his discretion'.[85] This approach accords more with the modern English case law[86] and with academic opinion[87] in this country. It takes serious account of the fact that the court must necessarily *satisfy itself* that the official was 'satisfied', and on that basis alone is preferable to the judgment of Rabie CJ. It cannot be doubted that the judgment of Rabie CJ finds extensive support in the older South African cases,[88] but it is nevertheless a pity that the Acting Chief Justice was so determined to reject the English and Transkeian[89] authority on which the court a quo relied. Quite apart from questions of precedent and pedigree, some of the most elementary notions of justice were at stake: a person had, after all, been detained without trial.

(iii) 'Opinion' and emergency detention

As might be expected, the Appellate Division has held in *Minister of Law and Order v Dempsey*[90] that the prerequisite of an 'opinion' that the arrest and detention is 'necessary for the maintenance of public order, the safety of the public or the termination of the State of Emergency'[91] falls into the second category referred to by Corbett J. The judgment of Hefer JA closely parallels (and approves)[92] that of Rabie CJ in *Katofa*:[93] the 'onus' on the arresting officer may be discharged merely by asserting that the opinion was held, while the applicant bears the far more onerous burden of persuading the court that the arresting officer was mala fide, failed to apply his mind to the matter or acted with ulterior motives. Since Hefer JA made it plain that inferences of such an abuse of discretion are not lightly to be drawn from silence in the respondents' affidavits,[94] applicants after *Dempsey*[95] will carry a heavy burden indeed.

---

[85] At 741E–H, quoting the words of Innes CJ in *Shidiack v Union Government*; see n 79 above.

[86] *Secretary of State for Education and Science v Tameside MBC* [1977] AC 1014 (HL) ('is satisfied'). For a general discussion of the interpretation of subjectively phrased clauses in English administrative law, see H W R Wade *Administrative Law* 6 ed (1988) 445–62.

[87] See inter alia Hannes Schoombee (1986) 2 *SAJHR* 74; M L Mathews (1986) 2 *SAJHR* 333, especially at 336–7; Hugh Corder (1988) 4 *SAJHR* 281, especially at 284ff.

[88] Amongst others, *Shidiack v Union Government* (n 79 above) ('to the satisfaction of the Minister'); *Union Government v Union Steel Corporation* 1928 AD 220 ('is satisfied'); *Sachs v Minister of Justice; Diamond v Minister of Justice* 1934 AD 11 ('is satisfied').

[89] *Sigaba v Minister of Defence and Police* 1980 (3) SA 535 (Tk); see the judgment of Levy J in the court a quo (n 83 above) at 221..

[90] 1988 (3) SA 19 (A).

[91] Emergency regulation 3(3) promulgated by the State President under the Public Safety Act 3 of 1953, Proc R109 of 12 June 1986.

[92] At 35–9.

[93] Note 77 above.

[94] At 40I–J.

[95] Note 90 above.

The approach of Hefer JA contrasts sharply with that of Marais J in the court a quo.[96] There it was emphasised that the officer must hold an opinion that it is *necessary* to arrest and detain the person *in order to achieve the purposes* set down in the regulation. The officer would also have to consider the necessity for continued detention in the light of alternative courses of action, such as arrest under the ordinary law of the land. As in the *Katofa*[97] case, we are presented with very different views of the proper role of the courts: to contain executive and legislative excesses, or to allow those arms of government all the latitude they claim.

(iv) Can objective language confer a subjective discretion?

Common sense (not to mention the cases discussed so far) suggests that it is impossible to confer a subjective discretion on an official by means of objective wording. After all, 'if the moon is made of green cheese' is not the same as 'if the official thinks that the moon is made of green cheese'. The first may be proved by objective means to be true or false, whereas the second is difficult to disprove unless one goes in for lie-detecting equipment. None the less, in *Van der Westhuizen NO v United Democratic Front*[98] the highest court in the land has held that

> '[A] purely subjective discretion may be conferred without expressly consigning the question . . . to the opinion of the repository of the power. The same result is achieved when a discretionary power is conferred unreservedly and in unqualified terms, unless there is reason to believe that such a result could not have been intended.'[99]

The case concerned an emergency regulation which empowered the Commissioner of Police to prohibit the holding of gatherings 'for the purpose of the safety of the public, the maintenance of public order or the termination of the state of emergency'.[100] This rider (as Hefer JA correctly remarked)[101] cannot be regarded as in the nature of a prerequisite to jurisdiction; rather, it is a co-requisite.[102] On the

---

[96] *Dempsey v Minister of Law and Order* 1986 (4) SA 530 (C). Having been followed in *Bishop of the Roman Catholic Church of the Diocese of Port Elizabeth v Minister of Law and Order* EPD 1 August 1986 Case No 1101/86 (unreported), the scope of the *Dempsey* judgment was restricted in *Nqumba v State President* 1987 (1) SA 456 (E), confirmed on appeal (1988 (4) SA 224 (A)); see Clive Plasket (1987) 3 *SAJHR* 76. The decision a quo in *Dempsey's* case is paralleled in *Swart v Minister of Law and Order* 1987 (1) SA 452 (C), confirmed on appeal (1989 (1) SA 295 (A)). Cf *Bloem v Minister of Law and Order* 1987 (2) SA 436 (O); *Gumede v Minister of Law and Order* 1987 (3) SA 155 (D); *Peters v Minister of Law and Order* 1987 (4) SA 490 (NC).
[97] Note 77 above.
[98] 1989 (2) SA 242 (A).
[99] Per Hefer JA at 250J–251A.
[100] Regulation 7(1)(*b*A), Proc R225 of 28 October 1986.
[101] At 249E–F.
[102] *All* the principles of good administration embodied in the idea of legality— including the requirement that legislative purposes be properly pursued—are in the nature of 'co-requisites' to the exercise of power. In other words, absence of one of the co-requisites *at the time when the power is exercised* will lead to invalidity.

other hand, it can hardly be said that this was a power conferred 'unreservedly and in unqualified terms'. This description suggests that the court would be powerless to deal with a blatant failure to observe the purposes specified, and moreover ignores the fact that legality imposes *implied* constraints on the exercise of all discretionary powers, even when there are no express constraints—that it is, in truth, impossible to confer a completely unfettered discretion on anyone.

Notwithstanding the objective wording of the power and the express qualification attached to it, the court—taking into account such factors as the nature of the powers and the fact that they were conferred in the context of a state of emergency—found that 'there is every reason to believe that the intention was to constitute the Commissioner the sole arbiter of the necessity or expediency of exercising his powers'.[103] This decision has the effect of blurring the crucial distinction between *wide* discretionary powers (the Commissioner's powers were undoubtedly wide) and *subjective* discretionary powers. It seems that in emergency cases at least, one can no longer rely on the logic which says that subjective discretions are often wide, but that wide discretions are not necessarily subjective.

2 Misinterpretation of the law

We now turn to the situation where the jurisdiction of a public body depends on the interpretation of law rather than on the existence of a fact or a state of affairs. Though it sounds surprising—judges are, after all, experts on law—there is controversy as to who is to have the last word on the correctness of legal interpretations. As Baxter[104] says, the trouble is that 'the "legally correct" view can also be a matter for subjective assessment, affected by considerations of policy as well as clear-cut rules'. In other words, the public body may have what has been called an 'interpretive discretion'[105] to decide what the legal position is. Moreover, a court of review does not ask whether the public body was 'right' or 'wrong' in its conclusions, but only whether the conclusion was arrived at in an acceptable manner. How, then, can a court of review question the substantive correctness of a public body's interpretation of what the law is? On the other hand, how can a public body possibly be permitted to base its authority on a mistaken perception of what the law is?

This problem, too, is dealt with by means of a compromise: our courts will review a mistake of law when the mistake has prevented the public body from appreciating the nature of its powers, or has otherwise prevented the proper exercise of its discretion. As Stratford JA[106] put it,

---

[103] At 251B–D.
[104] Baxter 468.
[105] Etienne Mureinik (1986) 103 *SALJ* 615 at 642.
[106] *Union Government v Union Steel Corporation* 1928 AD 220 at 234.

'If a discretion is conferred by Statute upon an individual and he fails to appreciate the nature of that discretion through misreading of the Act which confers it, he cannot and does not properly exercise that discretion. In such a case a court of law will correct him and order him to direct his mind to the true question which has been left to his discretion.'

Reviewable mistakes of law are sometimes called 'distorting errors' (because they distort the nature of the discretion) or 'jurisdictional errors', but it would be just as appropriate to call them 'fettering' errors, since they prevent the discretion from being exercised properly or at all. But the apparently simple explanation of Stratford JA conceals a considerable difficulty: how does one tell the difference between a (reviewable) error which *does* fetter or distort the discretion, and an (unreviewable) error which does not? The case law is not particularly helpful in this regard. In one of the leading cases, *Johannesburg City Council v Chesterfield House*,[107] a compensation court had the discretion to determine 'whether any person is entitled to compensation' under the relevant legislation. The compensation court had decided that the appellant was not such a person, and it was argued that this was a mistaken interpretation of the law and that it should be corrected by the court. The Appellate Division declined to do so, Centlivres CJ asserting[108] that this error was not of the kind referred to by Stratford JA.[109] This ignores the fact that the incorrect interpretation of the law effectively prevented the compensation court from exercising its powers. Having made the mistake, it was prevented from 'directing its mind' to the appellant's claim at all. The opposite approach may be illustrated by the case of *Reynolds Brothers Ltd v Chairman, Local Road Transportation Board, Johannesburg*.[110] Here the Board had a discretion to refuse a permit where it was satisfied that the applicant could reasonably be expected to use an 'available' railway service instead. The board refused the permit. The Appellate Division found[111] that the great distance to the nearest railway station prevented the service from falling within the meaning of 'available' as intended in the Act, and that the board's faulty interpretation of the word 'available' had prevented it from properly considering the application. It is difficult to reconcile this decision with that in *Chesterfield House*,[112] all the more so when one takes into account the subjective wording of the discretion in *Reynolds Brothers*.[113] One has sympathy for the cynical

---

[107] 1952 (3) SA 809 (A). See also *Doyle v Shenker and Co Ltd* 1915 AD 233; *Harpur v Steyn NO* 1974 (1) SA 54 (O). For a general account, see Arthur Chaskalson (1985) 102 *SALJ* 419.

[108] At 826A.

[109] Note 106 above.

[110] 1985 (2) SA 790 (A). See also *South African Broadcasting Corporation v Transvaal Townships Board* 1953 (4) SA 169 (T); *Theron v Ring van Wellington van die NG Sendingkerk in Suid-Afrika* 1976 (2) SA 1 (A).

[111] Per Miller JA at 804.

[112] Note 107 above.

[113] Note 110 above.

view that *any* error of law can be made to be reviewable or unreviewable by simple assertion—and that the real issue is not the nature of the error, but the court's willingness to interfere. As in other jurisdictional problems, the English courts[114] have demonstrated that they perceive their role to be a large and important one. By comparison, our courts have opted for a walk-on part.

[114] The case of *Anisminic v Foreign Compensation Commission* [1969] 2 AC 147 has been largely responsible for breaking down the distinction between jurisdictional and non-jurisdictional errors of law. For an overview, see Wade op cit n 86 at 299–303.

15   Fairness and Reasonableness

As we indicated in chapter 11, the judicially created concept of legality requires that administrative action be both 'fair' and 'reasonable'. These requirements are of the kind which are not usually obvious on the face of the enabling legislation, so that their existence and development is peculiarly dependent on judicial creativity and on fluctuations in judicial attitudes towards justiciability. In relation to both requirements, the usual method adopted by our courts for dealing with problems of justiciability continues to be the outdated and artificial system of classifying administrative functions.[1]

In the case of fairness, the system of classification has proved to be an insensitive and vastly inadequate way of deciding when a fair hearing is required. In the case of reasonableness, the courts' determination not to encroach on the executive preserve has resulted in the creation of three 'different' tests which apparently overlook both the natural overlapping of administrative functions and the common ground underlying the various forms of unreasonableness. There is tremendous uncertainty as to the precise meaning of certain grounds of review, and many grounds overlap to an extent which suggests the need for the recognition of a single, all-encompassing ground of unreasonableness. In both areas, statutory reform can provide only some of the answers to the many problems which we outline in this chapter.

I   FAIRNESS

It is in the interests of better and more informed decision-making that public bodies exercise their discretionary powers in accordance with the principles of natural justice or, more simply, procedural fairness. The requirements of natural justice are expressed in two famous maxims: audi alteram partem ('hear the other side') and nemo iudex in sua causa ('no one should be a judge in his own cause'). While both of these have to do with fair hearings, it is convenient to deal with them separately; the nemo iudex principle is fairly clear in both its meaning and its application, whereas the audi alteram partem maxim is the subject of considerable judicial controversy.

A   Nemo Iudex in Sua Causa[2]

This maxim, also known as the rule against bias, requires that decision-makers be impartial. It extends not only to the decision-

---

[1] See generally above, 85–9; 258.
[2] In relation to judges and magistrates, see above, 204–6.

322

maker who literally prosecutes and judges the same case, but to a variety of less obvious forms of impartiality. It is based on two common-sense principles of good administration: first, that administrative decisions are more likely to be good ones when the decision-maker is unbiased; and second, that faith in the administrative process will be assured where justice is not only done, but *seen* to be done. Decision-makers must therefore be prevented from making decisions which are based on illegitimate, usually personal, motives and considerations.

1 Bias and the classification of functions

Thus stated, the rule against bias has a great deal in common with many other principles of good administration which we will consider later on in this chapter. As so often happens, there is a considerable overlap between those principles (in the negative, grounds of review). However, the extent of the overlap is reduced by the courts' inevitable practice of classifying administrative functions. Like the audi alteram partem principle, the rule against bias finds its classic application in *judicial* and *quasi-judicial* contexts, epitomised by the judicial trial and the proceedings of disciplinary and other tribunals. This does not mean that an official concerned with a 'purely administrative' decision has carte blanche to be biased, however! As the cases show, allegations of what amounts to bias are frequently made in other contexts, but they will usually be couched in the language of unreasonableness (mala fides, failure to apply the mind, improper purpose) when the decision-making function in question has been classified as *administrative* or *legislative*. Unfortunately, there are many cases where, because of an 'administrative' label, an allegation of bias has been ineffective. In *Hack v Venterspost Municipality*,[3] for instance, the court found that the chairman of the Municipal Licensing Committee (the mayor of Venterspost) was debarred by an ordinance from hearing an application for a general dealer's licence by reason of his employment by a company which owned business premises in the municipal area. Had he acquired a licence, the applicant would have been trading in competition with the company's tenants, thus reducing the letting and selling value of the company's property. But in terms of the common law, Roper J was forced to conclude that the mayor's indirect financial interest was not relevant to the proceedings of the municipality: the court was bound by a long series of cases holding that the functions of local authorities were of a 'purely administrative' character!

2 The test for bias

'Bias' has received considerable definition in our case law. Generally speaking, it rules out decisions in which the body concerned had a financial interest, a personal interest (for instance, decisions

---

[3] 1950 (1) SA 172 (W).

involving the fortunes of friends or family members) or where feelings of substantial prejudice appear to have played a role—'bias on the subject-matter'. There is no reason why these three should be the only possible categories of bias, though the courts sometimes treat the list as closed.[4]

The precise nature of the test for bias is somewhat problematical, since it is not entirely clear from the cases whether a 'real likelihood' of impartiality is required before the decision may be set aside, or whether a reasonable person's *belief* in the likelihood will suffice.[5] Nor is it clear whether these different tests would produce different results in practice, since the reasonable person would surely hold suspicions only if these were grounded in a 'real likelihood'. Wiechers seems to favour the first test, since for him the question is 'whether, objectively speaking, there were circumstances . . . which would probably have caused bias'.[6] Baxter's formulation neatly combines the two tests by asking whether the 'reasonable lay observer would gain the impression that there is a real likelihood'[7] of bias. In view of the many judicial statements[8] which affirm that appearances are just as important as reality—that justice must be *seen* to be done—Baxter's formulation would seem to be preferable.[9] Naturally, proof of actual bias is also a ground for setting aside the decision, even if the facts are such that a reasonable lay observer would not have suspected its presence.[10] For instance, a suspicion of bias is regarded as less likely to arise where the decision-maker is judicially trained,[11] but that will not prevent the decision from being set aside on the ground that the decision-maker was in fact biased.

(a) Financial interest

Licensing cases abound with examples of bias arising out of financial interest, the facts in *Hack*'s case[12] being typical of these. The most famous is perhaps *Rose v Johannesburg Local Road Transportation*

---

[4] In *Crow v Detained Mental Patients Special Board* 1985 (4) SA 83 (ZH), for instance, Ebrahim J states that bias must be shown to fall into one of the three categories before the courts will take cognisance of it (at 98C).

[5] These two standards emerge from the judgment of Greenberg J in *City and Suburban Transport (Pty) Ltd v Local Board Road Transportation, Johannesburg* 1932 WLD 100 at 106.

[6] Marinus Wiechers *Administrative Law* (1985) 214.

[7] Lawrence Baxter *Administrative Law* (1984) 561.

[8] Some examples are to be found in *S v Bam* 1972 (4) SA 41 (E) at 43H (Kotze J); *Parag v Ladysmith City Council* 1961 (3) SA 714 (N) at 718F–G (Fannin J); *Slade v Pretoria Rent Board* 1943 TPD 246 at 251 (Barry J).

[9] This approach is supported by the case of *Jeffery v President, South African Medical and Dental Council* 1987 (1) SA 387 (C) where Berman J appears to have accepted without question Professor Baxter's formulation (at 394).

[10] See L A Rose-Innes *Judicial Review of Administrative Tribunals in South Africa* (1963) 173ff.

[11] Rose-Innes op cit n 10 at 175–6; *R v T* 1953 (2) SA 479 (A) at 483A–D; *Jeffery v President, SA Medical and Dental Council* 1987 (1) SA 387 (C) at 394F–G.

[12] Note 3 above.

Board,[13] where the chairman of the Transportation Board also happened to be the director of a taxi company. When the Board refused an application for an exemption certificate in respect of car-hire services, it was held that the chairman's interest in excluding competitors would induce an apprehension of bias in a reasonable man. In this case, as in a number of others,[14] the court appears to accept that the 'smallest pecuniary interest' will suffice to raise the suspicion of bias. However, it seems clear that the court will not be prepared to quash a decision where the interest is ridiculously slight or remote. One such case is *Jacob v Tugela and Mapumulo Rural Licensing Board*,[15] where the applicant unsuccessfully challenged the decision of the Licensing Board not to award him a general dealer's licence. One of the members of the Board, V, also belonged to a social and sporting club five miles away which already held an unrestricted general dealer's licence. The applicant reasoned that competition from his business would result in a reduction in the club's trading activities, which would induce the club to make up the shortfall by raising the subscription payable by its members—including V. Unsurprisingly, Fannin J found the financial interest involved too slight and remote to create an apprehension of bias.[16] The club's trading activities counted for only a small percentage of its profits, and were conducted more for the convenience of members than for profit; and the applicant had not been able to show that there would have been any real competition between the applicant and the club.

(b) Personal interest

A family relationship, friendship or emnity may give rise to a personal interest—real or apparent—which disqualifies the decision-maker. In *Rose*'s case,[17] two other members of the Transportation Board had, by their general attitude, shown such 'strong feeling' against the applicant that Lucas AJ felt that it would be wrong to allow them to decide on the application.[18] And in *Liebenberg v Brakpan Liquor Licensing Board*,[19] a decision to grant a licence to the mayor's brother was set aside where the mayor himself had sat as a member of the Board.

(c) Bias on the subject-matter

Bias on the subject-matter (or prejudice) can be much more difficult to identify, since there is no easy divide between significant or 'operative' bias and the ordinary opinions, preferences and tastes of men and women which do not necessarily prevent them from

[13] 1947 (4) SA 272 (W).
[14] See *Rose*'s case (above, n 13) at 287 and the cases cited there.
[15] 1964 (1) SA 45 (D).
[16] At 46H–47D.
[17] Note 13 above.
[18] At 290.
[19] 1944 WLD 52.

exercising impartial judgment. Thus, it is no doubt quite acceptable for a vegetarian to sit on a board which grants or refuses licences to butchers; and a self-confessed prude may doubtless act as a member of the Publications Appeal Board. Since everyone has likes and dislikes, the reasonable lay person would not automatically suspect such people of a lack of objectivity—unless, of course the vegetarian were chairperson of the League Against Butchers, or the prude had been heard to say that he would sooner die than expose the cinema-going public to the spectacle of a bared thigh. This sort of situation came before the court in *Patel v Witbank Town Council*,[20] where a decision to refuse the applicant a general dealer's licence was set aside for bias on the ground of the mayor's stated intention to 'move heaven and earth' to prevent an Indian from acquiring such a licence.

'Official bias', on the other hand, does not count as operative bias at all. The enthusiasm of public officials or tribunals 'for the discharge of their functions and for the . . . purpose at which those functions are directed'[21] is to be expected, and is acceptable provided it is unaccompanied by the illicit forms of bias. This is illustrated by the Zimbabwean case of *Crow v Detained Mental Patients Special Board*,[22] in which the applicant challenged the decision of the Board not to discharge him from a special prison, alleging that one of the doctors on the Board had approached his case with preconceived ideas and a closed mind. Ebrahim J found that the doctor's 'overly enthusiastic approach'[23] to his duties did not constitute 'bias' of the operative kind.

It is worth mentioning a different kind of 'official bias' which is equally inoperative. It arises in a variety of legal contexts when the law literally permits a prosecutor to be a judge in his own cause, or vice versa. For instance, s 30(1) of the Internal Security Act 74 of 1982 gives the Attorney-General—the ultimate prosecuting authority—a wide discretion to issue an order preventing a person from being released on bail.[24] Another example is the summary procedure for contempt of court on notice of motion, which permits a judge both to issue a rule nisi calling on the alleged miscreant to show cause why he should not be convicted of contempt, and, on the return day, to decide the case himself.[25]

---

[20] 1931 TPD 284.
[21] Rose-Innes 177.
[22] 1985 (4) SA 83 (ZH).
[23] At 99C.
[24] See also s 61 of the Criminal Procedure Act 51 of 1977.
[25] For a recent example, see *S v Harber: In re S v Baleka* 1986 (4) SA 214 (T). The conviction was upheld in the Appellate Division (1988 (3) SA 396 (A)). On the rule against bias as it applies to judges and magistrates, see above, 204–6.

B Audi alteram partem

It has been said,[26] with justification, that the rules of natural justice are applied in an all-or-nothing fashion[27] in our law. This is the natural result of employing the classification of functions as a limiting device to prevent the administration from having to dispense natural justice in every case. The *application* of the audi alteram partem rule (as with the rule against bias) is limited to 'judicial' and 'quasi-judicial' decision-making; but the lucky few to whom it is applied tend to get the full benefit of its *content*, so that the hearings which are given can properly be said to be fair ones. Reducing the number of available hearings in this way is one method of lightening the potential burden on the administration; another would be to have an unlimited application of the rule but a highly variable content—an alternative which is explored below.[28] We begin by considering the content of the rule, which is its less controversial aspect.

1 The content of the audi alteram partem rule

Apart from the need for an impartial decision-maker, it is generally accepted that a fair hearing contains two elements at common law: the hearing itself, and notice of the intended action. Adequate notice is regarded as an essential prerequisite of a fair hearing for the common-sense reason that a party who has not been notified in time of the intended action—disciplinary proceedings, for instance—will be prejudiced at the hearing. Where there is insufficient notice, he will not have had sufficient time to prepare, and where there has been no notice at all, he cannot meet a case of which he has no knowledge.

How much notice needs to be given? Does the hearing have to be an oral hearing? Is there a right to legal representation? In determining the *detailed* content of the audi alteram partem rule, the court will look for the answers to questions like these in the enabling legislation or, in the case of private tribunals, in the contract between the parties. These answers are seldom complete, however, so that the courts have had to evolve their own principles for deciding what the rule requires in the circumstances. Generally speaking, for these purposes our courts recognise that administrative decision-makers (whether officials or tribunals) are not courts of law, and that they should not have to adopt the strict procedures of such courts (an interesting concession, considering how eagerly the comparison is drawn when it comes to the application of the rule).[29] The technical rules of evidence, for instance, need not be complied with even in disciplinary tribunals, which are probably the most 'judicial' of

[26] Baxter op cit n 7 at 593.
[27] See the critical remarks of Corbett JA in *Attorney-General, Eastern Cape v Blom* 1988 (4) SA 645 (A) at 664–6.
[28] Below, 338–40.
[29] See below, 331ff.

administrative proceedings. In fact, decision-makers (be they officials or tribunals) may adopt whatever procedures they like, provided that they 'observe the principles of fair play'. In broad terms, those principles imply that

> '[T]he person concerned must be given a reasonable time in which to assemble the relevant information and to prepare and to put forward his representations . . . he must be put in possession of such information as will render his right to make representations a real, and not an illusory one'.[30]

Thus there is no *general* right to legal representation, to cross-examination, to discovery of the evidence against one, to be heard in public, or even to be heard orally at all; the precise meaning of 'fair play' will depend on the particular circumstances of the case. In a disciplinary case where the charges are serious and the consequences of conviction are harsh, the court is likely to require a higher standard of fairness from the tribunal. It might insist on some form of legal representation, for instance, or on the right to cross-examine witnesses. An example is *Turner v Jockey Club of South Africa*,[31] a case involving serious charges of corrupt practice, and one which resulted in the accused's being 'warned off' for 20 years. Since the contract between the parties did not permit the accused jockey to be legally represented, the appeal court took the view that the board of inquiry concerned should have compensated for this by adopting a more inquisitorial attitude and taking extra care to elicit the truth. In short, what makes a hearing 'fair' depends on the circumstances. On one hand, written representations may suffice in cases where it is not practicable to afford the affected person an oral hearing; on the other, an oral hearing in public may be regarded as an essential component of natural justice. In a matter of urgency, it may be impracticable to afford a hearing *before* the decision is taken, in which case a hearing afterwards may suffice, provided that this does not cause prejudice and that the hearing is a fair one.[32] As far as the detailed content of a fair hearing is concerned, the hallmark of the audi alteram partem rule is its flexibility.

---

[30] Per Colman J in *Heatherdale Farms v Deputy Minister of Agriculture* 1980 (3) SA 476 (T) at 486D–G. See also H Corder 1980 *THRHR* 156. In our law, the giving of reasons is not yet recognised as a component of natural justice, though a failure to give reasons in certain circumstances can lead to (or strengthen) an inference of unfairness; see above, 312–13.

[31] 1974 (3) SA 633 (A).

[32] *Sachs v Minister of Justice* 1934 AD 11; *Everett v Minister of the Interior* 1981 (2) SA 453 (C). A subsequent hearing will be of no avail where the decision has had irrevocable consequences, and the hearing will not be fair where the decision-maker has closed his mind to the possibility of changing the decision; see the remarks of Hoexter JA in his dissenting judgment in *Omar v Minister of Law and Order* 1987 (3) SA 859 (A) at 906.

2 The application of the rule

(a) Statutory provisions

The most obvious (and least controversial) instance of the rule's application is whenever there is a statutory duty to comply with particular requirements of natural justice. It is always open to Parliament to insist on the need for notice of intended action, or a hearing, or both; and it may, of course, empower its delegees to make similar provisions. Likewise, Parliament is at liberty to exclude the audi alteram partem rule expressly in statutes, and to empower delegated legislators to do the same. As Stratford ACJ put it in *Sachs v Minister of Justice*,[33] '[s]acred though the maxim is held to be, Parliament is free to violate it'. Legislative intention is, as always, treated as paramount.

Acts of Parliament which themselves exclude the need for a hearing are, of course, immune from attack. Where delegated legislation purports to exclude the rule, it can be challenged on various grounds—the most obvious being unreasonableness and lack of authority. The field of security legislation is rife with instances of exclusion, and the case law abounds with examples of challenge on these grounds, though precious few have been successful. An important case in this regard is *Omar v Minister of Law and Order*,[34] where the appeal court found to be valid emergency regulations which excluded the right to notice, a hearing and legal advice in the context of detention.

(b) Absence of statutory provisions

Security legislation excepted, it is usual for legislation to be silent on the subject of natural justice. In this case, the orthodox approach of our courts is to presume that Parliament intended the audi alteram partem rule to apply. The classic dictum is that of Centlivres CJ in *R v Ngwevela*,[35] where the Chief Justice stated that audi alteram partem must apply

> 'unless it is clear that Parliament has expressly or by necessary implication enacted that it should not apply or that there are exceptional circumstances which would justify the Court's not giving effect to it'.

This dictum creates a presumption that the audi alteram partem rule will apply in the absence of the conditions stipulated by Centlivres CJ. In other words, the affected individual has a *right* to be heard unless the statute excludes that right or unless exceptional circumstances justify the court in not giving effect to that right. The right to

[33] 1934 AD 11 at 38.
[34] *Omar v Minister of Law and Order, Fani v Minister of Law and Order, State President v Bill* 1987 (3) SA 859 (A). See further below, 353.
[35] 1954 (1) SA 123 (A) at 131H.

a fair hearing (including an impartial decision-maker) may, however, be waived by the individual, in which case it is forfeited.[36]

While there has always been much support[37] for the presumption in favour of natural justice, the Appellate Division has not always adhered to it; there are cases in which that court has disregarded the *right* to a hearing and made the application of the rule dependent upon statutory implication. The most famous of these is *South African Defence and Aid Fund v Minister of Justice*,[38] where Botha JA held that the first question to be decided must always be whether the enactment concerned impliedly incorporates the maxim. If it were found not to be impliedly incorporated, audi alteram partem would not apply. The absence of an *intention* to exclude it would be irrelevant, since 'where it (the rule) cannot be implied, there is obviously no need to exclude it'.[39] The confusion created by this case and its offspring[40] has recently been dispelled by the decision of Corbett JA in *Attorney-General, Eastern Cape v Blom*,[41] where the learned judge of appeal expressed an informed and unequivocal preference, both 'logically and in principle',[42] for the *Ngwevela* formulation and the prima facie right which it creates.

The presumption does not, however, mean that there is a prima facie right to a hearing across the board. This is precluded both by the 'exceptional circumstances' proviso, which may be used to justify breaches of natural justice in emergencies (typically in security cases)[43] and by the fact that Centlivres CJ expressly confined the operation of his dictum to statutes which empower public officials to make decisions 'prejudicially affecting the property or liberty of an

---

[36] *Volschenk v President, SA Geneeskundige en Tandheelkundige Raad* 1985 (3) SA 124 (A).

[37] In *Publications Control Board v Central News Agency Ltd* 1970 (3) SA 479 (A), Rumpff JA said (at 488H–489A): 'It is, of course, firmly established in our law that when a statute gives judicial or *quasi*-judicial powers to affect prejudicially the rights of person or property, there is a presumption, in the absence of an express provision or of a clear intention to the contrary, that the power so given is to be exercised in accordance with the fundamental principles of justice.' The presumption was also supported in *Laubscher v Native Commissioner, Piet Retief* 1958 (1) SA 546 (A); *Minister of the Interior v Mariam* 1961 (4) SA 740 (A); *Administrateur van Suidwes-Afrika v Pieters* 1973 (1) SA 850 (A); and it has received decided academic approval: see Baxter 572–3 and the references cited there.

[38] 1967 (1) SA 263 (A).

[39] At 270F.

[40] See *Winter v Administrator-in-Executive Committee* 1973 (1) SA 873 (A) at 888H–889A, where Ogilvie Thompson CJ seems to approve the approach of Botha JA; *Omar v Minister of Law and Order* 1987 (3) SA 859 (A), where Rabie ACJ appears to have disregarded the presumption.

[41] 1988 (4) SA 645 (A).

[42] At 662G–I. See also *Moodley v Minister of Education and Culture, House of Delegates* 1989 (3) SA 221 (A) at 235H–236D.

[43] See *Minister of the Interior v Bechler* 1948 (3) SA 409 (A) at 452; *Winter v Administrator-in-Executive Committee* 1973 (1) SA 873 (A) at 890–1, both security cases involving the deportation of aliens. The proviso was not applied in *Dhlamini v Minister of Education and Training* 1984 (3) SA 255 (N), in spite of the 'practical difficulties of a high order' inherent in communicating with exam candidates before cancelling their results (per Leon J at 260–1).

individual',[44] or, in other terms, judicial and quasi-judicial decisions. This selective application of the audi alteram partem principle has always been accepted in our courts. In our law, therefore, acts of other kinds (administrative and legislative) simply do not entitle the persons affected to a fair hearing in the absence of a provision to the contrary. The presumption in favour of natural justice does not apply to them at all.

This tight-fisted attitude, regarded with hostility by many, is doubtless prompted by practical considerations. The courts are extremely reluctant to bury the administration in the avalanche of hearings which would result if virtually every administrative decision entailed a duty to hear the affected person's case. Hearings (even if they are not oral hearings) are expensive and time-consuming, so that while they may be the fairest way of reaching decisions, they are not necessarily the most expedient. There is also a fear on the part of some judges[45] that to apply the audi alteram partem rule across the board would be to lessen its value; that inevitably, the tremendous burden of all those hearings would result in lip-service being paid to the requirement. In order to avoid these difficulties, the courts have felt obliged to draw a line somewhere between the ideal and the practical, and the classification of functions provides an ever-convenient way of drawing it.

Unfortunately, the compromise which the courts have reached is by no means satisfactory to all concerned—mainly due to the lack of meaning of the term 'quasi-judicial'. From the administration's point of view, their own actions and decisions do not come in packages labelled 'quasi-judicial' or 'purely administrative', and when the legislation in question gives no guidance as to the observance of natural justice (most often the case) it must be highly inconvenient to have to dispense hearings if and when the court decides to slap on the magic label. From the affected individual's point of view, injustice is frequently done: a hearing will be denied in a case where common sense would dictate the need for one, but where the trappings of a 'quasi-judicial' decision are absent. From the courts' point of view, the system of stare decisis has largely bound judges to follow previous labellings, no matter how inappropriate or inept those labels might now appear. Expropriations, for instance, are 'purely administrative' decisions—a devastating label, but one which will stick unless and until the Appellate Division unglues it.[46] The words of Schreiner JA in *Pretoria North Town Council v A1 Electric Ice-Cream Factory (Pty) Ltd*[47] have been quoted many, many times, but they bear repeating: '[O]ne must be careful not to elevate what may be no more than a convenient classification into a source of legal rules.'

---

[44] *R v Ngwevela* 1954 (1) SA 123 (A) at 127F.
[45] See the remarks of Schreiner JA in *Laubscher v Native Commissioner, Piet Retief* 1958 (1) SA 546 (A) at 549.
[46] See below, 334.
[47] 1953 (3) SA 1 (A) at 11.

(i) Attempts to define a 'quasi-judicial' decision

To say that 'quasi-judicial' means 'like judicial' is intrinsically unhelpful: decisions of the administration can *all* be contrasted with judicial decisions proper (that is, judgments of courts of law) by the very fact that they are made by the administration, and not by officers of the courts.[48] In what way can such decisions sensibly be said to resemble those made by a court of law? Not surprisingly, the cases have never been able to give a coherent answer to this question. Many of the earlier cases relied on external appearances, such as the presence of legally qualified decision-makers or the existence of a lis inter partes—an existing dispute.[49] The embarrassing number of instances in which hearings have regularly been granted in the absence of such features has, however, led to a different focus on the essential functions performed by courts of law.[50] On this approach, the most characteristic function of courts of law has generally been identified as their ability to make far-reaching pronouncements on the rights and liberties of individuals. Thus, as we have seen, Centlivres CJ recognised in *R v Ngwevela*[51] that those decisions 'prejudicially affecting the property or liberty of an individual' cannot be taken without hearing the affected party. The Chief Justice in that case was relying in part on a dictum of Tindall ACJ in *Minister of the Interior v Bechler*,[52] where the audi alteram partem maxim was said to apply to decisions 'affecting rights or involving legal consequences to persons'. Both of these dicta were approved in *Laubscher v Native Commissioner, Piet Retief*.[53] Here Schreiner JA was not prepared to bestow the quasi-judicial label on a decision which had not affected 'any legal right' already held by the applicant, and which had no prejudicial effect on his liberty or property.

These and other attempts to make sense of the term 'quasi-judicial' reveal the essential futility of the comparison between administrative decisions and judges' decisions. In relation to rights already in existence (the 'existing rights' approach), it has been pointed out that one's right to a particular decision is quite irrelevant to one's right to a hearing when the decision is made.[54] In a criminal trial, for instance, the accused does not have to prove a right to a verdict of 'not guilty' before he has a right to be heard. Why, then, should the applicant for a permit or a licence be denied a hearing (as was the

---

[48] In relation to the content of the audi alteram partem rule (as opposed to the circumstances of its application), our courts are at pains to point out that the tribunals and officers of the administration are *not* courts of law and that they need not observe the rigorous procedural standards of those bodies! See 327 above.

[49] See Rose-Innes 39–41 and the cases cited there.

[50] For instance, Rose-Innes points out (at 40) that many ex parte applications in the Supreme Court need not involve any dispute between two or more parties.

[51] Note 35 above.

[52] 1948 (3) SA 409 (A) at 451.

[53] 1958 (1) SA 546 (A).

[54] Baxter 578.

applicant in *Laubscher*)[55] on the ground that he has no existing right to the permit itself? The test of prejudicial effects to property and liberty, too, could have startling results if strictly followed: it would not be necessary to hear the accused, whether in the Supreme Court or in an administrative tribunal, where the rights in question have no bearing on property or liberty. In *Hack v Venterspost Municipality*,[56] a case which preceded *Ngwevela*[57] and *Laubscher*,[58] Roper J acknowledged the potentially harsh effects of reasoning solely in terms of rights and burdens by formulating a wider test:

> [A] tribunal, or a body, even if administrative, must exercise its functions in a judicial or quasi-judicial way whenever it is empowered to make decisions, not in its own arbitrary discretion, but as a result of an enquiry into matters of fact, or of fact and law, and these decisions may affect the rights of, and involve civil consequences to, individuals.

This dictum has since been applied in the Appellate Division.[59] Apart from the unfortunate reference to 'arbitrary discretion', which modern writers would regard as a complete contradiction in terms,[60] this more liberal dictum is arguably preferable to the 'existing rights' approach and to that in *Ngwevela* because it allows for a far more flexible application of natural justice. But flexibility can be carried too far, and the formulation turns out to be so flexible as to lack objective meaning. Since *all* administrative decisions involve some sort of enquiry (should we promulgate this piece of delegated legislation? Is it, in our opinion, necessary to detain this person?), and since there is no indication that the decision *must* affect rights and involve civil consequences to individuals, it is difficult to think of *any* administrative decision or action which would fail to qualify as quasi-judicial in terms of it. It is no exaggeration to say that most administrative decision-making could be made to conform to the principles of natural justice by means of the test in *Hack*.[61] Judicial caution and a lack of inventiveness on the part of certain counsel no doubt explain why they have not been!

(ii) Excluding legislative and administrative decisions

But even the stricter 'rights' tests quoted above do not logically exclude from the category 'quasi-judicial' many decisions of the administration which are not, as a rule, accompanied by hearings: the expulsion of aliens,[62] the dismissal of public employees,[63]

---

[55] Note 53 above.
[56] 1950 (1) SA 172 (W) at 189–90.
[57] Note 35 above.
[58] Note 53 above.
[59] *Minister of the Interior v Mariam* (n 37 above); *Van den Berg v Direkteur van Ekonomiese Sake* 1983 (1) SA 106 (A).
[60] See above, 301.
[61] Note 56 above.
[62] *Minister of the Interior v Bechler* 1948 (3) SA 409 (A); *Winter v Administrator-in-Executive Committee* 1973 (1) SA 873 (A). Cf the 'legitimate expectation' cases discussed below, 338–9.

thewithdrawal of passports,[64] and so on. Most 'legislative' and many 'purely administrative' decisions *do* in fact affect existing rights, especially rights to property and liberty. To explain away these exceptions, and to avoid the consequence that such decisions are 'quasi-judicial' and can only be legally made if accompanied by a hearing, our courts have had to resort to some very strained reasoning. Two illustrations are offered below.

In *Pretoria City Council v Modimola*[65] the Appellate Division held that an owner whose land had been expropriated under the Group Areas Development Act 69 of 1955 was not entitled to a hearing prior to the expropriation. In order to reach this conclusion, it was necessary for the court to classify an expropriation as something other than 'quasi-judicial'—not an easy task, since expropriation has such obvious and extreme effects on a person's proprietary rights. Botha JA succeeded in classifying the decision to expropriate as 'purely administrative', surmounting the difficulty by reasoning that the legislation authorising the expropriation was not 'directed against any individual', but authorised action required 'in the interest of the community as a whole':[66]

> 'In . . . statutes where a public authority is authorized to take a decision prejudicially affecting the property or liberty of members of a whole community, e g to levy taxation on them or their property, or to restrict their movements, no principle of natural justice is violated by a decision taken under a statute without affording an opportunity to every individual member of the community to be heard before the decision . . . is taken. In exercising its powers under such an enactment, the public authority is guided solely by what is best for the community as a whole, and the peculiar conduct of circumstances of any individual member of that community is a completely irrelevant consideration.'[67]

The problem of infringed rights has also been surmounted in the case of delegated legislation which makes no reference to the need for a hearing. An example is *E Snell and Co Ltd v Minister of Agricultural Economics*,[68] a case which arose out of a government notice prohibiting the sale of spirits under the name 'Brandy Liqueur'. The applicant, who had been marketing a beverage by that name, claimed that the Minister had acted contrary to the principles of natural justice by purporting to exercise his powers under s 10 of the Wine, Other Fermented Beverages and Spirits Act 25 of 1957 without affording the applicant the opportunity of a hearing. Page J relied on

---

[63] *Le Roux v Minister van Bantoe-Administrasie en Ontwikkeling* 1966 (1) SA 481 (A). For a recent example, see *Swart v Minister of Education and Culture, House of Representatives* 1986 (3) SA 331 (C), discussed at 337–8 below. Cf the 'legitimate expectation' cases discussed below, 338–9.

[64] *Boesak v Minister of Home Affairs* 1987 (3) SA 665 (C).

[65] 1966 (3) SA 250 (A).

[66] At 262F.

[67] Per Botha JA at 261H–262A.

[68] 1986 (3) SA 532 (D).

Modimola's case[69] in rejecting this contention.[70] But as to the point that the legislation *had* in this case been directly aimed at the applicant, and therefore at the deprivation of individual rights, the court could only reply that this did not alter the 'essential nature of the function',[71] which is legislative—not quasi-judicial![72] Definitional assertions of this kind show that while 'legislative' may have acquired a meaning of its own, that meaning cannot be distinguished from 'quasi-judicial' merely by reference to individual rights.

(iii) Quasi-judicial decisions and contracts

To make matters worse, there are cases in which hearings have been denied in respect of decision-making which is obviously and pre-eminently quasi-judicial. This may be illustrated by reference to cases dealing with disciplinary action in colleges and universities, a context in which administrative law and contract law frequently meet. These cases again reveal the use of reasoning which deflects the focus of attention from the coercive nature of the power and its effects on individual rights and liberties (as in *Modimola*)[73] or which simply characterises the power as 'purely administrative' by means of a definitional assertion.

The orthodox (and, we believe, correct) view recognises that disciplinary action is the epitome of 'judicial' administrative decision-making, and that a contractual basis for the disciplinary action makes no difference to its disciplinary character. In accordance with the Appellate Division authority contained in *Turner v Jockey Club of South Africa*[74] and *Theron v Ring van Wellington*,[75] it recognises that statute and contract are the 'twin pillars'[76] on which natural justice rests. Thus, public or private bodies which are contractually entitled to take disciplinary or coercive decisions should ensure that these be preceded by a hearing, either on the basis of an implied term which incorporates natural justice into the contract (as in *Turner*)[77] or on the simple and obvious ground that the decision is a quasi-judicial one. This last was the basis for quashing the decisions in both *Rampa v Rektor; Tschiya Onderwyskollege*[78] and *Mathale v Secretary for Education, Gazankulu*,[79] where students who had allegedly indulged in prohibited political activities were expelled without being afforded hearings. There is, however, a line of cases

[69] Note 65 above.
[70] At 536.
[71] At 537D.
[72] At 536J.
[73] Note 65 above.
[74] 1974 (3) SA 633 (A).
[75] *Theron v Ring van Wellington van die NG Sendingkerk in Suid-Afrika* 1976 (2) SA 1 (A).
[76] H W R Wade (1969) 85 *Law Quarterly Review* 468 at 469.
[77] Note 74 above.
[78] 1986 (1) SA 424 (O).
[79] 1986 (4) SA 427 (T).

which challenges this approach. By focusing exclusively on the terms of the contract between the student and the institution, and by characterising the student's misconduct as a breach of contract which justifies rescission, the punitive essence of the expulsions and exclusions has been overlooked in cases such as *Jacob v Council of University of Durban-Westville*,[80] *Sibanyoni v University of Fort Hare*[81] and *Mkhize v University of Zululand*.[82]

Mkhize's case concerned a decision of the Council of the University not to readmit students who had contravened hostel rules by entertaining female students in their rooms. It was argued for the applicants that, since the decision was punitive, it should not have been taken without hearing the affected students. Relying on the Appellate Division decision in *Jacob*,[83] Booysen J regarded the relationship between the parties as purely contractual. In terms of s 23 of the University of Zululand Act 43 of 1969, the Council clearly had the power to refuse admission to any student, and s 20(2), which requires annual registration of students, clearly indicated that the contract was one in respect of each academic year. Thus the Council's decision was merely a decision not to accept the student's offer for the forthcoming year, and

> '[t]he decision of a person not to accept an offer to enter into a contract with another person is ordinarily not a reviewable decision and not one which has to be arrived at after application of the rules of natural justice'.[84]

In the absence of an implied term guaranteeing readmission to successful examinees, there was no reason why an applicant for admission *or readmission* should be in any better position than an applicant for membership of a club, or the applicant for a job.[85] In the result, the hearing was denied. It is interesting to reflect on whether the same purely contractual view would have been taken of the case if the applicants had had the good fortune to be excluded in the middle of the academic year instead of at the end—and, if so, whether a student's entitlement to a hearing ought to depend on the time of year.

Sibanyoni's case[86] provides an even more extreme example of this ouster-by-contract of the ordinary principles of administrative law. During a spate of student boycotts, the rector of the University gave notice to the students to attend lectures on a certain day on pain of being 'deemed to have elected to discontinue their studies at the University'. The appellants failed to attend lectures on the appointed day and were subsequently excluded without being given a hearing. The full bench of the Ciskei Supreme Court held that the appellants

---

[80] 1974 (3) SA 552 (A).
[81] 1985 (1) SA 19 (Ck).
[82] 1986 (1) SA 901 (D).
[83] Note 80 above.
[84] Per Booysen J at 904F.
[85] At 904D.
[86] Note 81 above.

were not entitled to a hearing. Pickard ACJ (Erasmus and Rees AJJ concurring) rejected the contention that since the measures were disciplinary, they ought to have been taken in terms of the disciplinary procedures of the University's statute. Instead, the court reasoned that the students were in breach of their contractual obligation to attend lectures regularly, which meant that the University was entitled to rescind the contract. The resulting 'exclusion' was not, therefore, a (punitive) 'expulsion'.[87] As for the possibility of implying a term into the contract requiring observance of the audi alteram partem rule, Pickard ACJ went so far as to say that

> '[t]he rules of natural justice, on the basis of audi alteram partem, have no application in matters of contract; contractual rights and obligations are governed by the laws of contract as they are known to us.'[88]

Fortunately, this is Ciskeian and not South African law—though one might be forgiven, on the basis of *Jacob*[89] and *Mkhize*,[90] for thinking that it applies in the rest of the country too.[91]

In *Ngubane v Minister of Education and Culture, Ulundi*[92] a teacher rather than a student was subject to punitive treatment following allegations of misconduct. The punishment took the form of a summary transfer in terms of s 19 of the Act from the post of rector of a college to that of principal of a high school. Since the transfer entailed no reduction in salary, the teacher's consent was not required by law; the only question was whether the decision to transfer the teacher was invalid for failure to comply with the audi alteram partem rule. Howard J decided that it was, since the exercise of the power in s 19 qualified, in terms of the test in *Hack v Venterspost Municipality*,[93] as a quasi-judicial function.

There was no mention of contract in *Ngubane*,[94] but one must not leap to the conclusion that this had any effect on the result in that case; for an exclusive focus on the contract is not the only loophole out of natural justice. This is supported by the case of *Swart v Minister of Education and Culture, House of Representatives*,[95] where a hearing was denied teachers who had been suspended in terms of s 17 of the Coloured Persons Education Act 47 of 1963, and where there was also no discussion of contract—or, unsurprisingly, of *Ngubane's* case.[96] As in *Ngubane*, counsel relied on the *Hack*[97] formula. But though Selikowitz AJ appreciated both that the

---

[87] At 30B.
[88] At 30I.
[89] Note 80 above.
[90] Note 82 above.
[91] For criticism of these cases, see Etienne Mureinik (1985) 1 *SAJHR* 48; John Hlophe (1987) 104 *SALJ* 255.
[92] 1985 (3) SA 160 (N).
[93] Note 56 above.
[94] Note 92 above.
[95] 1986 (3) SA 331 (C).
[96] Note 92 above.
[97] Note 56 above.

suspensions were preceded by an enquiry into the alleged misconduct of the applicants, and that 'very serious hardship' could result from the suspension, he found that Parliament did not intend the respondent to give the applicants any form of hearing.[98] The suspension procedure was not, in his view, intended to impose a penalty on the person accused of misconduct; it was merely intended to provide

> 'a procedural step to enable the Minister to ensure the orderly and proper continuation by his Department of the task entrusted to it, namely the control of education for Coloured persons'.[99]

Translated into the language of the classification of functions, a decision defined as a 'procedural step' is surely the same thing as a 'purely administrative' function. The definition just as surely subverts what the established case authority regards as the crucial key to a quasi-judicial function: the effects of administrative action—especially coercive action—on the rights and liberties of individuals.

3 The Road Ahead

The cases discussed above show that the application of the audi alteram partem rule is a sadly haphazard business. The various tests for what is quasi-judicial are infinitely flexible, it seems, so that the classification of functions has become an increasingly unsatisfactory method for discovering those decisions whose legality ought to be conditional on the giving of a hearing. In apparent recognition of this problem, two solutions are beginning to emerge from our case law which would seem to avoid the pitfalls of classification: the 'legitimate expectation' test and the so-called duty to act fairly.

The legitimate expectation test has its roots in English law, where it is now firmly established.[100] Instead of reasoning in terms of rights, this test asks whether the affected person had a legitimate expectation of a fair hearing in the circumstances. In *Everett v Minister of the Interior*[101] the test operated in favour of alien who had been expelled from the country without being given an opportunity to make representations to the authorities; a significant result, as Baxter[102] points out, since the explusion of aliens had always been classified as an 'administrative' act. More recently, the legitimate expectation test has been applied with a liberal hand in a series of cases concerning the dismissal of hospital employees[103]—another

---

[98] At 342H.
[99] At 343H.
[100] Lord Denning first enunciated the test in *Schmidt v Home Secretary* [1969] 2 Ch 149. For an overview, see John Hlophe (1987) 104 *SALJ* 165.
[101] 1981 (2) SA 453 (C).
[102] Baxter 580.
[103] *Langeni v Minister of Health and Welfare* 1988 (4) SA 93 (W); *Mokoena v Administrator, Transvaal* 1988 (4) SA 912 (W); *Mokopanele v Administrateur, Transvaal* 1989 (1) SA

significant development, since public employees have seldom had the benefit of the audi alteram partem rule in the past.[104] The test has also been referred to in a case dealing with the withdrawal of a passport,[105] an area in which natural justice has always been conspicuous by its absence. In spite of these developments and the enthusiastic reception which the test has received in academic circles,[106] it has not yet been applied in the Appellate Division. In *Castel NO v Metal and Allied Workers' Union*,[107] however, Hefer JA conceded that there might be 'a need for legal reform',[108] and this suggestion has been taken up boldly by Howie J in the recent case of *Lunt v University of Cape Town*.[109] Here it was held that a post-graduate student who was refused re-entry into the University's Medical School had a legitimate expectation of being heard before being labelled as an unsuitable candidate—a decision which the judge found to be 'censorious to a damning degree'.[110] In view of Howie J's careful distinguishing of *Castel's* case[111] and his reasoned criticism of certain of the 'student cases'[112] discussed earlier in this chapter,[113] it would be surprising indeed if this decision failed to inspire further judicial interest in the test.

The 'duty to act fairly', another product of English law[114] which has been adopted in other common-law jurisdictions,[115] is merely a restatement of the ordinary principles of natural justice. Its attraction is that it avoids the problems of classification by applying to all forms of administrative decision-making. While it applies generally, the content of the duty is utterly flexible: what is 'fair' for the purposes of the duty depends on the circumstances of the case, and its requirements will vary accordingly. Though the duty has some support in Zimbabwe,[116] it has so far received a mention in only a

---

434 (O). The first two cases were decided by Goldstone J, who also presided in *Traube v Administrator, Transvaal* 1989 (1) SA 397 (W); see n 110 below.

[104] See n 63 above.

[105] *Boesak v Minister of Home Affairs* 1987 (3) SA 665 (C) at 684C–H (Friedman J, Van den Heever and Vivier JJ concurring).

[106] Baxter 580; Hlophe op cit n 91; Hlophe op cit n 100.

[107] 1987 (4) SA 795 (A). The test received some support from Wilson J in the court a quo (1985 (2) SA 280 (D)) at 286J.

[108] At 810H–I.

[109] 1989 (2) SA 438 (C).

[110] At 446G–J. See also the approach of Goldstone J in *Traube v Administrator, Transvaal* 1989 (1) SA 397 (W), where medical practitioners had been judged 'unsuitable' for reappointment.

[111] Note 107 above.

[112] At 448–50.

[113] Above, 335–8.

[114] Attributed to Lord Parker CJ in *In re H K (An Infant)* [1967] 2 QB 617, though the equation of natural justice with fairness is much older than this case.

[115] Australia, New Zealand and Canada; see Baxter's account at 594–5.

[116] See the judgment of Ebrahim J in *Crow v Detained Mental Patients Special Board* 1985 (4) SA 83 (ZH) at 95–7.

handful of South African cases.[117] However, such a duty may be the outcome of future legislative reform. The South African Law Commission, apparently recognising the advantages of general duty with a variable content, has recommended the adoption of a general requirement of compliance with the principles of natural justice and a general ground of review of unfairness. It has also supported the abolition of the distinction between administrative and quasi-judicial acts.[118]

One is tempted to assume that reform along these lines can hardly fail to be an improvement on the present system, but there is danger inherent in it too. Just as the legitimate expectation test leaves it to the judge to decide who deserves a hearing, the general duty to act fairly gives the judge the widest possible discretion to decide what is fair in the circumstances. One does not have to be a cynic to suppose that three factors—the political climate of restraint, the perennial judicial reluctance to overburden the administration and the system of stare decisis—could combine to ensure that the content of fairness turns out to be meagre indeed.

The danger would, we believe, be diminished by addressing a related and underlying difficulty, which is that real agreement has not yet been reached on the sorts of decisions which require hearings or other forms of natural justice. The need for such agreement has been obscured by the courts' reliance on the classification of functions (and on the classificatory tests which apparently dictate the correct result), but the incorrigible subjectivity of judgments as to what is 'fair' would make such agreement essential. It could be achieved by making a statutory list of factors which point to the need for notice and a hearing, or by any other means which allow for the articulation of the factors by which judges decide issues of natural justice. The classification of the administrative decision in question would surely be one of those factors, but, we hope, only one of many.

II REASONABLENESS

Judgments as to what is *unreasonable* are often thought to be both hopelessly subjective and incurably substantive—and thus quite inappropriate to the business of judicial review, or 'not justiciable'. It is not surprising, then, that reasonableness is the most controversial requirement of our administrative law. More than any other requirement, it exposes the tension between two conflicting judicial emotions: the fear of encroaching on the province of the executive arm of government by entering into the merits of administrative decisions, and the watchdog-like desire for adequate control over the decisions of public authorities. Again, the limiting device used by our courts is the classification of administrative functions: our courts

---

[117] *Roberts v Chairman, Local Road Transportation Board (2)* 1980 (2) SA 480 (C); *Lawson v Cape Town Municipality* 1982 (4) SA 1 (C); *Terry v University of Cape Town* CPD 21 August 1987 Case No 9093/87 (unreported).
[118] *Working Paper 15,* Project 24 (1986), especially at 105.

have recognised two different tests for the unreasonableness of 'legislative' and 'purely judicial' acts and decisions, and a third test of 'symptomatic' unreasonableness for 'administrative' decisions. We begin with this last category, which takes in the vast majority of administrative decisions.

A Administrative decisions

According to the cases, a test for the unreasonableness of adminstrative decisions does not exist. The locus classicus, *Union Government v Union Steel Corporation*,[119] denies that unreasonableness itself is a ground of review.[120] Instead, the test has been described as one of 'symptomatic unreasonableness':[121]

> '[N]owhere has it been held that unreasonableness is sufficient ground for interference; emphasis is always laid upon the necessity of the unreasonableness being so gross that something else can be inferred from it, either that it is "inexplicable except on the assumption of mala fides or ulterior motive" . . . or that it amounts to proof that the person on whom the discretion is conferred has not applied his mind to the matter. . . .'[122]

This dictum has prevented, and continues to prevent, the recognition of a single ground of unreasonableness for testing the validity of administrative decisions. Instead, it has stimulated the development of various fragmented and overlapping grounds of review, a patchwork approach which is the subject of considerable controversy. The controversy relates to two issues in particular: the problem of substantive judgments, and the problem of subjective judgments.

1 The problem of substantive judgments

The *Union Steel*[123] test relies on the inference being drawn of some recognised irregularity, and not on the unreasonableness itself— thereby avoiding the problem of pronouncing on the merits and of usurping the powers of public authorities. It has, however, been argued that this is an unnecessary manoeuvre: that courts are not in any event required to make judgments as to what is *substantively* unreasonable, but that they should—and do—decide on what is *dialectically* (or procedurally) unreasonable.

Using the example of an argument between two people, Professor Baxter, the proponent of the distinction, states that a proposition will be dialectically reasonable if it is supported by 'factors, values and

---

[119] 1928 AD 220.
[120] See also *The Administrator, Transvaal and The Firs Investments (Pty) Ltd v Johannesburg City Council* 1971 (1) SA 56 at 80; *Johannesburg City Council v Administrator, Transvaal and Mayofis* 1971 (1) SA 87 at 96A–D; *National Transport Commission v Chetty's Motor Transport (Pty) Ltd* 1972 (3) SA 726 at 735E–H.
[121] The term is that of Professor Taitz; see 1978 *AJ* 109 at 111.
[122] Per Stratford JA in *Union Government v Union Steel Corporation*, n 119 above, at 236–7.
[123] Note 119 above.

standards which the other party would recognise as legitimate given the context of the argument'.[124] Even if the arguers disagree violently as to who is 'right' and who is 'wrong' (substantively reasonable and unreasonable), it is nevertheless possible for them to recognise each others' views as dialectically reasonable *in that those views are supported by an appeal to legitimate considerations.*

As an illustration, take the student who complains about her examiners when she finds she has failed in her favourite law subject. Both examiners are wrong, or substantively unreasonable, in her view. When she consults them, one examiner admits to having decided the issue by tossing a coin; the other is able to explain that the student has failed because she cited no cases and because her answers were incomplete. The student may still feel that both examiners have made substantively unreasonable decisions, but she is bound to admit that the second examiner's decision was dialectically reasonable. The first examiner's decision is, of course, dialectically unreasonable; in making it, he appealed to a factor which is totally illegitimate and irrelevant in the context of marking exams.

If Baxter's analysis is correct, there is no harm in recognising unreasonableness itself as a ground for reviewing administrative decisions. Provided that they confine themselves to the dialectical side, judges may pronounce on unreasonableness without crossing from review to appeal and without usurping the functions of the executive arm of government. In fact, Baxter argues that our judges do pronounce on unreasonableness in this way, since the recognised irregularities listed in *Union Steel*[125] are themselves forms of unreasonableness. He unites these 'irregularities' and other apparently unrelated grounds under the one heading of unreasonableness (an approach we have adopted in this chapter), pointing out that they appear to be unrelated only because they have evolved on an ad hoc basis over many years.[126] Moreover, Baxter argues that the different tests applied to administrative, legislative and judicial functions all conform to the same standard; that, notwithstanding their apparent mutual exclusiveness, they all deem to be 'unreasonable' the type of conduct which no reasonable person would accept.[127] Similarly, Rose-Innes takes the view that the test of unreasonableness applicable to 'administrative' proceedings 'is the same concept'[128] as that applicable to subordinate legislation. There is no doubt that these writers are correct in identifying a tremendous amount of common ground between the various forms of unreasonableness recognised by our courts.[129] So far, however, the Appellate Division

---

[124] Baxter 485.
[125] Note 119 above.
[126] Ibid 489–90.
[127] Ibid, especially at 490, 496–7, 534.
[128] Rose-Innes 217–18.
[129] See further below, 359–60.

has been unreceptive to these suggestions, and remains adamant in its adherence to the symptomatic (and safe-sounding) *Union Steel* formula.[130]

2 The problem of subjectivity

The problem of subjectivity arises most acutely in the case of *substantive* judgments as to what is reasonable or unreasonable. But even if we confine ourselves to the dialectical, my idea of what is a legitimate consideration in the context of our argument may well be different from yours. Everyone agrees that it is unreasonable for an examiner to toss a coin in order to decide whether a candidate should pass or fail, but issues in discretionary administrative decision-making are seldom so clear-cut. When a magistrate is deciding whether to allow the holding of an outdoor gathering in terms of s 46 of the Internal Security Act, is it unreasonable for him to refuse permission on the ground that the noise of the gathering might disturb the neighbours? Is noise a legitimate consideration in the context, or should the magistrate confine himself to security issues?[131] Even dialectically, what is unreasonable in the eyes of Judge X may be reasonable in the eyes of Judge Y. The problem of subjectivity seems to be insurmountable, whether (like Baxter) one focuses on the unreasonableness itself or whether one employs the *Union Steel*[132] inference from 'gross' unreasonableness. It is import-ant to realise, however, that the difficulty is not unique to the grounds of unreasonableness. It is likely to rear its head whenever there is particular scope for judicial interpretation in judicial review.

The problem of subjectivity should not be exaggerated; after all, lawyers contend with it every day. The law of delict continues to function notwithstanding the subjectivity of opinions about the proper behaviour of the 'reasonable man'; and legal documents are not invalidated when they make provision for a 'reasonable' income or a 'reasonable' time. On the other hand, one cannot ignore the problem. Its implications in administrative law are especially significant because they strike at the heart of the controversy about the proper role of the judicial arm of government.

3 The grounds in *Union Steel*

(a) Improper or ulterior purposes

Though Stratford JA did not expressly refer to ulterior purposes in the *Union Steel* case, the modern case law tends to treat this ground as included in the dictum by virtue of the reference to 'ulterior

---

[130] See the strong remarks of Hefer JA in *Castel NO v Metal and Allied Workers' Union* 1987 (4) SA 795 (A) at 812J–814D.

[131] In *Metal and Allied Workers' Union v Castell NO* 1985 (2) SA 280 (D) Wilson J found this and the other factors taken into account by the magistrate to be irrelevant considerations. The Appellate Division took a different view in *Castel NO v Metal and Allied Workers' Union* 1987 (4) SA 795 (A).

[132] Note 119 above.

motives', some judges (inappropriately, it will be suggested) treating the two as synonymous. In any event, it is firmly established in our law that the court will interfere

'... in those well recognised cases in which powers, given to public bodies to be used for certain purposes, are wrongly used by them to achieve some other purpose ...'.[133]

This ground of review, also (confusingly)[134] known as fraus legis, applies not only to 'administrative' decisions, but also to other acts of the administration.[135] The purposes for which powers are given will sometimes be apparent from the statute in question, but will more often be found to be implicit in the statute. Where the legislation seems to give no indication at all as to proper purposes, the court could fall back on the residual rule that public powers must always be used in the public interest.[136] If the court finds that the powers have been used for unauthorised purposes, or purposes 'not contemplated at the time when the powers were conferred', it will hold that the decision is illegal. This will be the result even where the powers are mistakenly used for praiseworthy purposes, as happened in the wartime case of *Van Eck NO and Van Rensburg NO v Etna Stores*.[137] Here a War Measures regulation empowered the Director of Food Supplies and Distribution to seize foodstuffs in order to obtain evidence of failure to comply with the regulations. An official acting under the Director's authority seized some bags of rice in order to further a food distribution scheme. Davis AJA, remarking that the appellants had no doubt acted with good intentions,[138] nevertheless held that the seizure was illegal; the purpose was an unauthorised one. The result might have been different if the regulation had not been limited by a specific purpose, since the seizure would probably have been judged as 'in the public interest'.

In most cases, however, the intentions of the public authority can hardly be described as laudable. A less-than-heartwarming example is the infamous case of *Rikhoto v East Rand Administration*

---

[133] Per Watermeyer CJ in *Sinovich v Hercules Municipal Council* 1946 AD 783 at 792. See also *Orangezicht Estates v Cape Town Town Council* (1906) 23 SC 296; *Fernwood Estates Ltd v Cape Town Municipal Council* 1933 CPD 399.

[134] As with mala fides (see below), there is no certainty as to what it means to act 'in fraudem legis'; it is a term used to describe both *innocent* and *dishonest* uses of power for unauthorised purposes. For examples, see *Van Eck NO and Van Rensburg NO v Etna Stores* 1947 (2) SA 985 (A) 998–9; *Metal and Allied Worker's Union v Castel NO* 1985 (2) SA 280 (D) at 287D–E; *Castel NO v Metal and Allied Workers' Union* 1987 (4) SA 795 (A) at 811–12.

[135] In relation to legislation, see *University of Cape Town v Ministers of Education and Culture* 1988 (3) SA 203 (C), discussed below. Improper purposes pursued in judicial or quasi-judicial cases (such as the use of university disciplinary powers to terrorise the students) would seem to be very rare, and are likely to be brought under other headings, especially that of bias.

[136] Above, 247; 309.

[137] 1947 (2) SA 984 (A).

[138] At 997.

Board,[139] where the board was held to have frustrated the purposes of s 10 of the Blacks (Urban Areas) Consolidation Act 25 of 1945. Under that law, black workers could acquire residence rights in an urban area if they had worked continuously in the area for a period of ten years. The Board made the acquisition of such rights impossible by instituting a system of annually renewable labour contracts— thereby ensuring that ten years' work could never qualify as 'continuous'!

A more recent incident which aroused equal indignation arose when, in 1987, the Ministers of Education and Culture and National Education purported to impose certain conditions on the grant of subsidies to universities in terms of s 25 of the Universities Act 61 of 1955. This section enables the Minister to grant subsidies out of moneys voted by Parliament subject to conditions determined by him, and 'with due regard to the requirements of each university in relation to the general requirements of higher education in the Republic'. The conditions demanded, among other things, that the universities should take steps to prevent staff and students from engaging in boycott action, unlawful gatherings and many other forms of 'disruptive conduct', and required the university Councils to report on all transgressions and on the preventive and disciplinary steps taken by them. In terms of s 27 of the Act, failure to comply with these conditions would enable the Minister to withhold all or part of the subsidy voted by Parliament in respect of the errant university. The imposition of the conditions was challenged on a number of grounds in *University of Cape Town v Ministers of Education and Culture*.[140] Not surprisingly, one of the findings of the full bench of the Cape Provincial Division was that the conditions were directed towards the achievement of purposes relating to 'law and order'—purposes which were not contemplated by s 25 of the Universities Act.

It is tempting, in such cases, to conclude that the public authorities concerned cannot possibly believe that they are entitled to use their powers for such unlikely purposes. But one must resist the temptation: dishonesty is a very serious matter and is extremely difficult to prove. For these reasons, there are few cases in which dishonesty is alleged, and the courts are usually careful to point out that the probity of the respondent is not in doubt. In the *University of Cape Town*[141] case, for instance, the court uses the terminology of ulterior motive, but makes it clear that in the context, the term does not connote 'a sinister motivation';[142] it merely covers the situation where powers are used for a purpose not expressly or impliedly

---

[139] 1983 (4) SA 278 (W), confirmed on appeal in *Oos-Randse Administrasieraad v Rikhoto* 1983 (3) SA 595 (A).

[140] 1988 (3) SA 203 (C) (Howie J, Nel and Conradie JJ concurring).

[141] Note 140 above.

[142] At 212G–H, quoting the words of Corbett JA in *Goldberg v Minister of Prisons* 1979 (1) SA 14 (A) at 48E.

authorized by the statute. We suggest that the use of the word 'purpose' is more accurate in this type of situation, since 'motive' does tend to mislead by suggesting the presence of subjective, 'hidden' or 'sinister' aims of which the decision-maker is *conscious*. As such, ulterior motives refer most obviously to the *dishonest* use of power rather than the mistaken use of power. Improper purposes are judged objectively, improper motives subjectively; and though they may coexist in particular cases, they can also appear on their own. There is nothing to be gained by confusing the terminology of mistake with that of dishonesty.

(b) Ulterior motives or mala fides

Notwithstanding what has been said above, there seems to be doubt as to whether dishonesty is a ground of review in our law at all! There are two main sources of confusion in this regard. First, though 'ulterior motive' has clearly been recognised as an 'irregularity', and appears to have been equated with another well-recognised ground (mala fides) in *Union Steel*,[143] there are cases which establish that the (subjective) motive of the public authority is irrelevant provided that the (objective) purposes are properly authorised. In other words, the courts are not consistent in their approach to dishonest motives. Secondly, there is no unanimity as to the meaning of 'ulterior motive' and 'mala fides'. Both have been used in their ordinary sense to mean an abuse of power which is conscious (and therefore dishonest), but both have also been used to describe abuses of power which are induced by honest mistakes or mere stupidity. In this last sense they have been equated with that catch-all ground called 'failure to apply the mind'.

(i) Motives 'not relevant'

As regards the first source of confusion, the case of *White Rocks Farm v Minister of Community Development*[144] provides an illustration. Here the applicants' land had been expropriated by the respondent in furtherance of a mountain catchment scheme. The applicants objected to the fact that the expropriation was made under the Expropriation Act 63 of 1975 rather than under the Mountain Catchment Areas Act 63 of 1970, whose provisions would have operated to the greater benefit of the applicants and involved greater expense to the respondent. The court was prepared to assume that the respondent had used the Expropriation Act for financial reasons, but refused to set aside the expropriation order: since the purpose throughout was a 'public' one, it satisfied the requirements of the Expropriation Act, and the motives of the respondent were therefore

---

[143] Note 119 above.
[144] 1984 (3) SA 785 (N).

irrelevant. As Corbett J put it in another expropriation case, *L F Boshoff Investments (Pty) Ltd v Cape Town Municipality*,[145]

'Provided that the expropriation is a *bona fide* one for a municipal purpose, those motives would not be relevant to the question as to whether the power of expropriation had been validly exercised.'

The principle that motives (the subjective reasons for a decision) are irrelevant once a proper purpose has been shown to exist, was approved by the Appellate Division in *Broadway Mansions (Pty) Ltd v Pretoria City Council*.[146] Here, as in *White Rocks*,[147] 'cheaper' legislation was used for an expropriation to the detriment of the applicants. Thus, though it is not clear whether the authorities in these cases *did* in fact act dishonestly, it seems not to matter whether they did—provided that the decision was supported by an objectively valid purpose.

(ii)   The meaning of 'ulterior motives' and 'mala fides'

The second source of confusion relates to a lack of unanimity as to the meaning of 'ulterior motives' and 'mala fides'. They are clearly accepted as grounds of review, but do these terms refer to dishonesty? As appears from the *University of Cape Town*[148] case, is standard practice to equate the former term with ulterior purposes; and yet the word 'motives' used without the prefix 'ulterior' (the usage in *White Rocks*,[149] *Boshoff Investments*[150] and *Broadway Mansions*)[151] is generally understood to mean the subjective reasons for acting in a certain way, actuating reasons which can and must be distinguished from objectively proper purposes. And, as we have indicated, 'mala fides' is used in two completely different senses: one meaning dishonesty, the other referring to a mere lack of due mental application.[152]

Rose-Innes[153] uses the term in the first (strict) sense, equating it with fraud, and illustrates its operation with *Adams Stores (Pty) Ltd v Charlestown Town Board*.[154] Here a licensing authority (the Town Board) was found deliberately to have ignored a valid objection, made false statements and condoned a fatal irregularity. The court could not 'escape the conclusion'[155] that the board had acted mala fide. Baxter appears to support the use of the term in the strict

---

[145] 1969 (2) SA 256 (C) at 270C.
[146] 1955 (1) SA 517 (A).
[147] Note 144 above.
[148] Note 140 above.
[149] Note 144 above.
[150] Note 145 above.
[151] Note 146 above.
[152] See the remarks of Didcott J in *Anchor Publishing Co (Pty) Ltd v Publications Appeal Board* 1987 (4) SA 708 (N) at 711B–F.
[153] Rose-Innes 142.
[154] 1951 (2) SA 512 (N).
[155] Per Carlisle AJP at 517B.

sense,[156] as does Wiechers when he says that mala fides presumes 'consciousness of wrongfulness';[157] though he differs from the other authors in arguing that mala fides is not in itself a ground of review.[158]

While these authorities are agreed on the strict meaning of mala fides, there are many instances of the less pejorative usage. A typical example is the *Etna Stores* case,[159] in which Davies AJA noted that the respondents had committed an abuse of power which 'amounts to *mala fides*'; but, he hastened to add, he was not attaching to them 'any moral obliquity'.[160] Similarly, the court a quo in *Metal and Allied Workers' Union v Castell NO*[161] found that a magistrate who withheld permission (in terms of s 46 of the Internal Security Act 74 of 1982) to hold an outdoor gathering, had based his decision on matters which were irrelevant; so much so that he acted mala fide. But, said Wilson J, 'I do not, for a moment, suggest that [he] was motivated by any improper motives'.[162]

Powers of arrest and detention under the emergency regulations have produced more examples of the inconsistency, all the more pronounced because the facts in most of the cases are so similar. The typical facts obtained in *Bloem v Minister of Law and Order*,[163] where the applicant alleged that the arresting officer had acted mala fide in that he could not conceivably have entertained the opinion that her arrest was 'necessary' for the purposes stipulated in regulation 3(1) of the emergency regulations. The officer alleged that he formed the opinion on the basis of information received from a 'reliable source'. Van Coller J, in holding that allegation of mala fides had not been proved, clearly equated mala fides with dishonesty: in his view, the officer would have acted mala fide only if the evidence should prove that he did not in fact receive the information, or that he did not believe the information[164]—in other words, only if the officer acted dishonestly. A similar approach was adopted in *Gumede v Minister of Law and Order*[165] and in a number of other cases[166] dealing with arrest and detention under reg 3(1). However, in *Radebe v Minister of Law and Order*[167] the court seems not to have regarded mala fides as involving dishonesty. Here Goldstone J came to the conclusion that

---

[156] Baxter 515–19.
[157] Wiechers op cit n 6 at 254.
[158] Ibid 256.
[159] Note 137 above.
[160] At 997.
[161] Note 131 above.
[162] At 289A–B. The decision was overturned on appeal (1987 (4) SA 795 (A)), but it is not clear whether the appeal court disapproved of this looser usage; see the judgment of Hefer JA at 811–14.
[163] 1987 (2) SA 436 (O).
[164] At 440J.
[165] 1987 (3) SA 155 (D).
[166] See, for instance, *Nkwinti v Commissioner of Police* 1986 (2) SA 421 (E); *Dempsey v Minister of Law & Order* 1986 (4) SA 530 (C).
[167] 1987 (1) SA 586 (W).

the officer could not bona fide have formed the requisite opinion, the probability being that he 'did not properly apply his mind to the precise terms of reg 3(1)'.[168] This looser usage seems also to have been adopted by Kannemeyer J in *Nqumba v State President*.[169]

(iii) Resolving the difficulty

There is an obvious and pressing need for clarity as to the meaning of ulterior motives and mala fides, and as to the status of dishonesty as a ground of review. If dishonesty is a ground for setting aside the administrative decisions—and, conflicting authorities aside, it is almost inconceivable that it should not be!—then it is important to indicate the presence of dishonesty by an unambiguous term: 'dishonesty' itself would seem to be the most obvious choice. 'Ulterior motives' and 'mala fides' would then be redundant terminology, since the irregularities not involving dishonesty could be indicated by the existing terminology of improper purposes and failure to apply the mind. If Wiechers[170] is right and dishonesty is not in itself a ground for setting aside administrative decisions, those confusing and ambiguous terms are equally superfluous. This terminological difficulty could be eradicated quite easily by legislative means, and it is to be hoped that it will not be overlooked by the Law Commission.

(c) Failure to apply the mind

'Applying one's mind' is a rather nebulous concept which might mean almost anything. The same is true of the corresponding ground of review: 'failure to apply the mind to the matter' is a sort of catch-all phrase which trips easily off the tongue and is capable of covering most instances of bad decision-making quite comfortably. There does not seem to be any certainty in the cases as to its precise meaning, probably because of its tendency to overlap with other grounds of review. On one interpretation, failure to apply the mind refers to a failure to exercise authority at all, which is a ground of review in itself;[171] on another (more popular) interpretation, it means failure to exercise the power properly. When used in this second sense, the phrase is generally synonymous with one of two other recognised grounds of review, to which we now turn.

(i) Relevant and irrelevant considerations

When decision-makers fail to take relevant considerations into account, or when they give undue weight to irrelevant considerations, it is frequently said that they have 'failed to apply their minds to the matter'—though the first two phenomena are also recognised

[168] At 595I.
[169] 1987 (1) SA 456 (E) at 475D.
[170] Above, n 158.
[171] Per Colman J in *Northwest Townships Ltd v The Administrator, Transvaal* 1975 (4) SA 1 (T) at 8. On failure to exercise authority, see above, 306ff.

as grounds of review in themselves.[172] Thus in *Bangtoo Bros v National Transport Commission*,[173] Henning J concluded that if a tribunal were to relegate a factor of obvious and paramount importance to one of insignificance, and give another factor a weight far in excess of its true value, this would amount to a failure properly to apply its mind to the matter.

Unless there is fairly detailed statutory guidance as to the factors which ought to be taken into account in a particular decision, one's view of what constitutes a relevant or irrelevant consideration tends to be a highly subjective matter on which different judges might easily disagree. A typical illustration is to be found in the divided opinions of the full bench in *Anchor Publishing Co (Pty) Ltd v Publications Control Board*,[174] a case which arose out of the Board's decision to ban the applicant's magazine, a guide to 'glamour' photography. The decision applied to two existing editions and all future editions of the magazine. All three members of the court agreed that the board had failed to apply its mind to the issue of the subsequent editions: on the basis of only two published editions, it had concluded that *all* subsequent editions would be 'undesirable' in terms of s 9(1)(*a*) of the Publications Act 42 of 1974. As to the banning of the two published editions, however, there was disagreement. The majority of the court (Thirion and Booysen JJ) found that there was ample ground for the board's decision to ban the magazine; Didcott J, dissenting, found that the board had given too much weight to one factor—the probable circulation of the magazine—and too little to another factor, the manner in which the magazine portrayed nudity.[175]

(ii) Arbitrariness and capriciousness

A decision may be said to be arbitrary and capricious when it is irrational or senseless, without foundation or apparent purpose. Again, capricious decision-makers can sensibly be said to have failed to apply their minds to the matter.[176] There is also a potential overlap with improper purposes and dishonesty, so that arbitrariness itself seldom appears as the sole, or even the most obvious, ground for setting aside a decision.

B Legislative acts

While Acts of Parliament cannot be declared invalid on any grounds except non-compliance with the constitutional formalities laid down for their enactment, our courts have always recognised that

---

[172] See Rose-Innes 132ff; Baxter 501–7; *Castel NO v Metal and Allied Workers' Union* (n 131 above) at 812H–I.

[173] 1973 (4) SA 667 (N) at 685A–D.

[174] 1987 (4) SA 708 (N).

[175] At 720D–G.

[176] *Northwest Townships (Pty) Ltd v Administrator, Transvaal* 1975 (4) SA 1 (T); Rose-Innes 211n5.

non-Parliamentary or subordinate legislation is treated differently. A distinction has been drawn between the two types of subordinate legislation for these purposes: *original* subordinate legislation and *delegated* subordinate legislation. The former consists of provincial ordinances and the enactments of the 'homelands' assemblies, and is (rightly or wrongly) treated with particular respect by the courts because it emanates from legislative bodies which, though subordinate to Parliament, are themselves 'original' legislators. Apart from the usual need to comply with formalities and the principle that such legislation may not be repugnant to an Act of Parliament, it is virtually immune from attack.[177]

The term delegated legislation applies to all the other forms of subordinate legislation. It may be declared invalid on much wider grounds, though there is said to be a doctrine of 'benevolent interpretation' in the case of delegated legislation emanating from elected legislators such as municipal councils and other local authorities.[178]

1 The rule in *Kruse v Johnson*

Four grounds of attack are enumerated in the English case of *Kruse v Johnson*,[179] where Lord Russell elaborates on the various forms of unreasonablenesss applicable to by-laws:

'If, for instance, they were found to be *partial and unequal in their operation* as between different classes; if they were *manifestly unjust*; if they *disclosed bad faith*; if they involved such *oppressive or gratuitous interference with the rights of those subject to them* as could find no justification in the minds of reasonable men, the Court might well say, "Parliament never intended to give authority to make such rules; they are unreasonable and *ultra vires*."'

While our courts have been determined not to impose standards of this kind on the exercise of 'administrative' discretion, they have not hesitated to employ the far-reaching *Kruse v Johnson*[180] formula to delegated lawmaking.[181] Three of its legs focus on the effects of legislation; the fourth—the disclosing of bad faith—is concerned with the process of enactment, though its meaning has not been much explored in the cases. The formula is flexible, and may be used to declare invalid either the piece of legislation in question, or a particular application of the legislation.

Many of the cases which illustrate the operation of *Kruse* are criminal cases where the invalidity of the legislation (or action taken

---

[177] See further above, 172–5.

[178] *Sinovich v Hercules Municipal Council* 1946 AD 783 at 790 per Watermeyer CJ. See Baxter at 492–4, where the author relates the doctrine of benevolent interpretation to the concept of justiciability.

[179] [1898] 2 QB 91 at 99–100 (Our italics).

[180] Note 179 above.

[181] As Schreiner JA put it in *Sinovich v Hercules Municipal Council* (n 178 above) at 802–3, 'The law does not protect the subject against the merely foolish exercise of a discretion by an official, however much the subject suffers thereby. But the law does protect the subject against stupid by-laws, however well intended, if their effect is sufficiently outrageous.'

in terms of it) has been raised on appeal by the accused. Thus they also illustrate a form of indirect—but none the less effective—judicial review.[182]

(a) Inequality, injustice and oppression

The apartheid policy officially pursued by the South African government since 1948 has resulted in legislative authorisation for many forms of racial discrimination which would otherwise be unreasonable. Their hands largely tied by Parliament's all-too-obvious intentions, our courts have generally accepted that 'separate but equal' treatment of different races (or other classes) does not fall foul of the *Kruse* formula,[183] though it might constitute an 'oppressive and gratuitous' interference with rights if the division of the community for these purposes were sufficiently absurd.[184] Inequality is a different matter. It was on this ground that municipal regulations providing for separate beaches for whites and 'non-whites' were declared ultra vires in *R v Carelse*,[185] the beaches in question being distinctly unequal in their attractions. In *R v Lusu*,[186] where a railway waiting room had been reserved for whites but not for other race groups, the reservation was declared ultra vires. And in *R v Abdurahman*,[187] a similar reservation of a railway coach for whites only was held to be unlawful. In both of these last two cases, the reservations made in terms of the legislation were set aside for inequality; the legislation itself remained valid, since it envisaged merely separate treatment. Where the validity of the legislation itself is in question, the case of *S v Adams, S v Werner*[188] has established that its reasonableness is judged at the time it comes before the court. This means that legislation which was once reasonable can, over a period of time, come to be judged as unreasonable because of inequalities which have arisen since its promulgation.[189]

But even substantial inequality can be authorised by Parliament, as it was found to have been in *Minister of the Interior v Lockhat*.[190] This case arose out of a proclamation of the Governor-General made under the Group Areas Act 77 of 1957, one of the effects of which was

---

[182] See above, 241–2; 293.
[183] See *Minister of Posts and Telegraphs v Rasool* 1934 AD 167, where the Appellate Division (Gardiner JA dissenting) held that a by-law which compelled 'non-Europeans' to transact their business in a separate room at a post-office was not unreasonable, the facilities being equal to those in the 'European' room.
[184] In *Rasool*'s case (n 183 above), De Villiers JA expressed the view (apparently without irony) that separate-but-equal discrimination based on the colour of one's eyes would be unreasonable because of its gratuitousness (at 182).
[185] 1943 CPD 242.
[186] 1953 (2) SA 484 (A).
[187] 1950 (3) SA 136 (A).
[188] 1981 (1) SA 187 (A) at 199A–200C.
[189] But it does not mean that unreasonable legislation which might become reasonable should be judged favourably: in *R v Carelse* (n 185 above) the fact that the inequality could have been cured by improving the 'non-white' beach was found to be irrelevant.
[190] 1961 (2) SA 587 (A).

to convert an Indian group area into a white area. Dealing with the validity of the proclamation, Holmes JA decided that although no express power was given to the Governor-General to discriminate substantially between different race groups, such power was clearly implicit in the Act:

> '[T]he Group Areas Act represents a colossal social experiment and a long-term policy. It necessarily involves the movement out of Group Areas of large numbers of people throughout the country. Parliament must have envisaged that compulsory population shifts . . . would inevitably cause disruption and, within the foreseeable future, substantial inequalities.'[191]

Similarly, Parliament can authorise other forms of unreasonableness, such as 'manifest injustice' and 'oppressive interference with rights', though it seldom does so expressly. In such cases, the applicant's only hope is that the court will be slower than that in *Lockhat*[192] to find an implied authorisation. In the context of the emergency regulations, a prime example of oppressive delegated legislation, the hope has often been in vain. The much-criticised case of *Omar v Minister of Law and Order*[193] illustrates a judicial willingness to recognise Parliamentary authorisation for delegated legislation which deprives individuals of their ordinary rights. Here the appeal court found, inter alia, that a regulation which allowed the Minister of Law and Order to detain a person without notice and without a hearing, though 'very harsh', fell within the 'extremely wide powers' conferred on the State President for coping with the emergency.[194] In other contexts, our courts may be less willing to find that the wide scope of powers is enough to authorise legislative excesses of this kind. In the recent case of *Vereeniging City Council v Rhema Bible Church, Walkerville*,[195] for example, a town-planning ordinance was held not to authorise a racially discriminatory clause in a town-planning scheme. The wideness of the council's powers in respect of town planning did not *in itself* authorise discrimination, since 'statutes are presumed not to sanction discrimination or inequality'.[196]

(b) Disclosing bad faith

Using 'bad faith' in its strict sense of dishonesty, there is no doubt that delegated legislation can be set aside on this ground in our law. In *Feinstein v Baleta*,[197] Roos JA conceded that the motives of a lawmaking body, though not normally relevant to the court's enquiry, would become so where 'a charge of bad faith or corrupt

---

[191] At 602D–E.
[192] Note 190 above.
[193] *Omar v Minister of Law & Order, Fani v Minister of Law and Order, State President v Bill* 1987 (3) SA 859 (A). For criticism, see the 'Focus on *Omar*' in 1987 (3) *SAJHR* at 295–337.
[194] Per Rabie ACJ at 900I–901A (Hoexter JA dissenting).
[195] 1989 (2) SA 142 (T).
[196] Per Goldstone J at 151D–G.
[197] 1930 AD 319.

motive is laid'.[198] Legislation knowingly enacted for improper purposes would thus, it seems, 'disclose bad faith'. As we have seen, legislation which pursues improper purposes *innocently* can be set aside in any event,[199] so that little turns on the correct interpretation of 'bad faith' for the purposes of Lord Russell's formula. In accordance with the analysis above,[200] however, it seems quite unnecessary to confuse the issue by using 'bad faith' in two different senses. Here, too, greater clarity would result from the use of exact terminology—that of dishonesty and improper purposes.

2 Vagueness or uncertainty

For years our courts have recognised that, quite apart from the grounds of attack in *Kruse v Johnson*,[201] delegated legislation can also be declared ultra vires on the ground of vagueness or uncertainty. The accepted test is that of Broome J in *R v Jopp*:[202]

'[T]he Court must first construe the bye-law or regulation, applying the usual canons of construction with no bias towards "benevolence". Having ascertained the meaning, the Court must then ask itself whether the bye-law or regulation, so construed, indicates with reasonable certainty to those who are bound by it the act which is enjoined or prohibited. If it does, it is good; if it does not, it is bad; that is the end of the matter.'

The rationale for the rule, as with the *Kruse* formula, is that Parliament does not intend lawmaking powers to be exercised unreasonably.[203] Here, the unreasonableness emerges from the failure of the legislation to guide the public, its failure to inform citizens of what they must and must not do. Thus in *R v Shapiro*,[204] the accused traders had been convicted of contravening regulations which prohibited the granting of credit to blacks 'at or near any coal mine in the province of Natal'. On appeal, the vagueness of the prohibition resulted in the convictions being set aside. As Feetham JP indicated, the scope of the prohibition was so uncertain that the traders could not know whether they were subject to it or not:[205]

'If a by-law or regulation is uncertain, then it is unreasonable, and statutes do not empower the authorities to make regulations so uncertain that people will not know how to comply with them or whether they are subject to them or not.'[206]

Though the older cases do not seem to envisage any extension of the rule, at least one court has been prepared to apply it in the case of a banning order—an order which, because it applies to an individual,

---

[198] At 326.
[199] See the *University of Cape Town* case, discussed at 345 above.
[200] Above, 347–9.
[201] Note 179 above.
[202] 1949 (4) SA 11 (N) at 13–14.
[203] *R v Pretoria Timber Co (Pty) Ltd* 1950 (3) SA 163 (A).
[204] 1935 NPD 155.
[205] At 159.
[206] Ibid.

lacks the generality associated with legislation. In the famous case of
S v Meer,[207] a banning order which prohibited Mrs Meer from
attending a 'social gathering' was found to be 'incorrigibly' obscure
by the court a quo, and her conviction for breaching the order was set
aside. The Appellate Division reversed this decision,[208] but did not
appear to disagree with the application of the vagueness rule to a
non-legislative administrative act. This and other[209] instances of the
rule's extension are undoubtedly justified on the basis that the
citizen's need to be informed and guided by administrative
decision-making does not alter with the classification of the decision.
Parliament may, however, 'authorise' vagueness, thus doing away
with the citizen's entitlement to be properly guided. This is
illustrated by the case of *Gumede v Minister of Law and Order*,[210] which
dealt with the validity of a detention notice made under s 28 of the
Internal Security Act, and specifically with the 'reasons' and
'information' which that section requires the Minister to furnish to
the detainee. A full bench of the Natal Provincial Division found that
the notice could not be attacked on the ground that the information
supplied was vague, since s 28 requires the Minister to furnish only
so much of the information as can, in his opinion, be disclosed
without detriment to the public interest.[211]

(a)   The decision in Staatspresident v United Democratic Front

The ground of vagueness has been used frequently and to
considerable (if short-lived) effect on a number of regulations during
the various states of emergency which have operated since 1985.[212] Its
status as a ground has since been thrown into doubt by the Appellate
Division decision in *Staatspresident v United Democratic Front*,[213] a
case dealing with the validity of certain media regulations issued by
the State President in terms of the Public Safety Act 3 of 1953. Relying
on a narrow definition of ultra vires (and thereby ignoring the import
of virtually every precedent in our law relating to vagueness),[214] the

---

[207] 1981 (1) SA 739 (N).
[208] 1981 (4) SA 604 (A).
[209] For examples, see *R v Pretoria Timber Co (Pty) Ltd* (n 203 above); Baxter 531.
[210] 1985 (2) SA 529 (N).
[211] At 542H–543J (Van Heerden AJP, Kriek and Broome JJ concurring). The Appellate
Division did not pronounce on this point when it overturned the decision (1986 (2)
SA 734 (A)).
[212] See, for example, *Metal and Allied Workers' Union v State President* 1986 (4) SA 358
(D); *Natal Newspapers v State President* 1986 (4) SA 1109 (N); *United Democratic Front
v State President* 1987 (3) SA 296 (N).
[213] 1988 (4) SA 830 (A). See also *Staatspresident v Release Mandela Campaign* 1988 (4) SA
903 (A), decided on the same day by an identical court. For criticism of these cases,
see Nicholas Haysom and Clive Plasket (1988) 4 *SAJHR* 303; Etienne Mureinik
(1989) 5 *SAJHR* 60, especially at 69–72; John Grogan (1989) 106 *SALJ* 14.
[214] The leading cases (discussed above) leave one in no doubt as to the justification for
the courts' interference: that Parliament does not countenance or authorise the
making of vague subordinate legislation.

majority of the court[215] found that the regulations could not be held ultra vires for vagueness. The reasoning was as follows: the Public Safety Act does not expressly require the State President to make clear regulations or prohibit him from making vague regulations; it simply empowers him to make regulations under certain circumstances. Though some of the regulations might be so vague that they should be considered to be invalid, and though they might constitute an imperfect or ineffective exercise of the State President's discretion, this does not mean that the State President has (literally) *exceeded* his powers, or acted ultra vires;[216] on the contrary, it means that the regulations have in fact been made 'under' s 3 of the Act, and are intra vires the State President's powers. Accordingly, the ouster clause in s 5B of the Act applies to the regulations, so that no court of law is competent to enquire into their validity. This court cannot, therefore, strike the regulations down on the ground of vagueness.

(b) Problems raised by the decision

Leaving aside the extraordinary constitutional implications of this decision, which have already been discussed,[217] two further issues remain to be considered. The first relates to the scope and effects of the decision, while the second concerns the practical problem of implementing it. As to the first, it is clear that vagueness will only operate as an *effective* ground of review in cases where no ouster clause is present. In such cases, the vagueness itself—and not the ultra vires doctrine—will justify the court in setting aside the legislation.[218] Where there is an ouster clause, it will prevent the court from enquiring as to the vagueness or clarity of the legislation in question. The question is whether this will apply also to the other grounds which have to do with *abusing* power rather than literally *exceeding* it; the requirements of legality which are *implied* as well as those which are *express*. Unfortunately, an affirmative answer has already been given in relation to the unreasonableness of subordinate legislation: in *Natal Indian Congress v State President*[219] Friedman J found, with the utmost reluctance, that the ouster clause effectively prevented him from invalidating regulations on the grounds set out in *Kruse v Johnson*.[220] The prognosis seems grim for other grounds of review which have to do with abuse of discretion. At best, the effects of the *UDF* decision will be confined to the contexts of subordinate legislation and ouster clauses. At worst, the decision signals the end of judicial control over all abuses of discretion, and thus makes nonsense of all the implied or judge-

---

[215] Rabie ACJ (in whose judgment Hefer and Vivier JJA concurred); Hefer JA (in whose separate judgment Vivier JA concurred); Grosskopf JA (in whose separate judgment Hefer and Vivier JJA concurred); Van Heerden JA dissenting.
[216] See the judgment of Rabie ACJ at 853D–F.
[217] Above, 261ff.
[218] See the judgment of Hefer JA at 867A and 868G–H.
[219] 1989 (3) SA 588 (D).
[220] Note 179 above.

made requirements of legality, including the requirements of reasonableness and fairness.

The second issue concerns the problems inherent in distinguishing between excess and abuse; between illegalities which can be exceeded in a literal sense, and which therefore go to ultra vires, and breaches of implied, common-law or judge-made requirements, which do not go to ultra vires. In the *UDF* decision, as in the writings of authors such as Rose-Innes[221] and Wiechers,[222] it seems to be assumed that the different types of illegality fall into two clear categories. But while it is true that some of the requirements of legality will be fairly obvious on the face of the relevant enabling legislation, and that others owe their existence entirely to judicial choice, this distinction cannot be pressed too far. The ground of improper purposes,[223] for instance, is given by Rose-Innes[224] as an example of an illegality of the kind that goes to ultra vires. In fact, it falls clearly into that category only if one makes the far-fetched assumption that all statutes provide express *and absolutely irrefutable* statements of the purposes which may be pursued legitimately under the legislation. In real life, even the clearest legislative provisions leave room for judicial interpretation, and the vast majority of statutes give no express indication of proper purposes. Judges faced with such legislation must choose between competing purposes, or they must imply into the statute some sort of legitimate purpose; and this means that they have a *choice* of interpretation, a creative function similar to that exercised in relation to the 'implied' grounds of review. What happens to the ground of improper purposes in these cases? If the answer is that this ground falls into a different category whenever judicial interpretation is needed, one can only reply that judicial interpretation and judicial choice are *always* relevant: where there are words, there is interpretation. Indeed, the 'express' grounds themselves only qualify as grounds of review because they have been recognised and interpreted as such by judges. As we have seen, judicial interpretation can convert an express and apparently compulsory statutory provision into a non-essential or 'directory' provision, and it can find an implied power to exist where there are no express words to suggest its presence.[225] In the same way, it is judicial interpretation which decides both the existence and scope of the grounds of review in a particular case: illegalities are not self-defining. The distinction between express and implied requirements (or excess and abuse of power) is not necessarily an easy one to draw, as subsequent courts will inevitably discover.

[221] Rose-Innes 89–94.
[222] Wiechers 174–9.
[223] See further above, 343–6.
[224] Rose-Innes 91–2.
[225] See above, 300–2.

C Judicial Decisions

1 The 'no evidence' rule before 1976

It is a well-established rule of our law that proceedings before an inferior court or an administrative tribunal may be set aside if there is 'no evidence' to justify the tribunal's finding. In two Appellate Division decisions involving special *statutory* review of the proceedings of the Medical and Dental Council,[226] the rule was extended to cover decisions which could not reasonably have been reached on the evidence.

2 The rule after 1976

The rule has since been extended to cases of ordinary (inherent) administrative law review. Since the important decision of Jansen JA in *Theron v Ring van Wellington van die NG Sendingkerk in Suid-Afrika*,[227] our courts have been able to set aside 'purely judicial' decisions of the administration for unreasonableness.

The case arose out of the proceedings of a disciplinary tribunal of the NG Kerk, which had found a minister and certain members of his congregation guilty of contravening the Church Ordinance. At a contentious meeting to discuss the appropriate sentence, the tribunal voted in favour of a warning; but this decision proved so unpopular that a second meeting was held, where the first meeting's decision was rescinded and a vote was taken in favour of a severer sentence. The applicants appealed against this sentence to the General Synodal Commission, who remitted the matter back to the tribunal on the ground that the decision taken at the first meeting, and everything flowing from it, was invalid: the members of the tribunal had been confused and the voting procedure irregular, and the decision could not be said to reflect the true intention of the majority at the meeting. The applicants then instituted what turned out to be very lengthy review proceedings in the Supreme Court, appearing first before a single judge of the Cape Provincial Division and then appealing to a full bench. Both courts disclaimed jurisdiction to hear the matter, there being no apparent ground for interference in terms of the *Union Steel*[228] test, and leave to appeal was refused. Nothing daunted, the applicants petitioned the Chief Justice, and a full bench of the Appellate Division constituted by him finally granted leave to appeal to that division.

The appeal court decided by a narrow majority that the commission's decision should be set aside, Jansen JA (Van Blerk ACJ concurring) holding that there was no evidence upon which it could reasonably be concluded that the members at the first meeting were

---

[226] *SA Medical and Dental Council v McLoughlin* 1948 (2) SA 355 (A); *SA Medical and Dental Council v Lipron* 1949 (3) SA 277 (A).
[227] 1976 (2) SA 1 (A).
[228] Note 119 above.

confused, that the procedure had been wrong, or that their intention had not been accurately reflected. In reaching this decision, Jansen JA approved the presumption that Parliament intends powers to be used reasonably. Drawing boldly on two Appellate Division decisions[229] which involved special statutory review of a disciplinary tribunal—and not the inherent jurisdiction of the Supreme Court— Jansen JA found that decisions which cannot reasonably be supported on the evidence available may be set aside as unreasonable. However, he emphasised that a decision could only be struck down on this ground if it were 'purely judicial':[230] that is, a decision involving the same sort of discretion as that normally exercised by courts of law, and being characterised by the application of legal rules or principles rather than by its policy content.

D Unreasonableness as a single ground of review

We began the second half of this chapter by proposing that the classification of functions has been used as a limiting device to ensure that the court, while retaining its watchdog role, does not encroach on the preserve of the executive arm of government. If this is correct, it would certainly explain the persistent refusal of the courts to recognise a test of reasonableness in the case of purely administrative functions—an attitude which is particularly significant when one considers that our courts *have* been prepared to pass judgment on the reasonableness of delegated legislation for nearly a century. It would also explain the preparedness of Jansen JA[231] to admit such a test in the case of purely judicial decisions: decisions which involve the sorts of skills with which judges are wholly familiar, and where their interference is justifiable on the basis of their superior qualifications.

The necessity for the elaborate, three-tier structure which has resulted is, however, in doubt. As Baxter[232] has shown, judicial restraint in relation to purely administrative decisions becomes quite superfluous once the difference between substantive and dialectical reasonableness is appreciated; and while there is no getting away from the subjectivity of judgments about what is reasonable, the problem *already* exists in the case of the *Union Steel*[233] formulation. It is a problem unlikely ever to be solved, but the recognition of a test for reasonableness for administrative decisions is equally unlikely to make it worse.

Furthermore, there are cogent reasons for recognising a unified requirement of reasonableness which would apply across the spectrum of administrative decision-making. One of these is the artificiality of the assumption that there are clear lines to be drawn

---

[229] Above, n 226.
[230] At 19–20; 23E; 24–5. See further Baxter at 499–500.
[231] *Theron v Ring van Wellington*, n 227 above.
[232] See above, 341–3.
[233] See above, 343.

between the various administrative functions.[234] That there are no such clear lines is suggested by the undeniable overlapping[235] between the various grounds of review. It is difficult to resist the suspicion that behaviour which would be judged as unreasonable in the case of a judicial officer would amount to failure to apply the mind in the case of an administrative official, and that the resulting decision, if it appeared in legislative form, would fall foul of the *Kruse v Johnson*[236] formula.

The Law Commission has given implicit recognition to the truth of this suspicion by proposing a new (and apparently general) ground of unreasonableness.[237] The ground is qualified, however, by the breathtaking proviso that 'policy considerations' will not be reviewable—presumably the Law Commission's way of ensuring that the courts do not encroach on the executive's territory. Since it is difficult to think of a single decision which involves no policy considerations at all, the recommendation of the Law Commission, if accepted, might herald the withering away rather than the flowering of unreasonableness as a ground of review; assuming, of course, that the *United Democratic Front*[238] decision has not already seen to that.

[234] See the discussion at 331ff above.
[235] For an extreme illustration, see Baxter's convincing suggestion (Baxter 500–1) that the 'no reasonable evidence' test has already been applied outside its 'purely judicial' context in the case of *W C Greyling & Erasmus (Pty) Ltd v Johannesburg Local Road Transportation Board* 1982 (4) SA 427 (A).
[236] Note 179 above.
[237] *Working Paper 15* op cit n 118 at 105ff.
[238] Note 213 above.

Index